Now that my 115,0... horseback ride is nearing i... is my firm belief that somew... there in the mountains a... ranges of the west there is a young cowboy, mounted on a roan horse whose ears are pointed forward, while his dogs stand at attention, that is just beginning his 100,000 mile horseback ride. I wish him good luck through all of the experiences he is going to have while traveling along his long winding trail.

Long Winding Trails

4,434,174 Miles on the Back of a Horse

By

Dave Secrist

Illustrated by Jerry King

ISBN 978-1-4507-4857-5

For additional copies of this book:
Contact:
e-mail: secrist100m@gmail.com

or by writing to Long Winding Trails,
2504 Twin View Lane, Twin Falls Idaho 83301

Caxton Printers, LTD
Caldwell, Idaho

Printed in U.S.A.

Dedication

I dedicate this book to my wife, Jane, who spent untold hours helping to make this book presentable and to the cowboys and cowgirls that have ridden or are still riding along their long winding trails in the mountains, deserts and valleys of this great land we call America.

ACKNOWLEGEMENTS

I would like to thank my wife, Jane, for her unwavering support, up beat attitude and input while I was writing this book. Without her help this book would not have been written. When cowboy lingo and terminology meet a well educated school teacher, hell bent on putting verbs and nouns in their right places, sometimes sparks fly. We often jokingly said, "If we don't get this book finished soon, we were going to have to go see a marriage counselor." I would like to thank Mary Branscomb. She gave of her time as well as her advice. Her positive attitude and encouragement helped get this project off the ground and through to completion. I would like to thank the Nevada Cattlemen's Association, the Cowboy 100,000 Mile Club members and their representatives for the information they provided. Input from Bob Secrist and Harold Crothers, who were present when many of these stories happened, helped me keep my facts straight. Again many thanks to all of the above.

Jane and I would like to thank Teresa Sales representing Caxton Printers for the help she gave when we were compiling my writings for publication. Teresa and Caxton Printers were professional, knowledgeable, and patient through out the entire process and we appreciate that.

DISCLAIMER

First I would like to say I've written these stories from many years of memories and to the best of my ability they are factual. I am well aware that several people being in or seeing the same event will sometimes come away with different opinions of how things happened. These stories are written from my perspective and I am not liable to anyone that may remember things differently. The same reasoning applies to the authors of the documentations that appear in this book.

TABLE OF CONTENTS

ILLUSTRATIONS BY JERRY KING

AN EXPLANATION OF STORIES

I've had many experiences along my 115,000 mile horseback ride where the horse, cow and I were the only ones involved. I have described a few of these events in the stories I remember, but these stories are not unique to only my long winding trail. Every cowboy that has lived and ridden on the big ranches, back country and wilderness areas of America has personal experiences known only to him and the animals and the nature that surrounded him at the time.

I am sure, when reading these stories, it seems as if I stumbled from one catastrophe to another and this is not true. Over the span of seventy plus years the incidents that stand out in my mind are the good, the unusual and the bad. The majority of days along my lifelong ride were just normal work days, with no unusual events cropping up. Many days were spent enjoying the company of the people and animals I worked with. The stories I remember are events that happened during everyday cowboy work.

The documentation of the miles ridden by the members of the "Cowboy 100,000 Mile Club" only touches the tip of the iceberg. These documents only unlock a very small part of the personal incidents and stories other "Cowboy 100,000 Mile Club" members have encountered. It is my hope that memories from my horseback ride will provide some insight into the lives of the other club members, as well as the many working cowboys that still ride many miles each year just doing a day's work. My hat is off to each and every one of you who have ridden or are still riding along your individual long winding trail.

I would also like to tip my hat to the Nevada Cattlemen's Association. They and other associations like them, help us continue to ride our ranges as independent operators by providing us with a united front. I think this is the best chance we have of preserving our environment and our cowboy way of life.

During the seventy plus years of my life I spent untold days doing what many people would think of as being alone. I would characterize these days spent with horses, dogs, and livestock in the mountains and sagebrush basins of the west as being self-sufficient. Because people were not present during many of these long days spent surrounded by nature and animals, both became an important part of my life. I learned to understand and respect most that was around me. Most of all I learned to respect, appreciate, and understand the horses that I rode every day.

It is important to note that spending a lifetime in the back country of the west does not necessarily mean living the life of a hermit. There is much intermingling and interaction with the more civilized people of the outside world.

The stories I am going to recall only include the people, horses, cattle, and wildlife that were actually involved while I traveled along my lifetime 115,000 mile horse back ride. These stories do not reflect another part of my life that is very important to me; close ties to a supportive family, good neighbors, and the loyal friends that have made my 115,000 ride through life possible.

To help me put this information together I solicited the help of two qualified people: my school teacher wife, Jane and our friend, Mary Branscomb.

Even though Jane knows I cannot spell a word correctly enough to find it in the dictionary she is still very supportive. With a sly grin she says, "Hon, anyone who can only spell a word one way has no imagination." Mary is well known for her ability to research, document facts and write stories. Together with Jane and Mary's expertise and my knowledge of the western range and the cowboy way of life, we have compiled the following documentations and stories.

This is a good place to say Jane and Mary do not always condone my choice of words or the terminology I use. They tell me I am butchering the English language. I understand and I appreciate their efforts to keep me on the straight and narrow. They correct what they can and accept what they can't. By way of background information I've included their stories later in the book.

COWBOY LINGO

As with any occupation, cowboys and ranchers have some lingo that is specific to their work. These explanations of the words may help to understand some of the stories being told.

Allotment ....noun: government grazing land that is attached to privately owned deeded land called base property: a rancher has to own enough base property to support his livestock for 5 to 7 months out of the year to qualify to own a permit to use an allotment.

Bald hornet nest ......noun: a large cone shaped nest built by hornets (large very aggressive bees) the nests usually hang from a tree limb

Black Ballies ....noun: Calves half Black Angus, half Hereford (black colored cattle with white faces)

Bootlegger ....noun: a person who sells liquor illegally

Bronc ....noun: a bucking colt or horse: any horse that is hard to handle

Buckaroo...................noun: name derived from Spanish for cowboy; used on certain big range ranches

Calavia ....noun: a horse performance with unbridle horses, costumes, acrobats and music

Calves ....noun: young cattle still following their mothers

Cattle guard ....noun; a structure usually made from parallel metal bars placed over a shallow pit in the road used to prevent cattle form crossing but allows vehicles and pedestrians to cross

Cinch .... noun: a strong girth used on stock saddles having a ring on both ends to which a strap running from the saddle is secured; it is usually made of mohair or cotton

Cinch binder............noun: a horse that pulls back and falls over backwards when it is first cinched up or cinched up too fast

Chinook....................noun: a warm wind usually blowing from the south or west causing a January or February thaw

Chowsing ....verb: harassing, teasing, and unnecessary chasing

Cow boss ....noun: boss of the cowboys or buckaroos

Dallies ....noun: turns taken around a saddle horn with a rope

Dude ....noun: a city person on a ranch, a person unfamiliar with ranching activities

Gykhanas ....noun: a speed pattern racing event and timed games on horses

Hackamore ....noun: a piece of riding equipment usually made of braided rawhide used to control a horse without a bridle and bit

Hematoma................noun: a severe bruise on a bone causing an abscess

Hobbles ....noun: a piece of equipment used to hold a horse's front feet together

Jigger boss ....noun: a person in charge of the ranch hand crew

Lass rope..................noun: the lasso or rope a cowboy uses to rope cattle, carried on the saddle; a term used by cowboys out on the open range

Lariat.......................noun: a long rope cowboys carry on their saddles to rope cattle

Latigo ....noun: a leather strap on the saddletree of a western saddle used to tighten the cinch that goes under the belly of the horse to hold the saddle on

Macarte....................noun: a horsehair braided rope

Moon shiners ....noun: a person who operates a still and produces liquor illegally

Outhouse..................noun: an outdoor toilet with no water plumbing

Quakies ....noun: Aspen trees so called because of their leaves shaking in the wind

Quirt ....noun: a whip with a leather thong on the end

Rango ....noun: the person who gets the horses in for all in the morning

Remuda....................noun: a name derived from Spanish for a large group of horses from which a cowboy selects his mount

Rep............................noun: a cowboy representing a certain ranch when cattle that run in common are gathered and worked (separated by brand) on the open range

Repping....................verb: the act of being a representative

Rodeer......................noun: an area where cattle are held and worked on the open range

R.O.T.C. ....noun: acronym for Reserve Officer Training Corp used on college campuses for groups of students that are trained to become officers in the armed services

Screw worms ....noun: larva of flies that eat flesh from an open wound

Siwash ....verb: to camp out without a tent or supplies

Stud ....noun: a male horse, stallion

Taylor Grazing Act ..a law passed by Congress in 1934 that required ranchers to own enough deeded property (base property) to run their cattle, horses or sheep on during certain months of the year in order to qualify to own a permit to graze cattle on government land

Ubiquitous................adjective: existing or being everywhere, ever present feeling

Weaners ....noun: young calves newly taken form their mothers

Wrangler..................noun: a person who gathers or tends the horses at round up

Introduction

When I was President of the Nevada Cattlemen's Association I came up with an idea and I named it the "Cowboy 100,000 Mile Club". I thought there should be a way to document the lives of the western range cowmen and cowboys in such a way that it would be recorded and interesting to the general public. Jane and I worked up guidelines and Paul Bottari helped implement them. We thought it was important that the minimum miles ridden by a club member were high enough to capture attention and also that the miles ridden were well documented.

There isn't a cowboy in the west or in America for that matter that ever said, "I'm going to start out and ride 100,000 miles on the back of a horse." The 100,000 miles traveled is a byproduct of the life they have chosen. This award, given by the Cowboy 100,000 Mile Club, is intended to honor those that have reached this milestone and to bring attention to other cowboys and cowgirls that have obtained this goal. To these cowboys, the distance ridden is not measured by miles but remembered by incidents that happened during warm spring days, cold winter storms, and hot dusty cattle drives. Miles remembered are also measured by the people, horses, dogs, wildlife, valleys, rivers and mountains that surrounded them while they traveled along their long winding trails. Never or nearly never are miles ridden thought about when a cowboy rides out to do a day's work.

The longest distance a Cowboy 100,000 Mile Club member has documented riding horseback during his lifetime is 287,000 miles. 287,000 miles does not sound like much in this day of spaceships and rockets, so let's put it in perspective. I've been told the average distance is 238,857 miles from earth to the moon. This means this Cowboy 100,000 Mile Club member has ridden the equivalent of going to the moon on horseback and still had 48,143 miles to spare. When people look up at a full moon on a clear night, I hope they stop and visualize a cowboy, just living and working on the western ranges, riding this distance horseback. Maybe the "Man in the Moon" is a cowboy. It seems just as plausible to me as the cheese theory.

I am a junior member of the Cowboy 100,000 Mile Club but I have ridden 115,000 miles on the back of a horse. I didn't make it to the moon but I did get about halfway there. Bringing this comparison back to earth, I have ridden the equivalent of four and a half times around the world at the equator. Using another example, this time on dry land I have ridden horseback the miles equal to crossing the United States from San Francisco to New York City nearly forty times in my lifetime. This was all done within a normal day's work .

Many stories are still being lived and told by the men and women who live and work in this Western environment. In our fast paced world, many of these stories are not being recorded in history and with the passing of time, are fading into unrecorded shadowy images of the past.

In many ways the western lifestyle is changing. Modern conveniences are being used to make ranch life easier. Cell phones and short wave radios make it possible for even the most isolated ranch to communicate with the outside world. New time saving machines have been developed. The four wheeler, the gooseneck trailer, cattle trucks, and big hay balers have all been incorporated into modern ranching operations. The pace of everyday life is moving faster than ever. Even so, the Western lifestyle and philosophy remains the same today as it was seventy years ago when I was that spellbound kid lying in front of the fireplace listening to the stories of the day being told.

There is no question that these modern conveniences have made ranching easier and more can be accomplished while doing a day's work. The gooseneck trailer has eliminated many line camps because horses can now be hauled into many of these areas usually in one to three hours. Many of those hard ten, fifteen or twenty mile trots, getting to and from the home ranch to areas on the range where cattle are gathered and worked, have been eliminated. One old cowboy told me, "I once worked for a rawhide outfit where we left the home ranch at 4:00 o'clock in the morning traveling in a long trot. At 4:00 o'clock in the afternoon we were still traveling in a long trot —- still going away from home." This was probably an exaggeration but maybe not as far fetched as you may think. I've driven cattle ten or twelve miles to a mountain pasture and then trotted twenty miles around the pasture's perimeter fence making sure the gates were closed before riding back home.

In my experience many of the horseback miles saved by using modern equipment are replaced by riding extra miles when the gathering and cow working areas are reached.

In today's media the rodeo cowboy is about the only image of the West the general public is exposed to. Many people think the big range cowboy died when the great trail drives of the mid-eighteen hundreds ended. They have no idea that there are still cowboys riding horseback thousands of miles every year just doing their everyday work.

Seventy years from now the machinery and equipment we use today will be as obsolete as the stage coach and the Model T Ford of days gone by. Many other things will change but I believe the horse will look pretty much the same in seventy years as it looks today. I think the horse and the cowboy will always have a significant part to play in the big range countries of the West. That is why the "Cowboy 100,000 Mile Club" was founded.

Long Winding Trails

*A glimpse into the western range cowboy's past
and a look into his present day way of life.*

VIRGIL PIQUET

Dave's comment: I first met Virgil in the 1960's and he soon became one of my heroes. His honesty, subtle sense of humor and gentle strength was captivating. From the cradle to the grave, Virgil was an honest to goodness western big range cowboy and rancher. His long winding trail typifies the lives of many of the Cowboy 100,000 Mile Club members as well as the lives of the thousands of men and women who have or are spending their lives in the saddle riding America's sprawling ranges.

Virgil told of an incident that happened during the early part of his lifelong horseback ride. I will relate it to you as an introduction to Virgil's documentation which was given by his wife, Ruth, when he was inducted into the Cowboy 100,000 Mile Club.

When Virgil left the Pendleton area and started working his way south toward the Miller and Lux Ranches, his horse went lame in Burns, Oregon. Virgil was about fifteen years old at this time. He found a livery stable and traded his lame horse for a horse the livery stable owner had. The man told Virgil the horse only had one fault. Every time you get on this horse he will buck, but other than that he was sound and reliable. Virgil said the livery man was right. Every time he got off the horse, even to pee, the horse bucked when he remounted. The rest of the time the horse was fine. Virgil said, "This recurring event became very tiresome and I soon learned to stand up in the stirrups, pee over the horse's right shoulder and the old horse was all right with that."

The following is the documentation written and presented by Ruth Piquet when Virgil was inducted into the Cowboy 100,000 Mile Club:

Virgil Charles Piquet

First member of The Nevada Cattlemen's Cowboy 100,000 Mile Club

Inducted in 1980

Virgil was born March 23, 1908 on the ranch his grandfather owned; Jules Adrian Piquet's ranch was located near Marcola, Lane County, Oregon. Virgil was the oldest child of Charles Adrian and Mary Dae (Hileman) Piquet. The family said that Virgil started riding around the corral horseback by himself at the age of two. When he was four years old his parents established a ranch near Guldane, Oregon, which was located three hundred miles east of Marcola. The family made the journey with one wagon loaded with their belongings, four head of saddle horses and twenty head of cattle. Virgil rode all the way, helping his mother herd the livestock while his father drove the wagon. His father did this because there weren't many roads in the area and driving the team and wagon across rocks, dry washes and steep hillsides was a dangerous job. Ruth said, "Virgil is not sure if the memories of this trip are his memories or memories of stories the family retold."

Gurdane consisted of a post office housed in a ranch residence, and a one room, eight grade, one teacher school house. This was the custom in rural areas at the time. It was thirty miles to the nearest store. All travel was done horseback with a team and wagon following along if supplies were to be purchased. A trip to town was made about once a month. At the age of six, Virgil attended the Gurdane School which was seven miles from his home, and he completed all eight grades. Thus he rode fourteen miles a day, two hundred days a year for eight years.

Total School Miles Ridden   22,400 miles

During the summers in this time frame, Virgil rode every day helping his father and/or his neighbors with their buckarooing and trips to town.

Summer Time Miles Ridden   14,000 miles

At age fourteen, Virgil started working full time. He operated a horse drawn Fresno scraper when the McCay Creek Dam was being built. It didn't take Virgil long to decide he liked riding horses better than driving them and buckarooing became the lifestyle he chose.

He started working on a cattle ranch near Pendleton and worked his way south toward his childhood dream of becoming a cowboy on the widely known Miller and Lux Ranches. The first Miller and Lux Ranch he worked on was in the Silvies Valley. He was about sixteen at the time. He became a cowhand for the company and was moved from one ranch to another until he arrived at the Alvord and White Horse Ranches in southern Oregon. Here, he continued to buckaroo on a daily basis, riding horseback from before daybreak to well after dark.

Virgil would ride up to fifty miles one way to attend a dance or sometimes a rodeo every month or so. During this stage of his life, he learned to do whatever needed to be done on the isolated ranches where he lived and worked. He learned to cut the other buckaroos' hair and he also trimmed his own. When Virgil remembered these events he would sometimes jokingly remark, "There's only a week's difference between a good and a bad hair cut." He repaired wagons and corrals; broke horses and did anything else that needed to be done on a ranch. He even ran the chuck wagon when the cook broke his leg.

In 1926, Virgil participated in a cattle drive from Oregon to the railroad corrals in Winnemucca, Nevada. They camped on Miller and Lux land every night of the drive. This was a long and tiresome drive and the sight of Winnemucca was a welcome exciting event. Virgil liked the area and commented, "Some day I am going to own a ranch here." When Charlie Ferrell, the owner of a horse raising ranch in Paradise Valley offered Virgil a job breaking horses, Virgil took it.

In a few days Virgil rode out to the ranch and was shown some horses that had been corralled the day before. Mr. Ferrell pointed out an ordinary looking sorrel that he wanted ridden. In the afternoon Virgil saddled the horse and when he mounted, Virgil was later quoted as saying, "All hell broke loose. The horse bucked, bawled and tore up a half acre of ground." Virgil said, "I was everywhere on that horse's back from his tail to his ears but somehow I rode that sorrel to a stand still." That evening Virgil told Mr. Ferrell he thought he would be moving on. He didn't think he was cowboy enough to ride Mr. Ferrell's horses. Charlie Ferrell said, "Son, you don't understand, if you can ride that sorrel horse, you'll have little trouble riding any horse I own." Virgil stayed for a year and broke horses for the Ferrell Ranch.

He further developed his horse training skills and learned something about how some ranch owners think. After a year he decided it was time to visit his family and look for a job closer to home. He continued to buckaroo in the Pendleton area for another nine years.

Miles Ridden From 1922 to 1937   92, 600 miles

Virgil married Ruth Porter, a fourth generation Oregon rancher's daughter, on December 26, 1937, and they started ranching on their own. Virgil and Ruth had four sons: V. John, and triplets David, Tebeau, and Allen. All of whom started riding horseback when they were three years old. They were helping drive cattle when they were four.

Miles Ridden From 1937 to 1952   82,125 miles

Over the next twenty-eight years Virgil continued to ride on a daily basis with fewer miles ridden during winter feeding and summer haying periods. The Piquets bought a ranch near Winnemucca, Nevada in the year 1967. This completed Virgil's dream of owning a ranch in the Winnemucca area. Virgil once again started riding on a daily basis and amassed many more miles.

Miles Ridden From 1952 to 1980   75,875 miles

GRAND TOTAL OF MILES RIDDEN   287,000 miles

Dave's comment: Virgil didn't know he was being inducted into the Cowboy 100,000 Mile Club. He knew Ruth had been working on documenting some family history and he'd even helped her compile some of it, but he had no idea he was going to be the first cowboy inducted into the Cowboy 100,000 Mile Club. After Ruth finished the presentation, Virgil got up and just stood there for what seemed like a long time. Then with a twinkle in his eye he said, "Yeah, and she doesn't know every place I've been."

LITTLE THINGS

A friend once told me when he was a kid, not long after electric fences were developed to keep livestock in pastures; like boys sometimes do, he was looking around for something to pee on and he decided to pee on the hot wire. Said he never did that again.

THE BEGINNING

In 1927 my folks moved from southern California to the back country in the northern part of the state. They established a homestead on Oat Ridge northwest of Rock Tree Valley and east of Willits, California. Mom and Dad were a young couple, just married and being independent by nature, they were looking for exciting challenges. They were following in the footsteps of my Aunt Mae and Uncle Vern Steadman.

Some years before, Aunt Mae and Uncle Vern travelled a distance of about 600 miles by horse and buggy from Los Angeles to Eureka, California. They returned to the Los Angeles area and the next year they again, traveling by horse and buggy, retraced their previous trip and stopped in Willits. At that time Willits was a frontier town, and Aunt Mae and Uncle Vern settled in the Rock Tree-Hearst area fifteen miles east of Willits. My Uncle Vern was a dreamer and lived a colorful life. In his early days his travels ranged from playing bit parts in early movies of the Mary Pickford era to taking part in the gold fever that followed the California gold rush.

My aunt Mae (my dad's older sister) told stories of panning for gold along the Uba and Sacramento rivers. She recalled the time they camped all summer along a sharp bend in a river, where Uncle Vern spent most of the summer diverting the river's channel. He did this to expose a huge boulder, where he expected to find a large amount of gold that had settled underneath the big rock. This didn't pan out, so for a short time they followed the early day rodeo circuit before making the two buggy trips north and finally settling in the Hearst area east of Willits.

For a period of time, Aunt Mae and Uncle Vern returned to Long Beach in the Los Angeles area of southern California where they founded, owned and operated the Falcon Archery Tackle Shop. They made, sold and demonstrated top quality bows, arrows and other archery equipment.

After that experience they moved back to the Willits area living in outlying places, taking care of property owned by absentee owners while Uncle Vern ran trap lines, fished and hunted.

In later years Uncle Vern became an accomplished small town gunsmith, photographer and artist. He painted pictures of the redwood trees and country scenery. Couple this with Uncle Vern's dry sense of humor and ability to remember and tell stories of his past experiences and you had a kid's paradise. My brother, Bob and I always enjoyed visiting Aunt Mae and Uncle Vern. One time Uncle Vern told us, while giving us a lecture on gun safety, that he considered himself to be one of the safest gun handlers in the world; but in spite of this he'd shot himself twice during his lifetime. Years before he shot off his right thumb with a twelve gauge shotgun while crawling through a wire fence and another time he shot himself through the thigh with a thirty-eight caliber pistol while quick drawing it from his holster. I think you can get the picture. Uncle Vern had the ability to drop a project without a backward glance and attack a new subject with all consuming youthful vigor. Uncle Vern was a dreamer and Aunt Mae was the glue that kept him in touch with reality. They were a great combination and he was a great guy.

By the time my folks made the trip north, the old cars had replaced the horse and buggy for long distance travel. This was the second phase of homesteading and the old trails and wagon roads leading to the first homesteads were gradually being improved so they could be traveled by these new fangled, high clearance, narrow tired cars. These cars looked more like wagons or buggies with engines than the cars as we know them today. I can remember my dad backing up several times to get around a sharp curve in the road leading to our homestead.

This homestead was where our folks lived when Bob was born. I was born a couple of years earlier on Foster Mountain. On the west side of this cabin along the base of the fireplace chimney is where a rattlesnake nearly ended my 115,000 mile horseback ride before it even got started. It was here, a few years later, that I was lifted onto the back of an old bay mare called Babe and the first steps of my horseback ride started when I rode to my first day of school. I will describe these events at a later time as I travel along my long winding trail.

One of the things that stands out in my memory of those real early years was following my dad to the cold spring located below the cabin. Butter and milk were kept cool in the cold water and I remember the excitement when Dad picked up what I thought was a huge watermelon that was floating in the spring box. He packed it back to the table where Mom was preparing a Fourth of July picnic. That watermelon was a real treat.

Another incident that for some reason stands out in my memory happened on a warm spring day when I was lying on my back in the soft green clover that was growing in the clearing that surrounded our cabin. I was lying stone still watching the white fluffy clouds drift through the blue sky when I noticed buzzards circling high above. The buzzards circled lower and lower until they were only a few feet over me. One buzzard cocked his head sideways for a better look and reached up and scratched the side of his head with one foot as he slowly glided by. I suddenly sat up and can vividly remember the swishing of wings and the surprised look as the buzzard desperately tried to gain altitude. I thought that was funny and tried to reenact the scene without success. I didn't realize it at the time but the meal those buzzards were anticipating suddenly and unexpectedly sprang to life.

The horseback ride to school slowly changed those innocent carefree days of youth. About two years after my first horseback ride to school, Dad built Mom a new house located farther back on the same homestead. The following are excerpts from the story of String Creek and Rock Tree Valley published around 1930. The Willits News revisited the history of String Creek and Rock Tree Valley in their Special Focus Edition during 1993.

Willits News Special Focus Edition

In the spring of 1931, John Secrist decided he would have to do something to find a way of making more money. John was a very handy man with tools and machinery, so he hit upon the idea of taking the engine out of their Model T Ford and making a portable saw mill.

"That just about broke my heart," Sarah recalls. "To have him tear down the little Ford car we honeymooned in, but I knew he was thinking about his family and wanting to do what was best for us."

John did all the work himself, with assistance of Uncle Dick Tenney; and an old retired sawyer and millwright, who lived in Willits. The old millwright heard about the project and came to volunteer his assistance.

The three men went to Branscomb to pick up an old donkey engine, which they repaired and hauled back to Oat Ridge. It was used to haul pine and fir logs which were cut on the property and then hauled to the construction site for cutting into lumber.

In the meantime the Secrists were also in the process of change. They had taken out a homestead on some property on the far side of Oat Ridge, looking out over the Circle W Ranch. The little mill was kept running from daylight to dusk to produce the timber to be used in what John planned as a real dream house for his family.

The home that John Secrist built for his family was one of the finest to be built in the area up to that time.

The walls were a double thickness of 1 x 12s with batting, left rough on the interior, which Sarah Secrist says provided plenty of insulation to retain the heat of two wood burning stoves throughout the cold winters.

"All my cooking was on a wood burner in the kitchen, and then we had a potbelly stove in the living room, near the stairwell going up to the second floor, so heat went up to warm the bedrooms." Sarah explains. "At night, the fires were banked so they kept smoldering all night and kept everything toasty."

There was no indoor plumbing, something that none of the houses in the area had at that time, but John did put in a fifty gallon water tank and piped water into the kitchen sink for Sarah, a rare luxury which up to that time had only been seen in the Rock Creek Ranch house.

"Every house had a small outdoor john, some distance from the house" Sarah says, "and bathing was done in wash tubs set up in the kitchen where it was easy to heat water."

"The Alfred Sheltons were the only ones to have a real bath tub. They had a regular old zinc tub on four claw feet which was set up in a small separate room, kind of a closet, just off the kitchen. Everyone thought that was really quite elegant to have a private tub and bathroom like that."

Another modern luxury which John provided for his family was radio. Mother Secrist, John's mother, brought an old battery radio with her when she moved up from southern California, but the radio had not worked for a long time.

One day John was looking at the old radio and said, "I think I'll fix that thing." So he went out to the car and took out the battery and fiddled around and finally went up on the roof and fixed up a kind of aerial for it, and told me to turn the knob on the radio," Sarah recalls.

"I'll never forget that. When I turned the knob a man's voice said, "The next sound you hear will be the sweetest music this side of heaven." It was Guy Lombardo and his orchestra, and the music came rolling into our little home and I was so excited I ran outside and hollered up to John, "It's working—-It's working! And from then on when ever we wanted to hear the radio, John would get the car battery and hook it up."

Sarah says that night as they sat around the supper table still listening to the marvel of the radio, she and John talked about the wonder of it all. "We both couldn't get over the idea that the music had been there all the time in the air, floating around us, and we just had to turn the right knob to tune it in."

One of the special features of the house was the use of beveled glass windshields out of some junked automobiles. John used these for the kitchen windows looking out on a covered back porch where they kept stacks of fire wood and a tall kitchen pantry which served as a food storage place and refrigerator.

"I used to sit at my kitchen table to have a cup of coffee and look out those pretty windows at the little juncos which would fly in to a bird feeder John built for me on the back porch." Sarah recalls.

"One day as I sat there looking out I became aware that the window looked awfully dirty and I went outside to take a look and guess what? There on the porch in the sawdust were prints of a big ole bear which

*stood up on his hind legs and leaned forward with his dirty paws on my
pretty windows to look in my kitchen.*

*I was so mad at seeing my windows dirtied up like that. If I had seen
that bear I'd have whacked him with my broom, that's for sure."*

*That pantry on the back porch was Sarah's pride and joy, with
shelves filled with her canned meats and gravies, jellies, jams, fresh
baked biscuits, pies and cakes.*

*"We had a rule around our place that anyone that went into the
pantry had to keep whistling the whole time. That way, I'd know they
weren't snitching bites of something I had out there cooling for dinner."*

It is hard to realize the conditions documented above were a vast
improvement over the original cabin on the homestead, but you can feel
the appreciation for having a new home in the words Mom used to describe this phase of her life. This was only eighty years ago but compare
the things Mom called luxuries to the living standards of today. Mom
often said during the time she lived on the homestead and the Circle W
Ranch, she had fewer worldly possessions and worked harder than at
any other time of her life. She also said they were the best and happiest
times she ever had.

Mom lived for years with saddles, boots, cowboys, fur pelts, and
rattlesnakes being in and around her house during this part of her life. I
do not remember her ever riding a horse or firing a gun but I knew one
thing, you were better off fighting a buzz saw than taking Mom on if she
thought that someone or something was threatening her family. This is
usually true of moms world wide but I think it is especially true of the
women and ranch wives who live and work on the big ranges of the west.

One incident Mom remembered from her youth was crossing the
United States from Pennsylvania to California on the train with her dad.
It was 1910 and she was seven years old when her dad decided to explore
the possibilities of moving his family west. At that time Arizona was
not yet a state so when the train reached this area, it stopped and waited
until daylight before crossing the Arizona Territory. This was done because the region was considered lawless and inhabited by Indians. This
incident happened only one modern day lifetime ago. Can you imagine
what will take place in the next lifetime?

Dad was an honest, hard working man that could be described as a
"Jack of All Trades."

Where he differed from the old proverb that ended by saying "Master of None" was the fact that he could do them all and do them very
well. He was an accomplished musician of the recreational type. Dad
could play almost any kind of musical instrument by ear though he
couldn't read a note of music. The violin or fiddle and the guitar were

his favorites. During his high school years he played with the then young
Eddy Peabody. Peabody later became known as "The Banjo King" per-
forming on many of the early radio and TV shows. Dad often played
with small pick up bands at country dances and other rural events. During my growing up years Dad was a carpenter, cowboy, ranch manager
and millwright. Sometimes he was doing many of these things at the
same time. In later years Dad built and operated sawmills and managed
logging operations in the Santa Cruz area of California. During World
War II he was chief of the Terminal Island Naval Station security police.
Later he was Commander of the Willits unit of the California National
Guard.   Dad constructed and sold houses until arthritis slowed him
down. He then built thirty two grandfather clocks. They were made
from redwood burl and other exotic woods. He gave most away. When
his hands got too stiff to operate the lathes, saws and other wood working
tools, he turned to building workable miniature steam engines. Simply
said, Dad was a good, hard working man.

   During Dad's cowboy days, my formative years, he had a serious
horseback wreck while heading a cow out on the range. Bolly, the horse
he was riding, fell and when Bolly got to his feet, Dad's foot was hung
up. The toe of his boot was wedged under the fork of his saddle and his
spur was hooked under the cantle. Bolly got up spinning in a tight circle
with Dad swinging straight out in the air on the off side. About the third
round, Dad, out of desperation, put his free foot against Bolly's side and
pushed as hard as he could. He felt his foot slipping out of his trapped
boot and he flew out landing in the brush and rocks. Dad was cut and
bruised but with no lasting injuries. If Bolly had gotten up running instead of spinning there might have been a much different ending to this
story. As long as Dad had that saddle, you could see the deep gash the
spur rowel left in the saddle leather.

   With Mom, Dad, Aunt Mae and Uncle Vern as mentors plus many
others, the foundation for my 115,000 mile horseback ride was formed.

   In my younger years I thought I was born fifty years too late. I
thought the history of the western way of life had passed me by. I grew
up in the range country reading Will James books. Listening to stories
of good and bad horses, cattle drives, wildfires, rattlesnakes, hard winters, blizzards, bear hunts, lion kills, warm spring days and tall grass.
All of these told by men who actually lived the stories they were telling.
I remember lying in front of an old fire place in a ranch house or beside
a pot-bellies wood stove in a bunk house, while stories of horse wrecks
and wild rides unfolded so vividly.

   There were stories, mostly told in bunk houses, about the shapely
young lady school teachers and the twenty-five mile horseback rides

traveling to Saturday night dances. The interesting part of these stories developed when several cowboys from different ranches arrived at the same dance with the same lady school teacher on their minds. Mix this with a little whiskey and the stories became very colorful.

Like the young boy playing cowboys and Indians said to his mother, who herself had been a teacher in a one room school house not long before, "Everything was fine until the lady school teachers came out west, marries the cowboys and they all settled down."

When Bob, my brother, and I were growing up everything we did, whether playing, doing chores, or working revolved around ranch activities. Even school was sometimes scheduled around the ranch year. Bob and I rode horseback to school (or at first pony back) four miles to school, eight miles round trip every school day. We were busy kids growing up but it seemed to me like time stood still. I couldn't wait to grow up and work with my dad and the ranch crew. This was especially true during the warm spring days looking out the window of that one room school house dreaming about all the exciting things I knew were going on outside. An example happened on a late spring afternoon.

My dad and Mr. Folsom, the owner of the Circle W Ranch, had gone to Lovelock, Nevada where they purchased about 200 yearling steers. The steers were shipped by rail from Lovelock to Willits, California where they were unloaded in the railroad yard. The next morning Mr. Folsom, my dad, and another rider had trouble getting thorough the noise and confusion that surrounded the railroad corrals. You can imagine how those steers, coming off the Nevada desert, reacted when the corral gate was opened. By the time the steers were rounded up and under control, the ten mile drive to the Circle W Ranch headquarters was well behind schedule.

We couldn't see the steers when they went by the school house that afternoon but we heard them going down the county road. The next recess Bob and I rushed out to the barn behind the school and saddled our ponies. At the time we were riding two Shetland ponies given to ranch kids by the Willits Volunteer Fire Department, sponsors of the Willits Frontier Days Parade and Rodeo. The only stipulation was the ponies had to be ridden every year in the annual parade. Well, when the teacher finally rang the bell, signifying the end of the school day, Bob and I were mounted and headed for home.

Those ponies were probably the most stubborn; bull headed animals I have ever ridden but man were they tough. We caught up with the trail drive about a mile from home. Although the steers had stampeded out of the railroad corrals that morning, by afternoon it was hot and the steers had gone about as far as they wanted to go. Dad was glad to see us and Bob and I were busy riding around trying to be a big help.

I rode up behind a big, long-legged steer that had stopped to rest in the shade of some Manzanita bushes. I whopped him across the rump with my quirt, just as my pony put his head down to get a bite of grass. That steer, being surprised, kicked over the pony's head and hit me in the pit of my stomach with both hind feet. I stayed in the saddle but every bit of wind was knocked out of me. I gasped, chocked and wheezed for what seemed like forever. I couldn't even call for help and just before I thought I was going to pass out, a rush of air hit my lungs and I started to breathe again.

This turned out to be more excitement than I planned while sitting at my desk in school, but before long I had my wind back and was helping to drive the steers home.

I guess hands-on learning really does work, because even though this happened some sixty years ago I can still feel that first rush of fresh air and I never made that same mistake again.

LITTLE THINGS

A man was once heard to say. "I am their leader. Which way did they go?"

LESLIE J. STEWART

Les was inducted into the Nevada Cattlemen's Association Cowboy 100,000 Mile Club in 1982.

This presentation was written by Leslie's wife, Marie, and presented by Bob Wright.

Les Stewart was born in 1920 and spent his entire life on the Ninety-Six Ranch in Paradise Valley, Nevada. He has never worked anyplace else nor has he ever lived any- place else. His father was Fred B. Stewart and his mother was Edith Stock Stewart, the daughter of William Stock, who started the ranch in 1864.

At one time the ranch ran cattle, sheep and horses. During this time they used much grain. The sheep and the commercial horse herds were sold and the "96" raised only enough horses for ranch use. The raising of grain was also discontinued and the "96" evolved into a strictly cattle ranch.

At about age six, Leslie started going along with his father and other buckaroos while they worked cattle on the ranch. During the pre-high school years he learned a lot about working cattle from observing the "old-timers", men like his father: Fred Stewart, The Holt Brothers, Charlie Sheldon, Jim Grigsby and many others, all top old-time buckaroos.

Leslie started doing serious riding about the time he entered high school. He was never much interested in school sports and social events, but rather spent most weekends working cattle horseback on the ranch. During summer vacations he rode with the wagon for about two months on the open range, working cattle and gathering horses. During this time the ranch used many work horses and they were gathered from the open range prior to each haying season. During this two month period he would average about twenty miles a day in the saddle. During the rest of the summer he would spend another two days a week horseback checking cattle on the ranch and moving horses between the hay camps. From age fourteen to twenty, Leslie rode well over 10,000 miles on a horse.

In the fall of 1938, Leslie enrolled in the College of Agriculture at the University of Nevada-Reno. All vacation time and as many weekends as possible were spent on the ranch. When he couldn't get home he still rode whenever possible; riding and breaking horses for several people in the Reno area.

In the spring of 1940 he decided that higher education was not for him. Near the end of the semester, while attending a class in ranch management, the professor was discussing the merits of a tidy farmstead. "When stacking the debris to be burned, don't stack it too close to the barn because you might burn the barn down," he admonished the class.

Leslie thought about this for awhile and decided his education was complete. He packed his saddle and other belongings and headed back to the ranch and never returned to college.

That fall at the age of twenty, he became the buckaroo boss and started running the wagon, riding year round. This he did for twenty-five years. During these twenty-five years when Les was mostly living on the open range, three incidents, from many others he experienced, stood out in his memory.

Les remembered when a rattle snake went swimming. After a day of riding, Les and his crew headed back to camp. Les spotted a large rattlesnake along the trail and decided to get rid of it. He killed the snake and threw it over the creek bank. Later on, back at camp, the buckaroos decided to take a swim and bathe before supper. While in the water Les felt something bumping against his neck. When he looked to see what it was, he was terrified to discover a big rattlesnake partially draped around his shoulders. He batted the snake away and jumped out of the water. When his heart stopped pounding Les realized the same snake he killed earlier in the day had floated down the creek and lodged against his neck. Years later long after this heart stopping incident, Les said, "In my mind's eye I can still vividly see that rattlesnake bumping against my bare shoulders."

In those days all work was done horseback, from the horse drawn chuck wagon with a cavy of about forty saddle horses to everyday ranch work. Leslie spent seven months a year on the range, averaging about twenty miles a day in the saddle or about 4,000 miles a season, plus another 1,500 miles a year on the ranch. During these years he rode at least 120,000 miles horseback.

Looking back Leslie thought this was the best time for buckaroos. They rode spring, summer, fall and quite a bit in the winter. Cattle carrying the "96" brand ran in common with several neighbors from Paradise Valley to the Oregon border, and the Quinn River Valley to the Owyhee Desert. Counting cattle worked in conjunction with the neighbors. The largest being the McCleary Circle-A Ranch, eight to ten thousand cattle a year were handled and about three thousand of these cattle belonged to the "96."

The buckaroo crew consisted of the boss, six to eight riders, a wrangler and a cook. Their home was the wagon. They never saw the inside of a bunkhouse until their work was done in the fall. Some of the better buckaroos who rode with Leslie during these years were Oscar Arnold, Antone "Wild Bill" Guerrica, Frank Sellars, Lil Davey, Lynn Kimball, Fred Raker and Jim Dewar, all of whom learned their trade from the real "old timers."

During this time, Leslie did some rodeoing in Northern Nevada, Northern California and Oregon. He concentrated on calf roping, team roping, and wild cow milking, having found out earlier that saddle broncs were not adding many miles to his time in the saddle.

(Dave's comment: "Along my long winding trail I have noticed that ranch and round-up cooks seem to attract trouble. I guess Les came to the same conclusion because the next two stories he remembered are about round-up cooks.")

Marie continues at the "96" Ranch, while packing up camp to take to the round-up wagon, the man hired to do the cooking decided to climb up on one of the horses that was saddled and ready to go to work. Not knowing much about horses and to no one's surprise, he got bucked off. He was pretty shaken up but otherwise seemed unhurt, so off they went to camp. During the night, terrible moans and groans were heard coming from the cook's tent. Believing the man must be seriously hurt after all, Les decided to take him to the doctor in town. They fixed a bed for him in the back of a pickup, and Les instructed two cowboys to sit with him. It was a forty mile trip across the desert. While going over a particularly rough spot in the road, the injured man began screaming in pain. Les immediately stopped the truck and hollered to the cowboys in the back, "My God, is the man dying?" "No they answered with a laugh. "We were rolling a cigarette and spilled some tobacco in his eyes." After some well placed expletives, the trip continued without any more incidents and the cook made a complete recovery.

On his way back to camp after a trip to the ranch for supplies, Les stopped in at the Circle-A camp where Lynn Kinball was the buckaroo boss. It being late and Les being tired, he decided to stay for the night and go on to the "96" camp the next morning. Several days later he ran into Lynn Kinball again and Lynn was pretty steamed up. He said to Les, "You know better than that. You can't take a man from another outfit to town without the boss's permission. Now we're without a cook."

Les responded, "I don't know what you are talking about. When I left camp, the cook was standing right over there cutting meat for dinner." It took several days for the truth to be known. It seems that the night before, while sitting around the campfire, the cook asked the buckaroos, "What's on the other side of that mountain"? The mountain the cook was referring to was a small rocky ridge not far from their camp. The answer was, "Boise, Idaho." The cook, apparently thinking he needed a drink, decided to be adventurous and walk over to Boise. Two days later, Tom Pedroli found him lost out on the Owyhee Desert, miles from nowhere. The cowboys neglected to tell the cook that Boise was two hundred miles on the other side of that mountain.

Marie continued, with the death of his father, Leslie took over the ranch and had to turn some of the riding over to others. In the early 1960's the range was fenced into individual ranch allotments. This, coupled with better roads and the use of trucks to haul saddle horses, reduced the miles of riding considerably. Even so, he spent three months of the year on spring and fall round-ups, plus nine months of riding on the ranch. He relied heavily on Indian buckaroos from Fort McDermitt during this period. The best of these were Albert and Oscar Skedaddle, Theodore Brown and Tex Northup.

SUMMARY OF MILES RIDDEN BY LESLIE STEWART:

Age 14-20

| Weekends | 4 months | 3,000 miles |

2 months of summer vacation riding with the wagon.

| Average 20 miles per day for 6 years. | 7,000 miles |

Balance of summers. At least 2 days per week on
the ranch. Average 50 miles a week, 6years.   2,500 miles

Age 20-45

7 months on the range. Average 20 miles per day
for 25 years.   100,000 miles
5 months on the ranch. Average 300 miles per
month for 25 years.   35,000 miles

Age 45-60

3 months on the range -2,000 miles per year
9 months on the ranch -1,000 miles per year
3,000 miles per year for 15 years

                                          45,000 miles

TOTAL LIFETIME MILES RIDDEN   192,500 MILES

Dave's comment: After being in the saddle for nearly 200,000 miles, Leslie slowed down. When he passed away on January 28, 2006 he was still living on the "96" ranch where he was born.

LITTLE THINGS

When you get bucked off, that hard thing that comes up and hits you is the ground.

HOMESTEADS

In the early days of my 115,000 mile horseback ride I was fascinated with the remains of homesteads scattered throughout the back country in the most inaccessible, out of the way places imaginable. The Eden Valley Ranch headquarters was thirty miles from town. It took two and half hours of travel time to get there in the winter providing we didn't get stuck in the mud or blocked by wash outs, landslides, downed trees or drifting snow. These old homesteads were located another ten, twenty, thirty or forty miles further back in the mountains. Even at the time I was riding these ranges, the old time homesteads were only accessible by foot or horseback and this was fifty years after they were established.

Some of the old home sites that come to mind are the Barney place, the Gibson cabin, the Crocker place, the Toney field, the Ford place and the Elk Creek cabin. There were others either I have forgotten or their names had already been lost in the past.

When I rode into one of these homesteads or maybe just a home site, I would stop, sit in my saddle and just look around. My first thought was usually, "Why in the world would some old timer pick such an inaccessible, isolated, starvation type patch of ground when at that time, there was so much accessible, good, open, fertile ground available?"

I've been told by people that lived during this time that many of these old homesteaders were soldiers just returned from World War I. Some still suffered from the effects of mustard gas and they just wanted to get away from civilization and be left alone. This may be true, because some were referred to as ex-officers and were addressed by the names of Sergeant, Lieutenant or Private, as they had been called in the military. At other times the old loners in these secluded cabins were there because of previous brushes with the law. Very often they were not seen by the occasional rider that passed by.

The homesteads I mentioned above and visited once or twice a year were remarkably similar. Of course, they were located along streams or springs. In most instances the cabins I am familiar with were located above the water source making it necessary to pack the water uphill to the cabin. This remains a mystery to me and I never did find an old timer who could give me a satisfactory reason for this. The only cabin I can recall where the cabin was located below the spring, was in the most remote, rugged canyon in the area. The cabin was still partially standing. It was made of sawed boards with a split shake roof while most other isolated cabins of the time were made of logs with sod roofs. Another thing that was unusual about this cabin was the twenty foot long fir poles that had been notched or veed out and placed end to end with overlapping joints. The veed out poles were placed on x shaped stands forming a trough that carried spring water down to the cabin below. A stand at the lower end of this pole trough was high enough above the ground to put a bucket or tub under and the remains of a galvanized tub were still close by. Of all these isolated cabins I used to ride by, this was the only one that had water running to the front door.

These old homestead sites could be identified by small areas that had been cleared, the remains of old rock fireplace chimneys, three or four old half dead apple trees with broken limbs that through the years had been stripped down by bear or coon climbing to reach fruit. In some areas parts of an old Monarch-type cook stove marked where the cabin had been located. Sometimes there would be a double row of daffodils that still bloomed in the spring, indicating the path to the cabin's door. This may have reflected a woman's influence. Anyway these hardy old flowers long out lasted the people that planted them. As indicated by the rocks or pieces of log walls still standing, these cabins were unimaginably small. Most were about ten by twelve feet in size. In the case of the Barney homestead located in this timbered wilderness, it is said the old settlers raised thirteen children. Talk about the Seven Wonders of the World. When riding by the Barney place, I imagined I could hear the commotion that still had to be echoing through the surrounding trees.

I was a kid working for the Eden Valley Ranch when this next incident took place and at the time I knew the names of the two deputies involved. As the story was told to me, the Mendocino County Sheriff learned a man wanted by the law was hiding at the Crocker Place, a deserted cabin located in the wilderness. Two deputized men were sent to investigate. These were not seasoned law enforcement officers. These were men who lived in and understood the back country. This was a common practice in northern California's wilderness during this part of the state's history.

Even though I rode these ranges in the latter part of this historical time frame, I was officially sworn in and was a Mendocino County Deputy Sheriff, but I never wore the badge unless called upon because of some incident that occurred on the range I was familiar with. When the two deputies approached the Crocker Place, they saw smoke coming from the cabin chimney. They tied their horse up a hundred yards back in the timber and slipped in close to the cabin door. They stationed themselves separately behind two trees and called out, "This is the law, come out with your hand up." After a short silence the cabin door burst open and a man firing a lever action Winchester rifle ran for the surrounding brush and trees. In the gun battle that followed, it was thought the outlaw was shot in the chest, but despite this he was able to disappear into the timber. According to the story, it was not known if he lived or died a lonely death somewhere back in the mountains. As far as I know he was never seen again.

Six or seven years after the incident I just described, while I was gathering cattle, I rode into the Crocker homestead. The Crocker Place was located about twenty miles from the home ranch back in timber along the east side of Mt. San Headron. The cabin was still standing although it had been deserted for years. The year before when coming by the cabin, I stopped and looked inside. There was a big packrat's nest in the middle of the floor. The door was closed, the old cook stove was still in place and the single window I looked through was not broken.

On this day as I rode toward the cabin, I smelled smoke and a tense feeling came over me. In this remote area it was extremely unusual to meet another person. My horse was nervous and my dogs that had been ranging out came in close behind. I was careful to stay in full view as I approached the cabin. When I got closer, it became apparent by the lazy curl of smoke coming from the chimney, that the cabin was occupied. I could see freshly split wood loosely stacked beside the front door. I stopped a ways from the cabin and my, "Hello. Is anybody home?" greeting was met by an eerie silence. I looked around at the brush and timber that surrounded the old cabin and the creepy feeling of being watched sent a shiver up my spine. Had I been seen or heard long before my arrival? After my second, "Hello. Is anybody home?" was again met by silence, I sat still for maybe two minutes just looking around. My horse and dogs stood like statues, their ears pointed toward the timber to my right. Could they hear or see something that I could not?

Upon hearing or seeing nothing during this period of time, the uneasy silence got the best of me and I turned and rode on. I didn't shake that creepy feeling of being watched until I was a mile or two further down the trail. The next year when I visited the Crocker place it was completely deserted as it had always been. There was no smoke coming from the chimney. The only evidence of recent human activity was a few sticks of split fire wood still piled beside the cabin door.

When looking back to the day I saw smoke coming from the chimney of that cabin, I sometimes wonder if I'd seen ghostly images from the past or if I had seen a true to life partial reenactment of the incident that happened at the Crocker cabin a few years earlier.

While riding by these isolated deserted homesteads, it was always easy for me to let my imagination run wild, but after the incident I described above, when I saw smoke coming from the deserted homestead cabin chimney, I always had an especially spooky feeling when riding by the Crocker Place. I still wonder if whoever was occupying the cabin on that long ago day just didn't want to be seen or if there was a real outlaw inside the cabin waiting to burst through the cabin door.

This remains another unsolved mystery I encountered along my long winding trail.

The only one of these old isolated homesteads that was still occupied by its original owner when I visited it was the Ford place. We were living at the Circle W Ranch and Bob, my brother, and I were riding eight miles round trip to the one room country school. It was a weekend and after supper Dad announced that he was going to be riding the back part of the ranch along the south fork of the Eel River in the morning. He was going to stop by the Ford place and wanted us to go with him. We were excited. This was wild country. We'd heard stories about the piles of flint chippings located on low ridges above the river where Indians sat and made arrowheads in times gone by. We'd heard stories of fishing trips during salmon runs and exciting adventures retold of running wild cattle through the brushy draws and canyons along the river.

Mom packed each of us a sandwich and not long after daylight we were saddled and on our way. Dad was leading with Bob and me following in single file up the steep brushy trail. Dad knew Mr. Ford from previous trips and around the middle of the day we reached the Ford cabin. As was the custom of that day, we approached the cabin in full view, stopped a short distance from the cabin door and Dad gave the traditional greeting, "Anybody home?" There was only silence. The cabin was nearly hidden by trees and the ground around the door was worn bare. This cabin was located closer to the timber industry than the isolated cabins I previously described, so it was built out of sawed boards and had a split shake roof. A double bitted axe stood to the right of the door. An old army type rifle that must have weighed twenty pounds leaned against the left door sill.

To me the rifle looked something like a crowbar with sights. Smoke was rising from the chimney and the door was open. Suddenly from our left, seemingly coming out of nowhere, an old man was standing in full view. The stern expression on his face turned into a broad smile when he recognized Dad. It was apparent the two men were glad to see each other while they walked forward with arms extended and shook hands. Mr. Ford accepted Bob and me with open arms; obviously a friend or Dad's family was a friend of his.

We loosened cinches, tied up horses, and Mr. Ford waved us into the cabin. The cabin was probably ten by twelve feet in size with a bed at one end. A cook stove and window were in the other end of the cabin. A board table and a homemade wooden chair sat in the middle. A black coffee pot was simmering on the cook stove where the stove lid had been removed. The lid was off the coffee pot and it appeared to be about half full of coffee grounds. Mr. Ford poured a cup and handed it to Dad. I was surprised that the black liquid poured and even more surprised that Dad drank it. Dad later said the coffee was strong enough to curl the hair on his chest. Bob and I both declined the offer. Mr. Ford, without saying a word, went out the door and a short time later returned with a bright shiny can of Dole's pineapple. He opened the can with an old wooden handled, hook billed can opener.

Now, talking to us all the time, he got out two cups, spooned a half can of pineapple into each cup and placed them on the table that Bob and I stood beside. At the time I didn't understand the significance of this, but in later years I came to realize that the pineapple was one of Mr. Ford's prized possessions and something he didn't eat every day. He'd packed it in on his back to be used marking some holiday or important event in his life and instead he gave it to us. While Bob and I ate cold, sweet, juicy pineapple, Dad and Mr. Ford drank coffee and swapped stories. Mr. Ford was eager to hear news and current events that were happening in the outside world and Dad was anxious to learn what areas the cows were using and when they had last been seen.

We got home, took care of our horses and did chores in the dark. Then we sat down to a hot dinner consisting of homemade bread, mashed potatoes, home canned vegetables, topped off with apple pie.

The last thing I remember of that day before going to bed was Mom and Dad doing dishes at the kitchen sink. Mom washed and Dad dried while Dad told her about the events of that day.

The things I remember most about Mr. Ford and his isolated cabin were his surprise appearance out of the timber, that black coffee pot, the pile of rusty cans and coffee grounds outside of the window partially blocking the view and, of course, the taste of that cold, sweet, juicy pineapple eaten at the end of a long hot horseback ride, generously given by an old man that had little, in surroundings where it was least expected. It remains one of the little things along my 115,000 mile horseback ride that stands out in my memory.

Other homesteads, not as isolated as the ones I just described, were located in the back country but in more open areas. They were surrounded by meadows, streams and valleys with fertile land and good grazing on all sides. They were first accessible by teams and wagons before the old cars, new and exciting in their day, came into use. The residents raised gardens, put up hay, milked cows, raised chickens, pigs, large families and built one room school houses. These homesteaders were nearly self sufficient. They went to town yearly or semi-yearly to purchase staples such as flour, sugar, shoes and cloth to make clothing. They often bartered for the things they needed. These people were strong, self reliant individuals and I worked and lived among them especially in the later part of their lives. I participated in and listened to the stories of incidents that took place during their lives.

Harvey was a mountain man and cowboy I worked with for many years. I learned many things about the mountains, nature, livestock, and wild animals during the time Harvey and I rode together. I wasn't involved in the next homesteader stories I recall, but I know them to be true.

One story was about a widow lady that Harvey knew in his younger days. Her husband died and she stayed on the homestead raising a big garden, along with chickens, pigs, a milk cow and a few sheep. Neighbors though few and far between, sometimes stopped by to visit and maybe stay overnight to help with butchering or cutting wood. As the years went by, she simply became known as the widow lady living on the homestead about twelve miles up the creek. On this day she was down on her knees picking string beans. As was normal when she worked in her garden, she wore a pair of baggy old bib overalls. She had been in one spot for some time and just before she started to move on up the row, she looked back and saw the last six inches of a rattlesnake crawling out of sight up her baggy pant leg. She kneeled there perfectly still, holding on to the stake that supported her row of string beans, until the snake, being stopped from crawling further up her pant leg by her bent knee, finally turned around and crawled back out. She continued to stay perfectly still until the rattlesnake was a safe distance away before she jumped up, grabbed her hoe and killed the snake. She threw the snake over the fence out of her garden, picked up her basket of beans and calmly walked to the house. People that think they are strong willed and in control of their emotions should try this some time. This is an example of how these old homesteaders survived in nearly unsurvivable circumstances. This story was told to me while I traveled along my 115,000 mile horseback ride.

Another story Harvey told that involved homesteaders was about a friend named Sam who was riding horseback across country. He had a pack horse carrying his bed roll, some food and a few necessities he used when camping out. Sam was looking forward to spending the night with a family of homesteaders that lived along the route he was traveling. In those days there was no way to call ahead or give advance notice so when he rode into the homestead just before dark, his arrival was a welcome surprise. He was met first by an old hound with a litter of half grown pups loudly announcing his presence. Then excited kids poked their heads out of the door and windows of the barn. His horses were taken care of and, as was the custom, he was invited to spend the night. The conversation was lively and after supper, overriding Sam's protest, the kids were sent to the barn to spend the night in the hay loft so Sam could stay in the house and sleep in a comfortable bed for a change. When the fire in the fireplace turned to coals and the conversation slowed down, everyone turned in for the night.

Earlier in the evening when Sam entered the house he noticed the screen door at the front porch had a large spring attached that slammed the door shut behind him. He also noticed the hound with her pups sleeping at the far end of the porch.

Everything was silent and Sam was just dozing off when that old hound let out a bawl and ran across the wooden porch floor, pushed the screen door open and it slammed shut behind her while she ran through the front yard barking at some real or imagined intruder. She was soon followed by the six pups in single file with the spring door slamming shut behind each hound. At this time doggy doors had not even been thought of but the screen door was old with a broken corner at the bottom and the hounds learned to open the door from the outside. In a few minutes the process was reversed with the old hound still leading and seven times the screen door slammed shut behind her and each of her pups. This process was repeated every hour or so throughout the night and no one else in the house seemed to notice. The next morning after- breakfast thank yous and best wishes were offered while several gifts of food were added to Sam's pack and he was on his way. Sam turned and waved to the family, still standing in the yard, one final time before he rode out of sight. When Sam left the house that morning he also noticed the hounds were all asleep in the far corner of the porch and he thought to himself, " No wonder they sleep all day."

Later recalling this incident, Sam said he was very appreciative of the hospitality he'd been given so he was very careful not to mention the sleepless night to his friends. But Sam did admit to thinking, as he rolled his bed roll out the following night, that sleeping under that stars on the hard ground wasn't so bad after all.

Left to right front row: Dave Secrist, Helen Shelton, Harold Crothers, Bob Secrist
Back Row: Bill Shelton, Mrs, Branch, our teacher, Don Graff, Mr. Branch

THE ONE ROOM SCHOOL HOUSE

My memories of a one room country school are given from the perspective of a six to ten year old and may not completely coincide with
an adult point of view. The incidents and stories I remember most did
not come from the book learning part of my education. I am including
these school stories in my 115,000 mile horseback ride because I rode
horseback to and from school most of the time while I was attending
grammar school.

Our school house consisted of one room with a woodshed attached
to the north end of the building. There were several rows of solid oak

desks with ink wells in the corners. The teacher's desk was elevated at the head end of the room along with the blackboard and a pot bellied wood stove. The American flag was on the wall as well as on the flag-pole outside in the school yard.

There was a horse shed with several stalls and two outhouses in back of the school house and an open sided well house out front. The well was equipped with a hand crank winch attached to a long rope. A bucket was fastened to the rope and when it was dropped down the well, the bucket filled with water. The bucket of water was brought to the surface by turning the handle on the winch. A long handled dipper for drinking hung on a nail and somewhere in the vicinity there was a bench with a wash basin, a bar of soap and a towel. The pasture in front of this was big enough to play baseball and the hillside had Oak trees to climb. A barbed wire fence enclosed the entire area.

All eight grades were taught in one room and it took a minimum of six kids to keep the school open. Of course, sometimes there were more kids, but at other times the teacher boarded a child to keep the school operating.

The teacher, or the older kids under the teacher's supervision, split and stacked wood, cleaned the school room, and raised and lowered the outside flag everyday. The book learning part of school was serious business. Each day started with the Pledge of Allegiance to the Flag of the United States of America. Each grade had the appropriate level of school work to do. There was a lot of hands-on instruction and when the school bell rang we came in, kept our mouths shut, and tried to pay attention. If we got into trouble at school and our folks found out, we were in double trouble when we got home. Now, recess was a different situation. The kids came from isolated locations and when we got to-gether, we played hard physical activities such as running, jumping, rac-ing, and climbing.

Everything was spontaneous and fiercely competitive. We played some standard games but for the most part we just made up games to play.

When I was in the second or third grade a girl and I were chasing a ball across the school yard running full tilt. I was ahead and when I slowed down to pick up the ball, we collided and I went head first through the barbed wire fence. (Those country girls were tough.) I came out the other side with an eight inch gash in my right forearm. I do not remember how we got there but I do remember my mother and I being in Dr. Babcock's upstairs office in Willits, California. Dr. Babcock was a huge man with a shiny bald head. He was a legend in his own time, making the transition from a horse and buggy doctor to the administrator of a then modern hospital. He put my forearm on a cold white table top, swabbed some mecuricom on the cut, and with a pliers-like instrument that had metal clamps looking something like hog rings, he started clamping the wound together. There was no anesthetic and it took eight clamps to close the wound. About halfway through this procedure I began to panic. My mother was trying to calm me down when Dr. Babcock bent his shiny bald head down and said, "Son, just reach up and grab a hand full of my hair and hang on." By the time I got through this distraction and couldn't find any hair to grab, the last clamp was in place.

My folks paid the doctor bill probably not all at one time or maybe they traded for services rendered. When we were on the homestead, Dad built a small homemade sawmill and sold lumber. He gave lumber to Dr. Babcock, who at the time was building his house. Another time Dad made a hand tooled leather belt with a hand engraved silver buckle and gave it to Dr. Babcock to help pay medical expenses.

After this experience was over my dad helped the school board take down the barbed wire fence that surrounded the school house and the entire incident was forgotten. In today's environment my folks could have sued the school district and at the ripe old age of seven I could have retired.

The first teacher I remember was Mr. Stoner. I was in the first grade and riding an old bay mare named "Babe" three miles round trip to school each day. There had been some problems with the lady teacher who taught previously at the Rock Tree School and the school board was scrambling to keep the school open. Paul, or Mr. Stoner, as we learned to call him, was a young cousin in our family just graduated from college with a teaching degree. He applied for the Rock Tree School District's teaching position. Because Paul was from the city, the Rock Tree School Board was already skeptical. They were concerned about Paul's ability to control the country kids and at the same time convert to the country way of life.

The story later told stated that the school board chairman told Paul the Board would hire him, then gave Paul the following advice (and I assume the chairman was at least partly joking when he said,) "Because you will be the only man in the valley that does not have a real job, part of your responsibility will be to hunt and furnish meat for the Rock Tree community." Maybe this was his way of initiating a young city oriented teacher. Paul and his young wife, Louise, moved into an empty farmhouse and quickly adapted to the country lifestyle. In the winter Paul ran a trap line while going to and from school and he was a very good hands-on teacher. After leaving the Rock Tree School, Paul pursued a lifelong teaching career and retired as a high school student counselor.

I am sure in later years he looked back on his first teaching assignment with fond memories and good humor.

The incident I remember the most, while Mr. Stoner taught at the Rock Tree School, happened on a warm spring day. It was recess and we were out around the well house snaring lizards using long slender wild oat stems with nooses tied in their tops. We would snare lizards one recess, tie them up to the well house with the oat stems and the next recess we would have lizard races. Mr. Stoner was sitting on the well house platform keeping track of what was going on or maybe watching for rattlesnakes when he asked Roland, an eighth grade boy, if he had completed his morning assignment.

Roland said something like he hadn't and wasn't planning to. Roland was a good kid but in this time and place, a country boy in the upper grades may have missed school to work for awhile, thus being older and more independent then the grade he was in indicated.

Mr. Stoner walked over and picked up a small redwood rail about six feet long, looked Roland in the eye and said, "I will make you a deal. I will give you a twenty yard start and if you can outrun me you do not have to finish the assignment. If I can catch you I am going to break this rail over your butt and you will stay after school until the assignment is done." This was not a hostile confrontation. It was deadly serious but more like a friendly competition and Mr. Stoner seemed to be enjoying the challenge.

As young as I was I knew what Roland had in mind. He thought he could outrun Mr. Stoner, have the afternoon off, still arrive home on time after school, and no one would be the wiser.

Roland accepted Mr. Stoner's challenge, got a head start, and they were off. They ran across the school yard with Mr. Stoner's stick waving in the air. We heard them splash across String Creek and start up through the timber on the other side. The lizard project was forgotten. We sat bunched together on the well house steps and waited and waited and waited. Finally we heard the whack, whack, whack of that redwood rail and Roland hollering for dear life. In a little while Mr. Stoner and Roland returned, walking side by side across the school yard. Mr. Stoner walked over and threw the broken rail on the wood pile. Roland went into the schoolhouse and school resumed in a normal manner. I do not remember hearing another word about this rebellious incident.

Years later I think I figured out what really happened that day. Mr. Stoner had a long hard run before he caught Roland and when he did they sat down to catch their breath. Then they had a very serious conversation. Mr. Stoner whacked that rail over a tree trunk until it broke while Roland hollered for dear life. Then they shook hands and returned to the school yard. However this confrontation played out, Mr. Stoner proved his point. One eighth grade student and a group of young school kids were seriously impressed.

About this time our family moved to the Circle W Ranch. Bob and I rode horseback eight miles round trip each day to school. The next teacher I remember was Mrs. Branch. She was a very compassionate lady. I remember several events while Mrs. Branch was our teacher. The first happened after a winter storm. Tomkie Creek overflowed its banks and new sand and gravel bars were dangerous to cross. Our folks made arrangements for us to stay with Mrs. Branch and her husband until the water went down and it was again safe for us to ride horseback to school. When Tomkie Creek receded and Dad could wade across, he drove Bob and me to the creek which was as far as the car could go. He then packed us across the creek so we could walk the rest of the way to school. We watched him again wade the creek and start turning the car around. Then we turned and started to leave for school. We'd just walked a little ways when suddenly we sank in some muck and silt left by the receding water. The suction was so great that we could not get out. By now Dad was turned around and leaving. We waved, hollered and screamed but because the creek was roaring and the car was running, Dad could not hear us. We thought for sure he was headed home but for some reason he looked back, realized we were in trouble and came running to our rescue. He pulled us out of the muck, but our boots didn't come out with us.

After we were safely on dry ground, Dad returned to the mud and had a hard time pulling our boots free. Dad was more concerned about this incident then we were because he realized the potential seriousness of the situation. While Dad returned to the car, Bob and I started walking the rest of the way to school.

Another experience I remember while Mrs. Branch taught school was the yearly visit from the Superintendent of Schools. His name was Mr. Good and he was a very stern looking man. When he came everyone in school including the teacher was nervous. Class adjourned while Mr. Good and Mrs. Branch discussed school matters. When the bell rang we returned to class and under Mr. Good's watchful eye continued our assignments. He came to each student's desk and made comments. In my case he removed the pencil from my left hand, placed it in my right hand and lectured me on the benefits of right handed writing. After Mr. Good's visit ended I switched the pencil back to my left hand and Mrs. Branch continued teaching as if she had not noticed a thing.

Yet another memorable incident took place when Mrs. Branch and her husband loaded the entire school into their touring car and drove to the 1939 San Francisco World's Fair. Some of us hadn't traveled on pavement before and the 145 mile trip down Highway 101 was an exciting experience. Mrs. Branch must have had a constitution of a mule and the patience of Job. Her single minded purpose was to see that we were safe and having a good time as she showed us some of the educational wonders of the world. We were dressed in the best clothes we owned. They ranged from an itchy new wool suit to outgrown pants that were too short. Through all of this Mrs. Branch didn't say one cross word even when I got car sick.

Mrs. Branch tried hard to impress us with the importance of a new invention called television. The display had two small wooden houses placed about 15 feet apart. There were hinged doors on the front of each building and these buildings looked like two outhouses to me. Mrs. Branch lined us up outside and the display operator put one of us in each structure and closed the doors. It was dark inside with a little lighted box maybe ten by twelve inches in size hanging on the wall. When standing in a certain position we could see, hear and talk to each other as if we were standing in the same room. This was the beginning of modern day television. Mrs. Branch knew this was an important invention and she wanted us to see it. I doubt if even she could comprehend the magnitude of the industry that was to follow.

My one room school days came to a close, and with these memories I continued along my 115,000 mile horseback ride.

LITTLE THINGS

I once saw a sign posted along a desolate country road in Modoc County, California. It was during mule deer hunting season and the sign read, "If it is standing still—Do Not Shoot—It may be our hired man."

JIM ANDRAE

Jim Andrae was inducted into the Nevada Cattlemen's Association Cowboy 100,000 Mile Club in 2006.

Jane and I spent some interesting time with Jim and his wife, Sharon, at their home located in the desolate sagebrush country in northern Elko County, Nevada.

Jim is another cowboy that is a real cowboy's cowboy. Jim and Sharon are gracious hosts but Jim is not much interested in talking about himself. It is easy to see Jim is more comfortable doing the things that happened along his long winding trail than talking about them. He isn't very interested in documenting the many miles he has ridden horseback either. These miles are just another byproduct of the life he has lived. If you doubt that Jim has ridden well over 200,000 miles on the back of a horse, just look up at his picture and look into his eyes, if you still doubt Jim's ridden over 200,000 miles horseback, you can challenge him if you want to.

The following are a few recollections from our visit with Jim. The early part of Jim's life was spent in a different time with different facilities to work with when compared to today. On the big ranges of the west, most horses of that day were raised in an open range environment. Jim often lived in isolated cow camps and much of the time worked alone using whatever methods he could to get the job done.

Remember, the horses Jim broke during this time frame were big stout five, six, or seven year old "colts." With the exception of being gathered from the range when they were branded and marked, they were never again touched by a human hand until Jim started to break them. These horses were not halter broke and were used to surviving by their instincts and the old law of survival of the fittest.

Jim said, "I was riding these horses outside by the second or third ride and before long I was working cows and roping on them."

I asked Jim if there was a humorous incident that stood out in his memory and without hesitation he told me this story.

He said, "One evening I rode a colt I was breaking into the barn at the Spanish Ranch headquarters. I rode the colt into one of the horse stalls. In those days the horse stalls had a deep manger in the front end and an open window behind the stall used when the stalls were being cleaned out. What I didn't know at the time was that another cowboy had roped a wildcat earlier in the day and somehow brought the cat in alive and put it in the deep manger in the front end of the stall I was riding the horse into." Jim continued, "The colt stretched out his neck, put his nose over the top of the manger, snorted, spun around and was running flat out when he tried to jump through the window behind the stall. The barn was old and the boards were brittle so the horse and I, being bigger than the window, took the whole side of the barn out as we went through. I finally got control of the horse a half mile out in the sagebrush. Jim said, "It was two or three weeks before I could get that horse back in the barn and for years people would ask why there were new unpainted boards in that section of the barn."

The following presentation was written by Sam Mori and given when Jim was inducted into the Cowboy 100,000 Mile Club:

Ladies and Gentlemen, I would like to introduce you to a man who is unique to our industry in many ways. This man had ridden a horse over 100,000 miles by the time he was thirty-five years old.

Jim Andrae was born and raised in the rough country of northern Nevada, mainly in the Tuscarora area. He attended Elko County schools and graduated from Elko High School while at the same time he was cowboying and working on local ranches. The only time he took a leave from cowboying was to serve his country in the United States Army.

When Jim got home from the Army he went right back to work riding horses. Also, soon after he got home he married Sharon Smith whose

Dad was the manager of the IL Ranch. Jim and Sharon had a son and their family and career expanded.

Jim first became cow boss and later manager of some of the largest ranches in the United States. He worked for the Spanish Ranch, the TS and IL ranches, as well as other sizable outfits. During this time every cow was moved by horseback and most salt was packed using horses. There were no gooseneck trailers in those days, so a 20 mile trot to get to where the circle started was common.

Jim became a cowboy in a different time. The horses that he made a living with were tough, mean and not as smart as today's horses. They were hard to catch. If you got one caught you couldn't saddle him. If you got him saddled you couldn't bridle him. If you got him bridled you couldn't get on. If you got on you couldn't get off. These horses were hard to shoe and dangerous to be around on the ground.

Jim showed me how to tie a horse's left front leg to the saddle horn, to foul him enough to be able to get on and then release the rope and be ready to go! Jim made a living on these horses for many years.

If you were to call Jim at 4:00 AM any morning you wouldn't have to worry about waking him up. Jim has a work ethic that is go, go, go. Anyone who has worked for him can attest to this fact.

Ladies and gentlemen, it is my sincere pleasure to introduce you to our newest member of the Cowboy 100,000 Mile Club, Jim Andrae.

Dave's comment: The point to be made here is that some horses are still raised and handled much as Jim described in his early days as a cowboy, but for the most part horses of today are raised under different conditions and broke to halter and to ride at a much younger age. This doesn't mean many of the challenges Jim faced as a young cowboy do not still exist today. It does mean that in Jim's early days working under the conditions of that time, "horse whispering" was not a practical method to use. Having said that, there never was a successful big range cowboy that didn't have a good line of communication with his horse. At times, all of us who have ridden horseback for a lifetime have used some form of horse whispering. We just didn't know it had a name.

LITTLE THINGS

An old saying, "Don't hire a man who rolls his own or wears a straw hat. If he isn't rolling a cigarette he's chasing his hat.

LITTLE THINGS

No matter how hard you try, you can't put an old person's head on young shoulders.

TRAIL DRIVES

I have been on hundreds of cattle drives during my 115,000 mile horseback ride and probably close to a thousand if all of the every day cattle movements from range to range and pasture to pasture were included. The largest cattle drive I was responsible for was 3,000 head. The smallest was one bull. Several things I have learned about driving cows during this time are as follows:

Sometimes it takes more cowboys to drive one cow than it takes to drive a one hundred head cow herd.

Sometimes the slower you go the faster you get there, especially when driving cows and calves.

An hour in the morning is worth two hours in the afternoon.

In the mountains a good cowboy with good dogs is worth two cowboys.

A cowboy with uncontrollable dogs isn't worth the trouble he causes.

Mothering cows and calves after a long hard drive takes a lot of patience.

The first cattle drives I remember taking part in, as a useful cowboy, took place during summer vacations when I worked for the Eden Valley Ranch. The ranch headquarters were located in a valley, surrounded by mountains, thirty miles east of Willits, California. At this time the ranch ran a total of one thousand head of livestock. This included cows, yearlings, two and three year old steers and bulls. Yes, they were three-year-old steers. Selling grass fat three year old steers, raised on the rough, steep coastal mountain ranges of northern California was the custom at this time. The three year old steers weighted about one thousand pounds when we gathered and trailed them to the railroad shipping corrals located on the eastern outskirts of Willits. During the latter part of this time frame the steers were sometimes driven to the Dutch Harmes corrals or the Don Coleman ranch where they were shipped to the Sacramento Valley by truck instead of by rail.

These three year old steers were born and ran out on the range year round. After they were marked and branded as calves, and dehorned as yearlings, they seldom if ever saw a man on foot. At times this made the yearly, two day, thirty mile beef cattle drive interesting, especially on the second day when we trailed fifteen miles down a country road, getting closer to civilization with every passing mile. The Red Hill, obviously named for the red colored dirt it was made of, was the last steep descent before reaching the Little Lake Valley. The county road going down the Red Hill was steep, narrow and crooked with sharp turns and few places for the old cars of the day to pass each other. When the lead steers of the cattle drive met a car coming up the Red Hill, the situation was tense.

Once there was a man who got out and stood in front of his new touring car apparently thinking he would keep the cattle from bumping into it. Then there was a lady in a colorful dress that got out of her car, left the car door open and stood in the middle of the road taking pictures. Another time there was a family car with the kids sticking their heads out of the windows hollering, while the family dog barked. Last but not least was a car that refused to stop and came toward the steers with the owner blowing the horn. Various scenarios of the incidents mentioned above happened every year during the annual beef cattle drives. These were all obstacles that had to be dealt with while trailing range raised steers down the Red Hill.

Roland Williams, the old time ranch manager responsible for getting the cattle delivered in good condition and on time took his job seriously. He usually rode in the lead, especially when going down the Red Hill. Sometimes when the pressure was on, he wasn't very diplomatic. I can still see those wild eyed steers milling around behind him as he menacingly whirled his romal overhead while he urged his horse forward, hollering "Get the hell back in that car, turn the motor off and sit still, so I can get these steers by you."

I took part in these cattle drives for a number of years and though I was only in my teens I became a seasoned trail driver. I learned to recognize and anticipate problems before they actually happened. In later years, after the youthful excitement of being on a cattle drive wore off and the cattle drives became more routine, Roland would tell me to take the lead when we reached the top of the Red Hill. I never knew for sure if he realized times were changing and a different approach was needed when range raised cattle and the general public met or if he was just getting tired of meeting the public. Either way I would lead the herd down the Red Hill and through the Little Lake Valley to the shipping corrals.

I soon learned that most of the problems encountered, when range raised cattle and the general public met, were caused by lack of understanding. When I saw a car coming up the Red Hill I would trot out ahead of the lead steers, stop the car and visit with the people inside. To the people I knew or who lived in the back country I would explain a trail herd was coming, pass the time of day with them and ride on. To the people that didn't understand the situation I would explain that the cattle were not used to seeing vehicles or people on foot. I would ask them to stay inside the car, turn off the motor, be quiet and sit perfectly still until the steers trailed by. I would then thank them for being helpful and ride on. In most instances the lead steers, being used to following my horse, would file by the vehicles without causing a problem.

One incident that happened while I was leading the yearly beef cattle drive through the Little Lake Valley made that particular drive stand out from the rest and vividly remains in my memory. We reached the Little Lake Valley and were having the usual problems with cars, people and barnyard distractions. When we turned a corner in the road I noticed the house up ahead, that had previously been vacant, was now occupied. No one appeared to be home but a large, well kept garden was now growing in front of the house. The garden wasn't fenced and was located close to the road we were traveling. There were rows of sweet corn, string beans on tepee type poles, tomatoes, squash, carrots, etc. The steers were traveling well and the trail herd was stretched out along the road for probably a quarter of a mile. It was past midday and the steers were hot, thirsty and hungry for something green. Knowing what was about to happen I hollered back for help but the next cowboy was around the corner and too far back to hear my call. I made a gallant effort and with the help of my dogs got the lead steers past the garden and traveling on down the road but the steers that followed were out of control. Harvey, the cowboy riding along the right flank of the herd, finally turned the corner and realizing I was in trouble came running to help. We hooped, hollered and beat steers with our ropes. But as soon as we would get one group of steers lined out down the road, the next group of steers spread out over the garden and it was hopeless. Sweat was running down our horses flanks and by the time I had to leave to again get in the lead of the herd, the garden looked like a moonscape. What those thousand pound steers hadn't eaten, they trampled flat.

I knew that garden was an important part of those people's livelihood. So still feeling bad about the incident when we got the steers corralled and not knowing what else to do, I went to the Safeway store and bought a barley sack full of sweet corn, some potatoes, several boxes of tomatoes, string beans, and squash. I loaded them into the old ranch Jeep and took them back to the house behind the garden plot. When I arrived I saw a boy, probably fourteen or fifteen years old, standing in the middle of the ruined garden. He had on bib overalls, with an old straw hat pulled down over his ears. He was just standing in the middle of that once green garden with his head down, leaning on his hoe. I tried to talk to him but he didn't have much to say, so I put the produce on the porch and left. The next day when we were riding back to the ranch, leading a couple of saddle horses, I was feeling especially apprehensive as we approached the place. When we got closer I saw an older lady, sitting on the porch in a chair, gently rocking back and forth. As I rode by she got up, turned to face me and in a strong voice said, "Thank you for the vegetables," before she again turned and disappeared into the house.

Now there was nothing outstanding or unusual about the cattle drive itself. There hadn't been any horse wrecks and we didn't lose any steers along the thirty mile trip. But the image of that young boy standing in the center of his ruined garden, leaning on a hoe, with his head down and the lady's effort to be gracious after losing a garden that was very important to her, has made this cattle drive one of the most memorable I have experienced on my 115,000 mile horseback ride. The image of that young boy is as vivid and clear today as it was all those years ago.

The next trail drive that stands out from the rest is the most difficult cattle drive I ever experienced. It surely wasn't the longest or largest I've been involved with but it was jinxed from the very start by uncontrollable events that nearly proved to be fatal. This cattle drive took place along the same route as the earlier cattle drives I had taken part in as a kid. The main difference was we trailed the cattle in a different direction at a different time of the year. Instead of trailing from the ranch to the shipping corrals in the late summer, we were trailing the cattle from the shipping corrals to the ranch in the late fall. The Eden Valley Ranch had been sold to Firco, a logging company, and Bob and I used the range as care takers for several years. We gathered and sold the few wild cows left in the area, replaced them with cows we owned and ran domestic hogs out on the range, utilizing the squaw clover, filaree and wild oats in the spring and early summer. The hogs grew fat feeding on the abundant crop of acorns in the fall and early winter. We hunted wild hogs and ran cows the year round.

This particular time we purchased about two hundred head of cows. The shipping date and time of arrival at the Don Coleman corrals was established and irreversible when a storm moved in from the coast. Harold Crothers, Bob and I started the thirty mile horseback ride from the ranch to receive the cattle before the storm hit. It was early December and in the coastal ranges of northern California it was not unusual to get two to five inches of rain in a twenty-four hour period. This particular storm hit with a vengeance and turned into a hundred year weather event before it was finished.

When Harold, Bob and I reached the Sadie Frost Corner, the bottom half of Little Lake Valley was flooded. Water covered the county road we were traveling on and we traveled some distance with the water above our horses' knees before we noticed our dogs were not with us. Looking back we realized the dogs were swimming. These were cow dogs not water foul hunting dogs used to swimming. Our dogs were getting tired and beginning to give out when we rushed back to rescue them. We got them to shallower water along the road right-of-way fence until they were rested enough to make it to the bare road above the flood water.

We reached the Don Coleman ranch and the cows arrived later that afternoon, Don and his wife Petey put our dogs, horses and cows up for the night. Early the next morning we started the cattle drive out of the corrals and headed for the winter range fifteen miles away. We knew we had to get the cows out of the flooded valley before the situation got worse. We also knew the Hearst road was closed to traffic because of mud slides, downed trees and wash outs. The phone line was out so there was no way of knowing what the situation at Hearst was like.

We had to cross the south fork of the Eel River before we could turn the cows loose onto Eden Valley range. We originally planned to cross the Eel River on a gravely riffle about a quarter of a mile above the old Hearst bridge. When we rode to town a few days before the storm arrived, the river was down and the cattle could have navigated this crossing without swimming. But by the time the cattle arrived at the Coleman Corrals, the river was estimated to be ten to fifteen feet above flood stage. It would now be impossible to cross the river at the gravely riffle, so we would have to trail the cattle across the Hearst bridge.

The Hearst bridge had been there forever, built before any of us were born. To us it was just part of the mountains that surrounded it and the bridge would always be there. In the winter we crossed the bridge regularly in pick-ups when the road conditions were right. We crossed the bridge with saddle and pack horses when the roads were closed. The bridge was fifty to seventy-five yards long. The decking was built out of wood boards with wire mesh railings on either side and it was a single lane suspension type bridge. To give an idea of the bridge's height, one calm summer afternoon, Frank flew his Piper Cub airplane under the center span of the bridge.

Anyway, crossing the bridge was the least of our worries as we approached the flooded area around the Sadie Frost corner. Sadie's house was located on a corner where the county road made a sharp turn to the east. Coming from the south as our trail herd was coming, the old weathered house looked like it was sitting in the middle of the road. The house had withstood many floods, looked tired and appeared to be settling down into the ground. Sadie was one of the last remaining members of the Frost-Colts family feud that originated in Missouri. The Frosts and Colts migrated to Mendocino County in northern California around the turn of the Twentieth Century where the final stages of their feud played out. There was never any activity around the house and the only time I remember seeing Sadie was once a year, when wearing a long black dress, she rode side saddle on an old white horse in the Willits Frontier Days Parade.

To help alleviate the yearly flooding, the county road crew dug a large ditch or canal along the west side of Sadie's property. This helped drain the water to the lower part of the Little Lake Valley. An eight foot culvert was installed, making a bridge farmers could use when crossing the channel to get to their fields and pastures.

On this morning, as we approached Sadie Frost's corner with our trail herd, everything was a sea of water. Except for the canal on the west side of the road, it was hard to tell if the water was six inches or six feet deep. The canal itself was brim full with swiftly running water filling the big culvert to capacity. The lead cows balked at the flood water's edge and refused to turn east where the road led to higher ground. Some of the cows crossed through the partly down fence into Sadie Frost's flooded yard. Bob and Harold had their hands full keeping the herd together. Bob said, "There was a large pile of firewood sticking up in the middle of Sadie's yard and the cows were trying to climb upon it to get above the water." When Bob and Harold finally got the cows out of the yard and looked back, the wood pile was gone.

I was riding Scrappy, my little roan mare, and I charged through the milling herd in time to stop the cows from crossing the canal at the culvert thus stopping them from getting into the flooded fields to the west. In the mean time several cows had been forced into the canal and were franticly swimming against the current trying to keep from being swept into the culvert. As they tried, they lost ground and one by one they disappeared into the culvert still swimming against the current. By this time Harold and Bob had the main herd going up the road in the direction they were supposed to go, so I could now leave the culvert. Two drowned cows washed out the bottom end and several others that got through alive turned and were swimming down the canal, going with the current that was carrying them into the lake at the lower end of the valley.

A quick look showed me that about seventy-five yards downstream the east bank of the canal sloped off and I thought the cows would be able to climb out. Not knowing how many cows were in the swiftly running water, I raced Scrappy down the berm that was still above water on the west side of the canal. When I got ahead of the swimming cows and the sloping bank was opposite me, I jumped Scrappy into the water thinking the commotion would force the cows over to the sloping bank where they could climb out of the canal and go back to the herd. Well, that part of my plan worked and the cows climbed out of the water.

The part of my plan where Scrappy and I were supposed to swim across the canal and follow the cows didn't materialize. When I jumped her off the bank and she went under the water, instead of swimming, every muscle in her body stiffened up, and we sank to the bottom like a rock. I was chest deep in water, when her feet hit the bottom and she lunged back to the surface. When her head appeared above water, her eyes were shut, her teeth were clamped tightly together and her lower lip was hanging loose. Without moving a muscle she again submerged and again lunged to the surface when her feet hit bottom. The third time she went down and didn't lunge when she hit bottom I kicked loose and started to struggle to keep my head above water. My boots were full of water, the full length yellow slicker was tangled around my legs, my chaps and wool winter coat were saturated with so much water the weight was pulling me down.

In the midst of my struggle I thought I heard someone hollering over the roar of the fast flowing creek. When I looked up I saw Leonard Munson. Sr. standing on the canal bank holding what looked like a coil of rope in his right hand. I learned later that Leonard had some sacks of grain stored in an old shack close by and he was trying to keep the grain dry and above the flood water when he saw me jump into the canal trying to save the cows from drowning. Seeing that I was in trouble he grabbed a coil of old electrical wire that was hanging on the shed wall and came running to help. Leonard threw the coil of wire toward me but it landed a couple of yards short. I made a tremendous effort and lunged toward it. When I had it in my hand a feeling of relief swept over me. I looked up at Leonard and he was just standing there with both hands in the air. That electric wire was stiff and Leonard had thrown it so hard, trying to get it to reach me that the trailing end of the wire slipped out of his hand. Now both ends of the life line were out in the middle of the canal with me. When I realized what had happened the elation I felt the moment before was short lived. With the lifeline useless self preservation took over.

I knew the only chance I had was to reach the sloping bank on the east side of the canal. I started lunging, rolling and thrashing in that direction. After what seemed an eternity one of my feet hit solid ground and I crawled half out of the water and lay back to catch my breath. I was cold, shaking and exhausted.

When I looked upstream I thought, "What the hell?" I saw Scrappy floating down the canal. I was so sure she had drowned and already washed out into the lake that I thought my mind was playing tricks on me but Scrappy really was coming down the canal head first, flat on her side with her eyes still shut, her teeth still clinched tightly together with her lower lip still hanging down. In disbelief I reached out and grabbed the reins as she swiftly floated by and the current swung her around to the canal bank.

Thinking she was dead I was sitting there trying to figure out how I was going to get my saddle and bridle off of her and up onto dry land, when out of frustration I slapped her on the neck and called her name. In an instant she exploded into action. Her head was flopping against the water, her legs were flaying in all directions and when she got her feet under her I really had to scramble to keep from getting trampled while she climbed up that sloping canal bank. I will never know if my cinch was too tight when Scrappy hit the water or if the magnitude of being so suddenly engulfed and submerged in the cold muddy water of the canal just shut her system down. Either way, regardless the cause, we both survived the ordeal and saved a number of cows from drowning in the lake below.

We were now up on the canal bank where Scrappy was vigorously shaking; sending water spraying in all directions, while I poured water out of my boots and reset my saddle. Leonard was still standing on the west side of the canal and I waved and shouted a heart felt thanks for the gallant effort he made trying to save me. I retrieved my hat that was lodged in some weeds along the canal bank, mounted Scrappy and trotted back to the trail herd.

Bob and Harold were having their own problems with the cows scattering everywhere.

They were so busy they were not aware of the problem I was having. With the cows all gathered on high ground and headed in the right direction, we took stock of our situation. Luckily Bob, Harold and I were all right, our horses weren't hurt, and somehow our dogs made it through the flood water and were accounted for. We were lucky that through the whole wreck we only lost two cows. Bob and Harold were wet to their waists and I was wet from head to toe with ten miles still to go. It was becoming crystal clear that this was not going to be a routine, pleasant, ride along, Sunday afternoon trail drive.

We knew that crossing Tomkie Creek along the old Hearst road at flood stage with its gravel bars and quicksand type sinkholes would be treacherous, so we took the Canyon road. We knew we could cross Tomkie Creek on a short wooden bridge at the Bargsten Ranch. When we reached the bridge crossing Tomkie Creek, the water was lapping at the wood decking while the cows filed across.

We made the sharp left turn where the road went through the Bargsten Ranch barn lot. It was one of those rare times during a cattle drive when the herd was completely silent. The cows were really moving out with their heads down, their ears moving back and forth in time with each stride. Not a cow was bawling, not a dog was barking and not a cowboy was yelling.

Part way through the barn lot the sun momentarily broke through and we must have looked like a ghost herd coming out of the clouds. As the day wore on we traveled up Tomkie Hill, went through Scott's Valley, past Calavetche Springs and went down Salt Creek toward Hearst.

As we approached Hearst, partly to get my mind off the bone chilling cold and my numb feet, I let my mind wander to crossing the Hearst Bridge. The old bridge creaked and rattled when a dog or horse crossed it and I knew it was important to get the cows started across the bridge on the first try. We would bunch the cows up on the approach to the bridge, get fifteen or twenty head started and while one of us followed them across, the other two cowboys would string out small bunches of cows until the herd was on the other side of the river. With a little luck we could cross the bridge without incident.

When we got to within a half mile of Hearst we could hear the river roaring and the closer we got, the louder it sounded. When we turned the last corner where we could look down on the bridge I was dumbfounded. There was nothing there, absolutely nothing there but a hundred yards of raging muddy water with an occasional tree or log swiftly floating by. We had driven these cows out of a flooded valley where two cows drowned, ridden for ten hours in wet soggy clothes and now the bridge that had been there forever was gone. The reality of the situation began to sink in: we were one hundred yards from the end of this trail drive and that was as close to the end of the drive as we were going to get. We drove the cows on up the river for a quarter of a mile to a small opening along the river bank. There were no fences but we figured the cows being tired, would stay in the area until early morning.

We had to change our thinking because we could not cross the river and ride to the Garcey Place and spend the night like we had originally planned. We were stranded along the south bank of the river fifteen miles from Willits and one hundred yards from where we wanted to be. We had 200 head of cows, three horses, four dogs and no place to go. The road was closed to traffic, the phone lines were down and it was late afternoon.

We decided Bob and Harold would ride a mile and a half to Emandal, a small summer resort. If the winter caretaker was there they could get dried out and their horses and dogs taken care of. They could be back where we left the cows about daylight the next morning and keep the herd from scattering out into the mountains to the south. I was going to ride back to Willits, explain our problem to the county road crew and return with a pickup load of hay as soon as the road was passable.

Harold was riding a horse named Reno. Reno was the fastest traveling horse of the three horses we had, so Harold and I traded horses and I started the fifteen mile ride back to Willits. After the events of the day, this turned out to be one of the longest fifteen mile rides I ever had.

The county had the road open to four wheel drive vehicles by midafternoon the next day and I got a load of hay hauled to the cows before dark. The cows hadn't much to eat for the past couple of days but one thing we knew for sure - they had plenty of water to drink.

Harold had to return to his regular job and the following week Bob and I more or less camped along the south bank of the river hauling a load of hay from the Little Lake Valley each day to feed the cows.

During this time the river receded to just below flood stage. The morning dawned bright and sunny and I remember the sky being exceptionally blue. Bob and I decided this was going to be the best chance we would have to swim the cows across the river. We gathered the cows and herded them onto a gravel bar that protruded out into the water. The river was still high and we were not planning on swimming across ourselves. We would just force the cows to swim across where they could scatter out over the range and get adequate feed. We planned on the cows angling across the river with the current, where a broad flat area on the other side made it easy for them to walk out onto dry land. Everything was going fine until the lead cows hit the strong current and started to turn back. Bob, who was on the down river side of the cows, knew the first effort we made was our best chance of getting the cow across and he was franticly pushing the cows back into the current. From my position at the back of the herd I could see that Bob was getting too far out into the river. I was hollering at the top of my lungs for him to stop knowing full well he could not hear me over the roar of the river and probably wouldn't have paid any attention if he had. About then Bob reached the point of no return and Dolly, the bay mare he was riding, disappeared under the roaring water. She reappeared a moment later swimming along side of the lead cow. I knew from former first hand experiences that watching helplessly as a wreck develops and not being able to do anything about it, is sometimes worse than being in the wreck yourself and this seemed to be the case now.

Dolly was a strong horse, a good swimmer and she was soon in the lead of the herd. Somewhere along Bob's past he read or an old timer told him that when you are in this type of situation the best thing to do is slip back over your horse's rump, grab your horse's tail and hang on and the horse would pull you through. That is exactly what Bob did. From where I was watching, not knowing what Bob was doing, it looked to me like he had slipped out of his saddle and when he disappeared under the water I thought he was drowning. My heart was in my throat until I saw Bob surface hanging onto Dolly's tail. He was stretched out, behind the horse, paddling with both feet. By now Dolly was halfway across the river, Bob was still hanging onto her tail, and the lead cows were following them. I knew I had to keep the drag herded into the water or the cows would turn back and once they turned back I wouldn't be able to get them in the river again. Those cows must have thought I was three or four cowboys that day as I charged back and forth, hollering and shouting until the last cow was in the river swimming across. When I looked up, Dolly was just dragging Bob out of the water on the other side of the river and the lead cows were coming out on dry land.

Bob was cold and shaking almost out of control when he headed for Frenchy's house. Frenchy, a bachelor, was the only person that lived at Hearst during the winter months. Frenchy wasn't home but Bob got warmed up and found dry clothes before he rode back to the river. Frenchy was a short, stout Frenchman about five feet five inches tall and Bob looked somewhat comical when he arrived at the river wearing Frenchy's dry clothes.

Bob and I couldn't hear each other over the roar of the river so we waved hats and each went on our own way. Bob rode three miles to the Garcey place, a cow camp, where he was batching and I went back to Willits.

The next day a friend hauled Scrappy and me thirty miles to Dos Rios where the state highway bridge crossed the south fork of the Eel River before it emptied into the middle fork of the Eel. I rode Scrappy over Brushy Mountain and back to the Eden Valley ranch.

The rest of the winter we crossed the south fork of the Eel River at Hearst in a rowboat and that is another story in itself, especially the time Bob rowed several hogtied wild pigs weighing about sixty-five pounds each across the river to sell at the Ukiah Livestock auction.

As I mentioned before, this trail drive wasn't the longest or largest trail drive I have been involved with but it is a trail drive that happened along my 115,000 mile horseback ride that is hard to forget.

Left: Dave Secrist   Right: Bob Secrist

OLD BLUE – THE FAMILY MILK COW

I remember one time when my folks got home later than planned. Bob, my brother, and I did our chores and then we decided to start the grown-up chores in order to help them get done before dark. We got along fine until the only thing left to do was milk Old Blue, the family cow. I hadn't milked her alone before.

We got her in the stanchion before we got the grain in the manger so right away the old cow knew something was wrong. Dad would let the calf in to suck on the off side while he sat on that one legged milk stool and milked from the other side. Old Blue gave a lot of milk! Well, we got the calf in and of course the calf went to the wrong side. By the time we got that situation straightened out, Old Blue was nervously switching her tail and stomping around. Manure was flying all over the place. By the time I finally got two inches of milk in the bottom of the milk bucket, the calf was done and as a parting shot it butted Old Blue. She stomped and her foot came down right in the middle of the milk bucket. Try as we would, we could not get her to move it. About then Dad walked in.

Later that evening at supper time, Mom gave us an "A" for effort but Dad, who had to clean up the whole mess, didn't think it was such a great deal.

LITTLE THINGS

WHEN IT'S SPRING TIME IN NEVADA

Walt Lebriski gave me this poem. It is probably a spoof of an old song entitled "When It's Spring Time in Nevada." Walt said he heard it when he was in high school and that's been a day or two. The author is unknown, it was found in a line camp and the cowboy who lived there was darn sure tired of the cold Nevada winter. This poem is short and to the point, a good example of cowboy humor.

When it's spring time in Nevada
And the gentle breezes blow
About seventy miles an hour
And it's fifty-two below.

You can tell you're in Nevada
Cause the snow's up to your butt
And you take a breath of spring time air
And you nose holes both freeze up.

The weather here is wonderful
So I guess I'll stick around
I could never leave Nevada
My feet are frozen to the ground.

EBBIE B. DAVIS

Ebbie B. Davis was inducted into the Nevada Cattlemen's Association Cowboy 100,000 Mile Club in 1983.

This presentation was written and presented by Connie Simpkins:

Eb Davis was born in May 1904 near the mining town of Beatty, Nevada. The time and location were such that the frontier was still very much with him. He was a cattle owner literally from the day of his birth. His brothers and sisters gave him calves as "welcome to the family" gifts. Horses and cattle in their many variations have been the focus of his life.

Eb was involved, as were all the children, with the family cattle and horses. His most memorable first horse event took place when he was about three and a half years old. A suitor, calling on his older sister, tried to curry a favor by letting Eb ride his horse. It was no elegant steed and didn't even have a saddle, but Eb rode back and forth on the horse happily roping a fence post. He recalled that the reins seemed to be getting longer and longer and suddenly, due to the horse not being long enough, he slipped over the horse's rump and off onto the ground.

Eb's first real horse was a little blue mare named Nellie. He doesn't recall how he came to consider her his possession. He was five years old when he laid claim to Nellie.

Eb's father was an engineer and miner. As a miner he could not mine in his back yard, so he was away a considerable amount of time working. This put a lot of the work on the boys in the family. Eb at an early age took some heavy responsibilities, usually related to horses.

About the same time he adopted Nellie, his father was involved in building a dam in Lincoln County, Nevada. Eb's mother leased a herd of Durham cows which she milked to provide dairy products to the townsfolk and workers. Eb, at the age of five, was given the daily responsibility of taking the cows and calves out to graze with the understanding that the cows were to be herded in one area and the calves in another and they were not to mix. He returned them home in the evening, still separated. Because his mother in his words, "was a pretty firm boss" he became a fairly good horseman and cowboy at a young age.

Dave Secrist said, "By the time he kept those cows and calves separated out on the open range I'll bet he was an experienced horseman and cowboy."

His first paid employment came again in relationship to his horsemanship ability. At the age of nine he was hired to take the mail from Sharp, Nevada, to Frieberg. This was a fifteen mile trip with another fifteen miles added to get back home.

The family moved to Alamo, Nevada, where Eb attended school and evenings, weekends and summers tended the family stock and worked for local ranches including the Johnny Wedge outfit, Leonard Wadsworth and the Gardner Ranching Company. When the family moved to Las Vegas they took their livestock with them. Of course, Eb made the cattle drive. In Vegas he finished high school, ran a dairy/ range cattle operation and got married. His skill as a horseman was well known in the area and he was selected to provide the horses, guidance and, at times, riding lessons for congressmen and engineers in the initial investigation and site determination for Hoover Dam (Boulder Dam). Ebbie was ranching in the area before the Hoover Dam was built or the United States Bureau of Land Management was formed.

Eb's means of livelihood during his life has always been livestock. The dairy operation he was running at the time of his marriage, evolved (thanks to the efforts of a newly acquired Brahma bull called Andy) into a beef operation. An arena was one of the first things constructed on the ranch, and when Eb was not practicing roping, he spent his time riding fence, checking livestock and bringing back strays.

The cattle range he owned had rights amounting to more than 1,500 square miles. As the area was generally arid, constant checking of range conditions, cattle, fences, windmills and watching out for friends and foes (inclined to brand indiscriminately) was necessary. It was a rare day when Eb was not on horseback for extended periods of time. It was common to spend dawn to dark searching for, gathering and driving cattle. During branding and roundup it was normal to spend eighteen to twenty hours on a horse.

When rodeo started to pick up in the 1940's Eb got involved at the ground floor of the movement. He became a capable and feared calf roper and in 1926 he was the World's Champion Calf Roper and runner-up for All–Around Cowboy. At this time he was a member of the Cowboys Association of America. The up and coming RCA was obviously the direction to go, but his membership was blocked for three years by members who were not looking forward to competing with Eb. He is now a permanent lifetime member of the RCA. He has rodeoed for more than three decades. He has attended rodeos in all the western states and a few states that only lay a frail claim to being western.

Eb bought and/or trained a long line of fine calf roping and team tying horses, as well. His talent with horses was widely recognized and his help or advice was sought by cowboys and rodeo sportsmen.

Eb involved himself with horses in other ways. He had a sizeable herd of fine Quarter horse brood mares and bred them to registered studs, some of which he owned. He bred, raised and trained some notable Quarter horses.

His large herds of cattle provided an excellent base of rodeo stock. He purchased a string of bareback and saddle broncs (and to his dismay he raised a few of his own.) Eb worked for many years as a producer of rodeos in the intermountain west.

He is an avid and talented hunter. For many years he spent most of two months providing guide services and, of course, horses for deer hunters. The routine consisted of dawn to dark guiding, searching, (sometimes for deer and sometimes for lost hunters) loading, packing out deer and always arriving in camp long after dark. When Nevada opened a limited Bighorn Sheep season, he had the honor of being chosen as one of a very few official guides. The guiding was done on horseback.

Ebbie and his wife, Nina, run cows on four BLM allotments, three in Nevada and one in California. The Nevada allotments alone encompass 398,616 acres.

Eb is still an active horseman and stockman. His pickup can seldom be seen not pulling a ubiquitous horse trailer complete with horse and tack. He still participates in rodeos and ropings. Eb shocks the "kids", who have pretty much taken over the sport, by winning with dismaying consistency. He is working on his twelfth saddle, having worn out almost a full dozen. He shows no signs of being put out to pasture, and if the past is any indicator of the future he will spend the rest of his life on a horse.

Ebbie is a slow talking, friendly, bowlegged charmer. He thanks everyone involved for considering him qualified to accept this award.

Here is how I came up with Ebbie's horseback mileage. I have purposely under estimated the last figure to make sure it is accurate.

Prior to 1924 – Alamo dairy herding

8 miles a day x 730 days (2 years)   5,840 miles

Freiburg Mail Carrier
Two trips per week for 104 weeks
208 miles x 30 mile trip   6,240 miles

1920 - 1924-   Alamo Cattle herding
Three days a week x 208 weeks (4 years)
624 x 5 miles a day   3,120 miles

1924 - 1929-   Las Vegas Dairy work
4 miles a day x 1,825 days (5 years) 7,300 miles

1940 – 1945-   Rodeo contractor
140 days a year x 5 years
700 x 15 miles per day   10, 500 miles

1940 – 1980-   Roping at rodeos
20 rodeos a year x 40 years
800 x 6 miles per rodeo   4,800 miles

1930 – 1980-   Hunting and hunting guide work
5 trips a year x 50 years
250 x 20 miles per trip   5,000 miles

1925 – 1945-	Longer cattle drives such as	
	Alamo to Las Vegas	100 miles
	Alamo to Jean	160 miles
	Alamo to Searchlight	170 miles
	Las Vegas to Searchlight	70 miles
	Las Vegas to Jean	60 miles
	2 trips a year for 20 years	
	40 trips x 110 miles average per trip	4,400 miles

1924 – 1983-	Day to day ranching operation – 59 years	
	59 years x 365 days = 21, 535 days	
	21, 535 divided in half = 10,767 days	
	10 767 days x 5 miles per day	
	(These are miles and days not detailed	
	anywhere above)	53, 835 miles

TOTAL LIFETIME MILES   101, 035 MILES

LITTLE THINGS

Red was a ranch hand that bounced around from ranch to ranch. He was a likeable guy who was full of big windy stories so this story I am going to recall may or may not be true but knowing Red it could have happened.

Red said that several years before he signed a contract to build eight miles of fence out on the desert. He soon found out that a foot down in that desert soil there was hard pan. He'd bid the job too low to take the time to dig through it and set the posts to the depth the contract called for. He was faced with the fact he was going to lose money on the deal.

The solution he came up with was to saw a foot off of the bottom of each fence post, making the posts look like they were set at the proper depth. He then sold the sawed off pieces of post for fire wood and made a profit on the contract. This was told for the truth. You be the judge.

JANE'S STORY

Dave says, "This part of Jane's story begins at the San Jacinto Ranch. The ranch is located in the northeastern corner of Elko County, Nevada and is the headquarters of the Salmon River Cattlemen's Association. This story took place before cell phones and instant communications arrived in our part of the world.

I wanted to check out a stock water pipeline and I asked Jane if she wanted to go on a working picnic. Now, Jane will hold dinner for hours when the ranch crew is late, take hurt cowboys to the emergency room, make a quick run for parts, pick up ranch hands at the employment office, fill in for a drunk ranch cook, move horse trailers and do the hundreds of things ranch wives do on an everyday basis. One thing she is not thrilled about doing is bouncing around all day on a dusty or muddy two-track mountain road in a four-wheel drive pick-up.

Because of Jane's past experience with working picnics, she is instinctively skeptical when I ask her to go on a back country pickup ride.

This trip did not do much to improve my image either. Jane hesitated a moment, but being a good wife, smiled and said, "That sounds like a good idea." It was Sunday morning. I found Clarence, the ranch cow boss, who was getting ready to go to a ranch hand rodeo in Wells, Nevada, and told him where we were going. I neglected to tell Jane that the Sidehill water line was located on the east side of Devil's Gap about thirty miles from the main ranch, but the trip went well.

It was a nice morning. We saw cows, a couple of coyotes, some antelope, and two golden eagles. Jane was having a good time. We arrived at the Sidehill water line. While I cleaned out the spring box, Jane got out the picnic lunch. We ate, rested for a while, and then drove the entire length of the Sidehill water line.

We were on our way back when Jane said, "I smell something hot." And I said, "That is not unusual. It is probably not very serious."

Well, serious it was! Some electrical wire above the gas tank had shorted out and the chaff and dust accumulated on top of the tank were now on fire. I couldn't reach the fire to put it out, so to avoid a range fire I drove to a bare spot of ground surrounding a salt lick. By then the whole top of the gas tank was burning. Thinking the tank was going to explode we grabbed an axe, the shovel, the water jug, and ran to a safe spot around the point of a hill. The gas tank did not explode it just went "whoosh" and a column of flames shot twenty feet into the air! Then the saddle tank erupted sending flames in all directions! The tires exploded! It sounded like bombs going off! A spiral of black smoke swirled a hundred feet into the air! Then, as if the pickup was giving its last gasp, the horn began to blow. That was one of the most pitiful sounds I have ever heard.

Just two hours after we had been quietly driving up that two track mountain road, we were standing beside the smoldering remains of our pickup. We had an axe, a shovel, a water jug, and we were thirty miles away from home.

We walked two miles back to the cross roads along the Sidehill water line. I told Jane when Clarence gets home and realizes we hadn't returned, he would come looking for us, and sometime during the night, he would come by this spot. Neither one of us mentioned the fact that if Clarence socialized too much at the rodeo he might not realize we were missing until we didn't show up for breakfast the next morning.

I chopped some limbs from a Juniper tree and we built a shelter next to the tree trunk. Then we settled down for the night. I unsuccessfully tried to convince Jane that the snakes and spiders would not bother us. The hot afternoon gave way to the chill of night. The night was pitch black and a million bright stars shone over head, but somehow it didn't seem very romantic. It was cold. The ground was hard and it was well after midnight before we finally drifted into a fitful sleep.

About four in the morning Jane sat bolt upright and said, "The pickup just went by."

When I looked up I saw the pickup's tail lights disappearing down the hill. We were only a few feet from the road but we didn't hear the truck coming in time. I crossed my fingers and told Jane that for all practical purposes, Clarence was headed down a dead end road and he would be back in about an hour.

I stuck the shovel up in the middle of the road, tied a red bandana on the handle and we went back to the shelter to wait.

We had the first good luck of the night. In about an hour we heard Clarence coming back. By the time the headlights appeared, we were standing in the middle of the road. When Clarence drove up and saw us, he really looked relieved. We found out later, when he came upon the burned out pickup, he checked for foot prints to see which way we went. In his pickup head lights, he could only find one set of tracks leaving the melted wreck and he thought one of us had burned up in the fire.

The warmth from the pickup heater was welcome. As we were approaching the ranch, the first rays of the morning sun came over the mountains casting shadows into the valleys below. It was the beginning of a new day.

The tree where we spent the night became known as "Jane's Juniper" and is still a useful landmark for cowboys working the area. I have since noticed that Jane is usually busy when I ask her if she wants to go for a pickup ride. Even though this happened twenty years ago, Jane has never again gone on a back country working picnic. For the life of me I can't understand WHY?"

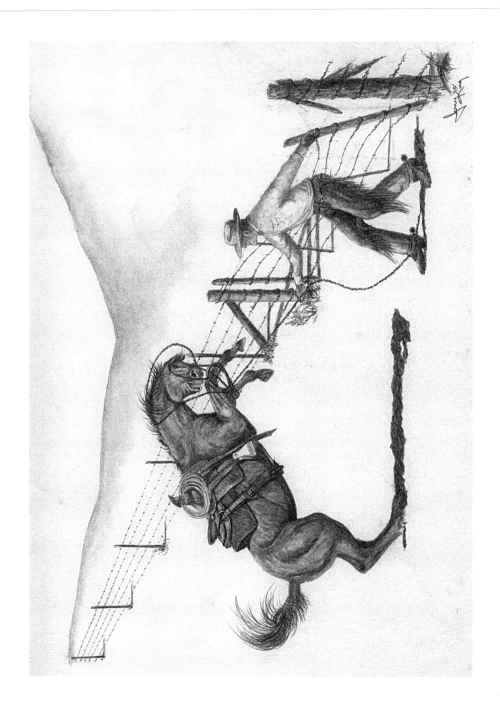

THE WIRE GATE

The wire gate has been around in the big range country for well over one hundred years. During this time it has been called many things. The most charitable or printable name I have heard it called is The Family Gate, meaning it takes a whole family, working together, to get the gate closed.

First the gates were built in drift fences dividing large ranges. They were then built in fences surrounding ranch headquarters, hay meadows and stack yards. On the big public land areas of the west they were built in fences separating deeded ranch property from their attached grazing allotments.

During my 115,000 mile horseback ride I built, cussed, begged and pleaded with the wire gate. Despite the invention of laser beams, jet planes, spaceships, high-definition TV, and atomic power the wire gate I went through yesterday looked exactly the same as the first wire gate I struggled to close when I was a kid some seventy years ago.

The wire gate is so simple that it is apparently complicated. I arrived at this conclusion after years of noticing the difficulty intelligent people have in trying to close the wire gate.

The wire gate consists of several barbed wires, a gate stick, one or two stays, a safety wire, a tightner or leverage stick and it goes through about four stages during its life time. In the first stage it may be so tight it is hard to close. During the second stage of the gate's life the tension is just about right and with reasonable effort the gate can be opened and closed in an easy manner. If you are careful you can even open and close the gate from the back of a horse. During the third stage the gate may get in such disarray it is nearly useless and during the fourth stage, after the fence braces have given way, you might have to stretch twenty yards of fence on each side of the gate to get it closed.

Over the years there have been a number of patented latches designed for use on the wire gate. But with time the wire gate, especially in the back country, usually reverts back to its original design. The only thing that I know of that replaces the wire gate on well traveled back roads is the cattle guard and the cattle guard, doesn't really replace the wire gate, it just relocates it. You seldom see a cattle guard installed on a country road that doesn't have a wire gate standing beside it.

During my lifetime I do not know how many miles I have ridden on cold winter days to avoid opening a wire gate. When it is ten degrees and you are stiff and cold with the wind blowing the snow and your slicker sideways, the chances of being able to get back on a cold cranky horse after getting off to open a wire gate are not very good to say the very least.

An old over used joke that circulates around in ranch country states: "You can always tell the real cowboy when three people are riding in a ranch pickup because the real cowboy will be sitting in the middle seat so he will not have to open the wire gates." There may be more truth to this joke than you think and I will relate an incident that explains why.

Some years ago I was feeding cows in the middle of winter using teams, wagons, and sleighs. The older cowboys who could handle the teams sometimes had trouble handling the hay and the younger ranch hands who could handle the hay sometimes had trouble handling the teams. So when feeding large numbers of cows, I would put the two together and this worked out fine except when they had a little trouble getting along because of the generation gap.

During this time frame the cowboy, the ranch hand and I would occasionally ride together in a ranch pickup. This particular time I was driving and Jake, the young ranch hand, reached the pickup and got in the middle before Lee, the older cowboy, arrived. Jake didn't do this on purpose; he just got there first and got in. When Lee reached the open pickup door, he stood for a moment, pointed down across the meadow and said something like this, "Jake, is there a cow in that stack yard way down there just south of those willows?" Jake, who could not see the stack yard from inside the pickup and couldn't talk without enough room to wave his arms around, got out of the truck. While he was explaining to Lee the cow wasn't in the stack yard, Lee slid into the middle seat and Jake got back in the pickup and closed the door. When we got to the first wire gate, Jake threw a fit complaining about the fact that he always had to open the wire gates, Lee just sat in the middle listening to Jake complain with a silent grin on his face.

Variations of this scenario repeated themselves a number of times during the winter and Jake never did catch on. In this case the real cowboy really did sit in the middle.

I remember one encounter I had with a wire gate very well. It was early one mid-summer morning. I was riding a young horse about five miles from the ranch headquarters when I spotted a small bunch of cows and calves grazing at the head end of a steep rocky draw. They were on the wrong side of an allotment fence so I worked my way up the draw, gathered the cows, made sure the calves were mothered up, and started them toward a wire gate I knew was located about a mile away. The cows took off in a long trot with a high headed roan cow in the lead. When the cows got to the gate, I had trouble holding them. I couldn't get them to settle down and that old roan cow was really looking for a way out. They wouldn't give me a chance to get off and open the wire gate. I decided to make a run for the gate, open it as fast as I could, remount my horse and head the cows off before they got out of sight. After that I planned to bring them back and put them through the gate. Nothing to it, I had done similar things a hundred times before. I made a run for the gate and the cows took off down the hill. I was on the ground before my horse had fully stopped. I grabbed my lead rope and in my hurry to open the gate I just left the reins of my hackamore hanging loosely over my horse's neck. The wire gate was stretched tight and in my haste to open it, the tightner stick slipped out of my hand and whacked me squarely on the chin. The commotion this caused, plus my fast movements, spooked the young horse I was riding and he promptly pulled back, stripping the hackamore off of his head. There I stood with a bruised chin, holding the gate stick in one hand and the empty hackamore in the other, watching the cows I had just gathered disappear down the fence line while my horse headed for home on a dead run. This all happened in less than twenty seconds. Chalk another one up for the wire gate!

Through the years I thought I had seen every conceivable way of closing a wire gate without slipping the safety wire down over the gate stick. Of course, most wire gates are closed properly, some are simply left open and a few people really show ingenuity in loosely putting a wire gate back in place. I have seen wire gates closed by using coat hangers, duct tape and shoe strings but I hadn't seen it all until I came upon a wire gate that crossed a narrow mountain road. The contraption that loosely held this gate shut was a lacey black bra. Now if that wouldn't make a cowboy wonder.

The normal way to close a wire gate, especially if the tightner stick is worn out or missing , is to press your shoulder and chest against the gate stick, wrap one arm around the gate post and press hard until you can slip the safety wire in place. This usually takes a reasonable amount of effort. Years ago there was a story circulating around the ranching community in Elko, Nevada. The story stated you could tell which lady was an Elko County rancher's wife because one boob was black and blue from opening and closing wire gates. I do not know who did the research that started this story in the fist place but it might have been an interesting project. My guess is they more than likely just came to a common sense conclusion.

Anyway, I think it is probably safe to say the last three things that will be left on this earth will be the magpie, the coyote and the wire gate.

BILL DeLONG

Bill DeLong was inducted into the Nevada Cattlemen's Association Cowboy 100,000 Mile club in 1984.

The DeLong family originally came from France traveling through Canada before coming to the United States. Bill was born September 27, 1913 at the Deer Creek Ranch located in the Jackson Mountains, fifty-six miles west of Winnemucca, Nevada. Dale Delong, Bill's wife, said, "As time passed Bill became known as a fair and just man. Many people passed through his doors seeking personal and financial advice. This he gave only if he felt the seeker was sincere. Any insincere person may as well not exist in Bill's opinion."

The following presentation was written and given by Les Stewart when Bill was inducted into the Cowboy 100,000 Mile Club.

One hundred thousand miles on a saddle horse – that is a long way. In 1962 when John Glenn made the world's first orbital space flight he only traveled 83,500 miles.

Granted, he did go faster.

Men who have ridden 100,000 miles know the desert and the mountains. They have felt the gentle winds of summer. They have felt the bitter winds of winter. They have known pleasure and hardship as they lived a hardy outdoor life in a land of scattered ranches in a time when people were few and cattle and horses were plenty.

Their memories are not of 100,000 miles ridden, but of events and incidents, some pleasant, some humorous and some tragic, of good faithful saddle horses, of rough string horses who would kick, strike and buck without warning, of friends and neighbors.

Ranching has changed. At this convention we have seen and heard of computers, helicopters, innovative methods that a rancher should use. Maybe? The 100,000 miler did not know or work in the jet era, but I don't think they missed much. If anything they feel the younger generation could not have known the way of life and values that were theirs and have missed out.

They have experienced the glories of hard, honest work and the pleasures of productive living.

The man, who I have the pleasure and honor of presenting this plaque to, is from Humboldt County born on the Deer Creek Ranch where he received his schooling. He is a real horseback buckaroo who never drove a car until nineteen years of age.

During his early years the cattle were driven from this ranch for three days to the railroad at Winnemucca, a distance of sixty miles. After 1939 with the purchase of the Jackson Creek Ranch, the cattle were driven to Quinn Crossing to be weighed and then to the railroad at Jungo, a distance of eighty miles.

In 1943 scales were installed at Jackson Creek and after this, the cattle were driven to Sulphur to be shipped. All this was done on horseback. And remember after the cattle were shipped, the buckaroos had to trot their horses back home. There were no trucks in those days. I figure that as a boy and just delivering cattle, he covered over 10,000 miles.

Bill spent a number of years from October to May at a cow camp in the "Sand" caring for cattle. During this period he added 25,000 miles to his riding. In 1948 a stock truck was purchased to haul saddle horses to work and to various camps. But this did little to detract from the miles actually ridden. This Outfit, which consists of the Jackson Creek Ranch, Old Hummel Ranch and the Alexander Ranch along with the Bottle Creek Ranch, comprises about 3,000 square miles.

Bill rode his own range from camps at Rattle Snake, Smokey Springs, Fox Farm, Rock Springs, Cedar Creek, Winter Camp, Thacker Well and Morman Dan's. At the same time, being a good rancher, he found time to help with his neighbors' riding and branding.

On his seventy-first birthday he rode from Rabbit Hole to Sulphur, down Rosebud Canyon gathering cattle as he went. Arriving at Sulphur Corral, he roped cows that had lost BLM ear tags and calves to brand.

Conservatively, he rode 75,000 miles during this phase of his life, putting him well over the 100,000 mile mark.

Bill DeLong of Jackson Creek is still riding and I would not really be surprised if he puts in nearly another 100,000 miles.

Dave's comments: "They quit counting miles when they reached the 110,000 mile mark along Bill's lifetime horseback ride but family and ranchers that worked with Bill say a total of 200,000 miles ridden would be a conservative number.

The DeLong family is a big family that dates back six ranching generations. Bill is truly a big range rancher and cowboy in every sense if the word.

An interesting diversion from Bill's cowboy life happened in the 1930's when Bill took up prize fighting. Dale DeLong said, "Bill was a very successful amateur boxer and soon gained a fearful reputation." She continues, "The big boys from the eastern cities soon learned to detour way around the "country kid" with such a hard right fist. Of Bill's seventeen bouts, only one ended in a draw, the others were knockouts. In the boxing ring Bill was known as "Cowboy Bill DeLong." About 1939 Bill gave up boxing to take care of his ranching responsibilities."

Another incident that happened along Bill's long winding horseback trail happened in 1981. Bill found a Mammoth skeleton on the Black Rock Desert near the Jackson Creek Ranch. The Mammoth is now in the Nevada State Museum in Carson City.

MARY'S STORY

Dave's story about Mary. I remember when Mary and Doctor Branscomb came to the Lamoille Valley south of Elko, Nevada. Dr. Branscomb, or Bruce as he became known to many, came to Elko to work with Dr. Cuthberson, owner of the Elko Veterinary Clinic. Bruce eventually branched out and established a veterinary practice of his own. The Branscombs raised their family in the Lamoille Valley and are respected members of that community.

Mary has bocame a local historian and author writing about ranching life in the big range country of northeastern Nevada.

She has an indelible spot in my memory because of an incident that happened some thirty or more years ago when she silenced a bunch of skeptical cowboys by just saying eight words.

Mary and "Doc" Cuthberson had extensive training and experience in jumping and English style horseback riding. I do not remember the reason Mary gave for organizing an English style jumping clinic in the middle of cowboy country but she did. Mary and "Doc" were the featured riders and the event was held in a pasture south of the Lamoille Church. I have always suspected the main reason for having this clinic had something to do with remarks some cowboy made about that flat English saddle. Maybe he was comparing that flat saddle to the hotcakes he ate for breakfast or maybe another grinning cowboy asked, "Hey, Mary, how are you going to take your dallies?"

Anyway the clinic started, and Mary and "Doc" were dressed in their English riding attire. There was a fair sized crowd of curious cowboys and ranchers lined up along the fence.

Mary gave a talk about the use of the English riding equipment while "Doc" took some warm up jumps. After her presentation, Mary joined "Doc" and they took turns jumping the hurdles with the top rail being raised after each jump. While "Doc' was making his jumps Mary would explain the different English style jumping techniques. By the time Mary cleared her last hurdle it looked to me like the top rail was five or six feet above the ground.

Mary came posting over toward the cowboys standing along the fence. She was still riding that flat little English saddle with the stirrups hiked half way up her horse's side. When she stopped, she offered the reins to the crowd and said, "Does anyone want to take the next turn?"

Well, except for a funeral, that was the quietest bunch of cowboys I have ever been with. No one said a word and I darn sure didn't raise my hand.

That morning, using just eight words and a gritty performance, Mary won the respect of the Lamoille Valley ranching community.

Since that time Mary has added western riding techniques and equipment to her lifestyle. She shows horses and has become part of the cowboy community.

LITTLE THINGS

The money you save is the easiest money you will ever earn.

HORSES I REMEMBER

The horses I remember mostly for the horses themselves, as well as incidents that happened while I was riding them, are small in number compared to the hundreds of horses I've ridden and been acquainted with, during my 115,000 mile horseback ride. With some exceptions, the horses I remember were remarkably good or remarkably bad. The rest remain shadowy blurs in my mind.

Of course, the first horse I remember riding by myself was old Babe. I rode her three miles to my first day of school. Babe was old and tall but she was honest. The only thing outstanding about Babe was the way she made me feel when I was riding her. When I was on her back I never felt alone. My mind wasn't yet cluttered with worldly problems or the pitfalls associated with horseback riding. When I looked at Babe's boney old frame, and she put her head down and nuzzled me with her soft nose, I only saw the strongest, shiniest horse in the west. When I was on old Babe I roped steers, rode bucking horses and led the ghost herd of horses through the mountains and valleys of cloud formations in the sky. Early on Babe helped me form a relationship with horses that lasted through my entire 115,000 mile horseback ride through life.

The next horses or relatives to horses I remember were the Shetland ponies my brother and I rode eight miles round trip to school for several years. These were the most spoiled, stubborn bull headed little animals I have ever been associated with. On the day the ponies arrived, Dad was out working so we were pretty much on our own. The first time we saddled them and rode about fifty yards from the barn they both reared straight up, whirled around and before we could get them stopped, they headed back to the open barn door on a dead run. As he went through the barn door, my pony nearly tore my leg off against the door frame in an effort to scrape me off. Once back in their stalls they refused to come out. After awhile with Dad not being around to help us, we decided to go back to the house and tell Mom our troubles. Well, that didn't take long. Instead of the sympathy we were looking for, we got a short lecture telling us we were the only ones who could solve the problem. So get back out there and show those ponies who was boss. With her broom still in one hand, she shooed us outside and shut the door. We sure didn't get the sympathy we expected. So with our lower lips sticking out, we pulled our hats down and headed back to the barn. I do not know how many times we hit the hard ground that afternoon but we punished and rewarded those ponies until we won the battle. The ponies finally realized it was safer and a lot more fun to go away from the barn than it was to rear up and run back to it, and that was the turning point. We rode those ponies to school and for ranch work for several years and they always had a bull headed, independent streak in them, but they became reliable partners. When they rebelled it was simply that they didn't want to do something, not that they intended to do bodily harm. We bonded with the ponies and they bonded with us and we had more enjoyable carefree years together.

As I began the transformation from a carefree ranch kid to becoming and understanding the ways and responsibilities of the big range cowboy, I learned many things. This learning process stayed with me all during my 115,000 mile horseback ride.

Other horses I remember were more realistic and part of the real cowboy world. The next horse I remember was called Happy. Why he was called Happy I do not know. Though I never touched or handled Happy, he stands out in my memory during the early years of my life long ride. Happy was just an average sized bay horse with average ranch horse abilities. He was probably eight or nine years old and he was well broke.

There was nothing memorable about him except for one trait. Old Happy was what is sometimes called a sleeper. It is not unusual for an old ranch horse to buck when saddled up on an early frosty morning. It is the usual custom for cowboy crews to start riding out at a fast trot first thing in the morning. This is to give a cranky horse a chance to get the kinks out of his system before the crew splits up out on the open range. Happy was a sleeper. He wasn't humped up or cranky when he started out in the morning but two or three times a year, usually during the middle of the day or late afternoon when his rider was relaxed and least expecting it, Happy would bog his head and buck and this old horse could buck. He bucked straight away and he put everything he had into it. He took high twisting leaps with his mouth wide open and every time his front feet hit the ground with pile driving force, he let out that low pitched gravely beller. Without the slightest notice of his intentions, this mild mannered ranch horse turned into a monster.

On this day Bob and I were home from school playing around the wood pile in front of the ranch house. The house stood on a knoll overlooking a small meadow that lay between the house and the corrals. Mom came out to watch as Dad and Mr. Folsom, the owner of the ranch, rode across the little meadow below. Dad was riding Happy and Mr. Folsom was riding his favorite horse, a big bald faced sorrel horse whose name escapes me. They were relaxed and visiting as they came into sight.

Suddenly the calm, pleasant, spring day was shattered by the pounding of horse's hooves and that loud low pitched beller some bucking horses let out every time their front feet hit the ground. Old Happy had exploded! Now Dad wasn't a bronc rider but to his credit he stayed with Happy for several jumps before Happy made his high twisting dive. He some how sucked his body back while all four feet were off the ground. Dad turned a summersault high up in the air before hitting the ground on the back of his head and neck. Dad never quivered. He lay as still as a stone. Happy bucked over the top of him still bellowing each time his front feet hit the ground.

Bob and I were up on the top of the hill watching. We had heard the tall tales and laughter around the kitchen table where cowboys laughed and joked about how high in the air a cowboy had gone when he got bucked off. So Bob and I were standing up on the wood pile laughing and hollering with no inkling of the seriousness of the situation in the meadow down below. Then we heard a cross word and saw the agonizing look on Mom's face. It was a cross between terror and love. After that look it didn't take long for two little boys to sober up.

Mom pulled her skirt up over her knees and went down over that hill in ten foot leaps. Every time she hit the ground her skirt billowed out creating the illusion she was flying. She reached Dad and cradled his head in her lap. We could hear her sobbing. Mr. Folsom dismounted and stood by her side with a stern look on his face. Happy was standing by the corral with his sides heaving back and forth. It was like the whole incident was frozen in time. Then Dad began to stir and come to. He had been knocked out cold.

What Bob and I didn't understand and learned in that five minute lesson was that cowboys never ever made a joke of a serious situation until everyone involved in the wreck was O.K. I also learned while traveling along the early part of my 115,000 mile horseback ride that a cowboy would risk death to help a friend, partner or anyone else that was tangled up in a serious horse wreck. That evening at supper Dad was sore but O.K. and the laughter and jokes were floating around the table. Mom was dubbed "The Flying Cook" and the cowboy's warped sense of humor was running wild. Everything was back to normal.

The next horse I remember was a little roan mare called Mescal. I was told she was named after a Mexican bush that grows in the southwestern part of the United States and Mexico. This was interesting to me and seemed to fit her personality. Mescal was the first real cow horse I ever owned. She was in the middle to waning years of her productive life. She was snorty and alert and not about to let a kid get by with doing something really dumb. On the other hand she was honest and trustworthy and would let a kid get by with things she would not let a more experienced cowboy do. Mescal taught me much more than I taught her.

About the only thing I could show her was what I wanted her to do. From that point on she showed me how to do it. It wasn't long before we learned to work together and I moved to the next phase of my 115,000 mile horseback ride. Before I moved on, Mescal taught me one more thing. Never ride a horse no matter how gentle without taking the time to saddle up or at least use the proper equipment so you could remain in control when the unexpected happens.

It was a summer morning before the heat of the day set in. Someone asked me to saddle up and go get the mail. I grabbed my halter and went to catch Mescal. I approached her too fast and she was a little snorty but she turned to face me, took a couple of steps forward, and lowered her head so I could put the halter on her. I notice a little shiver when I touched her shoulder but I led her out of the corral and instead of saddling up and putting the bit and bridle on Mescal, I just threw the lead rope over her withers and tied the loose end of the lead rope into the halter, making reins. I then spread the empty return mail sack behind Mescal's withers, jumped on her bareback and we were off.

It was a pleasant ride. Mescal and I were both feeling good. We loped along with Mescal shying at every imaginary booger she could find. We made the mile ride to the mailbox in no time at all. The only distraction was the red winged black birds that were nesting in the apple trees. When we rode by the little screeching monsters they dived down at me nearly touching my hat before they gained enough altitude to dive again. When we reached the mail box I sidled Mescal up to it like I was opening a gate. Without getting off I pulled the incoming sack of mail out of the box and placed the out going sack in its place.

I then spun Mescal around and headed for home. We loped along without a care in the world. We got by the screeching black birds and we came to the last corner in the road before a straight stretch led to the ranch buildings. About the middle of this straight stretch of road, a platform had been built. It was used to store fifty gallon barrels of gas and cases of oil. I guess as I approached the last major turn in the road I imagined I was a Pony Express rider packing the mail or maybe I thought someone would be watching and I would show off. For whatever reason as I neared this last turn that would put me in full view of the ranch house, I gave Mescal her head. She was more than willing to respond. I let out a Comanche yell. Waved the mail sack in the air and when we came around the last turn we were really smoking. We were going much faster than a kid riding bareback with a halter on his horse's head should go. I was leaning over Mescal's neck with my hat pulled down. Mescal's ears were pinned back and her head was low. She was flat out running. By the time we got close to that platform with the gas barrels and cases of oil on top we were really packing the mail. We were almost to that platform when Mescal saw something she didn't like. Within one stride she came to a complete cow horse stop. Gravel sprayed in all directions and the Pony Express rider that was on top became airborne. I flew over Mescal's head like a rocket stretched out flat in the air. When I eventually came down I made a perfect belly flop landing in the middle of that hard gravel road. I was gasping for air while I skidded to a stop. Mescal was still standing where she stopped. Her head was still down but her ears were now pointing forward and she had that "where in the hell did you come from" look on her face. She walked curiously toward me while I struggled to get to my feet. I looked around to see if anyone had seen the wreck. Satisfying myself they hadn't, I picked up the mail sack remounted Mescal and now, riding much slower, I delivered the mail to the front porch of the ranch house. I must have been the sorriest looking Pony Express rider in history standing there with my halter rope in one hand and the mail sack in the other. The front of my shirt was torn off and hanging down and I was gravel burned from my chin to my knees. Thinking no one had witnessed the wreck, I am sure my account of what happened, though truthful, was not as colorful as the event I'd planned.

Dad told me later that the next time I decided to pull off a stunt like that I should at least saddle and bridle my horse before I started out. This made me wonder if he had seen me make that wild fantasy ride.

I learned early on how amazingly fast a fun filled day can turn into a life threatening wreck when horses are involved.

I remember a young horse I was associated with for a short period of time. He had the potential of ending my 115,000 horseback ride almost before it began. The ranch ran a stud band of brood mares. They ran year round out on the range. We would wean the colts in the late fall and halter break them during the winter. Then when the colts were fat, shiny two year olds, we'd gather them from the range and work with them for two or three weeks. We would saddle, sack them out, break them to hobble using home made barley sack hobbles and ride them in the round corral before giving them five or six good rides outside on the range. After this was accomplished, the colts were again turned out until the following spring. This gave the colts a chance to develop into well muscled, sure footed horses before they were put in with the ranch horses to start working while continuing their training.

This spring the ranch boss gave me eight two year old colts to start breaking and as an after thought as he turned to leave he said, "Add that sorrel colt standing over there to your string and see if he is worth fooling with." The reason he made this statement was because some colts had gotten into a patch of Loco weed a year earlier and were completely use-less. When they were not excited, they stood around with their heads down as if asleep; oblivious to what was going on around them. Period-ically they would come to and spooked easily at seemingly nothing. The ranch had gotten rid of all of these colts except this sorrel who at the time seemed to be all right.

This was my first and only contact with a horse that had eaten Loco weed and I do not know if his reaction to the weed was typical or in fact the weed really caused the problem. What I do know is that this bunch of colts ran together in one pasture and they all came down with the same symptoms and the symptoms did not go away. The old timers said it was Loco weed and I accepted that.

In the next day or two I caught the sorrel colt and right away I got the feeling he wasn't quite all there. I knew Roland, the ranch boss, was hoping the colt would turn out to be O.K. so I thought I had better work with him for a little while to see if my first impression was correct before talking to the boss.

I did some ground work and saddled the colt. Except for being kind of listless and not paying much attention to what was going on, he seem normal. In fact he was so quiet about what was going on, I got careless. I was standing in front of him holding the lead rope loosely in my hands. I was watching my dog come over and lay down outside the corral when suddenly the colt came to life. As if seeing me for the first time, his eyes got big, his ears pointed forward, his nostrils flared and he snorted as he whirled around. His hind quarters were now toward me and he kicked with both back feet. This wasn't just a little tap from the hind feet of a scared colt. He put everything he had into it. He meant to hurt whatever he hit and both of his hind feet were coming directly toward my head. I was just far enough behind the colt to be near the end of his kicking range which is the worst possible place to be. I can still see the frog and soles of those two hind feet as they flashed by my face and brushed on both sides of my hat.

This all happened in a split second and I was standing in the corral trying to comprehend what had just happened or maybe what had not happened. The colt was now calmly standing in the corral not paying much attention to what was going on around him. I wasn't hurt, I hadn't even lost my hat but the realization of what had nearly happened began to set in. If I had been a couple inches to the left or a couple inches to the right when those feet came whistling past both sides of my face my 115,000 mile horseback ride would have been over. This horse didn't even have a name. I worked with him less than an hour and I don't even remember what happened to him. That part is a blur in my memory but the sole and frog of his hind feet are still clear pictures in my mind's eye, making him another horse I will never forget.

Perhaps the horse I remember the most among the long list of horses I have ridden and been acquainted with during my 115, 000 mile horseback ride was a little roan mare named Scrappy. During my younger years I broke and rode a lot of colts and young horses. Sometimes these horses had a tendency to become one man horses and this is a detriment or at least a waste of time on the big range outfits where horses are herded in large remudas and ridden by many different cowboys. In the more confined mountain ranges in northern California where mares and geldings are raised and worked together all of their lives, there is more opportunity to keep and ride colts for a longer period of time. This was the case with the little roan mare named Scrappy. She wasn't very big. It might be a stretch to say she weighted a thousand pounds but her heart was as big as all outdoors and she had a spirit that wouldn't quit. Though she had an independent streak and was snorty, I never rode a horse that tried harder to do what I wanted done. Scrappy was too small in size to catch the boss's eye so I was able to keep her in my string until she was a broke cow horse. During this time the little roan mare and I developed a very strong bond and I spent more time than normal training her.

One incident I remember that happened when Scrappy was a broke horse is a good example of the spirit this little roan mare had. I could crack a whip, call her name and she would come trotting across the corral to me. I expanded this training until I could call her name and throw a rock in her general direction and she would come trotting across a field, go through the gate and without a halter follow me to the saddle room.

This incident happened on a late winter day. I recall feeling the warmth on my back when periodically the sun broke through the clouds while I made my way through the pasture out behind the corrals. An inch or two of snow had just melted and the top of the ground was muddy and slick. It was the last days of winter and the horses were getting tired of hay so they were at the far end of the pasture where they could get the first taste of new green grass that had just started to grow. I called Scrappy's name and tossed a rock in her direction. Up came her head, her ears pointed forward and she came toward me at a fast lope. When she got close she skidded to a stop, making perfect elevens in the mud, splattering slush and mud all over me. Somewhat irritated I put my hand out and when she came sliding to a stop, I reached out and lightly touched her neck. She snorted, whirled around and took off on a dead run going back to the horses still standing at the far end of the pasture. This time, as she took off, she again splattered me with more mud and slush.

A little way out into the pasture her pace slowed and her stride short-ened to stiff legged hops. She raised her tail high in the air. She lifted her neck as high as possible and swinging her head from side to side she snorted at me every time she looked back over her shoulders. As un-happy as I was with the mud splattered all over my face, I could not help grinning at the picture she presented. She was telling me she had pulled a good one and she was getting away with it. She was enjoying her vic-tory dance so much she forgot to look where she was going and didn't see the half frozen mud puddle in front of her. In an instant all four feet flew out from under her and in all her glory she came crashing down flat on her side. She got up, turned to face me and with her head bobbing up and down she calmly came trotting back to where I was standing, pushed her muddy nose up against me and just stood there. It took a moment for me to fully realize what had happened. Scrappy knew she wasn't sup-posed to turn tail and run after she came up to me. She learned that les-son well in the round corral several years before. But on this day when she was feeling good with the promise of spring in the air and green grass just around the corner, her independent streak came through and for the moment it was stronger than the training she had previously received.

There was no doubt in her mind that I was some how responsible for the fall she had just taken and she somehow connected that fall to spinning away from me a few moments before. I guess if you wanted to stretch the imagination you could say Scrappy was reacting to her guilty conscience. But being more realistic the truth is more than likely as fol-lows: Scrappy knew she wasn't supposed to come up to me, then whirl and run away. When she fell while showing off, she apparently thought I was reprimanding her for running away and realized it was easier, more fun and less painful to come to me and stand than it was to whirl away from me and run.

I bought Scrappy when I left the ranch where she was raised and I was the only cowboy that ever rode her during her working years. In spite of the fact that she nearly drowned me during a very difficult cattle drive, the thing I remember the most about her after all these years is the special bond that existed between this young cowboy and that little roan mare.

George
Wilkinson

"Mustangers" in Box Canyon: George on the left

GEORGE E. WILKINSON

George E. Wilkinson was inducted into the Nevada Cattlemen's Association Cowboy 100,000 Mile Club in 1993.

Kimble Wilkinson, George's son gave this presentation when George was inducted.

George E. Wilkinson was born September 18, 1930. He started riding horseback at the age of four, leading the work horses to and from water. At the age of six George had to start school, and at that time the cars and road were not very reliable, thus his horseback riding continued as he rode the four miles to and from school in McDermitt. At the age of fourteen he went away to school in St. George, Utah. Although in the winter months his riding was limited, he always came home in the summer months and helped his Dad, George W. Wilkinson and the other ranchers in the McDermitt area. This joining of all the ranches was known as "riding with the wagon."   This means covering the open range with the other cattlemen such as the Lucy 7 Ranch, Oregon Canyon Ranch and several others. George would stay with the wagon during the summer months, branding calves, gathering steers, and at times running and herding the wild horses that roamed Northern Nevada and Southern Oregon.

When George graduated from high school in 1948, he married his high school sweetheart, Annetta Tanner, bringing her home to McDermitt to take over his aging father's ranch. Since then George has been ranching and riding non-stop for nearly forty-five years, promoting the cattle industry in every way he could.

George continued working toward his goal of being a successful cattle rancher and in 1978, he, along with partners, Kimble, his son, and Fred, his brother, added 1,200 head of cows to the newly bought McCormic Ranch. This brought the two ranches together to cover fifty square miles east and west of McDermitt.

Furthermore, George believed in the old time motto "that if it couldn't be done on horseback it wasn't worth doing." That motto still stands today.   There are few ranches left in the west today that have genuine cattle drives to their range. In the spring the Wilkinsons trail their cattle four days to the far end of their ranch where the cattle are left to graze for seven months. In the fall on a thirty mile trip, the cattle are trailed home. In addition, George's ranch is one of the few left that does not own a gooseneck trailer. He would rather ride and do the work horseback.

At the spry age of sixty-two, George continues to do the two things he has always loved, ranching and riding horseback. Therefore, I would like to nominate George E. Wilkinson to the Cowboy 100,000 Mile Club. It is very difficult to add all the miles a working cowboy would ride in forty-five plus years, but if anyone deserved the honor, it would be George. Just ask anyone who knows him around the McDermitt, Winnemucca and Jordan Valley areas.

Footnotes on George E. Wilkinson's mileage:
1. Age four: George riding around the ranch leading work horses to water and just pleasure riding.

2. Age six: rode to school eight miles a day until age fourteen.
3. Age fourteen to seventeen: rode three months in the summer along with the wagon on the open range round-ups.
4. At age seventeen: George took over his father's ranch and ever since has stayed with it. He is now sixty-two years old which makes forty-five years of non-stop ranching and riding.
5. Fifty mile cattle drives one way every spring for four days, thirty mile cattle drives in the fall, plus other small cattle drives off of the mountains (steers, bulls, etc.) all at least thirty miles one way.
6. The many weeks spent on the range during the seven months the cattle were there.
    A. Spring brandings
    B. Bull drives
    C. Heifer drives
    D. Steer Drives
    E. Plus numerous August rides over the mountain, a distance of thirty miles, leading a pack horse just to check cattle.
7. Miles in the winter riding around the ranch in the five months the cattle were home.
    A. Riding to check water pumps.
    B. Going through the cattle checking for problems.
8. The starting of hundreds of horses in forty- five years, which requires a lot of riding just for the fun of it.
9. Helping other ranchers gather and brand cattle.

Dave's comment: "Up to the age of seventeen George documented riding 12,000 miles horseback. From the time he took over his Dad's ranch in 1948 until he was inducted into the Cowboy 100,000 Mile Club in 1993, a time span of forty-five years, he averaged riding eight miles per day for a conservative total of well over 125,000 miles. The grand total miles George's ridden horseback adds up to 137,000 miles. George has ridden many more miles since he was inducted into the Club which prompts me to say he is another Cowboy 100,000 Mile Club member who is over qualified.

REPLACING HORSES AND COWS WITH MOOSE AND BROWN BEAR —I

In 1948 Don Linsteadt and I were young cowboys working for the Eden Valley Ranch in northern California. We had been inseparable friends during high school, though fiercely competitive. A new coach, in an effort to improve competitiveness and school pride proposed dividing all physical education classes into two groups that would play sports against each other during the school year. Don was elected captain of one group and I was elected captain of the other. All of the boys were called into the gym and Don and I alternated while picking kids for our respective groups. Don called his group "The Gauchos". I called my group "The Panthers". We competed throughout the school year and in the end "The Gauchos" won out. Our friendly competitiveness continued throughout our lifetimes. I was elected president of the Future Farmers of America chapter and Don and I had a number of projects together during this time frame.

Bob, my younger brother, and I spent our winter school vacations running trap lines with our Uncle Vern. We learned the ways of fur bearing animals and how to stretch and handle the furs from Uncle Vern, and we learned patience from Aunt Mae. Don spent his winter school vacations working in logging camps around the Willits area. I spent my summers working on the Eden Valley Ranch as a cowboy, while Don spent his summers on a fishing boat a family relative owned. They fished along the coast in the Juneau area of southern Alaska.

By the time we graduated from high school we'd known each other for much of our youth and we got along well together. We both felt we had been born fifty years too late and we each had an intense desire to be part of the American West. The Eden Valley Ranch gave us a good chance to be in the wilderness. We worked long hard hours with horses and cows but we also found time to run wild hogs, fish, trap and hunt bear. A lot of this was accomplished while we were doing a day's work. It was a learning process and we had fun doing it.

The enthusiasm, energy, and imagination of youth is boundless. Don and I dreamed and planned toward carving a cattle ranch out of the wilderness or owning a cow outfit on the open ranges of the west.

Don came back from his summer fishing trips with stories of boundless areas of grassland on some islands in the Aleutian Island chain that were warmed by southerly currents in the Pacific Ocean, making them useful for growing livestock. I came back from my summers working on the Eden Valley Ranch with first hand stories from old timers that lived the experiences they were telling me about.

After graduation from high school, we worked together on the Eden Valley Ranch. During the summer we decided the only way we were going to find out for sure what possibilities we had, was to go check things out ourselves. So in the bunkhouse at night, we began to work out a plan. We decided to start by exploring Alaska and by the first of September we had a plan in place. We worked up enough courage to tell the ranch boss we were quitting and explained why. He sat quietly with a strange smile on his face and to this day I do not know what he was thinking. I don't know if he thought "there goes two kids that are too dumb to know what they are getting into" or if he was remembering something from way back along his long winding trail.

Anyway, in true youthful style of thinking time was running out and passing us by, we stored our saddles and equipment, pooled our money and rode the greyhound bus to San Francisco, California. We bought a used canvas top Jeep for five hundred dollars. We drove the Jeep home where we loaded four five-gallon gas cans in the brackets along the sides and back of the Jeep. Then we packed our rifles and camping gear in the back along with some groceries and said goodbyes to our families. We headed for the Al-Can Highway.

This might be a good time to explain that neither Don nor I had been in subzero temperatures before. Bob and I were born while our folks lived on homesteads in the mountains in northern California and we were used to hard winters and heavy snow. One night when Bob and I were very young, our Mom and Dad packed us through knee deep snow several miles because they were afraid the high winds were going to blow two large snow laden fir trees over onto the house. Don and I were used to night time temperatures in the twenties and mid-teens but we hadn't lived where subzero temperatures were sustained twenty-four hours a day for long periods of time. We were well aware of this and didn't plan to buy clothes and equipment until we got into areas where these kinds of things were used.

Well, we were on our way. We crossed the Rockies and were going through flat grassland in western Montana. The Rocky Mountains looked like they were cut out of cardboard on the horizon to the west. We were zipping along in our canvas topped Jeep with a maximum speed of forty-five miles per hour. Everything on the highway was passing us but we were steady. The Jeep didn't have a heater so that weight wasn't what was slowing us down. Every time we came to a gas station or small community we would pass cars that had previously zipped by us and were now stopped for snacks or restroom facilities. So we were holding our own. The weather was good and we didn't have any problems until night time and we were in a steep mountainous area, maybe the northern Rockies. There was snow piled up on both sides of the road. We were suddenly passing Cadillacs, Lincolns, and pickups. You name it and we were passing them. They were all poking along about twenty miles per hour. About a quarter of a mile into these conditions we hit black ice, spun around about three times and slid tail first into a snow bank. It was degrading sitting there while all those cars we had just passed came by. We'd driven in all kinds of weather on country roads. We'd driven in foot deep mud and slush, snow drifts, frozen mud puddles and we knew how to drive in winter conditions but we hadn't driven on asphalt covered with black ice before. We put the Jeep in four-wheel drive and easily drove out of the snow bank. We continued on our way with a lesson well learned.

Don and I were changing drivers and traveling at a steady pace and nothing unusual happened until we reached a small border crossing in the western part of Montana. There wasn't much traffic but a group of ten or twelve Mennonites was trying to cross into Canada and they were apparently trying to slip one young lady across who was not supposed to go into Canada. Things got very tense for awhile. In an hour or so it was our turn. It didn't take long to discover we could not take our rifles into Canada without a certain permit which, of course, we did not have. After some discussion they told us they could mail our guns to Anchorage, Alaska, and we would not have any trouble picking them up there. With no other options available we skeptically agreed, gave up our guns, and entered Canada. We headed for Edmonton. There were miles and miles of sparsely occupied country. We soon began to recognize when we were approaching urban areas. In the sparsely populated areas everyone, including farmers on their tractors working in the fields, gave us a hearty wave as we drove by. When this custom slowed down or stopped we knew we were approaching an urban area with more people around. With no signs posting distances, this became a reliable indicator when the Jeep's gas gauge began flirting with empty.

We reached Edmonton and thinking we were far enough north to purchase winter clothing, we stopped to shop. We bought winter coats, gloves, parkas, long johns, and wool socks. Our original plan was to reach Alaska and get well enough acquainted to purchase a trap line and get settled before the real winter set in. So far we were on track. We had done a lot of research and knew about what we were going to need. We purchased the type of snowshoes for the conditions we expected to be in and headed for Dawson Creek, the beginning of the Al-Can Highway.

The Al-Can Highway at this time started at Dawson Creek, British Columbia, and ended 1,522 miles later at Fairbanks, Alaska. The road went through rugged, unmapped wilderness and was heralded as a near impossible engineering feat. After Japan attacked Pearl Harbor it was thought they were going to attack Alaska by coming through the Aleutian Island chain thus gaining a foothold in North America. When Japan invaded Kiska and the Allu Islands in the Aleutian Island chain, efforts to complete the Al-Can Highway intensified.

It has been reported that the Unites States Army used 10,670 troops working twenty-four hours a day in temperatures as low as seventy-nine degrees below zero to build the Al-Can Highway in eight months and twelve days. Construction on the highway started on March 8, 1942 and the road was completed on October 28, 1942. Even though the road was completed in October, it was not opened to public vehicles until 1943. Even then, permafrost melt and frost heave made the Al-Can Highway nearly impossible to travel during June and July.

Don and I reached Dawson Creek in early September of 1948. The weather was getting colder and signs of civilization were thinning out. The maximum speed our Jeep was capable of going didn't matter any more because it was impossible to go that fast anyway. There were miles and miles of cribbed road, logs and poles placed tightly together across the road over permafrost, muskeg and frost heaves. In between these spots the road surface was a constant line of washboards and potholes.

Don and I were doing well. These roads were not much different than conditions we were used to. We were going slow but steady. We could camp and cook any place we wanted to. There were road houses about every seventy-five to a hundred miles where we could fill up our gas tank and restock our meager food supply. Our big problem was flat tires. We had good tires on the Jeep and two spares, but at times we would have two or three flat tires per day. We carried a tire repair kit with casing boots and tube patches along with a hand operated tire pump so we just repaired tires and continued on. The only signs I remember seeing along the entire Al-Can Highway besides an occasional road house sign were signs saying, "WE ARE BUILDING TODAY FOR YOUR DRIVING PLEASURE TOMORROW."

We once stopped to see if we could help a man standing by his beat up old car that had a flat tire. This man looked dejected and his head was hanging down. His wife was sitting in the front seat with three or four rambunctious kids fighting in the back. He looked up and pointed to the sign ahead and said, "WE ARE BUILDING TODAY FOR YOUR DRIVING PLEASURE TOMORROW." He was in the middle of a wilderness, a thousand miles from nowhere and his patience and the pot of gold at the end of the rainbow was losing its luster. This was his third flat tire of the day.

We were breaking camp one morning and I splashed a little water on my head. I was having trouble getting the comb to go through my hair and on closer inspection I found the comb was clogged with flakes of ice. It was getting colder. Because our Jeep didn't have a heater the moisture from our breath was forming ice inside the windshield. We stopped at the next road house and bought a can of deicer. We sprayed two spots on the inside of the windshield, one on the driver's side, one for the passenger's side and we could see reasonably well for a period of time. We were now occasionally coming to road houses that were out of gas and we began to rely more on the extra cans of gas we had in reserve.

Three or four days later we were traveling along and we started going slower and slower. We were going down hill in low axel, four-wheel drive and hardly moving. Finally the motor sputtered and quit. We had gas and spark and could start the motor with the clutch pushed in but when we let the clutch out the motor died. Thinking the transmission had gone out; we discussed what our options were. We could sit and hope someone would come by, we could walk back the way we came or we could walk forward. Just sitting there didn't seem appealing; we knew the last road house we passed was fifty to seventy miles behind us so our decision became a no brainer. We loaded our packs with things we would need to survive and started walking down the road ahead. After we walked ten or twelve miles we lucked out and saw the road-house we were hoping to find up ahead.

The man who came out to greet us was a kindly, patient looking fellow. He gave the impression he'd seen about everything that could possibly happen in his part of the world. We explained our situation to him and he asked several questions before he put a large canvas tarp and four kerosene burning blow torches in his old pickup. He said, "Get in. I think I can help you boys." When we reached our Jeep it looked pitiful sitting there in the middle of the wilderness with icicles hanging off the front bumper. We helped our new found friend start the blow torches and put them at strategic places under the Jeep. Then we covered the entire Jeep with the big canvas tarp and went back to his pickup to wait. He told us it was going to take about an hour so we settled down to visit. When he finally said, "Let's give it a try" it was starting to get dark. We put the torches and tarp back in his pickup and our Jeep started and freely moved back and forth. We drove the Jeep to his road house and parked it in the small garage that was heated by a pot-bellied wood stove. We unrolled our sleeping bags on the garage floor and spent the night. The

California transmission oil that was in our Jeep's rear end, transfer case and transmission had frozen to the point it would no longer allow the gears to turn, thus slowing the Jeep down until it killed the motor. The oil had frozen while we were traveling along!

The next morning the road house owner drained the heavy oil from the Jeep's gear boxes and replaced it with oil suitable for subzero weather. We filled the Jeep and our four five-gallon gas cans as full as possible, paid the bill we owed, which wasn't much, shook hands with the station owner and we were on our way. As we traveled along, the road houses seemed to get farther apart and after we passed two in a row that were out of gas, we began to get concerned. We had already used three of our four five-gallon gas cans we had in reserve and we would have to use the fourth can before long. It is amazing how fast the gas gauge goes down when you are watching it. After we used our last five gallons of gas and the gas gauge dipped to a quarter of a tank, we shut the motor off and coasted down the hills. We could do this because we didn't have power steering or power brakes. By using the hand pulled emergency brake now and then, we could keep the brakes from getting too hot. We'd just coasted down a long hill, turned the motor back on to round the next uphill turn when we saw the road house.

We let out a war hoop and pulled up to the gas pump, when the owner came out, we told him we were out of gas, our gas cans were empty and we'd been coasting down hill to save what little gas we had left. The man shook his head and said, "I'm sorry boys but I ran out of gas several days ago." Seeing the look on our faces he quickly added, "I'll tell you what," and he looked at our gas gauge. Then he said, "These Jeeps usually have more gas in the tank than the gauge indicates. You probably have three more gallons left in the tank. Don't turn that motor off and I can fill your tank with diesel. Just remember don't turn the motor off or kill it or you will be up the creek because the motor won't start again. You can make it to the next road house and I think they still have gas." He filled our gas tank with diesel and we took off in a huge cloud of blue smoke. The man knew what he was talking about because we made it to the next road house and they had gas. We drained the gas tank, cleaned the carburetor, filled everything up with gas and we were on our way as if nothing had happened.

Don and I left the Al-Can Highway at the Slana-Yok Junction. We were in the middle of the Alaska wilderness, miles from nowhere and there was a 'Y' in the road. There was nothing else there. There was no sign post, not even a sign pointing north and south. I'd always been good at keeping my directions straight in the mountains. I almost always knew where north, south, east and west were. But a strange thing happened going through Canada, I got up one morning and north was south and east was west. I knew which direction was right but the compass in my head would not accept that. When we came back through Canada, somewhere in the same area the directions straightened back out and they have been normal ever since. This didn't help the situation we were in now. If we were in the right spot, Anchorage was about three hundred miles down one road and Fairbanks was two hundred miles down the other. I told Don I thought we should take the left road and he said, "That's as good a guess as any. If we're wrong we can back track and get started in the other direction."

We made the right decision. The highway got better and in a day or so we were in the Mantanuska Valley. This was a farming area where the trees had been cleared and the fertile soil, with the help of twenty-four hour a day sunlight during the growing season, grew exceptional crops. This didn't mean it was easy. We were told on certain years the stooks of grain had to be chopped loose from the ice with an axe. We learned that farming got started in this area when the United States government transplanted droughted out farmers from the Midwest dust bowl during the 1930's and sent them to Alaska. These hardy pioneers carved farms out of the Mantanuska Valley wilderness.

By now our bankroll was running low. This is a nice way of saying we were broke. It was harvest time in the Mantanuska Valley so Don and I decide to get a job to build up our grubstake. We went to work for a farmer in the Palmer, Alaska area about forty miles from Anchorage.

We didn't have any trouble retrieving our guns from the Anchorage Post Office and we settled down on the Alaskan farm to work.

Don and I knew how to work. We had an agricultural background and we were used to working long hours. Some crops were different than we were used to and the crops we were familiar with were handled using different methods, but the farmer helped us and it didn't take us long to understand and we soon fit in pretty well. We ate with the family and really appreciated the ranch type meals. There were plates heaped with what they called "government beef" (caribou and moose meat) and we took a good natured ribbing about how much we ate. The farmer took a liking to us and when he learned something about our background and what we intended to do, he became very helpful.

One day when he returned from Anchorage where he bought supplies, he told us he had visited with an old trapper-prospector. The trapper was in the Anchorage hospital recovering from a hernia operation and he wanted to sell one of his trap lines. I don't remember how the farmer came to find this old timer but he gave us a phone number and directions to the hospital. We made phone contact. The old trapper's name was Fred Humes. On most evenings after work, Don and I would drive to Anchorage and sit by Fred's bedside visiting. Fred had a colorful past. In his early years he had been a successful actor in the silent movies. When the movies changed to talkies, the sound track made his voice seem high and squeaky and the studio couldn't use him anymore.

Fred said he was so dejected he decided to go to Alaska. He vowed to himself that he wouldn't return to the States until he struck it rich. When we met Fred he was probably in his early sixties and still trying to strike it rich. He trapped in the winter to make a grub stake so he could prospect in the summer. He told us he'd found a number of gold ore prospects over the years, but they were either too small or in the middle of wilderness where they had little commercial value. He told us about the time he was prospecting one summer and came face to face with an Alaskan brown bear. The bear turned and ran down the trail away from him for about twenty yards before the bear suddenly whirled around and charged. Fred said after several shots the bear finally went down and he reached out and poked it with the end of his rifle barrel just a few feet from where he was standing. Fred's standard operating procedure was to hire a bush pilot to fly him and his supplies into the interior wilderness. He went in the winter to trap and in the summer to prospect. He set a specific date (weather permitting) when the bush pilot was to return and the time span was usually four to six months. Fred said one time the bush pilot was over a month late returning to pick him up and it nearly cost him his life.

Anyway, as several evenings went by and we got better acquainted, we became convinced Fred was an honest man and he saw something in Don and me he liked. So we struck a deal.

At this time you could not buy a trap line from the U.S. Alaskan Territorial government. You paid a small one time payment and received a ninety-nine year lease for trapping rights in a specific area. Beyond that, the trapper involved owned the cabin, traps and whatever private property he used to trap within the designated area.

We bought one of Fred's trap lines for five hundred dollars. It was remote and for this winter Fred wanted to trap closer to civilization until he fully recovered from his operation. The base cabin for the trap line we purchased was located at the lower end of Tonsina Lake, where the Tonsina River started. Tonsina Lake is seven miles long and is located below the Tonsina Glacier.

One trap line went several miles down the Tonsina River. One went west from Tonsina Lake to timberline. Another trap line went up the mountain to the northeast and also ended at timberline. There were two trap line camps located seven or eight miles from the main cabin. Fred stayed in these camps in the late winter and early spring trapping beaver and muskrats. There were no trails along these trap lines because in the winter there were several feet of snow covering the frozen muskegs and ground. All of the traps we purchased were scattered along these trap lines. They were hanging from trees with four to twelve traps stashed in each group. These trap lines were only identified by local land marks and an occasional slash mark in a tree trunk along the way.

Don and I spent evenings at Fred's bedside while he explained the Tonsina Lake terrain. He told us of dangerous avalanche areas and where river and lake ice might be thin. He drew a map pinpointing where each cache of traps was located along each trap line.

We already knew from conversations before we bought the trap line that the only practical way to reach Tonsina Lake at this time of the year, with winter supplies, was to fly in. Fred helped us finalize our grocery list, pointing out things necessary to survive during a long, cold Alaskan winter in the wilderness. It was only twenty-five or thirty miles down the Tonsina River to Copper Center and Highway 4, but until the river was frozen over and the ice could be traveled on, getting through the mountains and muskeg to Tonsina Lake was not an option.

Fred was a soft spoken, self-reliant, straight forward type of man. He reminded me of the cowboys, homesteaders and mountain men I grew up with. During this time Fred, Don and I became acquainted. We'd exchange stories about our past and talked some about our plans for the future. Fred said he was going to make his last stand in the Brooks Mountain Range above the Arctic Circle. He was going to fly in enough supplies to last two and a half years. Then, on a prearranged date, a bush pilot was to return to pick him up. Fred offered to partner with us if we wanted to make the trip with him. This sounded interesting. We had the youthful energy and strength Fred needed and he had the knowledge and experience we lacked. Don and I told Fred we would see how our first winter in the Alaskan wilderness went and we would make a decision in the spring. (This was before we spent days on end with the temperature from forty to fifty-two degrees below zero.)

We finished our fall farm harvest job, got paid, and with wishes of good luck, we drove to Anchorage for the last time. We purchased our winter groceries and because of money concerns we probably skimped on some things more than we should have.

We found a bush pilot willing to fly us the hundred miles to Tonsina Lake but it would take two trips to fly us and our winter supplies to the lake. The bush pilot was a big, barrel-chested Swede. He had a thick Swedish accent and a twinkle in his eye. He had been a bush pilot in Alaska for twenty-five years and he knew exactly where we wanted to go. We asked him what the rate would be to make two trips and when he told us we said we didn't have that much money. He looked down at us with that twinkle in his eyes and said, "How much money you got?" Don said, "One hundred and fifty dollars." The bush pilot pondered for a minute and said, "Vee go first ting in the morning." Don and I hauled our winter supplies to the airport. We decided we would both fly into Tonsina Lake with half of our supplies on the first flight, Don would stay at the cabin the first night and I would return to Anchorage. The next day I would return with the rest of our winter equipment.

The next morning Don and I helped the pilot load the plane with what he said was all the weight the plane could carry. The plane was a small two engine seaplane with pontoons that I assumed could be replaced with skies for winter use. The pilot said it was a Weegen aircraft. It had three seats abreast across the front with limited space for cargo back in the fuselage. The pilot was to my left, I was in the middle seat and Don was to the right. It was very tight quarters. All I could see was a vast, snowy, white open space before us with snow covered mountain peaks sticking up on either side. There were large timbered canyons below. The air was rough and I was sitting there somewhat white knuckled when the bush pilot let out a belly laugh, whacked me across the chest with his beefy forearm and said, "Son, you never fly in a plane before?" When I admitted I hadn't I received some good natured kidding and the atmosphere in the plane lightened up.

In an hour or so Tonsina Glacier with the Lake below it came into view. It was windy and white caps were showing up on the small waves in the water below. When the plane hit the water it felt as if I'd been hit across the butt with a two by four. The plane skipped, slithered, and skidded across the waves for what seemed like a mile or more before we slowed down and started taxiing. It reminded me of landing on a washboard. We taxied up to a narrow rock strewn beach with a small log cabin with a cache on top of four six foot posts in the background.

I handed our supplies out over the pontoon and Don started stacking them above the waterline. When we finished unloading, the pilot was anxious to get back in the air so Don pushed the pontoon back out to deeper water. The pilot gunned the engine and we were soon turned around and taking off. I waved to Don and told him I would see him the next day. Don said the loneliest feeling came over him when he saw his last link to civilization disappear in the sky and he turned and saw that little cabin, that he had not even seen the inside of, quietly sitting there.

When I got back to Anchorage I was busy. I left the Jeep in the hospital parking lot and took the keys to Fred. Don and I had offered to let Fred use our Jeep for the winter. When he was sufficiently recovered from his operation he was going to drive the Jeep to Copper Center where he could use it to run a trap line he had along the highway. When Don and I were ready to come down the ice covered Tonsina River later, our Jeep would already be in the area. I don't remember where I stayed that night or how I got to the airport the next morning but I do remember I got there plenty early. I had a long nervous wait for the bush pilot to show up. When he did, we loaded the rest of our supplies aboard the plane and took off. We reached Tonsina Lake about the middle of the day. Don, who heard the plane coming, was standing by the lakeshore when we taxied in. We unloaded the rest of our supplies, shook hands with the bush pilot and while we stood there watching the plane disappear in the pale blue Alaskan sky, Don was excitedly telling me what he had discovered during the short time he had been here.

The cabin, cache, spring and everything in the immediate vicinity were exactly the way Fred represented them. Don had seen snowshoe rabbits, lynx tracks and salmon spawning along the shore of the lake.

We had traveled around 3,730 miles, overcome a number of obstacles, some caused by our own ignorance, and we were eager to start the second phase of our journey.

I will continue this story after more cowboy 100,000 mile stories are told.

LITTLE THINGS

It is strange how middle age keeps getting older. When I was 45, I thought middle age was 55. When I was 55, I thought middle age was 65. When I got to be 65, I thought middle age was 75. Now that I am 82, I've finally passed middle age.

COWBOYS AND WARS

From World War II through the Korean and Vietnam wars, many cowboys enlisted or were drafted into the services, leaving ranchers on the big range areas short handed. Young men of draft age had three choices: enlist, be drafted, or continue to work on the ranches under agricultural deferments. Of the four young cowboys that worked together for a number of years on the Eden Valley Ranch the armed forces took its toll.

Bob Secrist enlisted in the Air Force and became a top gunner on a B.59 Super Fortress. He was the highest ranking enlisted man on the crew with a rank of Staff Sergeant and controlled six fifty caliber machine guns. When Bob was transferred to Montana, the plane's bomb bays were refitted with fuel tanks and Bob was responsible for refueling fighter planes in midair.

Harold Crothers was drafted into the Army and fought in the Korean War. Harold was in the infantry and fought in the jungles and rice paddies of Korea until the war ended.

Don Linsteadt and I were the other two members of the original four cowboys working for the Eden Valley Ranch at that time. Don enlisted in the Marine Corps and became a lieutenant. I was now the only cowboy left of the original group and I was headed to the Army. Several years before, while I was in high school, I spent a stint in the Willits unit of the California National Guard. I remember tieing for first place in a marksmanship contest on the rifle range. The National Guard experience gave me some training and I was planning on enlisting in the Army when the local draft board called me to take the Army physical. They loaded thirty or forty of us on a Greyhound bus and took us to San Francisco where we spent the day in an Army barracks type building. There were five or six old doctors stationed around a large room. They looked like retired private practice doctors called up by the Army to give physicals. They were a stern, sober looking bunch, especially the old doc who examined for hernia and hemorrhoid problems. There certainly wasn't any humor in that place. This is the closest I have ever been to being treated like a cow. We were stripped, lined up in a straight line, and herded from doctor to doctor where we were pinched, poked, and prodded. The only thing missing was the livestock squeeze chute.

When I returned to the ranch from the bus trip I assumed I was in the Army. The mood at the ranch was somber. R.C.Williams, the ranch manager, was in a tough situation. During WWII the whole nation was involved and this was serious business. Gas, sugar, shoes and other commodities were rationed, farm labor dried up, ranches and farms all over the United States produced food with skeleton crews. Almost every able bodied man or woman was in the service or working in the defense effort. Older and younger people were pitching in to help fill the jobs they left behind. The whole nation was fighting to preserve our way of life.

This was the situation facing Roland Williams, the ranch manager. During the wars the local draft boards had the power to place a draftee in any position they thought would best benefit the country. Agriculture and feeding the nation was a top priority so Mr. Williams took me to a meeting with the local board and explained that three of his four man cowboy crew were already in the services. Therefore, I was granted a six months agricultural deferment. That deferment was renewed every six months until the war was over. I did my best to fulfill that obligation. The ranch was always short handed. We often worked what I called twofers, accomplishing two days work in one day.

The days, weeks, and months slipped by and I worked with older seasoned cowboys. Harvey Brightenstine was my mentor during this time period. What I learned from him about mountains, wildlife, horses, dogs, and livestock has been priceless as I traveled along my lifelong horseback ride.

Another long time friend that worked seasonally for Eden Valley was Don Martin. Don had a shock of straight hair with one little lock that curled down over his forehead. So, of course, to the ranch crew he became known as "Curly". Don attended Willits High School at the same time Don Lindsteadt and I were going there. Prior to this, Bob, Harold and I went to the same one room country school. In fact, we made up half of the student body. Don Martin went on to veterinary school and is a successful respected veterinarian. He practiced in central California for many years before going north and is now semi-retired but still operates a veterinary service in Hayfork, California.

Today we are fighting two wars: one in Iraq, another in Afghanistan, trying to halt a movement that threatens our freedom and way of life. Today, in mainstream America if it were not for the twenty-four-seven coverage by the news media, often critical of our country's efforts, the public would not even know there was a war going on. A lot of water has run under the bridge since Bob, Harold and I went to the one room country school where we pledged allegiance to the flag of the United States of America every morning, helped the teacher split wood, cleaned ashes from the pot bellied stove, swept the floor and took turns raising and lowering the American flag, being careful so it didn't touch the ground.

Yes, a lot of water has run under the bridge since those days. When I look back over my 115,000 mile horseback ride and remember what our country was like and what its values were when I saddled my first horse at the beginning of my lifelong ride and compare those values to our country and some of its values towards the end of my ride, I sometimes think part of those waters have been running in the wrong direction.

I think Abraham Lincoln said it best in just nine sentences:

You cannot bring about prosperity by discouraging thrift.

You cannot strengthen the weak by weakening the strong.

You cannot help the wage earner by pulling down the wage payer

You cannot further the brotherhood of man by encouraging class hatred.

You cannot help the poor by destroying the rich.

You cannot establish security on borrowed money.

You cannot keep out of trouble by spending more than you earn.

You cannot build character and courage by taking away man's initiative and independence.

You cannot help men permanently by doing for them what they could and should do for themselves.

ABRAHAM LINCOLN

I hope these values are never taken away from the part of America that still believes in them.

Enough said. Back to my cowboy memories at the end of WWII. I remember clearly where I was and what I was doing when I heard the war was over. I was re-riding the range, along the south fork of the Eel River, with Don and Roland Graff. The afternoon was hot and we were unable to find any of the crafty old cows that were missed during the original round up. We decided to ride down to a small ranch, situated close to the river, and see if my Aunt Mae and Uncle Vern had seen any cows going to the river for water.

We wanted to check before we left the area and climbed back up the mountain. When we rode into the clearing in front of their house, we were surprised to see the front door fly open and Aunt Mae and Uncle Vern running across their yard, waving their arms, making sure to attract our attention. This was unusual. They lived most of their lives in the back country and were always glad to welcome company but I had never seen this type of emotion and excitement before. Thinking something was wrong, we loped over to the yard fence and heard them both excitedly yelling, "The war is over! The war is over! Japan has surrendered!" Well, that was exciting news and we listened intently while they re-told the details of the news broadcast they just heard on their radio.

After WWII ended, the Korean and Vietnam Wars came along and they continued to have an impact on the ranching communities and rural areas of America. The country as a whole was impacted, but the intensity and commitment felt during WWII never again took place.

In time, Bob, Harold, Don and I were together again as cowboys working for the Eden Valley Ranch before we again went our separate ways. Bob moved to Elko, Nevada, and became a successful business man working and supporting the ranching community. Harold was a cowboy for a number of years before becoming manager and operator of the Brook Trails water system, west of Willits, California. Don came out of the Marine Corps and became a partner in a Certified Public Accounting firm in Sacramento, California. In later years he and his wife, Mary Lou, bought land and established a vineyard in the foothills on the east side of the Sacramento Valley where they lived until Don's untimely death. Don Martin expanded his veterinary practice and I continued along my 115,000 horseback ride.

Bob, Don, Harold, Don Martin and I, although involved in different endeavors, never strayed far from our roots. We still ride together once in awhile and cherish the days and memories when we were cowboys together.

The other day my neighbor and I were standing out front visiting when a young man came by. He grinned and said, "There's a couple of old timers' living in the past." My friend straightened up and said, "We don't live it the past, but now and then we enjoy remembering it." (I thought he hit the nail squarely on the head.)

LITTLE THINGS

The west was won in fifths, (referring to whiskey) inches, feet, yards, sections and townships. That is the way it should be. The metric system has no right here.

HARVEY DAHL

Harvey Dahl was inducted into the Nevada Cattlemen's Association Cowboy 100,000 Mile Club in 1992.

This brief introduction was given by Demar Dahl, and is as follows:

Harvey Dahl of Deeth, Nevada has been a cattleman all of his life. Part of his life has been away from his own ranch but he rode horseback while away and has always been associated with horses during his many endeavors.

Harvey put in more than fifty years as a pick-up man at rodeos. He has helped with an average of twenty rodeos per year and ridden approximately fifteen miles per rodeo.

He trailed cattle from ranches to railroad heads prior to, during and after World War II for at least ten years, thirty days a year for 300 days.

Harvey has done ranch work on ranches where cattle have run on year-round range for an average of forty miles a week for fifty-two weeks per year.

From the saddles he has worn out, the spurs that lost their rowels, the lariat ropes he's lost and the many good horses he's broke and ridden, these figures are conservative.

Harvey has owned his own ranch since 1938, or for fifty-four years.

He has picked up at rodeos in North and South Dakota, Florida, Utah, Idaho and Nevada.

He broke horses in Sweden, has ridden good horses in Canada and ridden the top Camp Draft Horse in Australia.

He cowboyed for many years in Florida.

Ranch work	83,000 miles
Pick up at Rodeos	15,000 miles
Trailing Cattle	9,000 miles
Grand total of miles ridden in his lifetime	107,000 miles

Dave's comment: "This is a presentation that is short and to the point. This is another example of a typical Nevada rancher that combined ranching with other horse oriented activities and excelled at both. He has been an ambassador for the ranching community all over the United States plus Canada, Europe and Australia. Harvey's ridden a lot of miles horseback while doing this."

LITTLE THINGS

You might be a rancher if you have convinced your wife that an overnight, out of state trip, to a bull sale is a vacation.

RANGE HOGS

During one part of my 115,000 mile horseback ride I rode many miles horseback hunting and gathering wild hogs. During this time many ranches in the coastal mountains of northern California let hogs run loose on their ranges. This was mostly by design to supplement income but sometimes by accident. To keep these hogs under control they were rounded up using cowboys, cow horses and cow dogs to do the work. The boar pigs were castrated, their tails were bobbed, and the ranch ear marks were put in each pig's ear. The domesticated sow hogs with litters of pigs, would occasionally come by the hog sheds and bed down for the night, stay around for several days knowing they would be fed some barley, before they again dispersed out on the range for days on end. The sows produced two litters of pigs per year. Each litter consisted of about six surviving pigs, so it was important to manage the range hogs that went wild or their numbers quickly got out of control.

The range hogs grazed on squaw clover, filaree, and wild oats from late winter through spring into mid-summer. They foraged on the abundant acorn crop produced by the many varieties of oak trees that grew profusely at different elevations all through the mountains during the fall and winter months.

Several times a year feeder pigs were gathered and driven to corrals at the end of country roads and shipped to market. The by-product of this activity was domestic hogs gone wild. Domestic hogs, raised under range conditions, will go wild in a single generation and they are a formidable animal to deal with. The full grown wild boars and barrows weighed between four and six hundred pounds. Wild hogs are the only animals I ever met in the back country that would consistently charge a man, whether afoot or on horseback, just because he was there.

In the early days part of our everyday work was hunting down and catching these wild hogs. This usually happened as a sideline to working cows. Working cows was our first responsibility but it was hard to pass-up a good wild hog chase. We would bay-up and kill the older hogs that were past their prime. Our dogs were also varmint dogs and liked to track and tree coon, lynx, bobcats, panther and bear but they especially liked to track and bay-up wild hogs. This was a dangerous business and it was not unusual to have a dog hurt. The wounded dog usually recovered and in time returned to the hunt with the same enthusiasm as before. Seldom was this encounter fatal.

The Eden Valley Ranch had a slaughter house, a hog dipping vat and a smoke house. The only time of year when running hogs took priority over working cows was in late January and early February. The entire cowboy crew with their dogs and horses would run and catch full grown wild barrows that had been caught, castrated and ear marked when they were pigs or young boars several years before.

This was exciting and dangerous work. We hunted the live oak roughs where the hogs bedded down and lived. These canyons were usually too steep and rocky for cows to graze. Therefore, they were wild areas seldom explored during the rest of the year.

We used three-eighths scant Samson spot cord cotton lass ropes when hunting hogs. The rope was strong, fast, could be half-hitched and drug through mud and snow and still hold its shape reasonably well. When we jumped a hog out of its bed or a dog cut a fresh track, the chase was on. Sometimes we would run the hogs all day long but usually the dogs would bay them up or they would break out into open ground where cowboys could rope them. If a hog bayed up in the brush where it was impossible to make a normal throw with a rope, we coiled the loop in the end of the rope up with the rest of the rope's coils and threw the coils underhanded into the area where the hog was charging around. After a few casts we usually snagged one of the hog's feet. Sometimes the hog would break and run before a foot was caught and the chase would start all over again.

After a barrow was caught we put one rope on a front foot, another rope on a hind foot, got back to the ends of the ropes and let the hog up. You have to remember most of these barrows weighed four to six hundred pounds with a surly disposition that wasn't helped any by the events leading up to this point. When the barrow charged, the cowboy holding the front foot jerked his rope hard and spun the hog around. If the hog started to charge in the opposite direction the cowboy holding the hind foot rope jerked his rope hard and turned the hog in the right direction; if all this failed you climbed a brush or tree; much faster that you thought possible. After a while the barrow would start traveling downhill and it would take about a day to drive him down the steep draws to the valley floor where he could be loaded on a stone boat or sled and hauled to the ranch.

For two or three weeks this process was repeated. The old boars and barrows that were past their prime were hunted and killed out on the range. The fat barrows were caught and brought to the ranch where they were put in a solid board corral until ten or twelve were captured. They were so wild they would not eat during the day time; they would only eat at night.

The hogs were then taken to the slaughter house holding pen. There they were killed one by one, scalded, and the bristles scrapped off the hide or rind. If I remember right the proper temperature for scalding a hog was 158 degrees. This temperature was hard to maintain using a wood fire under the vat. If the scalding water was not hot enough, the bristles would not scrape off. If the water was too hot, it set the bristles and they had to be shaved off. Needless to say, after shaving a four to six hundred pound hog, great care was taken not to overheat the water in the scalding vat.

After the hogs were killed, scalded and the bristles scraped off, the hogs were hung on the slaughter house rails. The next week was spent rendering lard and making hams and sides of bacon. The size of the hams and bacon slabs from four to six hundred pound hogs is hard to comprehend when comparing them to the size of hams and bacon sold in most modern day stores. In contrast, these hams and bacon sides were huge.

The two to three inch thickness of fat that covered the entire carcass was trimmed and cut into small squares along with fat trimmings from the hams and bacon and put into a large cast iron cauldron heated by a wood fire. When the lard was heated to a slow boil, it was poured through a sieve and put into five gallon crocks. There it cooled into soft white lard. The remaining trimmings, or cracklings as they were called, were placed in a press where the lard they contained was squeezed out. This press was screwed down by hand and the lard was again sifted before it was poured into the five gallon crocks.

At first, deep fried pork left in the crackling cakes was irresistible, but in a few days it seemed like the lard was seeping out of our pores and the temptation to eat them was gone. The dry crackling cakes were stored in a cool dry place and used to supplement feed for cow dogs during the winter.

The hams and bacon treated with Morton's salt were pumped by hand every few days to remove as much moisture as possible before they were placed in the smoke house with the sides of bacon where they were smoked for the proper period of time. Those hams and bacon were smoked with a smoldering Madrone wood fire started every morning. They were not the traditional Hickory smoked hams you hear about, but they were comparable.

The finished products furnished the ranch cook with lard, hams and bacon for the coming year and by the time the next year rolled around we were eager to start the whole hog hunting procedure over again.

You add to this food source, red meat in at least two square meals a day, raw milk, thick separated or skimmed cream, homemade bread, cakes, cookies and pies which were a part of the diet of that day and it would be enough to cause a modern day dietitian to have severe nightmares. In all fairness, the diets of those days were supplemented with canned and dried fruit, canned vegetables and home grown vegetables from the gardens. Apples and pears from ranch orchards were also plentiful, but all fresh fruits and vegetables were seasonal and the meals were a far cry from the recommended diets of today. Add whiskey, chewing tobacco, hand rolled cigarettes, pipes, and cigars to this mix and it is hard for many folks to understand how any of these cowboys and rural people survived well into old age, but many are still alive.

I am not knocking the modern dietary health trends of today. I am just pointing out what the old lady whose husband died at ninety-six said, " I've been telling John for years that eating red meat, frying steaks in lard, smoking cigarettes, chewing tobacco, drinking whiskey, and chasing women was going to kill him and I was right. It did."

LITTLE THINGS

When I was young I shod horses for six dollars a head an furnished the shoes. At that time ranch horses cost forty-five to seventy dollars per head. Today it costs sixty to eighty- five dollars to have a ranch horse shod and the horses cost seven to fifteen hundred dollars per head. If you really want a well broke horse the sky is the limit.

UNSCHEDULED SURPRISE

This incident happened early in my 115,000 mile horseback ride. I was probably nineteen or twenty years old. This day I was salting and checking replacement heifers on the Eden Valley Ranch just north of the Salt Creek Divide. I had a mixture of loose rock salt and bone meal in a tub shaped canvas bag known as a salt sack. The salt sack was about half full and draped over the horn and fork of my saddle. We used pack horses to carry salt to established salt licks in important locations, but today I was salting small bunches of replacement heifers wherever I found them. I would call the heifers while my dogs stopped the yearlings and brought them back toward me. I would put out small piles of salt, hold the heifers until they settled down, and then ride on until I found the next bunch. Even though the older cows ran out on the range year round and were pretty wild, they would usually come when called knowing they would be salted when they arrived. In the winter after a heavy snow storm we would load pack horses with one hundred-fifty or two hundred pounds of cotton seed cake. The weight loaded on each horse depended on the distance and the terrain we were packing into. We would call the cows and supplement them out on the range until the snow melted on the south slopes and the cows could again get enough forage. This was just another way of handling cattle in the steep, brushy, timbered mountains of northern California.

The day had been uneventful. I was heading home across a large grassy opening dotted with oak trees. The wild oats were already stirrup high and the Squaw clover was in full reddish bloom. I topped a steep, rocky ridge and in the middle of a clover patch about twenty feet away was a wild boar. The domestic hogs that go wild in this part of the country will weigh between three and six hundred pounds. This was a BIG BOAR! He raised his head and without provocation, charged. Pepper, the sorrel horse I was riding whirled out of the way and the boar went by. He turned and charged again before he headed for a brush patch some hundred yards away. My dogs were in hot pursuit. I turned Pepper around, caught up with the boar, and running along side, emptied my pistol, trying to place a shot at the base of his ear. Despite my efforts the boar was still going strong when he disappeared into the brush. Pepper slid to a stop. I dismounted on the fly, tied Pepper to a low hanging oak limb, and reloaded my pistol. Because of concern for my dogs, maybe youthful ignorance and the desire to make a clean kill, I crawled into the brush on my hands and knees. I was thinking that while the dogs kept the boar occupied I could sneak in close enough to get a clean shot. Twenty yards into the thicket, the brush canopy lifted a little and I could see ten or twelve feet ahead. About then the dogs quit barking and I couldn't tell where the boar was. This was a spooky situation but it didn't last long because the boar I had been hunting was now hunting me. The next thing I knew I was face to face with the charging boar. One eye was missing, his tusks were gleaming white, and red froth was flying from both sides of his open mouth. There wasn't time to think or shoot. I lunged to the left, my feet went out from under me and I fell hard. In an instant the boar was on me. The dogs were everywhere. Old Spike had a death grip on the boar's ear while Tip and Will were biting his flanks. After what seemed like an awfully long moment, the boar broke and ran with my dogs still hanging on. His right tusk tore my shirt; there was blood all over my chaps, and my left side hurt where I had apparently been stepped on. Miraculously, as far as I could tell, I was still in one piece. I crawled out of the brush, had trouble mounting an extremely excited horse, then turned my attention to the dogs barking about a quarter of a mile downhill. When I reached the spot, the boar was backed up against a granite rock with the dogs barking on all sides.

This time, hoping to avoid a six mile walk home, I hobbled Pepper before I tied him up. Then I located a safe spot within close range, called my dogs back, and killed the boar with a single shot.

Like most of these experiences when it is over, the silence is deafening. The murmuring of Salt Creek running in the distance and the dogs panting were the only sounds to be heard.

My dogs were not hurt, I was all right, and Pepper's shattered nervous system was getting back to normal. The rest of the ride home was uneventful.

Back at the bunkhouse I had been reading a story about a man in a life and death situation, and so the story went, he was so stressed that his hair turned gray overnight. The next morning I actually checked in the cracked mirror over the bunkhouse sink to see if I could find any gray hair. In part I think the story I was reading was true. In my case the gray hair just took thirty more years to materialize. Somewhere in my office I still have the tusks from that boar to prove this story.

A PARTNER LOST

During the winter months in the northern California coastal mountains, a large part of our cowboy work was packing cotton seed cake to the cow herds out on the mountain ranges and gathering a few old or young cows that were thin. These cows would be fed hay for a time until the late winter or early spring grass grew and the cows gathered could be turned back out on the range.

Harvey and I left the main ranch at daylight, which at this time of year wasn't very early. We started on the cold fifteen mile ride to the Garcy place, which was at that time a cow camp on the south end of the ranch where Harvey lived. I was going to stay with Harvey and work out of the Garcy Place packing cotton seed cake to cows out on the range for several weeks or until the snow melted. We were a couple of hours out riding through open country. The damp cold was beginning to seep into our bones and the low clouds and fog were just beginning to rise. For the last mile or so we'd ridden in silence, humped up against the cold.

Suddenly the dogs that were ranging out in front of us broke into a wild barking frenzy. No cows were bawling and the speed the dogs were traveling plus the sound of their barking told us they hadn't found cows but had jumped or hit a hot track of something else. It could be a lynx, bobcat, panther or a bear. The mood of the cold boring ride immediately changed. The bone chilling cold was forgotten. By now the dogs were a quarter of a mile ahead and we were running to catch up. In another five minutes the tone of the barking changed from trailing to baying or treeing. From the commotion it sounded like the dogs were baying something on the ground rather than barking treed. This made me wonder because I thought they were probably trailing a lynx or a bobcat. When we topped a ridge we were surprised to see a boar hog, weighing about two hundred pounds, bayed up on open ground. Our thinking immediately shifted gears and because we were together in the open with lots of room to work, instead of killing the boar we would rope him, stretch him out, castrate him, and put the ranch ear marks (crop in the left ear, under half crop in the right) and turn him loose. If we were lucky enough to catch the barrow again in a year or so, he would become ham and bacon in the ranch cookhouse.

Now sometimes a wild hog will run forever with a pack of dogs barking around his head but just one dog that bites his tail and flanks will cause him to sit down and whirl around facing the dog. Spike, my old dog, and Pete Harvey's dog were keeping the boar bayed up in the open by attacking his hind quarters. While I was taking my rope down,

Skeeter, my younger dog, charged the boar head on. Quicker than you could bat an eye, the boar lunged forward and caught Skeeter's forearm and shoulder in his mouth and shook Skeeter from side to side. A knot formed in the pit of my stomach when I heard the bones crunching. The boar threw Skeeter in the air like a ragdoll. Before Skeeter hit the ground the boar's left tusk ribbed open his ribcage. Skeeter still tried to rejoin the fight but soon gave up and crawled off to the side. The boar was sitting on his tail end with his snout in the air while the dogs nipped at his flanks. I made a good throw and the loop settled down behind his ears. Harvey picked up the boar's hind feet and we stretched him out. I tied hard and fast, castrated, ear marked and bobbed the boar's tail. Harvey held the boar down with a tight rope on his back feet while I carefully removed my rope and remounted. Then Harvey dragged the hog a safe distance over the hill and turned him loose.

I turned my attention to Skeeter who saw me coming and started to crawl toward me. I was dismounted, sitting on the ground with Skeeter's head in my lap, when I felt Harvey's hand on my shoulder. He said, "Why don't you ride on ahead. I'll ride down through Old Woman's Canyon and meet you at Box Springs sometime around noon."

Without another word I mounted my horse and rode on down the trail. In a short time I stiffened in the saddle when I heard the shot I knew was coming. With a friend and partner lost, I continued the day's work with a heavy heart.

Harvey and I met at Box Springs around the middle of the day and we discussed the cattle and range conditions we had seen during the morning but we didn't mention the act of kindness Harvey had done for me when he spared me from doing the inevitable. No thanks was asked and no thanks was given. This was just part of the unspoken bond that exists between the men that live and work on the big ranges of the west. This was another experience I had along my lifetime horseback ride.

Sherman Creek School House

JACK WALTHER

Jack and Irene Walther were inducted into the Nevada Cattlemen's Association Cowboy 100,000 Mile Club in 1993.

Russell Turner introduced Jack and Irene when each was induced in to the Club. The documentations given here are taken from memories Jack and Irene have of traveling their long winding trails and are written by Jane and Dave Secrist.

Jack Walther was born a native son of Elko County, Nevada in 1919. He was the tenth child of thirteen born to Joseph Crawford and Julia Ann Warr Walther on the family ranch in Halleck. Jack's grandfather, Valentine Walther, came from Germany in 1876. He took up land by squatter's rights and was one of the first settlers in Huntington Valley in the Jiggs area of Elko County, Nevada.

Jack got his name in a very unusual way. He had no name until he was old enough to talk. Then an aunt asked him what he thought his name should be. After a little thought Jack answered, "I would like to be named after Jack Dempsey or Pete Andersen." As you may know Jack Dempsey was one of the greatest prize fighter of his time, but you may not know that Pete Andersen was the local "bootlegger." The family chose the fighter's name. Jack was given the middle name of Halleck, after old Fort Halleck near the area where they lived.

Jack's dad was raised in Sherman, Nevada. He and his brother bought their grandfather's ranch at Sherman. Later they split the ranch and Jack's family moved to the part that was in the Fort Halleck area.

When Jack was about five years old he had a horse he named "Monkey' and sure enjoyed that horse. Jack remembers breaking his first horse when he was eight years old. It was a yearling filly and from that time forward breaking and training horses was an important part of Jack's lifetime work.

When six year old Jack started school, he rode either horseback or in a buggy one and one-half miles each direction for nine years. The family boarded the teacher and when Jack finished the eighth grade, his folks hired Marguerite Evans to come to the ranch and teach Jack for his first year in high school. She taught him Ancient History, English and Algebra. Jack says, "Miss Evans did not have an easy job. I was somewhat rowdy." During these years, Jack started his lifetime horseback ride by riding about 6,000 miles.

While Jack was going to school he also helped his folks and John Marble at the 71 Ranch. Jack said, "If you include my "foolin" around miles, you can add another 2,000 miles in this time frame."

After high school Jack went off to school in Logan, Utah to become a vet, but he says, "The school took one look at my high school grades and said, "Forget it. You're not going to make it." Jack settled for Animal Husbandry and stayed a couple of years. Jack noted that it was compulsory to take R.O.T.C. while in school but he didn't like it at all. He was required to take a physical examination in order to participate in the program. Jack figured out that the exam was given in a building at the top of a hill. Jack was inclined to have high blood pressure so on the way to the exam Jack ran all the way up the hill. When the doctor examined Jack he discovered he had high blood pressure (mostly from the exertion of running but the doctor didn't know that.) The condition caused Jack to be ineligible for the R.O.T.C. program. Now he had to choose either ballroom dancing or archery for physical education because he was out of R.O.T.C. Jack chose archery. Now Jack grins and says, "Maybe I would have been better off if I had chosen ballroom dancing."

Jack came back to Elko County and worked for the 71 Ranch again. He leased the Halleck ranch to the 71 for the right to run fifty head of cows on their range.

When Jack and Irene got married, they tell different tales as to why. Irene says, "I married Jack because he ran a ranch cookhouse and I wouldn't have to cook." Jack says, "I married Irene because she had fifteen cows. You see, I had the right to run fifty cows on the 71 Ranch and since times had been a little hard, I was down to only thirty-five head. With Irene's fifteen, I was back to my original fifty cows." Jack remembers he made $350 a month as superintendent of the 71 while cowboys made $150 a month.

Jack and Irene decided to save enough money to buy their own ranch. They looked at a ranch in the Lamoille Valley, but while one partner wanted to sell that ranch, the other didn't. Then the Eddie Martin Ranch came up for sale and they bought the one hundred sixty acres for $7,200. In a previous time, Eddie's son-in-law, Ira Sauder, dug a ditch to bring irrigation water to the meadows and they put up fifty tons of hay on the ranch. Today, with improvements Jack and Irene made, they now put up 300 tons of hay on the same meadows. As the years went by, they traded the Fort Halleck ranch for adjoining acreage, putting together the ranch in Lamoille Valley they now own.

Jack broke all types of horses. His horses became cow horses because one horse did everything. Compared to many of today's horses that are trained to do just one specific thing such as calf rope, team rope or cutting cows. With tongue in cheek Jack says, "A cowboy working on a ranch today would have to lead three of these type horses behind him to just do a day's work."

During the years from his teens to the present time, Jack estimated he probably broke an average of ten horses per year for sixty years (part of the horses he broke were work horse teams) so he guessed he rode each saddle horse at least 100 miles while getting them started. This easily adds up to 32,000 miles. Jack says, "When I got a horse into the bridle I was tired of him, and I was ready to see what the next one would be like. Every horse I've ever worked with has been different." He remembers his Dad saying, "Jack can do things with a horse that I can't do." Andrew Boyd broke colts but one time he sent Jack a horse he couldn't ride. Jack says, "I gentled him and sent him back." People said the horses Jack broke were extremely gentle. Jack liked to start work teams and saddle horses just to see what they were like.

Jack worked for the 71 Ranch for twenty years and said during this time he averaged riding horseback ten miles a day, four days a week. In those twenty years Jack rode at least another 31,000 miles.

We have not counted the many miles Jack rode caring for his own cattle. Jack and Irene have one of the best quality herds of Red Angus cows in the country and they take great pride in their herd. Jack estimates that during the last fifty-two years he's ridden about 30,000 miles for a grand total of 101,000 horseback miles during his lifetime ride.

Jack says, 'The estimated mileage ridden is pretty conservative but if you added the time I spent breaking and driving work horse teams, another 7,000 miles could easily be added.

Dave's comment: Jack's cowboy sense of humor and his ability to remember and tell stories make the Walther's Ranch a very interesting place to visit. Jack even recited some of his poetry at the National Cowboy Poetry Festival in Elko, Nevada and that is somewhat unusual for a cowboy that has ridden 100,000 miles in the saddle.

On one of our visits to the Walther Ranch, Jack told this story. It went something like this: Jack said, "I was starting a big long legged colt for a neighbor. The horse only had one or two rides on him and I was riding past the house where a tractor was parked. The horse was scared of the tractor, so as part of his education I was urging and coaxing the horse up to the tractor to build his confidence in me. He was very tense. I leaned over a little and I reached out to touch the tractor and at that same moment Irene came out of the house and slammed the screen door on the back porch.

I was hanging off to the side after grabbing the saddle horn and trying to regain my position of authority. This scared the horse even more. He continued jumping sideways until we got to the hard road before I finally hit the ground, knocking the wind out of me.

After getting my wind back the only injury I had was a big hematoma on one shin bone. Thinking I needed attention, I asked advice from a local veterinarian. I was advised to take a shot of terramiycin, the same dosage by weight as cattle were given. I had a half bottle left from doctoring calves in the spring so I decide to give myself a shot or two and see what would happen.

Ten days later the shin was still badly swollen so I went to see Doctor Seyferth in Elko. He lanced the swelling and really gave me hell for waiting so long. Dr. Seyferth told me the trouble with you ranchers is you think you can cure everything with sheep dip."

Jack would tell this story on himself and laugh when he got to the part where Dr. Seyferth commented on self-doctoring.

LITTLE THINGS

This happened in 1925. This "old timer" had never been out of Elko County, Nevada or ridden in a car before. One of his friends had a Model T Ford and talked the old boy into going to Winnemucca, Nevada with him. It was about 150 mile trip each way over a dirt road and when they got back to Elko someone asked the "old timer" what he thought of the trip. This is what he said, "Well, fellers, if this old world is as big to the east as it is to the west, it is a big S.O.B."

Spanish
Ranch
School
House

Irene with her dad, Bill

IRENE WALTHER

Irene was born to be a cowgirl and she enjoys her life as such. Irene was born on March 24, 1925 on her father's Independence Valley Ranch in Nevada. Her father was Bill Behn. Her grandfather, her Dad's father, was well educated. He spoke seven languages; however, he was an alcoholic. Men would bring him home in a straight jacket and he would end up with the snakes. He died of tuberculosis when her father was thirteen years old. Irene remembers her father telling about when he and his mother moved to the Spanish Ranch shortly thereafter. She was the cook and he was the wrango boy. Later on her Dad became a cowboy for the Spanish Ranch and they lived there for four years when Irene was young. Most people called her dad Bill but the cowboys called him "Dusty."

Irene says "I don't know much about my mother except that she had a high school education and that was special for those times." Irene remembers her mother didn't care much for her when she was young so she spent most of her time with her dad following the cowboy lifestyle.

Irene said "I spent my first and second grades going to the Spanish Ranch School. The building had once been used as a pump house and later the ranch put windows in both sides of the building and it became the school. It had a small wood burning stove in one corner and when the wind blew, snow drifted into the room through the window frames. The room always seemed cold in the winter." She remembers riding one mile horseback to school and another mile getting back home. One time she stopped to give her horse a drink from the creek and she dropped a rein. When she reached down trying to pick the rein up, she fell in the creek. She said, "Mom sure was angry with me." Later, after her folks got their own place, Irene rode five miles one way or ten miles a day to the same Spanish Ranch School. This time she went from the fourth to the eighth grades.

Irene's grandmother, Mary, married Oscar Miller, an old frontier freighter, who hauled freight from Elko to the mines with teams of horses. Oscar was a good man, but somewhat of a character. Oscar bought the ranch that Jim Wright owns now. He and Irene's Dad took out a 320 acre desert claim, and to irrigate it, they built a four and a half mile ditch with a team and fresno. This allowed them to take water from the Owyhee River.

"Later Dad and Oscar tried to buy the 45 Ranch, further down the Owyhee, but they went broke," said Irene. Around 1943 her dad took over Oscar's debts and bought the original ranch. The following spring he purchased cows from the 7 Wrench Ranch in Oregon for thirty dollars a head. Irene said, "He picked out all the calvie cows and had them shipped by train to Elko, Nevada. At this time her dad had about 400 cows and Irene remembers driving some of those cows from the Elko railroad yards to the ranch a distance of over fifty miles.

From the time Irene finished school until her dad was running his own cows, she continued to ride horseback every day. Irene remembers when she was small she sometimes fell asleep on her horse while helping to trail cows late in the day. She broke colts for neighbors, helped care for the family cows, followed her Dad on large open range roundups, took part in long hard trail drives, wrangled haying work horses before sun up and drove teams in the hay fields.

As Irene grew up she continued to help her dad, but also became more independent. She cowboyed for big range outfits such as the Spanish Ranch, the Quarter Circle S and the Hunter Banks Ranches. She recalls some long cold winters, especially 1948-49 and 1951-52.

The following are some of the memories of incidents Irene shared while riding along this part of her long winding trail. The following stories are told using her own words.

"The first incident I remember was about an event I didn't know happened until years after it occurred. One time, years later I was staying in an old house, where I had lived with my parents as a child. I noticed a small hole about three-fourth of the way up in the kitchen door. When I asked about it my Dad told me that when I was about three years old a man was fooling around with his "empty" gun and it went off. Dad said, "I was standing by the door and the bullet went over my head and through the kitchen door." Mom said, "Dad really gave that fellow a piece of his mind."

The winter of 1948-49 was very cold. Old Abe Snider and I went to a New Year's Eve dance at Tuscarora. Abe was about my Dad's age, but that didn't stop him from liking me. He would bring candy and marshmallows to me, then sit; and most of the time eat them himself. That winter it started to snow hard on New Year's Day. The morning of January 1, 1949, Dad and I started to bring the weaner calves to the place we were camped...a very cold day. Dad had the team and a load of hay. He sat there most of the day holding the team down so the calves could follow. I was riding a half broke colt and he would smart off and I would ride him back down the road to keep warm. When we got back to camp Dad was in bad shape because he was so cold. I drove the team to the house and he sort of fell off and went inside. I finished feeding the calves and took care of the team. It was sundown by then.

The snow was chest deep on a horse and fluffy. It was so cold you could ride a horse anywhere in it, it was just frost. Dad and I would drive a team six miles to the home ranch, leave the snow on the feed sleigh and build a fire on it. With the snow on the sleigh bed, we could move the fires around and not burn the floor of the rack. It was always fifteen degrees below zero when we went to bed and thirty to forty degrees below zero when we got up. Even the riffles on the river froze over.

There was also a lot of snow in the winter of 1951-52. It drifted so much that we couldn't use our high pole corrals. I broke some saddle colts for Dan Andrae. One was very ornery and tried to do everything in the book... stampeded, bucked, wouldn't turn to one side one day and the next day maybe wouldn't turn to the other side. I kept working with him and kept him busy. The days it was too cold to ride I would lead him behind the sleigh and make him drag an auto wheel. He wound up in a rodeo bucking string. The hay corrals would blow over and we had to feed a long way off so the cows didn't learn to walk over the fence and get into the hay stacks. We would unhook the team and drive them around the hay stack to break down the snow. I can remember rabbits came and they would eat around the hay stacks until you would think the cows had gotten in.

That winter Dad drug a short chain on the hind runners of the sled across from one runner to the other. This would roll the loose snow across the horse's tracks and make a smooth trail. If he hadn't done this the tracks would get deeper as animals tend to step in the same places. Also, the track would build up to a sharp point and cows would slide off into the deep snow.

My Dad was good at a number of things. He made furniture and was a good craftsman. He built dressers, folding tables and bedsteads. He learned to be a good welder. He was an excellent horseman. It didn't matter what kind of horse he was working with, he got along with it. He was a good roper and roped with a riata. He was a wonderful story teller and he was very patient with my mother. He died July 5, 1971. My mother died in 1975.

Once while Dad was still alive we had a rodeer at Summer Flat. There was a lazy man next to me and when a cow broke out of the bunch, he would never see it. It was always me, the one to bring the cow back time after time. Dad rode over to me and said, "Ride back down a ways and when you come back ride in by someone else. He is working you to death."

I remember one time the Spanish Ranch cow boss told us to ride Arthur Canyon the next day. We did. The boss was sure nasty and gave us hell. "That was not where I told you to ride," he growled. I thought, "You would think we worked for him." One old guy had a very red face that amused me. He was a sorry excuse for a cowboy.

Another time it was snowing and cold on a rodeer ground in June. A calf ran the wrong way and I was after him, running full speed. Before I could see it, there was a rattlesnake on top of the sagebrush. I'm sure my foot drug over and touched him. The chill I got, I can still feel it.

One time after a long drive to the railroad yards in Elko I was riding back to the ranch leading a saddle horse. I spent the first night at the Dinner Station Ranch. I remember that time, an old couple had a bar there and lived in the stone house. I got up early and went to the barn to feed my horses. When I opened the barn door it turned on the light plant they had there. I sure caught hell from the old gal because I woke her up too early. The horses were OK. I had breakfast and rode the rest of the way home. It was about fifty-two miles one way from Elko to the ranch.

I remember other cattle drives to Elko. It seems I made three trips with cattle to Elko when I worked for the Quarter Circle S Ranch. The cow boss was good to me. He had me up near the front of the herd so there wasn't as much dust. As he counted the cattle at the gate I would ride through when a good break was open so he could still count. On one of those trips with them, we stayed at the Dinner Station Ranch. Sewell's cowboys were going home to North Fork and they stayed there the same night. One cowboy was also a girl. They were getting oiled at the bar. They wanted me to join them, but I hid out and went to bed. My cow boss told them, "Leave her alone." The next time I stayed there the old gal was sure mad because the girl had peed the bed. That night there were mice in my mattress and they sure squeaked a lot. That old gal wanted to bed that girl down with me that night, but as it turned out, the mice were better. I lucked out that time.

One drive to Elko I remember sleeping in a ditch across from the Dobby house. The ditch was full of dried up cow tracks made when the ground was wet the previous spring. Not good sleeping because my bedroll didn't hide the bumps.

On one of the trips to Elko with the Quarter Circle S drives, as we approached the airport, there was a large row of dirt piled up with a red flag waving on it. The cow boss rode up and jerked the flag out so we could get the cows by. We almost got up to the spot when the ranch manager's wife drove her little airplane down in front of our herd. The cows stampeded up the hill to the beacon light, where John Carpenter lives now. The cows stampeded three times.

After riding our horses for five days, I was afraid they would play-out and we'd never get those cows to the stock yard corrals. The manager asked his wife why she did that. She said, "I only wanted to look at the cows." The cow boss said, "I wish she had to look at their butts for five day all the way to Elko like we did." I guess I'm the only "Old Buzzard" living who drove cows to the Elko stockyard corrals."

By this time Irene had ridden a horse nearly every day of her life for thirty-five years. Using 250 riding days per year for thirty-five years she had ridden 8,750 days averaging ten miles per day for a total of 87,500 miles. Some time during the end of this time frame, Irene was living on a small ranch in the Lamoille Valley and she married her neighbor, Jack Walther.

Irene said, "It took me two years to catch Jack. He was quite leery of marriage. We've had a very good fifty- two years (2007) together. We were both only interested in horses, so we had a lot of them. We broke and sold both saddle horses and draft teams. People say the horses we trained were very gentle and we did a lot of work to get them that way. By the time a saddle horse got in the bridle bit, we were tired of him and wanted to see what the next horse was like so we sold him. Now we are both old and stoved up. Jack seems in good health although he can't walk very well because his knees are worn out. Jack has been very kind to me. Guess I'm spoiled because he let me buy tractors, trucks and an equipment trailer. I also bought new saddles whenever I wanted."

Irene continues, "One time while in Twin Falls, I found a new John Deere tractor I needed and I wanted to talk to the salesman. The salesman thought that old gal is just talking in the wind and he went to talk to a man he thought was a better customer. The next day when I went back, I bought and paid for the tractor. Then the salesman was sure singing a different tune. I was amused and we became friends. When Russ Turner and I brought the tractor home, the only comment Jack made was, "It sure is green."

During our fifty- two years of marriage I broke horses, worked on trail drives and helped Jack take care of our herd of Red Angus cows. During this time Irene had ridden horseback another 45,000 miles for a grand total of 132,500 miles during her lifetime.

Jack said, "Irene now has trouble getting around, so I got a home health nurse to come by the ranch one day a week. The nurse brought a wheelchair for Irene to use and for several trips the nurse found the wheelchair sitting in the same place not being used. One day when the nurse came, the wheelchair had been moved. The nurse said, "Irene, I'm so glad you are using the wheelchair." Irene said, "Oh yes, several days ago I used it to go out to the shed. Then I used it to carry the chain saw and I cut those low limbs off the tree outside of that window. Now I can see down through the meadow better."

Dave's comment: "It is no wonder these hardy old timers won the west."

LITTLE THINGS

If you want to accidentally shoot yourself or someone else, fool around with an "unloaded gun" without giving it the respect you should give a gun that is loaded.

LITTLE THINGS

Two men got into a knock down, drag-out fight at a country dance and one man bit part of the other man's ear off. At the trial that followed a lawyer hoping to prove his client innocent, asked a cowboy that witnessed the fight, "Did you actually see my client bite the ear off?" The cowboy hesitated and said, "No sir, I did not actually see your client bite the ear off." The lawyer with a satisfied look on his face turned to leave when he heard the cowboy continue by saying, "But I did see him spit the ear out."

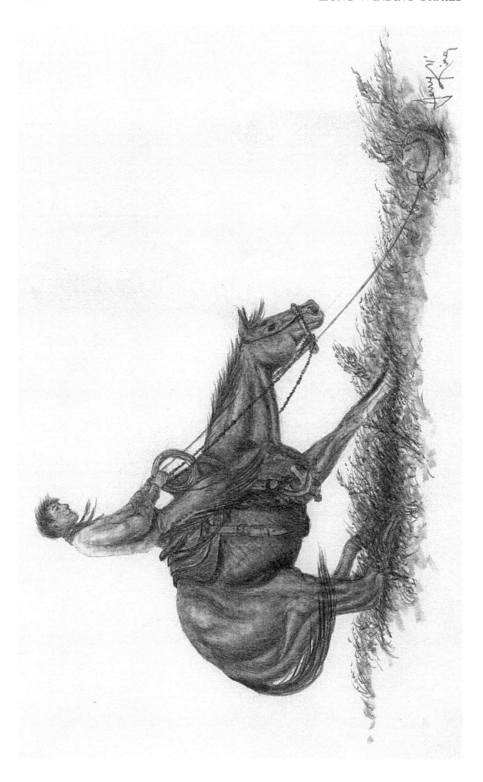

OLD HATS

I hate to break in a new hat. My old egg shape head doesn't fit the regular shape of a new hat. You can steam it, shape it and even dunk it in a water trough but it still doesn't fit right until you wear it until it fits and that's hard on the square corners of my head.

Have you ever gotten off to open a wire gate when the wind was blowing about thirty miles per hour and a wind gust comes up under your hat brim from the back and blows your hat off? I have a number of times in the last seventy years and this is what I have learned. The hat will fly about ten feet in the air, land twenty feet away, sit quivering in a low spot until you run over and reach down to pick it up. That hat knows you are about to catch it so it gleefully jumps up and starts cart wheeling across an open field, rolling on its brim. Next, on a dead run, you try stamping on the hat with your boot to hold it in place until you can bend down and pick it up. This rarely works and the hat will slither away at the last second. Finally the hat will plaster itself up against a sage brush and, all out of breath; you can reach down and pick it up. The last thing I learned about a runaway hat is this; even though you know you are alone, you can't resist looking around to see if anyone was watching while you were trying to catch it.

I was working on a stock water line in the bottom of the Cow Creek canyon. At the spot where I was working, the rock bluffs on either side of the canyon were forty to fifty feet high. On a hot afternoon the wind sickles up this canyon and does strange things. I got caught in a whirligig, dust devil or whirlwind and the updraft was so strong it sucked the old hat I was wearing off of my head and it swirled the hat around and around until it was about seventy feet in the air. The whirligig slowly moved my hat to the south rim of the bluff and sat it down on a rocky ledge about thirty feet above me. There was no way in God's green earth I was ever going to be able to retrieve that hat. I was standing there looking up thinking about Murphy's Law (Anything that can go wrong will go wrong) when another gust of wind came up the canyon. The updraft along the rocky bluff again picked up my hat, brought it back over the canyon and as the wind subsided, it gently let my hat float down until it landed within five feet of the spot where I was standing. Maybe this is nature's way of making up for the times she made me chase my hat across a windy flat.

When I was young and thought that anything that could not be done horseback was not worth doing, I was riding across a big flat. It was March and the wind was gusty. A big gust of wind came from behind and blew my hat off and it landed out in front of the colt I was riding.

Now, even old broke horses for some reason are scared of a wind blown hat bouncing along the ground and this colt was no exception. I knew I couldn't ride up to the hat, get off, and pick it up without losing my horse. So I decided to get as close to the hat as I could and rope it. I was carrying a Mexican Maquey hard twist grass rope. The rope was small, probably a three-eighths scant, and fast. The hat settled down for a moment, right side up, and I got the colt close enough to make a throw. The hat saw the rope coming, jumped up and took off. The second time my hat momentarily stopped, I lucked out and the loop of my rope settled down around the crown of my hat just above the hat band. It didn't take long to realize the easy part of my plan was over. When I started pulling that hat toward me, that little horse nearly turned inside out. I was able to keep him facing the hat but I had no idea he could run that fast going backwards. The colt finally wore down and I pulled the hat forward until it was on the ground in front of the young horse. I let him smell the hat and he snorted but held his ground. I gradually pulled the hat up along his quivering shoulder and as soon as I put the hat on, the colt began to relax.

I do not mean to imply that all a cowboy does is chase his hat. In fact, a cowboy under normal circumstances seldom loses his hat. I am just relaying to you a few of the things that happened to me on a windy day along my 115,000 mile horseback ride that some of you might relate to.

Another hat that was old enough to have a little personality got me in trouble. I was brazing a fitting in the end of a new water trough with an acetylene torch. It was a hot afternoon and I was working in front of the old shop at the Salmon River Cattlemen's ranch headquarters in northern Elko County, Nevada. I was bent over trying to braze the underside of the pipe fitting to the water trough when my hat fell down into the tank. After a while I could smell something burning but I continued working until I finished the job. When I took off my welding goggles I saw that my hat was on fire. I beat it against my leg but that didn't work so I dunked it in a bucket of water. The end result was about a two inch in diameter hole burned in the crown of my hat. The hole was above the hat band, it didn't go through the liner, and the old hat still fit so I continued to wear it.

I was still wearing that hat when fall round-up started and the Salmon River Cattlemen Association members and friends started coming down to help gather cows. On this early morning we had three horse trailers hauling four horses each with twelve cowboys and cowgirls crammed into the pickups pulling them. It was about thirty miles back through the mountains to the range we were going to gather. Somewhere along the trip Terrell Williams, the lady that took the picture of my hat with the hole in it, asked me what happened to my hat. Thinking I would tell a big windy that no one would believe before I told the truth, I said, "Well, I got struck by lightning and for awhile I was actually dead." To my amazement my joke was taken very seriously. Before I could tell the truth I was showered with so much concern and sympathy that telling the truth would have been a real embarrassment to all involved. I changed the subject and left it at that.

With the pressure of fall round up which entailed gathering, sorting, and shipping seven thousand head of cows plus their calves during the next four or five weeks, I immediately forgot about this incident and I didn't hear another word about it.

In a week or two Jane told me she had received several unusual phone calls from friends. Jane answered the phone in her usual pleasant, upbeat manner but she said, "The people sounded hesitant and never really said why they called." Finally she got a call from a friend that said, "I am so sorry for your loss. Is there anything I can do to help?" Jane said, "What loss?" Her friend said, "I heard that Dave had a terrible accident, got struck by lightning and was killed." Jane now was confused and said, "I don't think so. He was fine when he left the house this morning."

Well you know where this is going. When Jane told me about the phone call I immediately knew that unintentionally I had started the rumor. This is a good example of how a cowboy's warped sense of humor and a hole burnt in the front of an old hat can come together and cause unintended worry. Even to this day, when I occasionally think of this incident, it bothers me and I wish I had a second chance to do it all over again.

A TRIP TO THE SOUTH

One time a feed company put on a seminar promoting their feed. This was thirty-five years ago and the seminar was held in one of the southern states, maybe South Carolina. The University of Nevada-Reno contacted me and asked if I would like to go along and represent the big open range ranches in the state of Nevada. They said all I needed to do was give a short description of my ranching operation. I wasn't very good at making presentations but I thought that doesn't sound too complicated and I could do that. So we flew to the meeting.

There were about twenty states represented and we were seated around a long table. They asked each of us to introduce ourselves, give the state we represented along with a short description of our farming or ranching operation. The first man they called upon was from Georgia. He got up, gave his name and said his farm consisted of 320 acres. He ran something like two cows and calves, ten sheep and five goats per acre and every month he clipped his pasture to keep the feed from getting too rank.

The next three or four people called upon were all from the southern states and had similar stories. I was sitting there thinking, what in the hell am I going to say about Nevada that would compare to any of that. When my turn eventually came I got up. Thankfully I remembered my name and the state I was representing. Then I said, "Counting my deeded ground and permits, I control about 80,000 acres. I run two cows and calves per 640 acre section and if the cows happen to see each other we have to doctor them for claustrophobia." The funniest thing about the whole situation was they thought I was telling a joke.

I did give a brief explanation of my ranching operation. I explained that the ranch was largely self sufficient. Water rights went with the deeded land and water was gravity flow to the meadows. Hay was grown and fed out on the same meadows that produced it thus fertilizing the ground the wild hay was grown on. The privately owned base property plus the Forest Service and Bureau of Land Management permits balanced out the yearly operation and made the ranch a self sustaining unit. Each entity helped the other be more valuable and productive.

My presentation wasn't very long and I do not know if it helped the hosts of the meeting sell any feed, but like Nevada, it was unique. No other member at that meeting presented a story anything like that.

LITTLE THINGS

A cowboy told me this, "If you are driving your pickup at night and you are getting too sleepy to go on, stop. Get out. Put up the hood and grab the bare end of a spark plug while the engine is running. It will get you on down the road another seventy- five miles." He continued, "Just standing there looking at the spark plug for awhile and thinking you are awake enough to drive on won't do the job."

LEE WHITLOCK

Dave says, "You may not be able to see everything that is in this picture at first look. It is probably about zero. Steam is rising from the cow herd partly obscuring the second cowboy. Frost is frozen to the cows' backs and icicles have formed on the horse and cows' noses. Lee is sitting on his horse braced against the cold. "Yeah, I've been there, done that."

Lee Whitlock was inducted into the Nevada Cattlemen's Association Cowboy 100,000 Mile Club in 1994.

Lee's wife, Darlene, wrote and gave this presentation when he was inducted into the club.

Lee Whitlock was born November 28, 1919 in Mayfield, Utah. Mayfield is a small farming community in the foothills of a beautiful mountain with lakes and meadows. At an early age, Lee began riding the mountains. Horses were his first love and always have been. Working with cattle is his second love and being able to work with both horses and cattle have made a happy life for Lee.

As a teenager, Lee broke horses for others as well as himself. As they gentled, he rode them miles into the hills to train and get them used to streams, brush, rocky slopes and rough terrain. He managed his father's cattle while his father worked away from home. Lee's job required riding miles and miles on grazing land, pastures and the mountains.

At age twenty-one Lee married Darlene Swallow. Their first summer together was spent on the mountain working for the Gunnison Valley Horse and Cattle Association, keeping the "permitees" cattle off larkspur and getting salt to them. The camp was fifteen miles from town and he rode back and forth many times that summer as well as the many miles he rode each day checking the cattle and moving them to better feed.

In late October of 1941, Lee went to Nevada to work for the Swallow Ranches in Spring Valley. He rode for them for twenty-three years. For many years he rode out from the ranch fourteen to sixteen miles to reach the cattle, rode all day and then rode back at night. Later, the ranch got a small truck with a rack and tailgate ramp so he could drive out and accomplish more each day working cows. Swallow's cattle wintered at Murphy's Wash, Indian Springs and at Horse Camp, south of Conner's Pass. They summered on the pastures at the ranch which stretched about four to five miles long and two to three miles wide. Some cattle were taken to the Steptoe Range which is a two day drive up Cooper Wash and over the mountain to Cave Lake. Lee and Darlene rode all over the mountains the cattle were grazing on for seven summers. Lee rode alone one summer. These years Lee rode daily, even on holidays. Lee would excuse himself from the table to go get his horse and ride to the mountains above the ranch. He never seemed to tire of riding. He still rode and trained horses for others and helped to look after the lost sheep. Lee's entertainment during this time included roping wild horses and team roping.

In September 1964, Lee was sent to Twin Springs Ranch for ten months to help with the cattle. Those were long days and it took plenty of riding to gather the cattle. The circle around to each well and back to the ranch was one hundred miles by truck, so there were many miles ridden during those ten months.

From July 1965 to December, Lee helped care for steers in Spring Valley and on the mountain below Wheeler Peak, taking the steers to Bastion Basin Creek Ranch in the fall. (The above documentation was supplied by Darlene Swallow Whitlock.)

For a period of two years in January of 1966, Lee moved to Garrison, Utah to lease the Lee Dearden Ranch with his partner, DeVon Bellander. Lee was overseer of the cattle. In the winter Lee moved the cattle from one allotment to another as it was needed. He also roped and doctored any sick animals. In the spring Lee and other cowboys moved the cattle from the Ferguson Desert and Hamblin Valley to the meadows in Burbank, Utah. Lee was almost always on horseback, either working cattle or breaking horses in his spare time.

After 1968, Lee stayed on with Lee Dearden as cattle foreman. In 1973 Lee Dearden sold the ranch to John Carpenter and Lee worked for John until he went to work for the Baker Ranches, Inc. in February 1975.

Bill Dearden of Garrison has this to say about Lee, "I have personally ridden many a mile with Lee and a better judge of man and animal I have never met." As near as I can tell in this time period, Lee covered about 20,000 miles on a horse and that is being conservative. Lee Whitlock is one of the last true cowboys and I am honored to represent Lee and Darlene in saying, "Good job—-Well done, Lee." (Above material was supplied by Bill Dearden.)

When Lee went to work at the Baker Ranches his job was to care for the cattle on the range, in the meadows and in the feedlots. The winter range goes east approximately twenty miles and north about twenty-five miles. It is divided into rotation pastures in both directions. All of the moving to and from the range and between the pastures is done on horseback. This requires Lee to ride a horse almost daily during the winter. Lee's great skill with cattle and horses meant that most of the time he worked alone except when large moves were required.

From late September to May, Lee takes care of all the pen riding in the feedlot before he goes to the range. Summer means moving cattle to the main ranch for calf marking and then on to meadows or mountain range. All of this takes a great deal of riding which Lee does day after day.

Lee also irrigates the ranch where he lives. All summer long during the irrigation season, early in the morning and late in the evening, he rides his horse to tend to the water in the meadow.

If this does not seem like enough riding, Lee's pastime is team roping at which he is still very good, time after time winning money, buckles, and saddles. Last summer at the age of seventy- five he won the saddle at a roping in Delta, Utah, showing his great consistency.

Lee is the best of horsemen and when you add this to his cattle handling ability, it has made the Baker Ranches more profitable and productive.

Dean Baker says, "I know of no other man who has ridden as much or is as productive as Lee. In the twenty years he has worked for us he has easily ridden 40,000 miles. (Above material was supplied by Dean Baker.)

Dave's comments: "After reading this short sketch of Lee's cowboy life it is easy to see Lee Whitlock has ridden well over 100,000 miles on the back of a horse in his lifetime. The testimony of the men Lee worked for and with as he traveled along his long winding trail is a lasting tribute to the kind of cowboy Lee Whitlock is."

LITTLE THINGS

An old saying: Two things to remember and you pert near got it skinned don't whittle toward yourself and don't spit agin' the wind.

RANCH KIDS

Ranch raised kids sometimes grow up pretty fast. They are exposed to hard work ethics and responsibility at a young age. Many follow the ranch life into adulthood and many are drawn to the bright lights of the town where the work hours are shorter and the monetary rewards come quicker. Either way the work ethics, understanding of life's fundamentals and respect for the people, nature and animals that surround them usually stays with them for their lifetime.

It is amazing what an old honest ranch horse can teach a kid. They will stand while a kid struggles to get on and off, put their head down to be bridled and do a hundred things they wouldn't let a cowboy get away with while at the same time not letting a kid do something really dumb. The bond between a young person and a horse can sometimes be priceless. The old adage "You can take the kid out of the country but you can't take the country out of the kid" still rings true.

Some incidents that happened to our kids as I watched them grow up still stand out in my memory. I will relate a few for you. I remember the 4-H years when the kids learned to take responsibility for feeding and grooming their animals that were to be shown at the Elko County Fair. I remember after the market animal sale when the kids had to lead their animals to the trailers for the last time. Cindy cried all the way and had nearly all the people in the 4-H barn including me shedding a tear. I remember the kids running free through the ranch's barns, corrals and meadows when, besides a few squabbles, they didn't have a care in the world. I also remember when they became part of the ranch crew and at times they were the ranch crew doing a man's work.

During this time there was an incident that all involved will remember. A year earlier Joe Susatacha, a rancher who lived north of us, gave each of the kids a colt. The kids worked with the young horses and they became gentle.

A year later, a few days before this incident occurred, I asked the chore man to clean out a root cellar that was close to the barn. The contents hadn't been touched since we came to the ranch and I wanted to get it cleaned out so we could use the old rock building. After he finished cleaning and hauling the junk to the dump he noticed a sack hanging in one corner. On further inspection he found the sack contained a couple of hands full of poisoned oats. These were apparently used sometime in the past to control ground squirrels that were burrowing under the old building's foundation. The chore man, not wanting to make another trip to the dump, walked out to the meadow and flung the sack's contents in a large semicircle around him. The small amount of poisoned oats was well scattered and disappeared down into the meadow grass and the incident was forgotten.

A few days later I was working cows in the upper end of that same meadow and I noticed Cindy's colt grazing around in a small area for an unusually long period of time. When we finished working the cows, the colt was lying down so I rode down to have a look. Before I got to him I knew something was wrong. He didn't get up and after looking around I began to visualize what had happened. The horse spent most of the morning picking individual grains of poisoned oats out of the grass and the effect was beginning to set in. I called "Doc" Cuthberson. He did what he could and said, "If the horse makes it the next six to eight hours he might have a chance." Shortly thereafter the kids got home from school and hearing the news, Cindy came running out. She sat down and put the colt's head in her lap and gently stroked its neck while she talked to it between long drawn out sobs. This continued for nearly two hours and the colt finally died with its head still cradled in her lap. We got Cindy up and took her to the house where it turned out to be a long hard night for everybody. This is an example of what ranch kids sometimes face while growing up on the big ranches of the west.

Another incident that involved ranch kids took place when we lived on the Dinner Station Ranch, north of Elko, Nevada. At times Greg, Cindy and I were the whole crew. On this early morning we were gathering about 400 head of yearling steers. The steers were in the Sugar Loaf pasture south of the ranch and we were driving them to the corrals at the ranch headquarters where we intended to brand them before they went to Lone Mountain for the summer.

I was working along the left flank of the herd, Cindy was on the right and Greg was bringing up the drag. We had our hands full. One steer back where Greg was kept trying to quit the herd and Greg would let him get too far away before starting out to turn him. He would then have trouble bringing the steer back. I hollered and said something like, "Greg, wake up and watch that steer. If he breaks out again, get out around him before he gets a head start." The next time the steer broke out, Greg was right on top of him. They went up the side of a steep rocky ridge honey combed with badger holes. When they went out of sight over the top of that ridge, Greg was ahead, but they were gone out of sight so long I began to get worried. Suddenly the steer burst over the top of the ridge, with Greg so close behind that he could nearly reach out and touch him. Greg was sitting up on his horse's back like a wood tick and he was coming down through the rocks and badger holes at a breakneck speed that was no longer necessary. Now I was hollering at Greg to slow down or he was going to break his darn fool neck. Sometimes ranch kids can't win, but most learn fast and become seasoned cowboys at an early age.

We got the steers corralled and with the help of a little blue healer named Judy, working along the chute. Cindy, Greg and I got the steers branded and turned into the Lone Mountain pasture before dark.

When kids reach their teens they sometimes go through a phase where they know more than their parents do. Ranch kids are no exception. Sometimes when this happens on the big ranges in the west, ranchers swap kids for the summer. The kids would willingly do the same kind of work for a neighbor they would be doing at home only they wouldn't be arguing and fussing about it. It is interesting to see how much smarter and wiser parents get as their kids grow older.

LAURA   TRACEY

One more involvement with kids and ranching that comes from an entirely different background: These two young girls were born and raised in the city before they came to live at the Dinner Station Ranch. I don't think they thought they had arrived at the end of the world but they might have thought they could see it from there.

They got involved in outdoor activities and slowly began to get used to the ranch life. I remember the night I shot a pack rat off the outside rock wall of the Dinner Station house and the girls ran inside screaming. I remember them curiously watching while we butchered a beef. I remember them learning to drive an old stick shift ranch pickup in the field across from the corrals. The field was big and clear of obstacles so I gave them some instructions and turned them loose. At first the old pickup jumped, jerked and died, but it wasn't long before it was running smoothly around and around the field. The girls spent a lot of time driving in that field.

Some time later Jane took Laura to Puccinelli's Market in Elko to get a load of ranch groceries. When Angelo finished putting the groceries in the car he noticed Laura behind the wheel. He turned to Jane and asked, "That your daughter?" Jane said, "Yes." Angelo asked, "She learning to drive?" Jane said,"Yes." Angelo said, "Wait a minute." And he went back into the store. When he came back out he turned and handed Jane a bottle of beer and said, "Here, you gonna need this." A little cowboy humor.

Laura began to help Jane do the hundreds of things a ranch wife does each day to make a ranch run smoothly and Tracey began a life long love affair with horses.

This causes me to remember the following incident. Tracey was helping me turn a small bunch of cows out of the corral. The cows were anxious to go and as soon as they cleared the corral gate they began to run and scatter out. Tracey went to head a cow off and when her horse turned the cow back, Tracey continued to travel straight forward where she crash landed out in the sagebrush. I ran back to see if she was hurt and she said she wasn't. I knew the old horse she was riding would stand, so I hollered for her to get back on and catch up while I ran out to head the cows. Instead, Tracey thinking she was being abused returned to the ranch house to tell her mother her troubles. Jane couldn't get her to stop crying and kept asking, "Are you hurt?" Tracey kept saying, "No." Jane finally asked, "If you aren't hurt why are you still crying?" Tracey said, "Mom, You don't understand. The horse knew more than I did." Jane sent Tracey back out to finish the job. When this incident happened Tracey didn't think it was a laughing matter but now when she tells the story she laughs and says, "It is one of the best memories I have of growing up on the ranch."

The girls now have families of their own and they've been successful while traveling along their individual long winding trails.

I would like to think the time they spent on the ranch somehow contributed to this.

GENE DAVIDSON

Gene Davidson was inducted into the Nevada Cattlemen's Association Cowboy 100,000 Mile Club in 2006.

Dave's comment: Gene's not much on thinking about documenting the miles he's ridden, but the ranchers Gene's cowboyed for, his lifelong friends and anyone else that knows Gene, vouch for the fact that he passed the 100,000 mile mark years ago. They say he added another 75,000 miles to his lifelong horseback ride before he retired in 2001. Gene's the type of cowboy that ranchers in the west rely on and this type of cowboy is often treated like a partner or part of the family."

Fred Garrett's remarks when Gene was inducted into the Cowboy 100,000 Mile Club about say it all.

Fred's remarks:

At this time, it is my distinct honor to present this award to someone who truly deserves it. This is someone who for years is one of the best cowboys I have ever worked around and someone who made the job of cowboying his lifelong profession. For Gene it was never a job. It was a passion and a skill he wanted to perfect and be the best at, and in my opinion he has succeed at this task. He is a man who truly cares for animals in every aspect. His ability and knowledge of cattle and horses is rarely surpassed. He doesn't know he is getting this award, so at this time I would like to present the Cowboy 100,000 Mile Club award to Gene Davidson.

Gene was born in 1934 in Longmont, Colorado. His family moved to California when he was eight years old. He grew up around horses and livestock and after graduating from high school, he attended Pierce College in San Fernando Valley. He married and had a son, Mike.

In 1950 he went to work for BI Feedlot in Somis, California, he worked there for a couple of years. When the feedlot was subdivided for housing, Gene moved on.

In 1958 he went to work for Wolfsen Land and Cattle at Los Banos, California. He stayed there for ten years, moving back and forth with the cattle from summer to winter range. While at Wolfsen's he married Helen and was deputized to keep hunters off the ranch. Financial problems at the ranch caused it to be sold, so after ten years Gene again moved on.

In 1969 Gene went to work for John Marble at the 71 Ranch in Halleck, Nevada. He enjoyed his job there and the people he worked with. In 1974, the ranch was left to John's son, Pete Marble. As things changed, Gene decided it was time to look for something else.

In 1975 Gene went to work for Dirk Agee at the Twin Meadows Ranch in O'Neil Basin. He stayed there for twelve years until Dirk bought a winter range in southern Nevada and began moving cattle back and forth. Not wanting to move twice a year, Gene looked around for another job.

In 1986 he went to work for Glazer Land and Livestock. He had known them since 1969 because they neighbored the 71 Ranch. He stayed there fifteen years and in 2001, at the age of sixty-seven, he decided to retire.

As you can see Gene had a problem with employment. He would only stay at a ranch for ten to fifteen years or until it was sold. The same thing is true of Helen. After forty- five years of marriage, Helen says, "We're still waiting to see if it's going to work out."

As far as retirement went, Gene took about two days off.

In Helen's words, "It's let the phone ring and it's someone saying, 'Gene, we need help. Can you come'? Then it's out the door, catch a horse, set the alarm for in the morning, saddle, load, and down the road he goes to help." Helen thinks it's an addiction or just his love of cattle and horses and the care they need.

Part of the reason Gene is not very good at retirement is because so many of us won't let him. He's not just help. He's the kind of help you want on shipping day or anytime you have to have someone with the skills and the knowledge to do the job.

Gene is an outstanding horseman and I think proof of that is in his horses. When he shows up he's riding a good horse that he made himself and he has several of them.

Gene is always willing to help you with your horses, but you don't always get what you expect. You can tell Gene about your horse troubles and he'll often tell you a story about another horse. By the time you digest the story, you have the answer to your problem and he's done it without putting pressure on you or making you feel inadequate.

Gene has helped me with my horses and now he is helping my children as well.

Gene has touched many people's lives throughout the years and he does that in the same way he does everything else. When he makes friends, it tends to be for a lifetime. He's always a man of integrity and honest in all his dealings.

Gene's profession is not necessarily an easy one and over the years it has taken a toll on him. After a ruptured spleen, open heart surgery, pituitary gland surgery, both hips replaced, a pacemaker installed and a whole lot of other stuff that most people would have gone to the hospital for, Gene is still going strong.

When he gets horseback, he's a young man again and if something happens, you better lean over the saddle horn if you want to keep up with him.

One of the super abilities about Gene is that he deals with people the same way he deals with livestock. He reads them and helps them find a "soft spot" and most of the time you don't even know it. His sense of humor is outstanding in its subtleties and sometimes you have to listen to get the point.

Gene, along with his partner, Helen, knows how to be frugal. They have lived a very rich life by having a grasp of what is truly important and enjoying those things.

If you want to see perfection, just drive by their place. You will see trees in the desert and a place for everything and everything in its place with a quiet beauty that has been crafted by their labor of love.

There are a million other things I could tell you about Gene that I respect but because of time restraints I cannot tell you the many endearing stories about Gene that would come from hundreds of people Gene's life has touched.

The 100,000 mile mark is something most people will never see but Gene passed that many years ago.

Again, I can't think of anyone more deserving of this award and what an honor it is for me to be able to present it to you. I hope that I will have the opportunity to share part of the next 100,000 miles with you.

ROPES AND ROPING

I only roped in a rodeo arena one time in my entire 115,000 mile horseback ride. That wasn't successful, but during the early and middle part of my ride I would rather rope than eat. Out on the range in the timber, sagebrush, and badger holes you had to be quick to beat me to that first loop. Whether my loop went a little too deep or settled down where it was supposed to, I usually caught whatever I was after. In later years because of sore shoulders and declining coordination, I seldom roped unless I was trying to help in an emergency situation. I carried a rope and used it when necessary but now I carry one mostly because my saddle feels naked and out of balance without a rope coiled up on my saddle's right fork where it belongs. I've never lost my enthusiasm for roping and I still have a special respect for the cowboy who uses a rope on a regular basis just doing his everyday work.

During the years Bob and I rode ponies to and from school, we rode them in the yearly Willits Frontier Days Parade during the Frontier Days rodeo. We also rode them in the pony races around the thoroughbred racehorse track that surrounded the rodeo arena. This gave our family a chance to watch the rodeo and it was my first exposure to the trick ropers of that day. They had extensive acts on the race track in front of the grandstand. This was fascinating to a gawking country kid and I became hooked. It may just be a kid's first exposure to these rope handling events but those performers are etched in my memory as the best acts of this type I have ever seen during my 115,000 mile horseback ride. These weren't a sideshow to the main events; they were part of the main event.

During my youthful years these exposures to talented rope performers lead to many hours practicing out behind the barn. I actually got reasonably good at spinning a rope. I even partially mastered Red Shannon's half hitch hog tying act. I would have gotten better at it if I had not run out of kids available to practice on. Early exposure to these rope handling acts began my lifelong fascination with the lass rope. My respect for the ropes and the men and horses that learned how to use them has never diminished. All through my lifelong horseback ride, I have marveled at how the rope, being used as a tool, has lengthened the reach and usefulness of the cowboy's arm.

The first ropes I learned to use and that were available were grass ropes made by Tubbs Cortage Company based in San Francisco, California. They were good all around ranch ropes, though they had a tendency to be raggy in the summer and stiff when wet in the winter. The Mexican Maguey rope was a small hard twist rope that wasn't very strong but it was fast and the rope burns from a missed dally were tremendous.

In my youthful days the riata was still in everyday use. The riata took a special talent to use and special care to maintain. In today's world with more fences, less room and the talented professional ropers using short ropes to compete in specialized timed events, the riata is no longer practical to use for everyday work. The riata is hand made, using rawhide, and it takes a special talent to prepare the rawhide strings and to braid one. Having said all of this, I still think the riata in the hands of a riata man is the king of ropes. A well made riata seems to be alive. A certain twist of the thrower's wrist invites a response in the loop at the end of the rope. Old time cowboys who really knew how to throw a riata were a joy to watch.

R.C. Williams was a riata man, though he often used a grass rope during everyday ranch work. I have seen him throw the big loop in his riata underhanded, rolling it across the corral for twenty feet where the loop was only the size of a washtub when it seemingly jumped up and over the head of a running cow. Without moving his horse he would then jerk his slack, take his dallies and let the riata run for several feet while stopping the cow. I can still see the whiff of smoke rising above his saddle horn as he let his dallies slip by. Of course, this was before anyone thought of wrapping a saddle horn with rubber and ranch ropes were forty-five feet in length and riatas were sixty-five feet long.

We took a lot of ribbing from the professional arena ropers and the most common joke was the longer the rope the slower the horse. In reality out in the rocks, sagebrush and badger holes, the long ropes have a place.

One winter during the early part of my horseback ride, I made a riata. I fashioned a rawhide breakaway honda using an empty thirty-eight caliber pistol shell casing with a piece of steel bolt filed down to fit inside. I secured the honda shut with a small cotter key when I was doing serious roping. I enjoyed using this riata for a number of years and became good at handling it, though I never came close to using it the way an old time riata man could. I used my riata until I strained it roping a slick bull while running wild cows in the rough country. This happened at the mouth of Old Woman's Canyon along the south fork of the Eel River.

About this time nylon ropes began to make an appearance on the Western ranges and before long they became the rope of choice for big range cowboys as well as the professional arena roper. The transformation didn't take place instantly. It took some time. The first nylon ropes were so light that they would float up in the air when thrown instead of settling down around a cow's neck. I remember taking shotgun shells apart, prying the nylon strands open and shot loading the first ten or twelve feet of a nylon rope to make it heavy enough to settle down.

I remember one nylon rope I had that no matter what I did, it would form a figure eight when the loop tightened. It was a new rope and I hated to give up on it, so I stretched it over night, cut several feet off of the lead end and tied a new honda in the rope, thinking I would try it one more time.

About two weeks later, three of us were driving five hundred year-ling steers from the Basco Cabin to the Sprowl Cabin holding field. It was a hard drive, the day was hot, the lead steers wanted to run, the drag wanted to stop and the sagebrush along the drainage we were traveling was horseback high. Not long after we got started, I happened to look down at the rope coiled up on the fork of my saddle and there was that figure eight in the loop of the new nylon rope. We finally got to the Sprowl Cabin holding field and while I was closing the gate I noticed my rope was missing. The rope strap was broken and I'd lost the rope somewhere back in the four miles of sagebrush we had just ridden through. With a grin I called out, "Boys, I lost that miserable rope and it isn't worth going back to look for." Then the incident was forgotten.

About a week later I was driving my pickup down a two track road toward the Sprowl Cabin when about thirty yearling steers came out of a draw and started trotting down the road in front of me. I've never un-derstood why, but when cattle get on a country road in front of a vehicle they will trot down that road for a quarter of a mile without turning off which they could easily do at any time. One time I asked an old timer about this and he said, "Well, I guess they think if they can't out run you on a flat road, they sure as hell, couldn't out run you over there in the rocks, sagebrush and badger holes." I thought this was probably as good an explanation as any.

Anyway, as I pulled up closer and slowed down to follow the steers, I suddenly noticed a rope dragging from the right hind leg of the last steer in line. My first thought was disbelief. My second thought was the kids had been practicing and snagged a back leg and lost their rope. I knew this wasn't possible because I was out in the middle of the range and the kids were in school. When I got closer I recognized the special popper knot I tie in the end of my lass ropes. Then the reality of what happened hit me like a bolt of lightning. This was my rope! That mis-erable rope I lost in the sagebrush a week ago had come back to find me.

Somehow this steer stuck his foot through the noose of the lost rope that was lying somewhere out in the sagebrush and when he moved away the noose tightened up on his back leg. Miraculously the rope had not snarled up in the rocks and sagebrush, tying the steer up someplace where he couldn't be found, because that steer brought the rope I lost a week earlier back to the road I was traveling at the exact instant I was passing by. This might be a candidate for "Ripley's Believe It Or Not."

True to form, the steers trotted down the road for quite a distance before turning off to the side. During this time the rope was dragging straight down the tire track so I ran the right front tire of the pickup up on the dangling rope until I was only six or seven feet from the straggling steer. The steer lunged over the bank at the side of the road, I jumped out of the pickup, tailed the steer down and while he kicked and struggled, I finally got enough slack to loosen the rope on the steer's hind leg and he was free. The steer ran to catch up with the herd while I backed the pickup off the rope and I had that miserable rope back in my hands.

I threw the rope down the two tracker road and it landed with about a three foot loop lying flat on the ground at the rope's end. While I coiled the rope up, pulling the loop toward me, I couldn't believe what I was seeing. One side of that loop slowly rose up and flopped over making a perfect figure eight. It was as if the rope was saying, "I won." I coiled the rope up with the figure eight still in place and put it behind the pickup seat, thus demoting it to tying baled hay on a wagon or dragging a dead cow to the bone yard. I never tried to rope with it again.

This is another "truth is stranger than fiction" story I encountered along my 115,000 mile horseback ride. If that had been a good rope, I never would have found it in the first place and the rope surely wouldn't have found a way to come back and find me.

LITTLE THINGS

THE PRIZE BULL
By Dave Secrist

He's got big bone, good muscle and he's sound upon his feet.
He's clean around his brisket and his sheath is tucked up neat.

He's big and long and he stands on all four square.
His disposition's good and feel the thickness of his hair.

There is only one part of the bull that's not been talked about.
Without it he can't function ……. there isn't any doubt.

Well, the crowd grows quiet as the bull's led in the ring.
The bidding is brisk as the auctioneer begins to sing.

The rancher bids and bids and then he bids some more.
Then he bids again as the bull goes out the door.

The gavel bangs, "sold." And he hears the auctioneer begin to say,
"Congratulations, sir. You set a record for this day."

The rancher pulls into the yard at home, he's feeling mighty proud.
He blows the horn and hollers……his voice echoes kind of loud.

Boys come here because this you've got to see.
I want to show you what a good bull should really be.

The bull bawls and bellows…..paws dirt into the air.
Every bull around knows the new bull's there.

Folks, the next day is quiet…..it really is no joke.
When the prize bull comes walking in with his tallywacker broke.

Charlene and Floyd Slagowski

Floyd Slagowski—horseback,
Dave Slagowski—branding

FLOYD SLAGOWSKI

Floyd Slogowski was inducted into the Nevada Cattlemen's Association Cowboy 100,000 Mile Club in 2009.

J.J. Goicoechea, Floyd's son-in-law, wrote and gave Floyd's presentation for his induction into the Cowboy 100,000 Mile Club.

His remarks follow:

Floyd was born April 24, 1916, in Burntfork, Wyoming. He is the seventh child of six boys and three girls. The family's ranch was in the very sparsely populated area of the Henry's Fork River, fifty miles south of the Green River. Floyd's grade school years required that he travel fourteen miles round trip on horseback. For two more years Floyd drove the 'school bus', which was a canvas covered spring wagon pulled by a horse. He picked up nine kids on a seven mile route. He also attended some high school classes before the return trip after school.

Two major events happened in 1929 that brought great change to the family. After a long illness his mother died in September of 1929, and the Great Depression began that same year.

In the spring of 1933, Floyd followed his desire to work with cattle and horses. His brother, Doyle, who was six years older, was greatly respected for his excellent work and ability to train horses. With Doyle's help, Floyd soon gained valuable experiences. He was able to purchase a better saddle, and in late August, with Doyle leading a packhorse with their camping needs and Floyd leading a packhorse with their bedrolls, they were able to travel to places where they had a better chance of finding work.

A long trip of 150 miles north took them to Pinedale and the ranch of Nels Jorgensen, where they found work in the hay field. Doyle would drive a horse drawn mower and Floyd drove a horse drawn scatter rake. A dollar a day and board was earned. Doyle also received 25 cents for wrangling horses morning and night.

When the work ended, they made a long journey back to Green River City. Those depressed times caused some ranchers to work with limited help. Consequently some of them were unable to care for their many horses that were kept out on the range. This neglect brought opportunity for Floyd and Doyle. A rancher fourteen miles south of Green River offered to give them all the unbranded horses if they would find and corral as many of his horses as possible, so he could sell them. They began in October and by March they had many horses gathered for him and seventy-five unbranded horses for themselves.

Leaving there they soon found work with I.H. Dearth at the Eden Valley Ranch fifty miles north of Rock Springs. They were each paid a wage of thirty dollars a month plus board. Mr. Dearth had many horses out on the range that hadn't been managed for three years. He wanted those horses located, corralled and the young ones branded. Then he wanted the young horses started and given proper care. That lasted two summers and one winter with much hard riding. Mr. Dearth did provide some good saddle horses which were very helpful for them in corralling the horses. This was hard and dangerous work but also valuable experience for Floyd.

After leaving there, Floyd found work as a cowboy for Tom Welch at Burntfork. Tom's oldest son, Wix, was Floyd's boss. He was a great cowboy! Except during haying time, Floyd's work was in camp with Wix caring for their cattle. While there, Floyd purchased his first car which was a 1928 Model Ford touring car. The work ended in mid March of 1937.

It was with this experience that Floyd came to Nevada in search of ranch work. When Floyd arrived in Eureka, he was directed to Pete Laborde, who told him he could possibly find work at the Edgar Sadler and Sons Ranch in Diamond Valley, thirty-five miles north of Eureka. This proved to be a very good job, and they were fine people to work for. In a short time, Floyd was delegated to do the lion's share of their cattle work. Floyd rode as their representative with the fall roundup in Mound Valley near Jiggs, Nevada for four years. Those same years Floyd helped trail their beef to Palisade, a three day drive covering fifty-seven miles. He was then required to drive all the saddle horses home the following day.

Often in the fall, many trips were required to ride long distances to other ranches to bring home stray Sadler cattle. No truck or trailers were used in those days. After working for four years at the Sadler Ranch, Floyd went to work for Ross Plummer in 1941. Floyd helped put up the hay after the spring cattle work was done. The roundup gathering beef to sell in Pine Valley took about a month. There were eight "reps" from seven ranches. They rode about three days at each ranch. During the roundup, the cattle were gathered and moved from ranch to ranch. The beef were delivered to the stockyards at Palisade and sold. Floyd then, with his bed latched tight with a diamond hitch, drove the saddle horses to Bullion where a month was spent representing the Plummer Ranch to find cattle strayed into that area.

From there in late December of 1941, Floyd took a job at the JD Ranch for Charlie Damele to break ten head of colts to ride. This proved to be a pleasant year for Floyd. By the first of April those colts were all doing well. Floyd then was asked to stay on the payroll and continue with the ranch work. Some time was spent driving the cattle out to the range. In early May, the brood mares were gathered, the colts branded, and the mares placed where they would breed to their two good Morgan studs. The month of June was spent branding their calves. After haying season was over, they gathered the beef to be sold. Then it would take four days to deliver the beef to the railroad at Palisade and take two days to get the horses back to the JD Ranch.

After the beef were sold and delivered to the railroad, Floyd began riding with the Dan Fillippini wagon at the Dean Ranch. On October 25, 1942, he was inducted into the US Army. Floyd took the colts he had started and now were becoming very dependable saddle horses, back to the JD Ranch. Up to the time Floyd was inducted into the Army he documented riding 61,000 miles on the back of a horse.

Floyd was sworn into active duty on November 11, 1942. All of his years prior to the Army were mainly spent horseback, so during his Army training he found walking in flat heeled shoes and carrying a rifle and pack a severe change. This gave him a great respect for the good horses that had carried him many miles.

Floyd was sent to Hawaii to be trained for "jungle duty", but while there he was transferred to the 241st Quartermaster Troop Pack Train. He attended horseshoeing school where in three months he received his certificate of Farriers and Shoeing. This included Corrective and Pathological Horseshoeing. He was then given a platoon of seventy-five mules and six horses to keep shod. This was Floyd's duty for sixteen months.

On November 9, 1945, he received his Honorable Discharge. He was proud to have served his country in the time of war, and he was very anxious to get back into his saddle and on the range again.

After being discharged, Floyd returned to Pine Valley and went back to work at the JD Ranch for the Damele family.

On September 17, 1946 he married the love of his life, Charlene Walker Rand. They moved to the Cross Ranch in Pine Valley. This is where he began his own ranching life of sixty-three years as well as raising his family. Their five children all learned at a very young age how to ride and work horseback.

In 1987 and again in 1988, Floyd took his three grandsons; Joe, Will and Ira, on camping trips to push the cattle back up into the mountains and to scatter salt. During these two day trips, they packed their horses and rode up into Pole Creek, Willow Creek and around the Smith Creek Mountains. The young boys (ages 13, 11 and 11) had many learning experiences during those twenty plus mile trips, and they learned to tie Floyd's famous diamond hitch.

Most of the ranches, including the Cross Ranch, stacked their loose hay with horses until about 1952.

From 1952 until 1970, Floyd was a brand inspector for the State of Nevada. He was a member of the Mineral Hill and Eureka School Boards and also an officer for the Eureka Farm Bureau.

Floyd enjoys his ranch life and being able to ride and work the cattle with his children and grandchildren.

While visiting his family in Wyoming in 1988, Floyd and his brother. Leo, spent a memorable time horseback. They took their horses and camping gear and rode out to see the places where they grew up and ran mustangs when they were young.

To this day Floyd helps his sons and their families gather and brand all the young calves in the spring. Riding and roping, among many other things, have kept Floyd youthful, alert and active at the age of ninety-three.

Up until Floyd was inducted into the Cowboy 100,000 Mile Club he documented riding 110,000 miles horseback and probably more could be added.

Dave's comment: Floyd's accomplished many things horseback, but he also found time to write his autobiography specifically for his family entitled "Just the Way It Was". He is currently completing a book, soon to be published, that's entitled "The Pine Valley Puzzle".

LITTLE THINGS

Tiger was a good cowboy and the young cowboys looked up to him. When he brought his string of horses down to help with roundup, one of his horses was a big headed rough looking bay. The horse was probably seven or eight years old and hadn't been ridden much. Tiger thought some big, long, hard circle rides would do the old horse good. The first day out the horse bucked something like six or seven times and Tiger rode him five of those times. That evening in the cookhouse Tiger said, "Boys, I've got that bay horse figured out. He is never going to buck me off again." The young cowboys were all ears. The questions came fast. "Gee, Tiger, what are you going to do? How did you figure him out? When are you going to ride him again?" After a suitable silence Tiger said, "I've given it a lot of thought and it is simple, I am never going to get on that jug headed S.O.B. again."

AN OLD TIME RODEO CLOWN AS SEEN THROUGH THE EYES OF A KID

I've seen a number of talented rodeo clowns and bull fighters along my 115,000 mile horseback ride and they are exceptional performers. Their ability to mask the danger and courage involved in their profession with talent and bungling humor is exceptional. They are the professional arena cowboys' friend and help make rodeo the popular sport it is today.

The rodeo clowns of today have spectacular acts but like the modern day professional cowboy contestants, they specialize in single events. In today's faster moving, more professional managed rodeos, the rodeo clowns are not given the time or the opportunity to coordinate and banter with the grandstand crowd and the announcer throughout the day as they once did. I realize that rodeos have to be profitable and well organized but I wish there was a way to make them seem less regimented. In some instances rodeos have become so single event oriented that I once saw a bronc rider, who had just won the saddle bronc riding event at the National Finals Rodeo, fall off a gentle horse while trying to make a victory lap around the arena. I am not knocking modern day rodeo. I think the contestants, bucking stock and horses are spectacular. The talent displayed is almost unbelievable. But I do notice some of the changes that have taken place while I traveled along my long winding trail.

I remember an old time rodeo clown that crossed my path during the early part of my life. It should be remembered that the events I am recalling here were seen through the eyes of a kid. The rodeo clown's name was Red Shannon. His honest, straight forward cowboy sense of humor plus his ability to handle a rope and communicate with the cowboys as well as the general public has remained in my memory through all of these years.

During this period of time the cowboy contestants entered a number of different events in the same rodeo and one clown performed all during the rodeo, acting in many different capacities. He was the bull fighter, barrel man and stooge for the trick ropers, he might try to enter his mule in the thoroughbred horse races and when he was turned down, he would wait around until the horse races were over then charge around the race track leaning up over his mule's ears with the wind flopping the front of his hat up like a Pony Express rider packing the mail. All the time before and after his comical looking run, he was criticizing the arena announcer for not letting him enter the real horse races.

On the other side of the coin Red good naturedly made fun of the cowboys. He would follow behind a bucked off cowboy that was walking back to the bucking chutes, mimicking every move the cowboy made while fanning the cowboy's behind with his hat. He even limped like the cowboy did. Red never interfered with any of the arena or track events but he always seemed to be in the right place when needed. He might follow a cowboy that had just slipped down off of a pick-up horse, rope the cowboy's feet, trip him, throw his rope in the air and take off running for the arena fence with the supposedly angry cowboy in hot pursuit. Red would vault over the arena fence, cross the race track, leap into the grandstands, grab some embarrassed lady, get behind her and dare the angry cowboy that was now running back and forth along the track fence, to come and get him.

Red had many acts but he didn't use all of them at the same rodeo. He would ride a bucking Brahma bull in an old wicker easy chair cinched down backwards on the bull's back and sometimes he entered the real bull riding event. Red had an old beat up car that sputtered, backfired, and smoked when the front end of the car reared up in the air. Sometimes off centered rims made the car waddle like a duck. At other times the car would sputter and stop on the track in front of the grandstands. Red would jump out, kick the car in disgust while he walked around to the front and vigorously started cranking the engine. The car would not start but when Red finally gave up and started to walk away the seemingly driverless car would start and chase Red around. Of course, while all of this was going on Red and the rodeo announcer would be carrying on an amusing dialogue. The act ended with the car chasing Red off the track and the announcer hollering for him to run for his life or he was going to get run over and killed.

In another act Red had a mule and a flat bed trailer that he pulled into the arena. The bed of the trailer was about three feet above ground and Red would try to lead his mule up on it. He pushed, shoved, pulled, and begged while bantering back and forth with the announcer. When Red gave up and started to walk away, the mule would hop up on the trailer, stick his nose in the air and bray while the announcer explained that the mule was smarter than Red was. At other times Red would be out in the arena fooling around with his mule when the announcer would tell him to get out of the way. He was holding up the bareback riding event. Red wouldn't move while telling the announcer he had as much right to be there as anyone else did. His mule, standing behind him, would then put its forehead against Red's back and with his nose bobbing up and down, very forcefully push Red, who was vigorously protesting all the time, across the arena and out the gate by the bucking chutes.

These small acts didn't take much time and filled in when the rodeo activities slowed down.

Yet another act Red perfected was accomplished by using ten or twelve grape crates, sturdy boxes that were about two feet square by a foot and a half high. They were used to harvest grapes that grew around Ukiah and Santa Rosa, California. Red would start dragging grape crates into the arena while the announcer complained about him cluttering the place up. Red would continue to drag crates to a spot in the arena ignoring the announcer's threats. When he had the crates placed on a designated spot he would stack several boxes on top of each other, hop up and sit down. He would wave to some cowboy standing by the bucking chutes and when the cowboy came over, Red would get him to throw boxes up to him. Red would then stick his heels in the slots of the crates underneath him, carefully stand up and place the box on top of the column before sitting back down. He repeated this sequence with much clowning around until he was sitting on a column of boxes twelve to fifteen feet high gently swaying back and forth. The announcer was now telling him to get down off there before he killed his fool self. Red would look down as if to jump and the crowd would groan and Red would somehow right himself once again. It was amazing how far he could sway that column of boxes and still remain upright. Eventually the announcer would taunt Red into getting too far over and the column of boxes would come down stretched out on the ground with Red turning a summersault when he landed at the far end of the column. Of course, this stunt was a variation of an old circus act but in a cowboy atmosphere, somewhere around 1934, done with a western flare; it took talent that not many in the crowd had seen before. With Red's ability to act, it was a real crowd pleaser.

Red had many other acts, but the last one I am going to tell about impressed me at a young age because it was a rope handling act. It took place on the race track in front of the grandstands and usually happened after the rope spinning acts were over. Red never interfered with any of the rope spinning exhibitions but he complimented them by being a clumsy stooge. He would mimic what the rope spinners were doing in a fumbling fashion. Red was an accomplished rope handler so to finish his act he would spin a big loop around himself, flip it up over his head, and catch a running horse and rider that were going by.

After the rope spinners were finished, Red would stay on the track and banter with the crowd and announcer before eventually roping some seemingly unsuspecting cowboy that was crossing the track. When the cowboy protested and stuck his arms toward Red in a threatening manner, Red, who was standing at the end of his twenty-five foot rope, would begin to throw half-hitches on each of the cowboy's out stretched arms pulling them together. Red would now throw a couple more half-hitches over both the cowboy's hands thus tying them together. The cowboy, not being able to move his arms, would jump up and down in a rage while Red threw half-hitches around the cowboy's feet with each jump effectively hog-tying the cowboy who eventually toppled over. Red would then run to where he had an old branding iron stashed, run back and brand the cowboy's rump with some kind of fake smoke curling up in the air. Red then escaped to the arena while cowboys untied his victim, who, with his fresh hip brand still smoking, ran up and down the arena fence trying to get at Red. By now Red was out in the arena down on all fours, taunting the cowboy by pawing dirt like a mad bull.

Yes, Red was the cowboy's friend. He joked, kidded and good naturedly ridiculed them. But when things got serious and a cowboy was in real trouble, all pretenses at being funny were dropped and Red was the first one to reach the cowboy's side. Red always seemed to know what to do and added much to the rodeos of that day.

My neighbor, Ed White has been a barrel man and rodeo clown for thirty years and he reminisces over the changes that have taken place. One act Ed perfected is standing on his head out in the arena wearing his baggy clown outfit doing the YMCA with his legs in the air while the crowd sings along. I mentioned to Laurie, his wife, how comical this routine was. She laughed and said, "You haven't seen anything until you've seen him try to perform the act during a party at home after he's had a couple of beers."

As I mentioned before, these events happened a long time ago and were seen through the eyes of a kid. I understand that in today's more professionally managed, faster paced rodeos, with large amounts of prize money at stake, it is harder to find time for the rodeo clown and the arena announcer to banter back and forth like they once did, but I still miss the comedy and relaxed atmosphere these acts created. Maybe this comes under the heading of irreplaceable water that long ago ran under the bridge, because there are also times I miss being able to again see things through the eyes of a carefree kid.

LELAND ARIGONI

Leland Arigoni was inducted into the Nevada Cattlemen's Association Cowboy 100,000 Mile Club in 1996.

Matt Benson wrote and gave this presentation when Leland was inducted.

Leland Arigoni was born November 30, 1911 in Globe, Arizona. His folks and Leland's four older brothers moved to a homestead near Nyala, Nevada, called the Oxframe Ranch, when Leland was about two years old. The neighbors, several miles apart, included the Sharpes, Falinis, Bordolis, Lockes and Garrets, all of Railroad Valley.

All these ranches had cattle that ran in common. There were no fences in those days except to fence off a small homestead and a few acres of pasture and hay to feed saddle horses and milk cows.

Arigoni cattle could be found in Blue Eagle, Lockes Station, Cedar Pipe, Reveille Valley and Stone Cabin Valley. This range was for year round grazing and was approximately two hundred miles long and thirty miles wide.

The Taylor Grazing Act was not passed until 1934 and naturally there were no assignments of cattle allotments to the widely separated cattle ranches. Cattle often intermingled and it was common for ranchers to combine their efforts at roundups, brandings, trailing cattle to various ranges or shipping them to railroads at sale time.

Leland attended school five miles from home riding horseback for four years. School was only in session for four months out of the year, so his schooling in Nyala was rather short. After his folks separated when he was eleven years old, he was in Ely, Nevada, for a short time and finished school there.

Mileage in Nyala while attending school is estimated at 2,000 miles in four years.

When not attending school, Leland was helping his brothers and the neighbors move cattle to new range. He also helped with branding, salting and gathering on roundups for fall shipment of sale cattle to market. Ely was one hundred miles north and was the shipping point for most cattle from Railroad Valley.

In five years, as a youngster, Leland is estimated to have ridden about 5,000 miles for the Oxframe Ranch before his folks sold the ranch.

In 1922 Leland's folks separated and when the Oxframe was sold, all the Arigoni children went their own ways.

At age eleven, Leland signed on with the O.K. an Ed Reed outfit, as a horse wrangler. The Reed Ranches were a large outfit using the Hip O brand in the early 1920's. He became quite adept at recognizing each of the ninety to one hundred head of horses in the cavy. The buckaroo crew consisted of from eight to ten cowboys, each with eight to ten horses in his string. Leland wanted most to become a cowboy and after about a year, went to work in northern Arizona on the Fiddleback Ranch as a cowboy with his own string of horses.

The jobs with the Reed and Fiddleback outfits were seven days a week, thirty days a month with only occasional days off at Christmas time or a chance to get to a rodeo in Tonopah or Las Vegas for the Fourth of July.

Leland spent five years in southern Nevada and northern Arizona before deciding to look for new country farther north.

In those five years it is estimated that he covered over 30,000 miles, which is not an unreasonable amount when you consider desert country rides or circles covered from thirty to fifty miles per day for nearly thirty days a month. The pay matched the days —- $30.00 a month.

During my conversations with Leland, he recalled many "old timers" names, which I also know. Two in particular, worked for me at the Currant Ranch near Duckwater, Nevada, and the Hay Ranch near Eureka, Nevada, in 1952 and 1956. The first was Johnny Charles, a Shoshone from Duckwater, who had been a wagon cook for the Reed's wagon. The second was another Shoshone, Cooney Clifford, who at one time was a cowboy for A.C. Florio at Duckwater and Eureka.

The irony of this association was these two cowboys came to me in July 1956 at the Hay Ranch and borrowed $100.00 to go to Duckwater for the celebration. They celebrated too much and ended up in Tonopah for the Fourth of July. With Cooney at the wheel of his 1948 Chevrolet pickup, they managed to strike a fire hydrant and power pole on Main Street, rolled the pickup and both were pronounced dead at the scene. I had to make the trip to Tonopah for identification and make arrangements for their return to Duckwater for burial. They were two fine cowboys, sincere gentlemen and good friends.

From 1926 to 1928 Leland was with Lorigan Brothers Ranch in Nye County, Nevada. This was the same routine of hard-riding desert country that finally inspired Leland to move further north. He heard stories about a cattle country that seemed far better than the hot desert environment that had been his home for sixteen years, so he headed north for the Carson Valley. Meanwhile, he added another 7,500 miles to his horseback ride.

When Leland arrived in the Carson Valley, he hired on with the Fred Dressler Ranch and worked for Fred Dressler for one year. The Dresslers worked closely with the Plymouth Ranch which was owned by Norman Brown. Leland found himself working off and on for both outfits for the next six years.

The work schedule for Dressler and Brown were quite different from the daily routine Leland had known in the southern part of the state. Climate conditions required feeding of hay for several months in the winter and working with trains. However, Leland remained a cowboy for about eight months of the year. He also became the horseshoer, a job he carried on later in his life.

The cattle drives from Carson Valley for the Dressler Ranch were made in several stages. They went to Hope, Charity and Faith Valleys, then on to the main summer pastures in Bridgeport Valley. A reverse route was used in the fall.

The Plymouth ranch moved cattle from Smith Valley to Bridgeport. Several times a year a herd of steers and sale heifers were trailed from Bridgeport south, past Mono Lake to a shipping point at Benton, California. Of course, the trail to pastures or market was retraced while returning home with the horses and wagon.

While working for Norman Brown on the Plymouth Ranch, Leland was always involved with helping Norman with the renowned Belgian Six-Horse Team. Parades in Reno and Carson City on Nevada Day and Gardnerville on Carson Valley Days were always an attraction until Norman's health failed and they no longer kept up the tradition.

During this period from 1928 to 1933, while employed by Fred Dressler and Norman Brown, it is estimated that Leland rode close to 15,000 miles.

In 1933 Leland moved to Antelope Valley and was married. Two children were born of this marriage, a daughter, Lenore, who still resides in Coleville, and a son, Bruce, who lives in Yerington.

During this time Leland rode for Perry Morgan on the East Walker River. This was new country and covered Mason Valley, Shurz and up the East Walker River to Bodie, Mono Lake, Bridgeport, Fletcher Station and east toward Benton. Much of this area reminded him of Southern Nevada and Arizona. Riding distance with Morgan is estimated at 2,500 miles.

While living in Antelope Valley, Leland went to work for the Treloft Ranch. He particularly remembers gathering cattle at Soldier Meadow, north of Winnemucca for over a month, driving the cattle to Gerlach where they were loaded onto a train and shipped to Hudson, unloaded and trailed through Mason Valley to Antelope Valley, moved from Antelope Valley by way of West Walker River to Bridgeport, then returned to East Walker River for winter; adding another 2,500 miles while employed by Treloft.

There was a period when Leland worked day jobs for local ranchers in Antelope Valley, Bridgeport and Mason Valley, buckarooing and doing lots of horseshoeing.

From 1935 to 1944 the Little Walker Cattlemen's Association hired Leland to ride on the West Walker River and Little Walker River allotments. This association at that time was composed of twelve permittees with a permit for twelve hundred pairs. In cooperation with Ranger George Swainston and Germittee Equipment, an extensive system of water spreading ditches increased the grazing capacity many times over. The grazing season was from June first until October fifteenth with some variations according to climatic conditions.

In the seven years of moving cattle to various pastures, doctoring and fall gatherings, it is estimated that Leland put in over 20,000 miles. The job also included switching water on the water spreading system and salting which all had to be done on horseback.

In August of 1956, feeling he needed steadier employment, Leland went to work for the California State Highway Department from which he retired in 1976.

Working for the State of California out of Markleeville, Leland needed a place closer to the job, so he bought a small garage in Minden, where he resided until 1992, when he returned to Antelope Valley to live with his daughter, Lenore.

Working for the State of California did not stop Leland from riding. Weekends were free to do a lot of team roping, help with high school rodeos, chase wild horses and help local ranchers move cattle and gather in the mountains.

Between 1956 and 1976, the Park Cattle Company employed Leland on weekends to help with cattle movements, as did Arthur and Lawrence Settlemeyer, on drives from the Carson Valley to Pickle Meadows. Over this twenty year period, his mileage horseback is estimated at 8,000 miles.

When the Dangberg Ranch sold to Anderson and Nevis, the new owners hired Leland for eight months to ride their holdings in Hope Valley, Bagley Valley and Carson Valley. The estimated mileage for these rides is 1,500 miles.

The Junction Range Company (Settlemeyer and Heritage Ranches) employed Leland in 1980 to ride on its West Walker River property and forest permits. This job started in April when the irrigation of the meadow began. Then cattle were brought in to the deeded pastures about May fifteenth and forest cattle arrived about June first.

Trucking of cattle to summer range from Carson Valley started about 1960 when it was no longer feasible due to the increased traffic on U.S Highway 395. Leland was employed by Junction Range Company for twelve years. The estimated saddle mileage for this time is 25,500 miles.

In 1985 Leland Arigoni was voted the Carson Valley Man of the Year by the local 20-30 club for his participation in youth activities, high school rodeos and fundraisers.

In addition to his many years in the cattle business, Arigoni put many miles on horseback running wild horses on ranges in the Pinenut Mountains, near Hawthorne and in the desert near Benton and Mono Lake. As a teenager, he helped gather mustangs in Railroad Valley and Stone Cabin Valley. This mileage is not included in the summary.

If there is a riding job to do, cattle to be moved, or a chance to ride in the area, you can bet Leland , at the age of eighty-five (November 30, 1996) will be chomping at the bit to be there.

Total mileage ridden in seventy-five years — 119,000 miles.

Here is one of the few remaining old-time cowboys—my friend—
Leland Arigoni.

SUMMARY SHEET OF MILEAGE CONFIRMATION FOR LELAND ARIGONI

1. Oxbow - Schooling	4 years	2,000 miles
2. Oxbow - Riding	5 years	5,000 miles
3. Reed/Fiddleback	5 years	30,000 miles
4. Lorigan Brothers	2 years	7,500 miles
5. Dressler/Brown	6 years	15,000 miles
6. Perry Morgan	1 year	2,500 miles
7. Treloft	1 year	2,500 miles
8. Little Walker Association	11 years	20,000 miles
9. Park Cattle Company	20 years	
Lawrence & Art Settlemeyer	part-time	8,000 miles
10. Dangberg Company	part-time	1,500 miles
11. Junction Range Company	12 years	25,000 miles

TOTAL MILES RIDDEN   119,000 MILES

LITTLE THINGS

A camel is a horse built by a committee.

LITTLE THINGS

Some desert area ranchers still believe that when you dehorn a cow she loses her brains.

Our Trapper's Cabin in Alaska

REPLACING HORSES AND COWS WITH MOOSE AND BROWN BEAR II

Don and I hit the ground running. The first afternoon after I arrived we stored our winter supplies in the cache that stood on four sturdy posts about six feet above the ground. We cleaned out the spring, organized our camping equipment inside the cabin and placed our bedrolls on the two pole bunks located on either side of the cabin walls. The cabin was made out of logs and was weather tight with a foot thick dirt roof. One half of a heavy gauge fifty gallon barrel, lying down with a thick piece of flat metal welded on the top, was heater and cook stove in one unit. A small handmade table and two handmade chairs rounded out the furnishings.

Don and I arrived at our trap line later than planned so it was important that we prioritize the time left until the Alaskan trapping season opened. We had to locate each trap line and find the traps cached along the way. We had to hunt, kill and butcher a moose because we were depending on doing that for our winter meat supply. The last thing we intended to do was kill a bear. In the back country of California the old timers used bear grease as cooking lard and we were familiar with this practice. We were also familiar with the fact that bear meat could carry trichinosis, the same disease in raw pork. In northern California an entire homestead family had been wiped out because they'd eaten bear jerky. I have eaten bear meat and a ton of pork along the early part of my long winding trail and when cooked properly it is perfectly safe to eat. There was one thing we didn't realize or plan on. The black bear of northern California fattened up on an abundant crop of acorns. At this time of the year the Alaskan brown bear eat a lot of fish. It really didn't matter because by the time we were seriously ready to hunt bear and had our bear trap set, the bear had hibernated. This caused problems in our diet later in the winter. We did not have enough fat in our diet and we began to feel the effects.

I had one incident when I was very close to an Alaskan brown bear. It happened shortly after Don and I arrived at Tonsina Lake. It was the first and only contact we had with bear during our stay in Alaska.

I was exploring along the east side of the Tonsina River about a half mile from the cabin. A couple of days before I had been in this area and stopped in amazement at the sight of dry bear hair rubbed into the rough bark of a spruce tree from the ground to a point four or five feet above my head. In California I'd seen numerous places where black bear chewed the bark and limbs as high as they could reach in the white fir thickets. Old timers told me it was the male bear's way of marking his territory and showing any competition how big he was. I don't know if this bear impressed any other bear but he sure got my attention. The bear sign on the spruce was old, probably made in the late summer or early fall.

On this day I'd gone down the river about as far I intended and in another hundred yards or so I turned around and headed back toward the cabin. When I reached the area where the old bear sign was on the spruce tree, a huge bear track showed up in the snow covered trail ahead of me. The bear was going the same direction I was and my footprint looked like a day old baby's beside that bear track. The brush and timber was so thick on either side of the trail I was traveling that I could only see a short distance ahead or behind me. There was a thin line of roe or salmon eggs glistening on top of the snow between the bear tracks. I was so close to that bear I thought I could smell him and I knew he was going to be protective of the salmon he'd just caught. I also knew that the bear probably knew I was there. From stories I'd heard about the unpredictability of the Alaskan brown bear, I thought I was in a tight spot. Being at this type of a disadvantage wasn't the way I visualized meeting my first brown bear. Needless to say a shell was in my rifle chamber and the safety was off while I walked up the trail. I thought I had a better chance moving than just standing still. In another hundred yards my surroundings opened up and I could see a reasonable distance all around me. I began to feel better and the rest of the way to the cabin was uneventful. Even though I never saw that bear, his presence under those circumstances left a lasting impression on me.

It didn't take Don and me long to have our winter wood supply cut, so we turned our attention to our next priority. We would scout out the trap lines Fred had drawn on his homemade map and find the cache of traps he left hanging in the trees. We gave this our next priority because we could hunt for moose at the same time we were doing this. In a week or so we discovered each trap line and found all of the traps except four. During all of this time we hadn't sighted a moose or seen a single moose track in the snow. For the first time since we arrived at Tonsina Lake, we were beginning to get concerned. We were counting on killing a moose to supplement staple food items we flew in with us. Without a steady supply of red meat, those staples would not last the winter. So far we were doing well. We had ample flour, our sourdough starter was working and we made good sourdough hot cakes and biscuits. We occasionally snared a snowshoe rabbit and caught or shot salmon spawning along the lake shore. We knew this source of meat would not be sufficient to sustain us, especially after the lake froze over. We decided to hunt moose in a new area while locating the spring trapping cabin on Manker Creek. It was about eight miles from our cabin but we thought by leaving early in the morning we could make the round trip in one day. We packed a lunch, cleaned our rifles, and laid out our trail hatchets the night before. We got an early start the next morning but the terrain was difficult and it took us some time to find the right draw to travel up. We crossed Grayling Creek and by the middle of the day we were traveling up a steep sided, vee shaped canyon. The bottom of this canyon was only about twenty yards wide and the steep mountain ridges on either side were half a mile high. This was one of the avalanche areas Fred warned us about. He told us not to shoot a rifle and to be quiet when going through this part of the canyon. Looking up at those snow covered cliffs on either side of us it was easy to see why. By now it was obvious that we were not going to get back to our cabin by night fall. It was getting dark when we came out of the canyon we'd been traveling along and looked out over a vast area of willows and frozen ponds that was Manker Creek. Looking through the dim light we finally located the white side of a canvas tent about a quarter of a mile in the distance. When we reached the spot and looked inside the tent we found it was empty except for a frying pan and two five gallon tin cans. One can had a little flour in the bottom and the other had some kind of white lard in it. A cache of traps was hanging in a nearby tree and that was the extent of this trapper camp. We weren't surprised and we tromped the snow down in front of the tent. We made sure there were no snow laden trees over the area and we gathered enough wood to sustain a fire through the night. It was one of those situations where you roasted on one side and froze on the other but we had warm clothes and we were doing all right.

We were as hungry as two half starved coyote pups and we started thinking about the frying pan, flour and lard in those five gallon cans. We decided to make some sort of tough bread. I melted some snow and scrubbed out the frying pan while Don mixed some flour and lard together and we put it in the hot skillet. It cooked to a golden brown on each side and it really smelled good. At first, while it was still hot, the bread wasn't too bad but as it cooled off it became apparent that the lard was rancid. We burped rancid lard for the next three days. In fact, if I really put my mind to it, I can still taste that rancid lard.

Well, we settled down on opposite sides of the fire, lying with our backs toward the heat. The first one to get cold enough to wake up would put more wood on the fire and the night wore on. What we didn't realize was that during the night, in our fitful sleep, we moved closer to the warmth as the fire died down. Sometime during the late part of the night I leaped to my feet, hollering, "I'm on fire." The back of my coat was burning and the flames were reaching up over my head. Almost before I realized it Don was leaping across the smoldering coals, tackling me in the chest. The force of the blow took us both down into a foot of snow and immediately put the fire out. We got up, shook the snow off and checked to see how much damage was done. Due to Don's quick thinking and reflex actions, the damage wasn't as bad as it first appeared. I had a hole burned in the back of my coat and a small scorched spot on my back. We joked about the close call and sat up by the fire the rest of the night.

The next day we returned to our cabin. We'd found the trapper's camp and the cache of traps but we had not seen one single moose track. I spent evenings during the next week sewing a canvas patch in the back of my coat while Don kidded me about being a clumsy seamstress.

We hunted moose for several more days without success, then one morning Don opened the cabin door and let out a war whoop. There were moose tracks all around the cabin. One track was within four feet of the cabin door. We probably ate the fastest breakfast in Alaskan history and we were tracking moose in the early morning twilight. At this time of the year, in the part of Alaska we were in, we only saw the sun for about twenty minutes each day when it peaked over the horizon in a low spot in the mountains to the south. There was about a foot of snow on the ground and tracking was easy. We soon realized there were four or five moose in the herd. Apparently the rutting season was still on because the tracks showed a bull moose was following a cow that wasn't being very cooperative.

By mid-afternoon we were at timberline on a mountain six or seven miles west of our cabin. We hadn't been able to catch up with the moose we were tracking but by now other moose tracks were showing up and we'd found the area the moose were running in. Apparently the moose we'd been tracking left the mountains west of the lake, crossed the Tonsina River, passed by our cabin and traveled to timberline on the mountains east of our cabin. We started home and about halfway down the mountain, the Northern Lights began to put on a show. When we reached the cabin we were tired but satisfied. We knew where our winter supply of meat was.

The following day Don and I split up and hunted the tree line areas of the mountains and Don killed a moose. Now the real work began. The next day we took our backpacks, skinned and quartered the moose and packed the first loads of meat back to the cabin. We calculated we were each packing about eighty pounds of meat six miles over frozen muskeg criss-crossed with downed trees. We killed another moose in the same area and this process lasted for about another week. At the end of one of those days I wrote in my ledger that I felt more tired and deader than the moose I was packing. This also brought back memories of the moose that had been within four feet of our cabin door. Now we were set for the winter with our winter meat supply under our cache frozen solid. We were ready to start trapping.

Unbeknown to either Don or me, our trapping experience in Alaska was about to become something like the wedding where the preparation for the big event lasted longer than the marriage itself. We woke up one morning and the lower half of Tonsina Lake was frozen over. The lake was seven miles long and the next day the rest of the lake was covered with ice. The temperature hovered between zero and ten below. The temperature varied very little between night and the twilight days. The northern lights became more vivid and they were spectacular.

Our traps were set and our trap lines were working. We were catching lynx, otter, ermine, wolf, and tree martin. We were coping with the weather conditions very well. We were also coping with the stressfulness you find in any isolated line camp or trapper's cabin when one partner gets into camp at the end of the day before the other partner arrives. The partner that is still out knows where he is and what he is doing, but the first partner into camp doesn't know this and he begins to worry when his partner is past due and it is getting dark. On the big ranges of the west the worry is: "Did his horse fall?" "Did he get bucked off?" "Is he hung up in the stirrup?" or "Is he just staying with the herd of cows he's bringing home?" In the far north the worry is: "Did he fall through the ice?" "Did he get caught in an avalanche?" "Did he break a leg?" or "Has he just had a longer day than planned?" Either way, when you hear the familiar steps and the cabin door bursts open, it's a relief and all is forgotten until the next time.

The days were getting colder. When long cracks formed in the lake ice it sounded like rifle shots. The temperature was about fifteen degrees below zero day in and day out. Don had to cross Grayling Creek on the way to his trap line that ran from the cabin to the timber line on the east side of the lake. Grayling Creek was a swift running, boulder strewn creek treacherous to cross. One morning Don slipped on a boulder and fell through the thin ice. By the time he crawled out of the creek, he was soaked up to his chest in icy water. It was about thirty degrees below zero that morning and Don was a couple of miles from the cabin. He knew the only chance he had was to reach the cabin before he froze to death and he started in that direction as fast as he could go. When he reached the cabin his clothes were frozen stiff and he was having trouble moving. Don came through the incident without any frostbite but it put us in a somber mood.

The temperature settled in at twenty or twenty-five degrees below zero and it occasionally dropped to thirty below. It stayed that way for several weeks before a cold blast of air came down from the north and temperature dropped to between forty-eight and fifty-two degrees below zero. The temperature stayed in that range for more than two weeks. The situation was getting serious. Fur bearing animals stopped moving. We didn't have the right clothes to survive in this temperature and the lack of fat in our diet began to take its toll. Mistakes that are forgiven at twenty degrees below zero are not forgiven at fifty-two degrees below. You just don't make mistakes at fifty-two degrees below zero and live to tell the tale.

One morning we stayed in the cabin to review the situation we were in. We agreed that so far our Alaskan adventure proved that the reason we came to Alaska was not practical and the Aleutian Islands no longer looked attractive. We admitted to ourselves that some of the problems we encountered along the way were due to our lack of experience and we were now in a situation where we could not afford to make mistakes. This was a hard pill to swallow. We were used to finishing a project we started, but common sense suggested we should quit while we were still able.

After reviewing our situation and adding to it a little homesickness caused by the severe weather, we made a decision. We decided to swallow our pride and give up. There in the Alaskan wilderness inside an old log cabin sitting around a homemade table lighted by a flickering kerosene lantern, a dream ended.

The next step was not going to be easy. We were sitting in the Alaskan wilderness, we'd spent our last dollar getting there, it was fifty-two degrees below zero and we were 3,730 miles from home. To be continued.

JIM

Through the years I made life long friendships with many of the men I worked for, as well as many of the men that worked for me. One such person was a young man straight out of Ag. School from U. C. Davis. Jim was long on book learning and short on practical experience. This young man had more "want to" than many of the men I have worked with and in the two years he worked for me, he developed into a good ranch hand. No matter what the situation-calving, haying, fencing-Jim always tried. One incident I remember happened in the spring when each day's workload seemed like a week. We worked out a breeding herd of registered cows and calves and Jim and I drove them about a mile to the Ogilvie field where we mothered up the calves. I sent Jim trotting one way down the pasture fence closing gates left open during the winter. I went along the fence in the other direction doing the same thing. We were to meet at the far end of the pasture about two miles away.

In due time, when I got to the area where Jim and I were supposed to meet, I met a B.L.M. pickup coming down the rutted two track road. The two men in the truck were laughing. They said, "We met a young man horseback a little while ago. He flagged us down and said," "I work for Dave Secrist. Can you tell me where his ranch is?" Jim was lost inside the pasture fence two miles from the ranch headquarters.

Jim does not remember this incident but he remembers things that happened to me during this time frame, which I do not remember. So I guess we are even. You have to realize this happened forty years ago.

Another incident, during the early years that Jim worked for me, happened about halfway through calving season. We had a spring snow storm and there was a foot and a half of snow on the ground. We were having twenty-five to thirty calves each day and the weather was miserable. We were working night and day keeping as many calves alive as possible. There were calves in the calving barn under heat lamps, and one calf, nearly frozen to death, was in our bathtub in warm water getting thawed out. It was nearly dark when Jim, Marvin and I turned about thirty very calvy cows, cut out of the main cow herd earlier in the afternoon, into the calving lot where we could check them several times during the night.

We started riding toward the ranch headquarters and just before we got out of the calving lot, we came across a cow that seemed to be having calving troubles. If it had been earlier in the day and under different circumstances I would have given the cow more time, but it was nearly dark, about fifteen degrees, with a foot and a half of snow on the ground and I didn't want to take a chance. I told Marvin to rope the cow, which he did. I rode up behind the cow, slipped my rope around the calf's protruding front feet, took my dallies, turned my horse in the opposite direction, and when our ropes tightened there was a reasonable pull and the calf popped out. The calf came from ninety-eight degrees to fifteen degrees in less than five seconds. It was a slimy, quivering, steamy mess, lying in the snow. We took Marvin's rope off the cow. I gave my horse to Jim, hung the calf by its hind feet over a nearby fence post, shook the mucus out of his throat, laid the calf down and backed away. Luckily the cow mothered her calf, so we coiled up ropes, I mounted my horse and without a word we rode on to the barn. Jim watched the whole procedure which took about five minutes from start to finish. The cow was a good mother and the calf lived.

The next morning at breakfast Jim said, "I went through all of my vet books last night and couldn't find anything describing yesterdays calving procedure." Jim learned fast, became a good ranch hand and obviously he was quick to pick up a little warped cowboy sense of humor.

Another incident, Jim remembers, happened in the fall. I asked him and another ranch hand who was supposed to know where to go, to take the tractor with a wagon load of hay and feed some bulls in a pasture about a mile below the ranch. I asked the ranch hand if he knew where he was going and he assured me he did. Snow flurries had been coming through the valley all morning and soon after they started out with the load of hay, a real ground blizzard moved in. When the storm momentarily let up, I could see the tractor and wagon going in a big circle about half way to the bull pasture. Realizing the ranch hand was lost, I left the cows I was working and went to straighten out the situation.

Jim said he thought he was going to freeze to death and had never been so glad to see anyone in his life as he was to see me, on that little black horse, coming out of the low clouds and blowing snow. I think Jim credits me with saving his life. After all these years Jim and I still stay in touch and I am pleased to say he is my friend.

Loyd with son, Von in 1937

LOYD SORENSEN

Loyd was inducted into The Cowboy 100,000 Mile Club in 1990.

Throughout Loyd's life he was a staunch supporter of private property rights and in Loyd's world, as I knew it, black was black and white was white and there was no gray area in between. Loyd believed in striking while the iron was hot and you never had to wonder what side of the issue Loyd was on or doubt his ability to have the last word.

As an introduction into the documentation presented by Lorna Jones, his daughter, when Loyd was inducted into the Cowboy 100,000 Mile Club, I offer the following.

When I was President of the Nevada Cattlemen's Association, the first call I received at 3:30 a.m. in the morning was startling to say the least. My first thought, as Jane sleepily answered the phone, was that someone in the family had died or was hurt. Instead it turned out to be Loyd asking, "Is Dave still there or has he already gone out to work?" Then I heard Jane say, "Gee, Loyd I don't know if he is still here or not. Let me go see if I can catch him." Jane waited a minute, shook me more awake, and handed me the phone. The next thing I heard was Loyd discussing some public land issue. He wanted to make sure I knew and understood his point of view and Loyd wanted me to mention this at some meeting I was scheduled to attend later in the week.

To me this next story typifies Loyd's ability to have the last word no matter the circumstances. It happened several years ago and was told to me by Bob Wright, a Clover Valley Rancher. At the time Bob's brother, Steve, a rancher in the Ruby Valley area, was operating a hunting guide service in the Ruby Mountains and he had leased the hunting rights on Loyd's deeded sections of land. This land was high up in the Ruby Mountains, surrounded by Forest Service land and these deeded sections were summer range for Loyd's sheep operation. It was mid to late fall and the muzzle loading mule deer hunting season had just opened. I wasn't told why Loyd was this high up in the mountains horseback just as the sun was starting to hit the east side of the Rubies, but he was there, nearly to the top of the mountain, when he stopped to let his horse rest. While looking around he spotted a hunter sitting on a rock just above a pass at the head of a steep rocky draw.

Now Loyd knew he had leased the hunting rights on this deeded land to Steve but looking around he didn't see Steve anywhere and it bothered him to see the hunter on his land so he jumped to the conclusion that the man was trespassing. Loyd turned his horse and worked his way up through the rock outcropping until he and the hunter were within talking distance.

The conversation went something like this:

Loyd: "Mornin'. How did you get up here?

" Muzzle loading hunter: "I am out of Steve Wright's hunting camp and he stationed me here on this rock."

Loyd: "If that is so, where is Steve?"

Muzzle loading hunter: "Coming up the canyon, way down there in those Quakies. Any bucks in the area were supposed to come up through this pass."

Loyd: "Where are you from?"

Muzzle loading hunter: "Reno."

Loyd: "What do you do for a living?"

Muzzle loading hunter: "I buy old vintage cars and restore them."

Loyd: "Humph, I wouldn't think a man could make much of a living doing that."

Muzzle loading hunter: "Oh, I do all right. I just sold the last one I restored for $150,000."

Loyd, after a brief silence: "Well, I would think a man making that kind of money would be able to afford a better rifle" and without another word Loyd turned and rode back down through the rocks and disappeared through the mountain pass.

The following is a documentation of Loyd's lifelong 187,500 mile horseback ride written by his daughter, Lorna Jones.

Loyd Sorensen was born November 13, 1900 in Mt. Carmel, Utah. He was the seventh of ten children born to Hans and Miranda Sorensen. Loyd's father ranched in the Long Valley area, raising cattle, sheep and hay. Loyd began riding horseback as soon as he could walk. Horseback or horse drawn wagons or buggies were the mode of transportation in those days. Loyd rode back and forth to the family farm. The family ranch was a twelve mile ride from Mt. Carmel. Market animals were trailed to Marysville, which was a two hundred mile round trip from home.

As a young man of twenty-three he began working for his cousin, Ray Esplin, on the Arizona Strip (that portion of Arizona that is bordered by the Colorado River on the south, the Nevada state line on the west and Utah state line on the north.) For the next several years he herded sheep, taking sheep in lieu of pay. Once he accumulated 600 head of sheep he struck out on his own. During these years he wintered on the Arizona Strip and his summer range was on the East Fork River south of Bryce Canyon. The trail between his winter and summer range was roughly 100 miles. During those years he did his own herding and was with the sheep almost constantly. He rode ten miles a day for a period of thirteen years. It is estimated that during those years, combined with his early years, he rode horseback approximately 70,500 miles.

The passage of the Taylor Grazing Act in 1934 had a great impact on Loyd's operation on the Arizona Strip. Because he did not own any base property or water rights he could not meet the requirements to acquire a grazing permit on federal land. He was given a short amount of time to remove his sheep from the range. He trailed his sheep to the stockyards in Modena, Utah, loaded them on a train and shipped them to DuBois, Idaho, where he had leased range. In 1936 he purchased part of the Adams-McGill operation between Ely and Lund in White Pine County, Nevada. Loyd trailed his sheep eighty miles each fall from the summer range on Ward Mountain to the winter range in Coal Valley. In the spring the sheep took the same trek back. While in White Pine

County, Loyd acquired cattle to add to his operation and logged additional miles horseback managing them. During his fourteen years in Ely, Loyd added another 33,000 miles on horseback when estimating ten miles a day for 300 days a year.

In 1949 Loyd partnered with Bert Robison to buy the Gordon Griswold ranching operation in Elko County.   In 1958, Loyd and his son, Von, purchased the Ed Murphy Ranch in Secret Pass. In 1967 Loyd bought the Louis Goodwin Ranch in Clover Valley, south of Wells. In 1973 when his partner Bert Robison died, Loyd and son-in-law, Kenneth Jones, purchased the Robison share of the Robison-Sorenson partnership. (All of these ranches are in Elko County, Nevada.)

From 1949 until his semi-retirement in 1992 (at age 92) Loyd trailed sheep and cattle for substantial distances between summer and winter ranges, lambed sheep, irrigated, checked on and moved cattle mostly on horseback. During those years it is estimated that he rode an additional 84,000 miles by tallying an average of ten miles a day for 200 days a year for over 42 years. In all, it is estimated that Loyd rode horseback at least 187,500 miles in his lifetime.

Loyd was out before daylight almost every morning and he once said, "I may not work as fast as some people but if I get a two hour head start in the morning nobody is going to catch me." He was enthusiastic about life and loved the livestock business.

Dave's comment: Loyd passed away in Clover Valley, Nevada on October 9, 1997.

LITTLE THINGS

An old saying: One day you get the bear and the next day the bear gets you.

COWBOYS AND RANCH HANDS

Along my 115,000 mile horseback ride I worked for a number of ranchers as a cowboy and ranch hand and a number cowboys and ranch hands have worked for me. They range from young men like Jim that come with little experience and ton of "want to" that learn to be cowboys and ranch hands, to men that lived their entire lives on the big ranches of the west and were born to be cowboys. The group in between are usually seasonal workers and are also a very important part of a ranch's yearly operation. Regardless of their background, it is drive and dedication to a way of life that determines how successful they become. Many follow the cowboy way of life for a comparably short period of time before changing to other endeavors, but the experiences they have and the friends they make, during this period of time usually remain as cherished memories for the rest of their lives.

Most cowboys and ranch hands that I've been involved with are good reliable people. They are loyal to the outfits they work for. Some work for the same ranches most of their lives. Others move from ranch to ranch. They are respected members of the community and have the skills necessary to do this type of work. The lifestyle they have chosen requires them to really want to be a big range cowboy or ranch hand. To be good at it they have to be able to survive in all types of weather conditions, understand and respect the animals they work with, and maybe as important as anything, understand, respect and enjoy the rivers, valleys, meadow, mountains and wild life that surround them.

Another type of ranch hand that at certain times of the year is important, is the seasonal transient type workers. In years past when hay was put up in loose stacks and baled hay was stacked by hand, large numbers of workers were needed and came into Elko on the freight trains. They hid their bed rolls in the thick willows along the Humbolt River known as the jungle. The next morning, the employment office was full of men looking for haying jobs and sometimes a group of ten or fifteen men stood around outside. The Pioneer Hotel, Shorty's Club and the Snake Pit were also full of men looking for work.

During this time the Elko County Sheriff's office and the Elko City jail ran chain gangs. They consisted of eight to ten hung-over men chained together clanking up and down the Elko streets cleaning up trash and litter. They were under the supervision of two stern looking uniformed guards. Elko's chain gangs were famous from Stockton, California, to Salt Lake City, Utah, and they were used to help keep unwanted trouble makers from stopping in Elko.

During 1958, Marion and I along with her folks, Mr. and Mrs. Munson, purchased Lee Livestock Company, south of Elko, Nevada. With my family's help, I managed Lee Livestock for fifteen years. We ran a herd of registered horned Hereford cows along with a herd of commercial cows. We sold seventy-five to a hundred registered range raised Hereford bulls per year, plus yearling steers and heifers from the commercial herd. In the winter we fed the cows with four teams of horses using feed wagons and sleighs. In the spring, summer and fall we worked cows and hayed. The haying season at six thousand feet elevation is very short and on a good water year we put up four thousand tons of hay. I mention all of this because this is the reason we used a lot of seasonal and transient help and this is the source of many of my ranch hand memories. I would go to town, hire a pickup load of men, stop by the jungle while they disappeared into the willows and returned carrying their bed rolls. Then I would drive the twenty-five miles back to the ranch. I ran a twenty-four man crew during the haying season and some of my memories of working with these seasonal crews are serious and some are comical. In those days we didn't have a payday. If we paid our crew on a monthly basis, we lost half of our crew on a monthly basis. The men were furnished room and board at the ranch and we purchased the necessities and commissary they needed or wanted (except for beer, wine or whiskey, which was sometimes on their list). We kept a record of the wage advances they drew, along with their commissary and when the season was over or they quit, the commissary, advanced wages and withholding taxes were subtracted from the total wages earned. This was all itemized on a piece of paper and given to the men when they were paid.

The most used excuse for making a draw and going to town was to get a haircut. Most of those haircuts cost the men fifty to seventy-five dollars and the haircuts never materialized.

One incident I remember, and still grin when I think of it, took place in late winter. I had a truck load of concentrated livestock feed coming in. In those days livestock feed came to ranches in hundred pound burlap bags (gunny sacks). This was before feed was stacked on pallets and moved by front end loaders and most barns and sheds of that day were not designed for that kind of use anyway. The old trucks of that time were much smaller than the highway rigs of today but they still hauled fifteen to twenty tons of sacked feed that had to be unloaded by hand.

We were winter feeding cows and I couldn't spare my ranch crew (much to their delight), so on the morning the feed was to arrive, I was at the Elko Employment Office when they opened before daylight. I walked through the door with my old hat, winter down coat, boot overshoes and chaps on. I saw the only two men in the place glance at each other. I learned later they were two construction workers who had learned how to work the system. They worked construction most of the year but in the winter they drew unemployment. At this time, men drawing unemployment had to show up at the Employment Office for at least one hour each day and take any job they were qualified to do. These construction workers learned that if they came to the Employment Office early in the morning when the office first opened, it was seldom that anyone came in to hire them. After waiting an hour, their obligation to find work was satisfied and they were free for the rest of the day.

I filled out the paperwork, loaded the construction workers in my pickup and headed for the ranch. They kidded me all the way about how I was ruining their "sunshine pay". When we pulled into the barnyard, the truckload of feed was already there, backed up to the platform in front of the barn door. That truck looked like a railroad boxcar. I saw the construction workers look at each other when I explained the truck was loaded with eighteen tons of livestock feed in one hundred pound gunny sacks that had to be packed back into the barn by hand. I had explained all of this at the Employment Office and they were "gung ho" to go, but the full impact of the job didn't sink in until they saw that truck sitting in front of the old barn. The truck driver and I packed the sacks off of the truck and the two construction workers packed them back into the barn and stacked them chest high. In days gone by, truck drivers helped unload their own trucks.

These construction workers were two big strong young men but they had been lying around town all winter doing an occasional day job and they were soft. The truck driver and I kept packing sacks to the construction workers and they packed them into the barn. Soon the two men had their coats off, their sweatshirts were wringing wet, and sweat was running down their faces. We kept bringing the sacks of feed and the two men kept packing them into the barn. They were beginning to struggle but they were too proud to let a truck driver and a scrawny cowboy get the best of them. By noon the truck was empty and my feeding crews and feed teams were coming in, so we all went to the cookhouse for lunch. I paid the two men and took them back to town. I'll bet those two construction workers still remember the day I screwed up their "sunshine pay." I know I do and I still grin when I think about it.

One summer I hired a hay hand that was from the state of Pennsylvania. He was a good hand but nearly starved to death when I brought him to the ranch. The usual meals in the ranch cookhouses I've operated or been acquainted with consist of all you could eat beef roast, mashed potatoes and gravy, steaks, beef stews, some kinds of vegetables, gallons of hot coffee, butter and homemade bread with canned fruit or baked pies or cakes for dessert. This fellow, whose name escapes me, took full advantage of the situation; he sat down at the end of the table, grabbed his knife in one hand and his fork in the other and pounded them on the table while saying, "Just pass me everything."

He'd been working at the ranch for about ten days when he came to me and asked if I would do him a favor. I asked what he wanted and he said, "Would you advance me sixty dollars and send it to this address? I have my false teeth hocked at a pawn shop in Pennsylvania. I really enjoy working for you and I'd like to stay all year."

Well, asking for a draw wasn't unusual but the reason for this draw was a first for me. I made the check out to the pawn shop, put it in an envelope, put a note with his name in with it, and mailed it to the address he gave me. Then I promptly forgot all about the incident. In about two more weeks this fellow began to fill out and look normal. Everything was going fine and he was happy when something happened, I don't remember what, maybe a disagreement with another hay hand but what ever the reason, he quit. In about another two weeks I received a little square box in the mail. I wondered what it was and checked the return address. The false teeth had arrived. Since the owner of the false teeth was long gone, I kept them for several weeks and after no contact from the owner I sent them back to the pawn shop with address unknown written on the box. When I think of this incident, I conjure up a picture of this fellow moving from ranch to ranch with his false teeth following him, snapping at his behind but never quite being able to catch up.

In the early spring, one important job is dragging meadows. The drags can be factory made but most of the time, especially in the past, the drags were homemade using a piece of old narrow gauge railroad track or some other piece of heavy iron rail or pipe for the main beam. Old iron sulky rake wheels, chained together in two or three rows, were sometimes used behind the main beam. The drag is attached to a tractor by a heavy iron chain. The old tractors of that day didn't have cabs or heaters in them. At this time of the year dragging meadows seemed like the coldest job in the world. Those old tractors were like deep freezers on wheels. You could put on all the clothes you owned and still feel like you were going to freeze to death. When the drags were drawn over the meadows, they broke up the manure left from last winter's feed grounds and distributed it evenly, thus fertilizing the meadows.

On this spring day I had three tractors and meadow drags working when an early afternoon thunderstorm passed through. The talk that evening was about the lightning and how vulnerable it felt to be the highest thing sticking up, on a big flat meadow during a thunder storm. Sitting at the other end of the table one fellow said, "Lightning doesn't scare me because my tractor has rubber tires" and he went on and on about the fact that lightning wouldn't strike if you were on a piece of equipment that had rubber tires. He ended up saying, "You guys are wasting your time worrying about it."

Another hay hand, who didn't talk much, finally chimed in and said, "Ross, you are right. Tractors do have rubber tires and I don't know if that is a help or not when it comes to being struck by lightning, but did you ever stop to think about that two hundred pounds of iron meadow drag hooked to your tractor that you are dragging around on the ground behind you?" The look on Ross's face was priceless.

Hay hand Wino Bill gave me the next ranch hand incident I remember and Wino Bill is the name he used when he introduced himself. Bill worked for me for several haying seasons and never left the ranch until the yearly haying was over. Bill looked the part and the name Wino Bill fit him to a tee. He was a small skinny fellow that wore misfit clothes found or picked up at rummage sales. The pants were too short, the shirt was too big and he topped the outfit off with a well worn straw hat. Bill was a good hay hand with a sense of humor and as long as he stayed out of town he was reliable but he couldn't stand prosperity.

When haying season was over, Bill drew his wages and Wino Bill took over and he was a total loss. This year Wino Bill showed up after the Fourth of July when the haying season was just getting started. Bill wasn't in very good shape but in about a week he recovered and was ready to go to work. Some of my old side delivery rakes were too worn out to repair and I had purchased a brand new John Deere rake. It had a long green beam with seven large yellow rake teeth wheels attached to it. The rake could make windrows or be adjusted into a vee shape and used to roll windrows together. At the time the rake was supposed to be on the cutting edge of modern haying equipment. Bill and I serviced the rake and tractor and Bill followed me to the meadow where I made a few rounds, showing Bill how the rake operated. The rake was designed to make sharp turns to the left but sharp turns to the right could not be made. I took the time to demonstrate this fact to Bill. I watched while he made several more trips around the field. When everything was working smoothly, I left to take care of other haying activities. When I came back by about noon to pick Bill up, I saw the tractor and rake stopped at the far end of the field. The long beam on my new rake was bent into an L shape on top of the tractor tire. Bill had tried to make a sharp right hand turn. I was hot.

Four hours after my new rake was in operation it was sitting on top of my tractor looking like a piece of junk. I started across that meadow traveling over ditches much faster than I normally would. Firing Bill was the top priority on my mind. When I got half way across the meadow I saw Bill starting to run toward me, waving his arms in the air. When we came together before I could say a word Bill said, "Now, now, now, don't get upset. It was just a human miscalculation."

Those were the last words I expected to hear coming out of Bill's mouth as he stood there in his too short pants, his too big shirt, with his beat up straw hat in his hands and a very sincere expression on his face. This was all happening, while in the background; my new rake was sitting on top of my tractor with those big yellow rake wheels sticking up in the air. The scene was so pathetic and comical looking; I relaxed and started to laugh like an idiot. What else could I do? It was just another day in a rancher's life during haying season on the big high altitude meadows of northeastern Nevada.

I took the rake to the shop and repaired it. Wino Bill raked hay with that side delivery rake for a couple more seasons without any other problems and he never again tried to make a sharp turn to the right.

LITTLE THINGS

I once had a contractor giving me an estimate for a job I wanted done. I suggested maybe I could be his helper and it would save me a little money. When his bid came in the mail it stated: If I do the job it will cost you $425.00. If you help me it will cost $525.00. That wasn't very subtle, was it?

John DeLong 1966

JOHN DeLONG

John DeLong was inducted into the Nevada Cattlemen's Association Cowboy 100,000 Mile Club in 2007.

The following is the presentation written and given by his daughter, Christy Stanton:

I am here tonight representing our family in presenting John Delong with the Cowboy 100,000 Mile Club award.

My dad likes a horse on which his saddle fits well, a horse that has a desire to be a helper and friend, and most importantly, a horse that likes to reach out and travel in a ground covering trot.

There is a reason for this. Since he was old enough to ride, John DeLong, has averaged some 1,500 miles on horseback yearly, mostly at a trot. This is an explanation of those miles.

John, the second child of Bill and Dale DeLong, came to the Jackson Creek Ranch on the edge of the Black Rock Desert shortly after his birth in 1942. His first notable horseback miles were ridden bareback with his siblings Billie, Tim and Jeanne, following their father and uncle.

Those kids rode so far bareback that their parents, a bit guiltily, decided to get them saddles and bought three Fred Muler kids' saddles when John was in the second grade. About this same time, the first cattle trucks came rolling into the ranch to take delivery of steers. Thus John missed the miles driving cattle to the railhead as his father and uncle had done years before.

The bulk of John's horseback miles came from working cattle on the ranch and range. Each spring, from the time those saddles were purchased; he helped trail the Hereford/Shorthorn cattle some forty miles south as far as Seven Troughs.

The buckaroos would then trot home and go north another twenty-five miles to help Uncle Jude Delong gather and brand on a range that spread forty-four miles east to west around the Happy Creek Ranch.

As soon as school was out, John and his siblings would drive saddle horses southeast to Rattle Snake and then Fox Farm.

Their dad would meet them with the pickup and camp supplies and horse hay: from these points they would gather and brand. The routine was similar for the winter permit forty-five miles to the east.

The saddle horses were driven out to Sand or Morman Dan well, and from there they would ride to wean and pull bulls. The stock and the horses would then be driven back to the ranch and those same bulls would be driven out in the spring when the cows were back on the mountain.

For years these native desert cattle balked at the modern strangeness of the asphalt highway to the north and the iron rails to the south. Invariably something would have to be drug across these unfamiliar obstacles at the end of a rope.

The first stock truck was purchased in 1948 and did cut back on the horseback miles. However, good roads were few and there was lots of range to cover in between. The horse, like the cattle, did not take to modern conveniences. They could easily be loaded up a chute, but often would not jump in or out of the truck. You see, there wasn't a ramp. They'd just back the old Ford into a bank of some sort. Many a time somebody had to trot home because a horse just would not load.

After high school graduation, John left the ranch for four years, first working for Tom and John Marvel at the 25 Ranch. This job certainly added to his miles horseback as it's some one hundred miles from the 25 to the Stampede Ranch on a range thirty miles wide.

There weren't necessarily more miles to be ridden here than on the home range, but there were more horses —- young horses —- and excitement. It was here John actually did drive steers to the railroad.

The next two years John logged many miles, but very few horseback because he served in the United States Army.

John then went back to the Jacksons, which had grown with the acquisition of the Trout Creek Ranch in 1956. With this ranch came more miles to cover and the last outside mother cows to be acquired by the Delong Ranches. John and his wife, Judy, moved to the Trout Creek ranch after their marriage in 1966. It was there they raised their three children, Jhona, Will and me. They still live there today, enjoying visits from their six grandchildren.

At age twenty, John showed his first horse at the Elko County Fair and for the next forty-two years, he trotted and loped miles in a circle, conditioning his horse for stock horse shows.

In 1969 the Alexander Ranch was purchased —- making a whole ranch that spread approximately forty-five miles east to west and sixty miles north to south. Tim raised his family on the Alexander, and ironically, we five kids rode many a mile, sometimes bareback, following Dad or Uncle.

John bought the ranch's first horse trailer in 1979—an event my siblings and I remember vividly and I expect with great delight. It was powder blue C&J trailer and may have reduced the miles we trotted. However, it got us there faster, too, so we could certainly cover more country in the daylight.

In the 1980's the bulls became Limousin and in the 1990's Tim and his family moved to the Flying M Ranch. This became one more ranch where John rode miles helping gather and brand.

Nowadays, Delong Ranches' cattle are predominately Red Angus, Will and Katie live on the Jackson Creek Ranch, and the annual circle has changed a bit. After weaning at Trout Creek, the cattle are driven east to the Blue Mountain/Morman Dan Allotments. Then they are drifted southwest around Jungo Point to Fox Farm and Sulphur, before heading north to Winter Camp and gathered into Jackson Creek for late spring branding. The cattle spend the summer on the mountain until they are brought back to Trout Creek in the fall. On a map, this circle is 130 to 150 miles in circumference, but on horseback it is two to three times that, and John is there on every ride.

John averaged 1,775 miles horseback per year for sixty years for a total of 106,500 miles.

Just last winter, Dad trailed the dry cows out to winter range. Mom met him with the pickup and old blue trailer so they didn't have to trot home, but he could have, because you see, he rides a horse who likes to travel at a long trot. And now, when he looks around, a whole pack of grandkids are willing to follow at a trot, and still have lots of miles to go.

LITTLE THINGS

Some interesting facts compiled by the United States Department of Agriculture. The U.S.D.A. estimated the off farm costs such as marketing, wholesaling, distributing and retailing account for $.80 of every food dollar spent in the United States of America. The following examples were compiled by the National Farmers Union in 2008. From one pound of sirloin steak average cost $7.99 the ranchers share was 92 cents, one pound of bacon average cost $3.99 the producers share was 55 cents, a one pound loaf of bread average cost $2.99 the farmers share was 17 cents. The U.S.D.A. also said that 1% of the United States population produces the food for the other 99%. Most ranchers and farmers know this but it may be a surprise to many consumers.

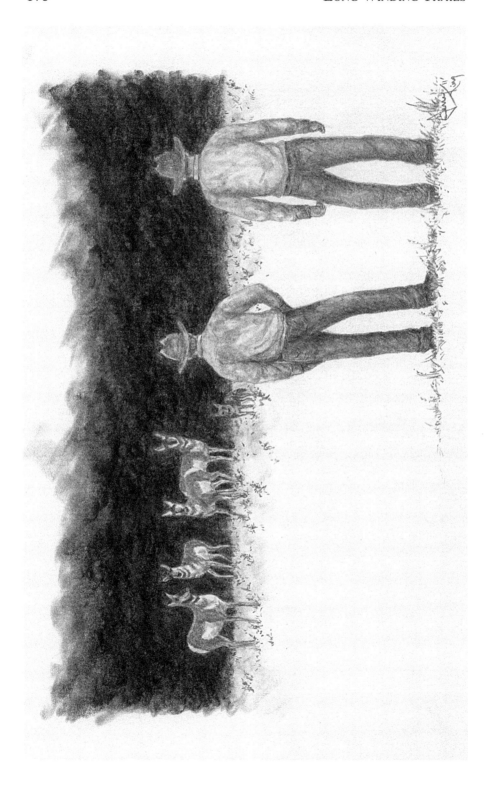

RANGE FIRES

From the beginning of my 115,000 mile horseback ride until now as I approach the end of the trail, range fires have been a constant. The only things changed are the methods and expense of fire fighting and the magnitude of catastrophic fires that have developed in the last twenty-five years. In the beginning of my horseback ride, the Forest Service in the areas I am familiar with relied on manned lookout stations placed on the highest mountain peaks to spot new fires.

They also relied on ranchers and rural people living in the back country to spot fires and many times these people were the first responders on the scene of newly developing fires. The Forest Rangers supplied ranchers with hand tools kept in a special place in barns or sheds. The tools consisted of shovels, axes, and McLeods. The McLeod was a special tool with a shovel-like handle attached to a heavy, foot-wide hoe with rake teeth on the upper side. This tool was used when building fire trail by hand in steep mountain country. Because of the lack of mobile pressurized water-wagons, which could travel in mountainous terrain, we kept gunny sacks in five gallon buckets of water. As silly as it sounds in today's mechanized world of chemical fire retardants and huge fire fighting tanker planes, a lot of range fires in the past were whipped out by using wet gunny sacks and controlled by using only hand labor.

At the Eden Valley Ranch headquarters a large school bell, no longer used by the one room school, was perched on a wooden tower behind the cookhouse. The old bell looked something like the Liberty Bell, except a long rope hung from the bell arm. The bell was used morning, noon, and evening to signal meals were ready. The bell used any other time of the day or night meant fire. Another universal distress signal, still honored in the back country today where cell phones are not available or usable, is three rifle or pistol shots fired in rapid secession at one minute intervals. These shots can be heard for miles and signify fire, a cowboy down, or some other life-threatening event where help is needed. Ranchers, cowboys and other back country people never use this signal unless in extreme danger and never in jest.

During this time frame, all big range fires were fought using man power, hand tools and if available, bulldozers and four wheel drive vehicles. Ranch crews were often the first to arrive at range fires. They put out many fires while they were still small and no one outside the area realized there had been a fire. Cattle, other livestock and wildlife used the ranges all year long. Elevation dictated deferred grazing long before rest-rotation grazing systems were thought of. The Indians and old timers set fires in the high country when they left their summer ranges in the fall and most lightning strikes burned themselves out. There seemed to be a workable balance between fire and forage.

Modern day government managers of public lands are beginning to recognize the importance of fire in their long term management of range and forest areas and they are trying to recreate the fire cycles of the past. This is difficult to accomplish. Part of the reason comes from the past and part of the reason comes from the present. Seventy–five to a hundred years of fire suppression policies, a large build up of fuel, and civilizations expanding into the wilderness have made it almost impossible to let a fire run free. Other factors making this difficult have to do with the present. After a range fire, management that allows or encourages range forage to rebuild to near its pre-fire volume before it is allowed to be grazed or used properly, perpetuates the burn-protect-burn fire cycle.

The rest rotation grazing system is a good forage management tool. I have helped set up and used many of these management programs but they too, under present management practices, have the potential to perpetuate the burn-protect-burn fire cycle. It seems to me we have reached a point where the tail (fire) is now wagging the dog and adjustments to help alleviate the negative unplanned side effects of modern range management should be considered.

A good way to start might be for the Bureau of Land Management and the Forest Service to consider input from the ranchers, farmers, and rural people that live, understand, respect and have feelings for the big ranges and forests of the west. This also applies to people living in other outback wilderness areas of America. I mentioned before, it seems to me the missing leg in modern public land management policies is the lack of implementing some of the input and knowledge the people, that live and derive their living from the land, possess. These people have learned how to coexist with nature from a practical standpoint. They know if you change nature's natural flow in one area it may cause unplanned or unwanted side effects in other management areas. In most cases people living on the land have learned to anticipate these changes and learned how to avoid them.

They learned long ago that you cannot starve a living out of a cow, sheep, horse or any other animal that grazes on private or public lands. They also learned long ago that you cannot starve a living out of the land their crops and livestock live on. They've learned the land can be used, maintained or improved all at the same time. They have seen first hand that the alternative to utilizing part of the yearly forage production by grazing it with livestock and turning that forage into food protein and other commodities for human consumption is a lot better than letting the forage build up and decay until it turns into fuel for an uncontrolled fire storm that consumes everything in its path.

I also observed it is possible to protect and love an area of land to death; and input from the people living in these areas should be considered when formulating range management policy on the public lands of which they are a part. The American public owns the public lands and the people who live and derive their living from the land are part of the American public.

One range fire that stands out in my memory from the long string of range fires I have encountered along my 115,000 mile horseback ride was caused by dry lightning. The fire started in the Shoshone Basin area of southeastern Idaho north of the Nevada-Idaho state line. The dry lightning storm started several fires that eventually burned together and moved south toward Nevada. It took two or three days before the fire worked its way into Nevada and the Salmon River Cattlemen's Association range. The fire crossed into Nevada at the old State Line homestead.

The State Line homestead consisted of a big spring and the log walls of the original cabin that were still standing. The roof caved in years ago and the only things remaining to show it had once been occupied were a rusty cook stove and bed springs still inside the cabin walls with several rusted out fifty gallon barrels located in the sagebrush outside. The unusual thing about the old cabin was its location. It straddled the Idaho-Nevada state line. The north half of the cabin was in Idaho and the south half of the cabin was in Nevada. When I asked Dale Messner, a long time association member, whose father was one of the founders of the Salmon River Cattlemen's Association in 1947, he told me the story his father told him. The old homesteader had a moonshine still and produced whiskey during Prohibition, which was his main source of livelihood. If Nevada lawmen came from the south, the old timer went into Idaho and the Nevada lawmen weren't inclined to follow him. If Idaho lawmen came from the north, he disappeared into Nevada with the same results. My guess is the lawmen were satisfied confiscating a little whiskey and let it go at that. This story has been handed down through the years and told as the truth. I can't testify to that but I can testify to the fact that during my seventeen years as manager of Salmon River's ranch holdings, the state line fence coming from the west ended against the center of the cabin's west log wall, and the fence line coming from the east ended against the center of the cabin's east log wall. It is true that the south half of the cabin is in Nevada and the north half of the cabin is in Idaho. You can come to your own conclusions, but knowing first hand the quirks and ingenuity of these old loner homesteaders, I'm going with Dale's story.

Getting back to the range fire I remember. The fire is now huge; it has crossed into Nevada and is burning on the Salmon River Cattlemen's range. The flames were seven miles from Gollaher Mountain, a twenty thousand acre pasture of deeded ground owned by the Cattlemen's Association.

The Bureau of Land Management fire camp headquarters are located on a flat along Cedar Creek and before the fire was out, it burned over seventy thousand acres. The fire camp contained two hundred fifty fire fighters, twelve or fifteen fire trucks, and several D7 or D8 bulldozers. They were supported by air tankers and helicopters dropping fire retardant and water from the air. In addition there was a state of the art communications trailer with computers instantly making maps of the fire's progress while processing information being sent in by observation planes. They also had a large kitchen trailer with supporting equipment, first aid facilities, several acres of tents, and an area for portable toilets. A large trailer equipped with hot water showers rounded out the facilities. All of this was supported by a fleet of trucks hauling fuel, food and other supplies to the camp. The magnitude of this fire and the methods of fighting it were a far cry from the range fires I helped fight as a young man using hand tools and wet gunny sacks.

Gollaher Mountain was Salmon River's main concern. The mountain is located directly in front of the approaching fire. Gollaher Mountain is surrounded by public land with the exception of isolated parcels of deeded ground around springs and stringer meadows, owned by Salmon River. The BLM owns and controls the surrounding area. Salmon River owns the grazing permits and the BLM regulates the use of the permits. Gollaher Mountain is excellent summer range. The winter snowdrift areas, quaky thickets, and mountain meadows produce an abundance of forage. The open ridges and steep draws are covered with Great Basin Wild Rye grass, growing stirrup high.

This was late July or early August and even the high country forage was drying and turning brown. About three weeks earlier the Salmon River cowboy crew, Association members and I finished gathering two thousand head of cows and calves from B.L.M. public land in lower elevation pasture and had driven them to the privately owned deeded range on Gollaher Mountain. We trailed them into the mountain pasture from all sides so the cows were well scattered. This was a timber box.

Two thousand cows and calves were scattered over the mountain and an out of control fire was seven miles to the north moving in our direction. I had Clarence, the Salmon River cow boss, and the Salmon

River crew already moving as many cows as possible to the south side of the mountain and I was begging the B.L.M. fire boss to put men and equipment on the north side of Gollaher Mountain.

This fire boss was a good guy and he understood my problem, but he obviously had orders from higher up. He told me the dry lightning storm had started six or seven fires in the area. His crews and equipment were stretched thin and at the present time his top priority was protecting private property further to the north. I argued that two thousand head of cows and calves and thirty miles of fence were private property. The fire boss told me by private property he meant "structures", so for the moment, Salmon River was on its own.

Clarence and the ranch crew were moving cows. I had already built two miles of fire line with the ranch bulldozer. Don Griswold from the Boies Ranch, thirty miles south of the fire, was on his way with his D7 bulldozer. Harold, my lifelong friend from our one room school days, was visiting and working with me.

I don't know why my friends come to visit. They are now involved in other endeavors and have been away from the cowboy life for sometime but they still bring their work clothes, boots, and saddles. We often work from daylight to dark and just for awhile we ride, joke and remember some of the experiences we had long ago. The amazing thing about these friends is they keep coming back.

Harold and I were on this fire for thirty-six hours straight and at times the flames were twenty feet high from canyon wall to canyon wall. Any wildlife, livestock or humans unlucky enough to be caught in this inferno had little or no chance of surviving. I didn't see it happen on this particular fire but on another fire, under similar circumstances, I saw several sage hens fly out of a burning canyon with their feathers on fire. They gained a little altitude, set their wings, and glided until they crash landed on a distant ridge thus starting a new fire.

At sun up the next morning Clarence had a fifteen man ranch crew, horseback, on top of Gollaher Mountain. If the fire burned into the Gollaher Mountain pasture and started up the steep northern draws and ridges, their job was to start moving cows down the south side of the mountain, opening gates and cutting wires in fence corners so cows reaching the southern mountain fence would have less chance of being trapped by the fire. Don Griswold arrived with his D7 bulldozer the afternoon before and that morning finished building a fire line along the north Gollaher Mountain fence. Harold and I were patrolling the fire break and, for the moment, the situation along the section of the fire we were working looked fairly calm. This situation however, didn't last long.

By midmorning the weather was scorching hot with a stiff wind, partially created by the fire itself, whipping the flames. Before the fire reached our fire line, spot fires began to start above the fire break well ahead of the main fire. Harold and I put out spot fires until it became obvious the situation was out of control and we retreated toward a high rocky ridge to the east. I told Harold the top of the ridge was bare and gravelly with very little forage to burn. My cell phone would work from the ridge top, and we could then drive the pickup east along the North Gollaher fence line until we were out of the immediate fire area.

We reached the top of the ridge. I called the B.L.M. fire camp and explained that spot fires just jumped our fire lines and the main fire was about to enter Gollaher Mountain. I was greeted with the same response I was given the day before. At this time the B.L.M. was only able to protect structures on private property.

Partly out of desperation and partly to inject a little humor into the serious situation, I called the insurance agent representing the Salmon River Cattlemen's insurance policy and told him I would like to extend insurance coverage to include two thousand head of cows and calves now grazing on Gollaher Mountain in case of injury or death by fire. Well, the humor part of my plan apparently worked. This fire happened several years ago and if the agent I contacted hasn't died from laugh exhaustion, he is probably still laughing. Needless to say, no coverage was offered.

Harold and I were not in any immediate danger but the fire had cut off our escape route to the east. I thought we could still work our way down through the fire to the west but I wasn't sure we could survive the smoke. A tremendous wall of black swirling smoke, jetting hundreds of feet into the sky was now about one hundred yards from us. It was decision time. We had to do something, and do it quickly.

The only escape route left was up that steep rocky ridge to the south and that was iffy. As we turned our attention to that possibility Harold said, "Look! That coyote is chasing those antelope!" Out of the black wall of smoke; four antelope with a coyote about fifteen feet behind them burst into view. Upon a second look it became obvious that this diverse group of animals was not paying any attention to each other. They had just one thought in mind; escaping the fire. They stood motionless for maybe half of a minute then plunged back into the swirling wall of smoke only to return in an instant with the coyote now part of the small group of antelope. For a while we all stood there, in that small area, two old cowboys, four antelope and one coyote, paying little attention to each other, all silhouetted against a raging inferno that was upon us. As Harold and I turned and started our four wheel drive up the steep rocky ridge I heard Harold say, "I hope they make it." And that was the last we saw of them.

We held our breath, as we slowly ground our way up the steep hill. We would almost spin out and stop before the tires would again gain traction and the pickup would jerk forward. After getting around a rock outcropping on a really sideling stretch of the ridge top, we began to breathe easier. When we came to a secondary ridge sloping steeply to the west, we were far enough above the fire to make a run for it so we turned down into the foothills and came out at the Vick Nelson spring. Here we met the end of a two-tracker road and started back toward the B.L.M. fire camp.

We were crossing a small wild rye grass basin just below the old Gollaher homestead. The homestead was established in the mid to late 1800s. Like the old Stateline homestead I described earlier, the quaky log walls of the Gollaher cabin were still somewhat in place but the dirt roof had long since caved in. I believe Gollaher Mountain got it's name from this old homesteader. It is said that Gollaher was a cranky, one-armed man, fiercely protective of his area. He was never seen without a shotgun at his side and at night he would harass the camps of pioneers and immigrants traveling through the flat country seven miles to the north. Presumably he did this to discourage these travelers from settling in his part of the world.

Anyway, while Harold and I were passing by the old homestead, a light came on in my head and the word "structures" jumped out at me. When we reached the next ridge, where my cell phone would work, I called the B.L.M. fire boss and asked him if he was aware of an old homestead structure on the north end of Gollaher Mountain situated directly in the fire's path. I explained that the old building did not amount to much but it did have some historical value. I guess that was the nudge the fire boss was waiting for. Within three hours, four fire trucks and two bulldozers were parked around those old buildings. During the afternoon and night, new fire lines were built along the north end of Gollaher Mountain and this part of the fire, coming south from Idaho, was contained. We fought the fire along eleven miles of Gollaher Mountain's east boundary for another day and a half. We worked in the foothills just below the mountain fence where the range had been grazed earlier in the season and there was less forage to burn so the fire was easier to control.

The backbone of the fire on Salmon River's range was broken when the remains of that old Gollaher homestead encouraged the fire boss to send crews to protect it with the side effect of stopping the rest of the fire before it entered Gollaher Mountain from the north. The fire never again gained the fire storm intensity it had when Harold and I were standing on that rocky point together with four antelope and one coyote. The fire only entered fringe areas of Gollaher Mountain and did little damage. Thus, with the help of the old abandoned homestead, a major catastrophe was averted.

After the fire was out and we were back at the ranch cookhouse, a cowboy said to Harold, 'Tell me again how much fun you are having on your vacation." Years before, the same question was asked of Don Martin, another friend from our school days, after a long day of gathering cows on Lone Mountain. Both men's answers were the same. They grinned, kept on eating and returned to the ranch again the following year.

LITTLE THINGS

Some years ago, after some laser surgery on my eye, I was still having problems. I went back to the very same professional, proper ophthalmologist that performed the original operation. He put on his magnifying glass, peered into my eye and blurted out, "Oh, shit!" This is the shortest diagnosis I've ever been given and the one I understood the best.

Merilyn on Star at nine months of age

MERILYN KANE SUSTACHA

Merilyn Sustacha was inducted into the Nevada Cattlemen's Association Cowboy 100,000 Mile Club in 2010.

The following presentation, written by Merilyn and presented by Bill McKnight, was given when Merilyn was inducted into the Club and is as follows:

My life began in Eureka, Nevada, where I was born to a rancher's son, Thomas Kane, from Clover Valley and a miner's daughter, Liberty Clifford, from Tonopah.

My great grandmother, Jane Laird, was matron of the Eureka County Hospital. In this modern day her title would be Director of Nursing.

After about ten days my parents brought me home to Lee, Nevada. My grandparents owned the Kane Ranches (now known as the 2U Ranch and the Woods Ranch, which Pete Paris owns at the present time.)

My family lived at the Woods Ranch. I am the oldest of four siblings. My brother, Bob, and sister, Patti, are now deceased. My brother, Bill, and his family live in Eagle Point, Oregon.

My first time on a horse was when I was nine months old. I have a picture to back it up. I was on a bay thoroughbred by the name of Star. It seems I've been riding a horse ever since.

Before I ever started school, my granddad would come and get me to help him move cattle from pasture to pasture on the ranch. At that time I rode a white horse named Cougar.

When I was small they didn't even know that kid's saddles existed. I rode an old time adult cowboy saddle with long stirrups, so I could get on easier. Boy, it was tough on your hide, especially the insides of your legs. You had to learn how to grip or fall off.

I attended the first four grades of school on the South Fork Indian Reservation. I learned to speak their native language and understood it well.

I rode a horse by the name of Jerry back and forth to school. After school some of the older kids would sometimes get under the Lee Bridge and spook my horse while I was crossing it. I really had some wild rides.

I rode a total of 6,808 miles in this time frame.

The Hilltop School was built across the road from the Woods Lane and I attended the fifth through seventh grade there, riding both ways horseback.

While I was still in school I would buckaroo from the Woods Ranch to Jiggs with no fences to bother me.

I would help hold the rodeer for the Jiggs ranchers, so they could work their cattle out and when my granddad worked his cattle I would hold the cattle he cut out of the herd.

I carried my school lunch in a gunny sack tied behind my cantle. One day I got a fancy new lunch pail for a gift. I was really proud of it. My Dad decided to fix a strap with a buckle to go around it and a ring to go over the saddle horn. That was a big mistake. Something spooked old Jerry, the thermos started to rattle and he didn't think that was too cool. Jerry started to run and buck and the lunch pail bounced and banged louder.

There was a ditch of water running along the side of the road and that's where I landed. Next came the lunch pail. There were a lot of dents in the fancy lunch box and that was the end of the thermos bottle.

Jerry ran home to the barn and I followed on foot. That was my first bronc ride at the age of seven.

We didn't have running water in the house. Mom had to heat some water on the wood cook stove so she could wash my hair to get the mud and gravel out of it. Then she gave me a bath and I put on clean clothes. I didn't have to go to school that day.

I rode 8,080 miles during this part of my life.

After the seventh grade my grandparents sold the ranches and my Dad took the job of manager for the Doheny Ranches in the northern most drainage of the North Fork area.

I went to Elko from the eighth grade through high school. I had to board out and I lived with a wonderful family. There weren't any school buses at that time. I went home every Friday evening and I hated living in town.

On weekends and summers I would buckaroo for my Dad, (Doheny Ranches), the Bing Crosby Ranch, (PX Ranch), J&H Livestock (Haystack Ranch) and Tom Tanner (Saval Ranch).

I was the oldest. All of the neighbors helped each other and because I was the oldest in our family I became cheap help.

The only ride I hated was when Jim McDermott, cattle foreman for the PX, would send me to the Truitt ranch. The sagebrush was as high as a person on horseback and it seemed to me there were rattlesnakes by the hundreds. The snakes liked to sun themselves on the tops of the sagebrush, sometimes when I got to this area it was almost dark and every time a cricket would make a noise especially at night, it would scare me to death and I would make my horse go faster.

As a child I remember taking turns pulling snow sleds with our horses as a form of recreation.

In 1953 I showed a stock horse in a youth class at the Cow Palace in San Francisco and won a silver buckle. In high school I rode in rodeos. At the first annual High School Rodeo held in Reno, Nevada also in 1953, I won the horse cutting event. In 1955 during the National High School Rodeo also held in Reno, I roped my calf in 4.6 seconds, a record time. That record wasn't broken for nearly forty years. (When Dave asked Merilyn, "How did you do that?" Merilyn replied, "I had a good horse.")

I rode a total of 27,580 miles during this part of my life.

In 1956-57-58 at the Elko County Fair in Elko, Nevada, I won the Women's Stock Horse Class three times in a row and retired the trophy sponsored by Paul Sawyer, which I still have.

On January 7, 1957, I married the love of my life, the late Jess Sustacha, Sr. For the next fifty-four years I've lived in the Lamoille Valley. Jess and I rode together for fifty years. The last year or so he rode on a four wheeler that he called his Japanese cow horse, but I still continued to ride my horse beside him.

In 1966 the Sustacha Cattle Company was divided.

We run commercial cows and a registered Hereford herd. Our headquarters is one mile east of the town of Lamoille, Nevada, and that is where I reside, on the old E. B. Lytton (Carden) Ranch. Most of the cattle winter here. Our lower ranch (Rossi or Cruzi) is nine miles north of the main ranch.

In the spring we move our cattle to the lower ranch to get away from mountain snow storms to calve. We brand there and then proceed to the summer range (Elko Mountain) which runs to the Humbolt River.

During the summer there is always something wrong on our range: a gate is left open, steers scatter and have to be gathered and put back in their field, someone runs through the fence at the heifer field and cows and calves get mixed up with the heifers. We constantly have to monitor the cows and calves to be sure they are safe and where they should be.

In the fall we gather, sort, vaccinate and eventually the cattle are brought back to the ranch headquarters for the winter. This completes the yearly fifty mile circle.

I thought I was in heaven when we bought our first Banett horse trailer. It sure made a difference and was much better than the stock truck.

At the stage of my life I am now in, I've graduated and lucked out. I get to take the pickup and trailer to get the rest of the crew at the end of the trail drives. If we are short handed I ride a horse and we all have to ride back to the ranch.

I also help our great friends Bill McKnight and George Donovan process and wean their calves.

In this fifty year time frame I rode 72,949 miles.

I take great pride in the horses I ride. I like a good cow horse and a well groomed one. My brother, Bill, is the same way. We learned this trait from our Dad.

A rancher's wife is an important part of a ranching operation. You have to be a wife, mother, grandmother, cook and a full time hired hand.

I have a wonderful and caring family: daughter, Tammi, son, Jess Jr., his wife, Shannon, and the grandchildren. They take good care of me. The rest of my special extended family includes my nephews, Todd and Tyler and their families, my niece and her husband, Paula and Jeremy, as well as many other wonderful friends. Jess and I raised Tyler and Todd and they grew up in Lamoille with Tammi and Jess Jr.

I belong to the Nevada Cattlemen's Association and I don't have time for any other organizations.

I have ridden approximately 115,417 miles in my lifetime. I can still buckaroo with the best and get the job done.

Dave's comments: "Merilyn is a neat lady. She has lived a colorful life and her life experiences have made her self-sufficient in many ways. She has been an inspiration and teacher to many young 4-Hers. Merilyn only has one gear and it is stuck in fast forward. She knows which side of the hotcake the butter is on and at times doesn't hesitate to explain it."

LITTLE THINGS

An old saying, "A man works from sun to sun but a woman's work is never done.

THE LYNX

Some time during the spring Al, a government trapper, caught a lynx and brought it back to the ranch alive. I don't know how he did that because he was horseback. The first time I saw the cat he was in a gunny sack lying in front of the bunkhouse. If anything got within twenty feet of the sack the lynx hissed, snarled and growled. He had the disposition of a rattlesnake.

We were just kids and we had a hound and cow dogs so we thought we would keep the cat around for awhile. We planned to use him to train our dogs to track and tree varmints, but by the time we got a dog collar on that cat, we weren't sure it was going to be worth the effort.

The east side of the horse barn was lined with work horse box stalls that weren't being used anymore so we snapped a long dog chain to the cat's collar and put him in one of the stalls. The long chain gave the lynx room to move around and the deep manger, with some hay in the bottom, gave him a good place to hide. It took all three of us hunting rabbits and ground squirrels in our spare time to keep that cat fed. As the summer slipped by, the cat's disposition didn't improve but he got fat and shiny while we wore ourselves out hunting rabbits and squirrels to feed him.

We attached a ring to a six foot long pole and threaded the chain connected to the lynx's collar through the ring. This kept the cat from attacking us while we led him a quarter of a mile back into the mountains and let him climb a tree. We would then go back to the ranch, turn our dogs loose and they would work out the track and bark treed when they found the lynx. The dogs really got good and looked forward to doing this.

When winter approached and the ground squirrels hibernated, we decided to turn the lynx loose and let the dogs tree him for the last time. One evening we took the lynx a short distance into the hills and turned him loose. This gave him a head start while we went back and started the dogs on the cat's track. The dogs were as excited as ever. The hound let out his first trailing bawl and the cow dogs followed with their high pitched yips.

They were following the hot lynx track. When the dogs reached the spot where we turned the lynx loose, their excited barking turned to confusion. From this point forward our dogs could not follow the cat's scent and the lynx got away.

We were dumbfounded. A number of times during the summer our young dogs followed the lynx's scent and barked treed when they found him. We told an old timer what had happened and he said, "Boys, it looks to me like your dogs were following your scent instead of tracking the lynx, because they learned there would be a lynx treed where your scent ended." Maybe the old timer was right because when our tracks were no longer beside the lynx tracks our young dogs could no longer follow the trail.

When I look back at the enthusiasm and effort we put into this project I have to shake my head and grin, but I really have to laugh when I think about the story that lynx must have told when he got back into the mountains with his old buddies.

LITTLE THINGS

I've noticed when things are going bad and the whole world seems to be tumbling down around you, things usually aren't as bad as you think. When things are going well and you don't have a care in the world, things usually aren't as good as you think.

A PANTHER HUNT

The Eden Valley ranch headquarters was thirty miles from Willits, California, and the trip over the rough crooked road took about two hours. Marion and I had gone to a Saturday night movie and were on our way home about midnight. The headlights on the Jeep that Don and I drove to Alaska and back made a narrow tunnel of light piercing the pitch black night.

About a mile east of Box Springs and coming from the left, a panther appeared out of the dark. The big cat was in midair and landed in the middle of the road in front of us before he leaped back into the darkness to our right. Gravel and dirt he kicked up rattled against the windshield. Then the cat was gone. Old Timers often said, "If you thought you saw a panther or mountain lion and didn't see the long tail, you hadn't seen a panther or mountain lion." This cat's long tail swished in the air like a bull whip.

Before the big cat leaped in front of us, I was getting sleepy as I drove, but the rest of the way to the ranch I was wide awake. Once home, I let two hounds and one cow dog loose so they could run around while I put my rifle, kerosene lantern and a flashlight in the Jeep. Then I loaded the dogs and started back up the road. When I reached the spot where we had seen the big cat I stopped.

Outside of the headlight beams it was so dark I couldn't see my hand in front of my face. Jenny, my lead hound, picked up the cat's scent and let out that first long drawn out bawl. I was careful to make sure she was tracking in the right direction before I let Pat, my cow dog and the other hound loose. They both chimed in and disappeared in the darkness. I lit the kerosene lantern, put the flashlight in my pocket, picked up my rifle and turned out the headlights. I was suddenly surrounded by a small circle of dim yellow flickering light about twelve feet in diameter.

For the first half hour the hounds made slow but steady progress. Their trailing bawls were frequent but still drawn out and once in awhile I could hear Pat's sharp yelp. The mountainside was getting steeper. I was crossing jagged gullies, working my way around large rock out croppings and carefully walking over slick shale. The timber was thinning and patches of oak brush were taking over. I knew the general area but because I was traveling within a small circle of dim light, I didn't know exactly where I was. Obviously I was in a section of the mountain that could not be traveled by horseback. I was picking my way through a shale rock slide when I slipped and took a hard fall. The lantern slammed into the rocks, the glass mantle shattered, the light went out, and I was lying on jagged rocks in the dark. My rifle wasn't damaged, the flashlight still worked and I could get up. The lantern was a total loss so I left it and continued following the hounds that were moving faster. I was glad to hear that because my flashlight was getting dimmer. I realized it needed new batteries.

Now the hounds' trailing bawls were shorter and more often and Pat's sharp yapping was constant. Suddenly their voices changed to a frenzy. Hounds were bawling, Pat was barking and they were running flat out. They'd jumped the big cat! Before long the dogs were barking "treed" and I tried to move faster.

When I finally reached the treed cat, the beam from my flashlight was only penetrating into the darkness a few feet. I could not see the panther but from the dogs' reactions I knew he'd jumped out of the tree. I was standing in a patch of short oak brush. The dogs went right by me and when they reached what I guessed was the top end of the oak brush thicket, they turned and were coming back directly toward me. I knew that cat was only one jump ahead of the dogs and the dogs passed within ten feet of me, but I couldn't see a thing in the darkness. Apparently the cat was reluctant to leave the oak brush thicket, because the dogs came by me two more times before the panther treed again. I was relieved. I'd had enough of the big cat, I couldn't see in the dark. That cat was passing so close to me I could nearly reach out and touch him. I went to the tree and when I pointed my flashlight up into it I could barely make out the dim outline of the panther. He was stretched out on a low limb of the Madrone tree. I held the dim flashlight along the rifle barrel so I could see the sights and when I had them centered on the cat's shadowy outline, I fired.

The panther came down and the cat and dogs disappeared in the dark. I followed cautiously and found the big cat dead in the bottom of the draw.

I drug the panther back up to a small flat spot around the Madrone tree, sat down with my back up against the tree trunk and thought about what to do next. My dogs came up to me with smiley faces and wagging tails and I assured them they had done a good job.

I didn't want to worry anyone by not showing up at the ranch in the morning and I knew I could not pack the cat out of this rough country in the dark. I doubted I could find this spot again if I left it, so I decided to skin the cat and pack out the hide.

This was a monumental task with the limited amount of light left in my flashlight. I finally finished the chore, draped the panther hide around the back of my neck and started working my way down the mountain. This was a mistake. I didn't get very far until the shale rock under my feet began to move. Before I knew what was happening I was flat on my back sliding feet first down the mountainside. I had triggered a rock slide! As luck would have it my legs straddled a scrubby little fir tree and I came to an abrupt stop while rocks slid by me on both sides. After things settled down I realized if I didn't start using more common sense I was going to kill my darn fool self, so I didn't try to get up. It was still dark. The panther skin was still draped around the back of my neck making a pillow and my dogs came over and lay down against me. We dozed until the first signs of daybreak showed up and I could begin to see around me. I was lodged just above a small rock bluff. I wouldn't have killed myself if I had gone over the bluff but during the night it would have felt like I was falling over Niagara Falls.

With daylight breaking, I could tell I was high up on the west side of Mt. San Headron just southwest of Impassible Rock. With enough light to see ahead, I had no trouble getting back to the Jeep. I reached the ranch in time to eat breakfast and do a day's work. This was another memorable night.

LITTLE THINGS

I was riding home from a long day in the mountains. It was late afternoon and I was about four miles from home when my dogs, which had been ranging ahead, broke into a wild barking frenzy. When I reached the small opening in the timber I saw an unexpected sight. A dead fir snag about three feet through stood in the center of a clearing. The trunk of the tree was broken off about twenty-five feet from the ground. A brownish gold colored yearling bear cub was at the top of the snag and a black yearling cub was right behind. Just below the cubs a full grown brown bear was urging the cubs to climb higher. At the bottom of the snag a big black bear stood on his hind legs reaching up with his front paws. There wasn't enough room left on the snag for him to climb up. This colorful totem pole of bears was sight to see.

JESS SUSTACHA

Jess Sustacha was inducted into the Nevada Cattlemen's Association Cowboy 100,000 Mile club in November 1991.

Jess's presentation was written by his wife, Merilyn. It was presented by their nephew, Tyler Seal.

Jess Sustacha is the son of Joe and Fransisca Sustacha and he was born in the small ranching community of Elko, Nevada. Jess has spent his entire life in the Lamoille Valley. He started attending the Lamoille School when he entered the first grade. Jess said, "The only language spoken in my home was Basque and at the time I couldn't speak English. Edna Patterson was my teacher and she was a fine person but one day I got upset and kicked her in the shins. She made me stay after school for punishment. After that, every function I attended where she was present she would laugh and mention this incident. The older I got the more she enjoyed telling the tale."

Both of Jess's parents came from Spain and had to learn to speak English and do things the American way, which they were glad to do. Jess's father was a prominent cattle rancher, as well as a sheep man. Jess took a great interest in the livestock industry. At an early age Jess took on enormous responsibility at the family ranch. The daily responsibilities that were asked of Jess involved making sure the cattle were well fed and prepared for what Mother Nature had to offer. This meant moving the herds to fields where there was plenty of shelter or maybe moving them to feed that was just a little better. Most of this work was done on Jess's first horse, Tommy. Jess said, "Tommy wasn't much to look at, but come rain, sleet or snow Tommy always started."

Jess remembers his first bronc ride at the age of six. He was riding an old white horse, called Spud. He was sent to a neighbor to get the family's Christmas turkey. Mr. Westlund put the big gobbler in a gunny sack, made two slits in the top of the sack, hung it over Jess's saddle horn and secured it with a saddle string. Jess said, "The trip went pretty smoothly until the turkey started to gobble and jump around in the sack, spurring Old Spud in the shoulder with his turkey spurs. The old horse started bucking. Jess said, "I rode Spud for several jumps with the sack full of turkey swinging out to the side before I got bucked off and Spud ran home." When Spud arrived at the ranch with only the turkey riding him, Jess's mom became worried and started back up the road. She met Jess, unhurt, walking home. ("I imagine the only thing really hurt was Jess's pride." Dave remarked.)

Jess recalls the many trips that had to be made horseback. Some of the most memorable trips were made in the fall when shipping time arrived. The cattle had to be driven from Lamoille to Halleck which is about thirty miles one way. Not only was it a long way, but the cattle had to be there before noon to meet the railroad switch engine or the cowboys had to move the railroad cars by hand using railroad tie tamping bars to pry the cars back and forth. This cattle drive took Jess from Lamoille to Halleck four times per year.

During this period of Jess's life he documented riding horseback 66,181 miles. (Dave's comment, "The 181 miles is there because Jess's wife, Merilyn, used a G.P.S. to document miles ridden. As far as I know this is a first when calculating distances ridden by Cowboy 100,000 Mile Club members.")

Another trip Jess remembers they made was from Lamoille to the Hay Stack Ranch. This drive was about sixty miles one way. He remembers how they would have to stop at the Dinner Station Ranch to water their cattle at a cost of two bits (25 cents) a head. This trip took place three to four times a year for many years. On most of the cattle drives Jess would spend from ten to fifteen days away from home. When asked about this, Jess simply said, "It was a way of life."

Jess remembers that the range had no fences so cattle wandered for miles and miles. The range that the Sustachas ran their cattle on went from Elko Mountain to the Hunter Banks Ranch, now known as Maggie Creek Ranch, and back to the Lee Indian Reservation. It wasn't uncommon for Jess to ride forty to fifty miles one way when gathering the family's cattle. Jess recalls one certain cow that had been missing for some time. One day he received a call and was asked to pick up his cow in Golconda, Nevada, a distance of about one hundred miles from the home ranch.

After they arrived at the Hay Stack Ranch they had to drive the cattle to the range and care for them during the spring and summer. In the fall the cattle were gathered and driven back to Lamoille. This routine was followed for many years. For many more years Jess and his brother, Joe, rode colts to Pleasant Valley to feed the family cattle. By the time spring came the colts were broke horses.

On other winters cattle were driven to Lee, Nevada, on the South Fork Indian Reservation where hay had been purchased. On one particular hard winter, over three feet of snow fell in twenty-four hours. The cows were out of hay and had to be trailed home. In those days bulldozers were not available. The snow had drifted and it was nearly impossible to drive cows through it. Jess and Joe gathered a small herd of saddle horses and drove them to Lee, breaking a trail through the snow. The next morning the horses were turned loose and they started for home along the same trail they traveled the previous day with the cows following them. This was a twenty mile drive and they all reached the home ranch by dark. These were long cold rides. During this period, Jess documented riding 83,796 miles horseback.

Jess and his family are active in the American Hereford Association. Jess's father started the registered Hereford cattle herd and Jess carried on the tradition for a combined time span of over one hundred years. One of Jess's outstanding accomplishments was having the Grand Champion steer at the Cow Palace show in San Francisco in 1931. Jess has been a lifetime member of the American Hereford Association, and a long time member of the Nevada Cattlemen's and the National Cattlemen's Associations. He was awarded a Gold Medallion as a Hereford breeder for fifty years in the state of Nevada.

Jess said, "My favorite breed of horse is the Quarter horse, especially the Peppy San breeding." His favorite horse was named Peppy, a nine year old sorrel with a white stripe down his forehead. "He is the best horse I have ever ridden, an excellent cow horse. All I have to do is spur and hang on. I really treat him well and he takes good care of me."

When asked about his favorite cow dog he didn't hesitate to answer, "Bozo, A blue heeler. He was a one person dog and would ride with me in the front seat of my pickup. When we went to town I would buy him a vanilla ice cream cone and he enjoyed that. When we were riding the range, he would catch a cottontail rabbit and put his paw on it and hold the rabbit down until we went by with the cattle, then he would turn the rabbit loose. Bozo was a great dog. He never let a stranger in the pickup. When we were working cattle and he was in the way I'd tell him to stay by the gate and he would stay by that gate forever. Sometimes I would forget him and have to go back with the pickup and get him. He'd still be there lying by the gate where I left him."

Jess, his wife, Merilyn, son Jess Jr., and occasionally daughter Tammi, and their four grandchildren still operate the family ranch in Lamoille, where the cattle work is still done on the back of a horse. Jess still averages five miles a day on one of his good ranch raised horses. There's one thing we can promise, when you come to the Jess Sustacha Ranch, you'll see good cattle and good horses.

Very seldom is there a day that goes by that you don't see Jess going to the corral with a bucket of oats in one hand and a halter in the other. From 1966 when the Sustacha property was divided until the time Jess was inducted into the Nevada Cattlemen's Association Cowboy 100,000 Mile Club, he added another 42,189 miles to his lifetime horseback ride for a grand total of 192,166 miles ridden. As you can see, most of Jess's time was not spent pulling a gooseneck trailer. It was spent sitting in a saddle built with a Weatherly tree in the sagebrush and dust driving a herd of cows.

When Jess was asked what he would like to pass on to the younger generation he said, "Work hard and treat everyone like you want to be treated. If you do that you will be successful."

Dave's comments: "Many years later when I was managing Lee Livestock Company a heavy snow storm came along the foothills of the Ruby Mountains. In the following days the temperature hovered around 25 to 30 degrees below zero. I rode out into the same country Jess and Joe crossed while trailing their cattle home during the hard winter years before. I intended to gather fifteen or twenty head of horses that were wintering out on the range and bring them to the meadows where they could be fed hay. About halfway to where I thought the horses would be, I came to a cattle guard. I got off and opened the wire gate that was beside it and carefully laid the gate back along the fence. After breaking a good trail through the snow where the gate was open, I remounted my horse. In due time, I found the horses and started them home on a long trot. They were following the tracks I made in the snow earlier in the day. When we reached the cattle guard all of the horses went through the open gate except one two year old work horse colt. In his excitement to catch up with the other horses he tried to cross the snow covered cattle guard. His big feet somehow slipped through the rails and try as I might I couldn't get him free. In the situation I was in I couldn't do any more for the horse so I rode on to the ranch and returned with my rifle intending to put the horse out of his misery. When I reached the cattle guard the horse was dead. He'd already frozen to death. That was a long, cold four-mile ride back to the ranch. I had worked up a sweat trying to get the horse out of the cattle guard, and when I got home, parts of my long johns were frozen stiff. This is just a small reminder of what the weather was like and the conditions encountered when Jess and Joe made that forty mile ride getting their cattle home."

LITTLE THINGS

Many ranches furnish cowboys with families room, utilities and beef. There is nothing like the wrath of a ranch wife that has gotten the front shoulder of the beef two times in a row.

LITTLE THINGS

This is an example of Murphy's Law in reverse. I purchased two loads of calves and the shipping date was set. I ordered two trucks to haul the calves on the given day. Soon after the cow buyer called and said he needed to set the shipping date back a few days. I said, "Fine. I will call the trucking company and cancel the trucks." About 10:00 o'-clock on the original shipping date I suddenly remembered I had forgotten to call the trucking company. In my mind's eye I could see the shipping corrals with the first truck pulled up to the loading chute with no calves and no cowboys around. Thinking I was going to have to pay for two empty trucks, I called the trucking company and was explaining that the shipping date had been changed and I had forgotten to notify them. When I got finished explaining he said, "What calves?" It turned out I'd forgotten to cancel the trucks and the trucking company had forgotten to send them. I wonder what the odds of that happening are?

RATTLESNAKES

Rattlesnake stories are somewhat like fish stories because they become bigger and more exciting with each telling. They are based on facts but enhanced by the teller's enthusiasm and the listener's imagination which puts them both in the actual situation so colorfully being described.

When I was growing up I heard snake stories about the first cars which were open underneath. Imagine running over a rattlesnake and having the snake thrown into the car by the spinning wheels. Imagine getting into one of those old cars and, while sitting down, you hear a rattlesnake that is coiled up in the open springs of the car seat just inches below the leather seat cover you are sitting on. Think about the rattlesnake that crawled into or coiled upon your sleeping bag to share your body's warmth.

One snake story I know is true, because I know the people involved, happened shortly after they were married. The man, after an evening of telling rattlesnake stories with neighbors, thinking he would play a joke on his new wife, put a piece of garden hose under the covers at the foot of their bed. Imagine that night when the wife got into bed and ran her feet down on that cold piece of garden hose coiled up at her feet. My common sense tells me he slept in the woodshed for the next six months. No, they didn't get a divorce.

At an early age I became acquainted with rattlesnakes and developed a healthy respect and a dislike for them. During my 115,000 mile horseback ride I have seen many rattlesnakes and I have never met one that I liked and very few that I met have lived to tell the tale. I know in this day and age it is not politically correct to kill a snake and I know people that think rattlesnakes are little cuddly serpents. But for the most part these people did not grow up and live with these creatures on a daily basis. In my experience the cute little snake with the bell on his tail you see in children's books and on Saturday morning T.V. shows bears no resemblance to the real life rattlesnakes I grew up and lived with during my long horseback ride.

The rattlesnakes I have been acquainted with are the most aggressive, ill-tempered creatures I ever met. They show up in the most surprising places imaginable. I have made that impossible ten foot step when looking down in midstride and seeing a rattlesnake stretched across the trail. I have reached for a stick of wood in the box beside a stove in a line camp and nearly touched the rattlesnake silently coiled up there. In both cases I was within inches of those snakes and they had the ability to kill me. That is what sends that shivery chill up my spine.

The first encounter I had with a rattlesnake occurred when I was two or three years old. We were living on the homestead and Dad was in the cabin meeting with several men from the area discussing some project he was working on. I only actually remember two things about the incident. The rest of my memories are from hearing stories retold. I had been playing outside and I came in, tugged on my dad's pant leg and said, "There is a big lizard outside." Dad, being intent on the conversation didn't pay much attention to me until one of the men said, "John, he seems to be pretty serious about this, maybe you should go take a look."

I took my dad's hand and led him around to the south end of the cabin where, along the fireplace foundation, a four foot timber rattler was stretched out. The tracks in the soft dirt showed I had been down on my hands and knees less than a foot from the snake apparently fascinated by the diamond like markings on his back. Well, of course, with all the excitement that followed, the snake coiled to strike and it was killed.

The first mystery of this encounter was why I had not been struck in the face when I was down on my hands and knees less than a foot from the snake. The second mystery was why, out of fascination, I had not reached out and touched the snake causing it to strike my arm. As I said, I remember two things from this encounter that I think are my memories of the actual event: the shiny greenish gray colors of the design on the snake's back and the cut off head of the snake with its mouth open, showing those long fangs that dripped venom when pushed up with a stick. All the time this demonstration was going on, my dad was trying to explain the dangers of getting too close to rattlesnakes.

The next memorable experience with a rattlesnake took place when I was about four thousand miles into my 115,000 mile horseback ride. I wasn't present at the actual event but the aftermath involved our whole family. It was a late spring day and Dad was repairing a drift fence about twelve miles from the Circle W Ranch buildings. He rode horseback and reached the fence about mid-morning, hobbled his horse and started to repair a section of the fence that had been heavily damaged by last winter's snow. He was walking from fence post to fence post splicing wire and replacing lost staples when he stepped on a silent rattlesnake. The snake was stretched out and blended in with the surroundings and didn't rattle until he was stepped on. Dad's foot came down about ten inches from the snake's tail. Quicker than lightning the snake swung around and struck, biting Dad with just one fang on his right leg just above the top of his boot. Dad leaped backward but the snake's fangs hung up in the denim of Dad's Levis and the writhing snake became airborne as Dad fell backwards. When he hit the ground, the snake came loose and struck again but this time Dad was out of reach. He killed the snake after this heart stopping experience, went back to his horse, sat down in the shade and tried to calm down so he could review the situation he was in. He was faced with a twelve mile horseback ride back to the ranch and another ten mile trip by car to get to Dr. Babcock for medical care.

In those days the best advice available for a snake bite was as follows: Stay calm! Take your knife and cut an x where each fang punctured the flesh causing the wound to bleed. If you could reach the area that was bitten and you didn't have a sore in your mouth you should try to suck the blood and venom out of the wound (presumably spitting the poison out instead of swallowing it.) I have seen those snake bite kits with a razor blade and a rubber suction cup inside, but in those days no one had one of these kits when they were needed and probably wouldn't have used it if they had. The last instruction in these snake bite kits said if you're bitten on the arm or leg place a tourniquet between the bite and your heart and seek medical help as soon as possible.

Now Dad was a common sense kind of guy so he sat there in the shade trying to figure out what his options were. I never knew Dad to leave the house without his pocket knife but this day that is exactly what had happened. So the first option was out. Instead he took a fence staple and scratched through the skin trying to make the wound bleed. This effort was met with only limited success. He couldn't reach the wound to try and suck some of the venom out so he took a chew of tobacco and slapped it on the wound thinking it might work like a poultice thus sucking out part of the poison. He tied that chew securely to the wound with his bandana. In today's sterile world, the treatment would have been worse than the snake bite. He mounted his horse and started home. When he reached the ranch he found there was no one there so he traded his horse for a car and continued toward town. About half way he met Paul, our school teacher, returning home. Paul said Dad was weaving all over the road and acting strange. When Paul found out what had happened, he insisted Dad leave his car and Paul drove him back to town where whatever Dr. Babcock did worked. Later that night Dad came driving himself home. I remember Mom changing the bandage on that snake bite all through the summer and into the fall before the black runny wound completely healed. If that snake had connected with both fangs Dad might not have survived this incident and a lot of things along my 115,000 mile horseback ride might have been different.

Along my ride I have only seen a few dogs, horses, and cows actually being bitten by rattlesnakes. But I have seen a number of these animals suffering from the effects of previous snake bites. Most cows do not die outright but never fully recover, remaining thin with a lump on the side of their head for the rest of their lives.

I have never been bitten by a rattlesnake in my entire life but I have had my share of heart stopping close calls. One close call that is memorable happened on a cold frosty morning in mid-fall. It was still hot during the day and the snakes had not hibernated for the winter. Roland, the ranch foreman, and I were gathering yearling heifers in the salt creek pasture about six miles north of the ranch headquarters. The first rays of the morning sun were just touching the mountain tops when we jumped the first bunch of yearlings. The heifers threw up their tails and took off down the hill. I was running flat out trying to head them off. The sorrel colt I was riding cut in close to a big flat topped rock that stood about waist high when I was horseback. As I passed the rock I saw a flash of motion and looking down, I saw a four foot long rattlesnake striking. The events that followed only took a split second but it seemed like a long time. The snake was so cold and stiff from the frosty night that he struck in slow motion. He was in the air coming toward me but it seemed like he was suspended there. My leg went by the striking snake but the colt's back leg that was stretched out behind him was just starting to come forward. The snake was still coming; he missed the colt's hind quarters by an inch and went under the horse's tail crashing to the ground. I was too busy to look back but I did head the heifers and we got them under control.

Then my imagination started running wild. What if it had been a few hours later in the day and the snake's reflexes had been back to normal? What if the snake had landed across the fork of my saddle? What if the snake's fangs had gotten caught up in the colt's out stretched tail? These after thoughts were worse than the actual event and this near miss could have turned into the wreck of the century! All of these thoughts are within the realm of possibility and occasionally do happen. That's what makes me wary when living with rattlesnakes on an every day basis.

LITTLE THINGS

One cure for chapped lips is to put chicken manure on them. It may not do much for the chapped lips but it will sure keep you from licking them.

TOM MARVEL

Tom Marvel was inducted into the Nevada Cattlemen's Association Cowboy 100,000 Mile Club in November 1996.

Dave's comment: "I sold registered horned Hereford range ready bulls to the 25 Ranch in the early 1960's. Tom purchased the bulls and when I delivered them to the 25 Ranch headquarters Tom's mother, Louise Marvel, took care of the paperwork necessary for the transaction. She managed and kept the W.T. Jenkins Ranching units, one of the largest cattle operations in the west, together and operating for many years. Louise was something of a legend in her own time. I found her to be a gracious, fair minded lady and when you left her living room and entering her office, it was all business from then on. Tom was superintendent of the cattle operation from 1946 to 1964. Tom inherited many of his mother's traits."

Some excerpts from: Tom Marvel: Always A Cowboy written by Mary Branscomb shows the compassion the 25 Ranch had for its employees and neighbors, as well as the true grit Tom Marvel possesses. The excerpt is as follows:

Cap and Louise Marvel had three sons-Dick, Tom and John and the family thrived on hard work and respect for the land, livestock and fellow human beings. The Great Depression hit hard in Nevada in the 1930s, but the Marvels pulled their outfit through while many others went under; partly because their key employees were so loyal they stayed on even when the ranch could not pay them. It could, however, provide them and many needy townspeople with beef and potatoes.

It was Dick's job, as the oldest son, to deliver food each week to those in Battle Mountain who needed it. He'd leave the grocery sacks on porches, never letting on where they came from.

Tom has ridden most every day of his life except for the years he spent in the United States Army during World War II, and the months, decades later, when one of his legs, broken in five pieces, was cast to the hip. When Tom was in the hospital with the newly shattered leg, the story goes that the doctor told him he needed to amputate the leg. It was broken that badly.

The news obviously disturbed Tom, who looked at the doctor and said, "Bring me a gun."

Fearing Tom might be despondent and ready to give up on life, the doctor launched into a soothing talk about all the things a one-legged cowboy could do. He said there was a psychologist on staff to help Tom adjust, and it was certainly better to live than to die.

Tom listened for awhile, and then said, "The gun isn't for me. It's for you if you take off my leg."

There was no amputation. The leg is still with Tom, a bit shorter than the other, but it works and he rides. There have been other broken bones since, and a lost thumb, but for the most part, Tom has saddled up every morning for as long as he or anyone else can remember. He rides the big country, a heritage passed down through generations.

Harvey Barnes, Tom's son-in-law, presented this documentation of miles ridden:

The Cowboy 100,000 Mile Club award is given by the Nevada Cattlemen's Association to recognize those who have basically spent their lives riding horseback. The earth's circumference at the equator is almost 25,000 miles. That means to qualify for this award, the recipient would have to have ridden the equivalent of around the world four times. This recipient has ridden 279,000 miles on the back of a horse. This is conservative because that is the way this guy is.

Tom Marvel was born in Battle Mountain, Nevada, June 7, 1924. His parents were Ernest and Louise Marvel who owned and operated the W. T. Jenkins Company with headquarters in Battle Mountain. Tom started riding when he was a young kid but those miles don't count Tom said because he wasn't working.

During school vacation from May 15 to September 15 in the years from 1934 to 1937, Tom stayed with his parents and brothers at Gold Creek in northern Elko County. It was a seventy-five mile trip to get there. The company did not use pickups. Everything was done with pack trains. Tom explains that during those school vacations his time was spent packing supplies to the sheep camps. During this time, the company ran about 50,000 sheep and some camps were from five to twenty miles from Gold Creek. "The closer camps we did in one day ,"Tom said, "but the further ones we packed in supplies, stayed overnight then rode back out and got packs ready for the next day." For four years that is how he spent his summers. He helped gather the steers at the end of the summer and trailed them forty miles to Carlin. This part of Tom's youth added up to a little over 7,000 miles ridden.

Clarence Jones from Carlin tells that Tom was not much of a school person. The fall of 1937 Tom's father, better known as Cap Marvel, came to get Tom and take him back to school. Clarence remarked, "I bet that kid will be back here in a week." Sure enough, in about a week Tom came riding back into their camp leading a pack horse. Clarence says, "For a couple of years it seemed all that Cap did was track Tom down and try to get him to go back to school. No luck."

At the age of fourteen he started repping full time for the 25 Ranch and the William Moffitt Company. Long circles were the norm; they rode over twenty miles a day. In 1941 help was scarce because of the war and Tom began running the cattle for the Jenkins Company on the 25 Ranch, part of their operation at this time. The W. T. Jenkins Company ranches ran about 50,000 head of sheep, 3,000 to 4,000 head of cattle and around 400 head of saddle horses on about one million acres of land. He did so until 1944 when he enlisted in the Army to serve his country. During this period of time 42,000 miles were added to his lifelong horseback ride. "Everywhere we went we rode horseback." Tom said.

Tom did something else of note in 1944. He married Rosita Petit December 28 of that year, while he was on Army furlough from Texas. Leah Swackhamer, a Marvel family friend, brought Rosita to Battle Mountain and that is how they met.

Tom got out of the Army in 1946 and from that time until 1964, Tom was cattle superintendent for the Jenkins Company. In those eighteen years, Tom rode another 130,000 miles horseback. The 25 Ranch itself was twenty-five miles long. Trailing the cavy of horses from Izzenhood Ranch to Stampede was a forty-five mile drive. Winter range in

Jersey Valley was sixty miles from the 25 Ranch. Those were long trails done every year, big, big areas. Every spring, for a month, they gathered the company horses. At that time, they had about three hundred saddle horses and around that many work horses.

In 1964 the W. T. Jenkins Company was sold and Tom and Rosita acquired the Martin Ranch which had been part of the original company.

It was a smaller operation, but still one of the larger outfits in the state with permits ranging over a big country. Rides of ten to fifteen miles a day were not uncommon. Daughter Suzy will vouch for that. She said she spent some awfully long days with her dad and Jim Dorrance. Over this twenty year period another 60,000 miles was ridden.

Most of you know or maybe guessed, Tom has a tremendous love of horses. His ability with stock and cutting horses is very well known and is documented by trophies, trophy saddles and by anyone who has knowledge of the horse world.

This part of Tom's time in the saddle is what makes him unique. No one that I know of has spent so many miles in the sagebrush as well as being recognized as one of the top horsemen in the west.

Gary Baumer, a noted horse trainer from California, told me, "Hell, Tom Marvel taught us all how to work a cow on the fence."

After working all day he would ride his show horses in the evenings for a lot of uncounted miles. I can remember Tom riding all day and then helping some of us another two or three hours with our horses.

There has never been anyone more willing or giving of his time and sharing knowledge about horses than Tom. Aspiring bronc riders were also helped by him.

The sharing of his skills is pretty much there for the asking. About all that's required is to be sincere with him. You might have to be there at 4:00 a.m. once in a while for help- he's an early riser. One other thing, the same mistake better not be made too many times because it will become very clear not to do it again.

Tom and Rosita sold the Martin Ranch in 1984 and moved to Visalia, California, where he trained cutting horses full time. Riding ten to twelve hours a day, another 40,000 miles were added to what I call his sagebrush cowboy miles.

Tom is back in Nevada helping his son, Joe, at the 6 Bar Ranch in Lamoille and helping the rest of us from time to time. He is adding another twelve to fifteen hundred miles a year.

Tom and Rosita have seven grandchildren and three great-grandchildren. Some are ours.

September of this year, 1996, Tom received the Vaquero award given by the California Reined Cow Horse Association to honor a unique few outstanding horsemen. The award says, "For contribution to the reining cow horse industry. For support, dedication and efforts in preserving the principles for which the association was founded."

It's a deep and true honor for me to recognize Tom with this Cowboy 100,000 Mile Club award on behalf of his thousands and thousands of miles in the saddle, not just because he is my father–in–law, but also because of the tremendous work ethic he has maintained throughout his life. 279,000 miles is a long winding horseback trail.

LITTLE THINGS

When spring of the year arrives on a ranch and each day's work load seems like a week's I used to tell myself to calm down and take things one day at a time. The first day winter weather breaks and spring begins there is a hundred things to do all at the same time: shoe horses, finish calving, brand calves, move cows off meadows, fix winter damaged fences, drag meadows, build irrigation dams while meeting with the B.L.M hoping to keep the year's A.U.M.s and turn out dates realistic. Last but not least is trying to stay on speaking terms with your wife, who is already over loaded with spring activities.

THE COWBOY AND THE BANKER

At times along my 115,000 mile horseback ride I have taken bankers out to back country ranches where, as we traveled along, we visited about the ranch's operation and inventoried livestock. There were a number of reasons to have the banker visit but the most common reason was to secure the next year's operating loan.

This is usually a meeting of men from two different worlds. Each is more knowledgeable in the world he represents. Most bank loan officers have had a lot of experience and understand the agricultural entities they loan money to. But in some instances they are not familiar with the conditions they encounter when inventorying livestock out on the big range areas of the west. In the early stages of my horseback ride, some bankers would saddle up and ride through the cows being inventoried. But later, in a faster moving world, this job was accomplished with the ranch owner or manager driving a four-wheel drive pickup along rough back country roads while explaining the ranch's operation and the type and numbers of livestock being seen.

I remember two banking experiences that were the exact opposite of each other. The first incident took place in the banker's office because the field work had already been done. Al Williams, an old style banker, was representing The Nevada National Bank and our family owned and I operated the Lee Livestock Company. Lee Livestock Company consisted of two cow herds. One was a registered Hereford herd and one was a commercial herd. The cattle market was in one of its down cycles and prices had taken a sharp down turn during the fall months. Because of the depressed market, the bank's appraiser valued the Lee Livestock Company cow herds at about half of the value they had given the same cows the previous year.

Through no fault of the ranch's operation and because of a situation I could not control, I was faced with the real possibility my operating loan application would be turned down. I could never understand why, at the lowest point of the cattle cycle when prices were down and a rancher should be maintaining or increasing his livestock inventory, money was so tight and hard to get, maybe even forcing a reduction in livestock herds. Then at the high point of the cattle cycle when prices were good and money was easier to get, ranchers were rebuilding their livestock herds instead of being able to take advantage of the good prices. Regardless of why, I was in a tough spot when I sat down in the plush chair and looked across the shiny oak desk and saw the stern face of the bank manager looking back. Mr. Williams asked how the fall work was going and I replied that the round-up was over, the cow herd numbers were up a little, the calves, cull cows and bulls had been sold, the hay crop was average and I had enough hay to feed the cow herds until spring turnout with a little hay left to carry over. As a last thought, trying to put my best foot forward, I mentioned that I had just finished running the cow herds through the dip vat treating them for lice and warbles. When I finished Mr. Williams said, "Dave, I don't know how to tell you this but when someone tells you your cows are lousy, they mean lousy. They don't mean they have little black bugs crawling all over them." As I tensely sat across from the banker, the look on my face must have been priceless because the stern expression on the banker's face slowly turned to a grin and then laughter and I slowly realized this was Mr. William's way of relaxing a tense situation. In a more relaxed atmosphere we reviewed my loan application which was approved before I left the bank. Of all the meetings I have had with bankers along my 115,000 mile horseback ride, I have never forgotten this one.

A number of years later another memorable banking experience occurred. The banking system had changed and the final decisions on ranch operating loans were usually no longer made at the local level. The information gathered by the local bank managers was now being forwarded to the regional offices where the final decisions were being made. During this time frame sometimes bank managers from other areas were transferred to rural banks, thus for several years Joe Blissenbach was my banker. He was originally from the New York area. Joe was a hard nose banker that went by the book. He had some agricultural background and was an all around good guy but Joe was not familiar with conditions we work under on the ranches of the west. The first trip he and I took together was at the Dinner Station Ranch twenty-five miles north of Elko, Nevada. I had a lunch and water jug in the four wheel drive pick up when Joe arrived. We started out toward Lone Mountain. This day we were inventorying two thousand head of yearling steers that were already turned out on the range.

During the middle part of my 115,000 horseback ride I learned from experiences, when taking bankers into the back country where they are not used to traveling, it is wise to go far enough in rough country to make them understand the ranch operations while at the same time getting a good honest look at the range and the livestock using it. But I also learned that is was not wise to go too far or get into unnecessary stressful situations because the results were sometimes counter-productive.

Another thing I learned from experience was how difficult it was for bankers not familiar with the range operations to understand that after a long, bumpy, four-wheel drive ride they may only actually see about forty percent of the livestock that are in the area. The other sixty percent are there but just shaded up back in the canyons and draws where they could not be seen.

On this day I unintentionally violated my own guidelines almost before the trip started. By the time Joe and I reached Lone Mountain I was traveling on old mining roads that were more like cow trails then conventional road ways. Not far up the mountainside I came to the first steep switchback corner and I had to back up to get around it. Being anxious to show Joe as many yearlings as possible, I was pointing out a bunch of yearling steers grazing on the hillside above while negotiating that corner. I noticed Joe had stopped talking and was sitting silently on the passenger side of the pickup. The side Joe was sitting on happened to be the outside edge of the steep mountain road. After we got around the turn and were driving on up the mountain, I started to point out the next group of steers when Joe poked me in the ribs and said, "Dave, you just watch the damn road and I will take care of looking for cows." This broke the ice and I drove on being more careful and for awhile the ride was less tense.

We counted steers, saw deer, antelope, sage hens, and a coyote as we traveled along.

The rye grass was as tall as the hood of the pickup and the conversation became relaxed until we got over the mountain into lower country. There we came upon a washout in the road caused by an earlier flash flood. This gully washer caused water to run down a normally dry canyon cutting a deep trench across this little traveled back country road. I knew the washout was there because I found it on a previous trip. At that time, realizing I could not get around the gully, and not wanting to backtrack over Lone Mountain, I went to the Basco Cabin and found a couple of railroad ties. I hauled the ties to the washout and made a makeshift bridge by placing the railroad ties length wise across the gaping hole in the road. I spaced them about six feet apart so they would match the width of the pickup tires and dug the ends of the ties down so they were flush with the road. On this day the makeshift bridge was still in place. When Joe and I approached the top of those two eight inch wide railroad ties, placed six feet apart, they looked pretty skimpy. By now Joe was beginning to joke about the condition of the back country roads and said, "You are not going to cross that thing, are you?" I answered, 'We are going to cross that thing unless you want to walk ten miles back to the ranch." I got out and looked to be certain that the front tires of the pick up were centered on the railroad ties then suggested Joe get out and stretch his legs while I drove across. Joe didn't hesitate to take my suggestion and I drove across the makeshift bridge without incident. Joe got back into the pickup but he was still looking back at the two railroad tie bridge as I drove down the road.

We continued counting steers while I answered Joe's questions. Yes, it was normal to only see about forty percent of the livestock in a given area in the middle of the day during a one day trip and yes, the sixty percent we did not see were really here. They were just shaded up, out of sight in the draws and canyons we came by.

My explanation was apparently successful because in due time the operating loan was granted with just one stipulation. The bank added an extra five thousand dollars to be used exclusively for back country road maintenance.

This banking experience is memorable because it was the only time during my 115,000 mile horseback ride I ever received more money from a bank than I asked for.

LITTLE THINGS

It is amazing how fast an hour goes by when you have too much to do or you are late for an appointment. It's also amazing to see how slowly it takes another hour to drag by when you are waiting for something important to happen or you can't get to sleep at night.

THUNDER STORMS

During my lifelong horseback ride on the big ranges of the west I have been involved in or witnessed hundreds of thunder storms. Most were routine events or bothersome inconveniences but from the towering, billowing thunderheads in the afternoon sky to the jagged blue white streaks of chain lightning, followed by earth shaking thunder, they were awe inspiring. Some were inspiring to watch, some were life threatening and a few left indelible marks on my memory.

If a person thinks he is important, he hasn't been caught out in the mountains about twenty miles from home with only his horse and dogs for company as lightning bolts hit the ground on all sides. The wind-driven hail raises welts on his back while the dogs try to cower under a horse that is now lunging nearly out of control. It puts things in proper perspective very quickly and makes a person feel really insignificant in the overall scheme of things.

The early part of my 115,000 mile horseback ride was spent riding the timbered mountain ranges of northern California. This is where I learned to respect the power of a bolt of lightning. When riding in the steep mountain terrain, it was not unusual to see a large oak, Ponderosa pine, or a Douglas fir tree that had been struck by lightning and sometimes be in the area when it happens. Often lightning strikes a live tree fifteen to twenty feet above the ground and spirals its way around the tree trunk until it hits the ground below. This leaves a long scar about four inches wide where the bark and splinters of wood are blown away. The tree usually lives and carries the scar for the rest of its life. The chances of starting a range fire are much greater if lightning strikes a dead tree and a dry lightning storm is really dangerous. I have seen a single dry lightning storm start ten to twelve fires as it travels along in a single afternoon. Sometimes a lightning bolt will strike a dead tree, igniting the tree roots, causing the roots to smolder under the ground for a number of days before the fire, caused by lightning, breaks out and starts to burn on a clear calm afternoon long after the thunderstorm that caused the fire has been forgotten.

The first lightning strike I remember that made me realize the extraordinary power of lightning happened when I was young. I was riding through timber on the east side of San Headron Mountain. I was following an old trail that was identified by slash marks cut in tree trunks years before I came along. I began to see signs of a lightning strike somewhere in the vicinity because the forest floor was strewn with pieces of bark and fresh splinters of wood. As I rode on down the trail, the splinters of wood became the size of fence posts. I began to get the uneasy feeling that comes with finding something you do not completely understand.

I came around a corner in the trail and saw a big Douglas fir tree that had been struck by lightning. The tree was probably eight feet in diameter at the bottom and four to five feet in diameter forty feet up where its trunk was completely blown off. The tree trunk was split from that point right down the middle until about ten feet from the ground where the bolt of lightning left the tree and traveled through the air before blowing a hole in the dirt below. The two halves of the big tree's trunk were still standing. They were about a foot apart at the top and I could see blue sky between them until the trunk came back together ten feet from the ground. I am sure the big tree stood there for a number of centuries and in the blink of an eye it was reduced to a grotesque snag by a single lightning bolt. It goes without saying that I felt very small sitting there on my horse looking up at the instant destruction one bolt of lightning had caused.

The next forty-eight years of my 115,000 horseback rides were spent in the big high desert sagebrush basins and mountain ranges of Elko County, located in northeastern Nevada. This is where the Ruby Mountains rise to over eleven thousand feet in elevation. Coming from the coastal timbered mountains of northern California where thirty-five to sixty inches of moisture per year is normal and sometimes eighty inches is recorded, it takes some adjusting to move to an area where two to four inches of moisture per year is normal in some desert valleys and seven to twelve inches of moisture is normal at the six to nine thousand foot elevations along the mountain ranges. It is amazing how different the big ranges of the west are but it is also amazing to realize how the skills learned in one range environment are so similar to the skills required to survive in a completely different environment. In my lifetime horseback ride, I have learned that all mountains are different but at the same time, similar.

Thunder storms in the sagebrush basins and high deserts of the west are just as awe inspiring as they are in the coastal timbered mountains, maybe more so because without being on a mountain top you can see twenty to seventy miles in one look. Lightning in this environment usually strikes rock outcroppings, rim rock, sagebrush, Juniper trees, and an occasional hay stack. I tell people I meet along my 115,000 mile horseback ride that the country is so desolate it is appealing.

One thunderstorm I remember happened on a late spring or early summer day. It was a pleasant morning and the sky was cloudless when I saddled up and started the five mile ride to repair a winter-damaged fence before I turned cattle into a pasture located in the foothills of the

Ruby Mountains. About a mile and a half from the main ranch I rode by two cows standing in a fence corner inside the pasture fence I was going to repair. The cows didn't belong in that pasture and while I was riding by I thought, when I return in the late afternoon I'll be on the right side of the fence and I'll put those cows through a gate and back on the range they came from. About three miles further on, I started working the fence where it left the low country along Haw Creek and started up the steep mountain toward Brennen ridge. The fence was old and was built with juniper posts. The terrain got steeper and the winter snow damage was considerable, so the going was slow. Off in the distance around the middle of the day I noticed a few big billowy thunderheads rising in the sky. By mid-afternoon a black thunder cloud formed about two miles north of the area where I was repairing fence and thunder was starting to rumble. The weather was calm and sunny where I was, so I wasn't concerned. The storm was moving away from me and going toward Ruby Dome. I was repairing a place in the fence where a winter snowdrift had broken and scrambled all four wires. To be safe, I moved away from the fence and sat down for ten or fifteen minutes. When I was satisfied the storm had moved on north, I returned to the fence and started splicing the top wire. I built a loop in one end of the broken wire with my fence pliers and pulled as hard as I could preparing to tighten the wire by using the hammer splice.

At this very moment a bolt of electricity came down the wire I was holding, went through me and, I assume, went on down the fence line. Now, I have had a number of electric shocks along the way, but my body certainly wasn't made to stand this kind of a jolt. I don't know if I threw the fence pliers or the electricity knocked them out of my hands but those pliers flew six or seven feet in the air and I was knocked down flat on the ground. The kernels or nodules under my arms felt as big as walnuts. I got up on my hands and knees and took a quick look toward my horse to see if he was hurt. He was standing there on three legs, half asleep with his head down, not noticing anything unusual. I checked myself over and couldn't find any lasting damage and I was thinking clearly. Skeptically I ran the old adage through my head, "Lightning never strikes twice in the same place." Anyway, I sat down for a half hour before starting to repair fence again.

On my way home in the late afternoon I came to the fence corner where the two cows had been standing earlier in the day. From a distance I couldn't see the cows and thought they had gone to water. When I got closer I could see the cows were still there but both were dead. They had been standing close to the fence and just dropped in their tracks.

Then I began to realize what had happened. A bolt of lightning, that wasn't close to either me or the cows, hit the fence between the spot where I was splicing wire and this fence corner. Part of the electricity went south along the fence wire and knocked me down while part of the electricity went north along the fence wire and killed the two cows. As I sat there looking at the little round spot of scorched hair under one cow's ear I remember saying to myself, "Old boy, you really did cheat the devil this time."

Along my lifelong horseback ride I learned that thunderstorms are like rattlesnakes. Statistics show the chances of being killed by either one is very low, but the potential for it happening is always present.

Another thunder storm that remains in my memory through all these years happened at night on the sagebrush flat below the Lee Livestock Company meadows. The flat is located between Lamoille, Nevada, and the South Fork Indian Reservation. It was a hot midsummer day. There hadn't been any moisture for days and dust devils swirled across the flat every afternoon. I had a breeding herd of registered horned Hereford cows and a bull in a pasture near the Ogilvie field. The feed was good in the pasture but in the summer during the dry hot spells, stock water had to be watched. On this particular evening two cowboys and I were riding home and we went out of our way to check this herd of cows. We could tell before we reached the pasture that the cows were out of water. Some were bunched up in the fence corners and some were walking the fence. During these hot summer days, cows can make the first day without water, but by the end of the second day they are in serious trouble. We decided to gather the cows, drive them about three miles across the sagebrush flat and put them in a pasture that was well watered. By the time we got the cows gathered and started across the flat, it was beginning to get dark.

We could still see the shadowy outline of the cows we were driving when I heard the first rumble of thunder and looking south I saw the first flashes of lightning. The thunderstorm seemed to come out of nowhere. The storm was low to the ground and fast moving. We tried to drive the cows faster but it soon became apparent that we were not going to outrun this storm. The wind picked up to nearly gale force and the first sheets of rain hit with a vengeance. In seconds we were engulfed in thunder with lightning bolts striking on all sides at the same time. In our part of the sagebrush flat, it was now light as day. We were wringing wet and the sides of the drenched cows were a fluorescent blue that flickered when each bolt of lightning hit. The cows looked like a ghost herd with ghost riders driving them. There was so much electricity in the air that for the first and last time during my 115,000 mile horseback ride, I actually saw blue streaks of electricity traveling between the tips of the cows' horns.

The thunder and rain were still over us, but the main force of the lightning was now moving to the north. In due time the thunder and lightning were in the distance still angrily rolling across the flat. The wind and rain stopped almost as suddenly as it began and the storm was gone. Now the part of the big sagebrush flat we were on was dark again. With the exception of the sloshing sound the cows and horses made wading through the pools of water, the flat was quiet. The urgency of getting the cows to water was forgotten and when we left the cows in the new pasture they soon spread out to graze. The moon rose above the horizon and we could see well enough to ride home.

After the conversation about what had happened died down, I began to realize how lucky we were. We were soaking wet and miserable but we were alive.

I was thinking maybe we had a little help from up above when I let my mind wander to a time long ago. It was during the war. I was just a kid and most of the young cowboys were in the service. I was riding and doing ranch work with older seasoned cowboys. I learned much during this time but sometimes these cowboys were a little gruff and didn't talk much, especially to a kid. On this occasion I was riding with an old cowboy when we got caught in an afternoon rain shower. Seeing a chance to maybe start a conversation, I said something like, "Jack, I'm starting to get pretty wet." Jack straightens up in his saddle and says," Wet! Wet! Kid you don't know what wet is. You ain't wet until both boots are full of water and your balls are wet." I had to grin when I thought back on this incident and I said to myself, "Wet! Wet! Old timer, I sure qualify for your definition of being wet this time."

I remember another thunderstorm that I wasn't even involved in. It took place years after the thunderstorm that I just described. I was manager of the Salmon River Cattlemen's Ranch holdings south of Jackpot, Nevada. I was working for forty association members and was directly responsible to an elected Board of Directors. The Association controlled about 380,000 acres and ran several bands of sheep and five to seven thousand head of cows during each seven month grazing season. During the seventeen years I was involved, the association membership was made up of ranchers and livestock people from three states. These were good people. Most of the time we worked well together and I made many friends, though at times I have to admit that working for forty strong-willed potential bosses, all at the same time, made me wonder about my intelligence.

This part of northeastern Nevada is prone to cloudbursts and thunderstorms and is the reason this thunderstorm is remembered. It was mid summer and two brothers were driving cattle on the neighboring Winecup Ranch. A summer thunderstorm developed and passed over them. A bolt of lightning struck the older brother and he and his horse were both killed, felled in their tracks. This incident put a somber mood over the ranching community and reminded everyone of the destruction even a small thunderstorm can produce.

Another thunderstorm that is memorable also happened at San Jacinto, Salmon River Cattlemen's Association Ranch headquarters. It was along in July, thunderheads were around the area and the air was calm, still and hot. This caused that eerie feeling that sometimes precedes a thunderstorm. Clarence and Joe were shoeing horses in front of the summer saddle room. About the middle of the day Clarence noticed a thunderstorm traveling down the valley along the Little Salmon River. By the time Clarence had shoes on the front feet of his horse, the storm was closing in. So he said, "Joe, let's go get a cup of coffee while this blankety-blank storm passes over."

They left the horses they were shoeing and walked the hundred yards to the cook house. Lightning was soon striking all around and the thunder rattled the cook house windows, but in about twenty minutes, the storm traveled on down the valley and the wind and rain stopped. When Clarence and Joe got back to the corral they couldn't believe their eyes. Both horses were dead, lying side by side, killed by a single bolt of lightning. I wasn't there at the time but from my own experiences I know what happened. Clarence and Joe looked at each other, looked at the dead horses, then looked over at the cook house, and I know what was going through their minds when they realized what could have been.

These thunderstorm experiences I remember may lead you to believe that I stumbled from one disastrous thunderstorm to another but there were many storms in between. I said at the beginning of these stories that during my 115,000 mile horseback ride, I was involved in or witnessed hundreds of thunderstorms and most were routine events or just bothersome inconveniences. The few storms I have written about, that stand out in my memory for one reason or another, happened over a long period of time. There were many more routine thunderstorms that caused inconveniences. Most thunderstorms are harmless; run their courses and leave much needed moisture behind.

One more thunderstorm that I remember was not life threatening or a danger to anyone. It happened in the late fall after the fire and thunderstorm seasons are usually over. Clarence and I were batching at the Clover Crossing cabin out on the Bruneau desert. Frank and Cindy

Bachman, my daughter and son-in-law, owned Clover Crossing at the time. With everyone's help we were wintering three hundred fifty cows on the desert. On this particular evening, just before dark, Clarence and I unsaddled our horses and fed them before we went inside the cabin. We lit the lantern and started a fire in the old Monarch wood cook stove, cooked supper and started to settle down for the night. Suddenly to our surprise, a deafening clap of thunder broke loose directly over head. The windows rattled and the old cabin shook. The thunder continued and seemed to stay in exactly the same spot. We went outside to take a look. It was completely calm. There was no wind. There was no rain. There weren't any lightning bolts striking the ground. Huge thunderheads had formed directly above us and they were stationary. The clouds were just churning around within themselves. There were long jagged draws spread out in all directions, reaching high into the night sky. Sheet lightning and an occasional bolt of chain lightning jumped from cloud to cloud in all of those cloudy canyons at the same time. Neon flashes of orange light worked their way up and down those cloudy draws intermingled with bright flashes of blue, green, yellow and reddish lights all bouncing and reflecting off the towering clouds.

All of this was punctuated by white streaks of chain lightning jumping from cloud to cloud. Thunder rumbled constantly while two old cowboys, who thought they had seen just about everything the open range had to offer, stood like statues, staring at the amazing lightning show in disbelief. The thunderstorm didn't move on. It stayed stationary for about forty-five minutes. The storm, without moving, finally lessened in intensity until it just faded away and dispersed as mysteriously as it appeared. Neither Clarence nor I had ever seen a light display in the night sky, either occurring naturally or man made, that compared to the spectacle we just witnessed.

We went back into the cabin, stoked up the old wood stove, pulled up a couple of chairs, opened the oven door, propped our feet up on the door, and leaned back to enjoy the heat. Thunder could still be heard lightly rumbling over head and a nostalgic mood seemed to settle inside the cabin. Clarence began to talk. He had worked for and with me for twenty years and never before or after this night did he ever talk much about himself.

I knew Clarence was from Encampment, Wyoming, and from a mutual friend who occasionally came to visit, I learned that Clarence was in the Vietnam War where he earned a Purple Heart and the Congressional Medal of Honor. I also knew the medals were on display in a museum in Encampment, Wyoming. Throughout all of the times we rode together, Clarence never mentioned this. He was a hard riding, hard working, hard cussing cowboy who was a little rough around the edges; but he could get two days work done in one day and he was fiercely loyal to the people and the ranches he worked for.

Anyway, the setting must have been right on this night because Clarence began to tell me about things he had done during his life. He said he was wild when he was young and if it had not been for a man he looked up to and respected being patient and not giving up on him, he probably would not have lived very long or ever amounted to a damn. He remembered the time he was drafted into the army. He had just qualified to ride saddle broncs at the National Finals Rodeo. The National Finals were just thirty days from the day he was called to be inducted into the army. Clarence said he tried everything he could think of to get his draft board to give him an extension of time so he could ride in the National Finals before he went into the army. Instead he ended up in Vietnam in command of a commando-type group of nine or ten soldiers who worked at night behind enemy lines. This group worked together for months until one night something went terribly wrong. That night Clarence came back from behind enemy lines packing the only other survivor of the unit on his shoulders. Sometime during this time frame, Clarence was wounded and Army doctors put a stainless steel plate in his skull. He said the army replaced his unit with raw recruits fresh from the states and he nearly got court martialed for refusing to lead them behind enemy lines where he was sure their inexperience would get them killed.

The stories slowed down about here and the fire was about burned out, so I slipped over and put more wood in the stove.

Clarence said when he was younger some place in Wyoming, (the name escapes me) they held a yearly sixty mile cross country ski race and he won the race five years in a row. I am assuming this is why, when Clarence got back from Vietnam, the army for whatever reason, made him a ski instructor and his job was to teach officers how to ski. He said he had Lieutenants, Captains, and other Army Brass under his control and he really enjoyed his position. I bet he did and I will also bet Clarence milked this position for all it was worth.

Another incident Clarence told me about that night involved racehorses. He'd gotten interested in and involved with racehorses somewhere along his travels. He went to work for a racehorse owner in Kentucky. One horse he was working with qualified to run in the Kentucky Derby. Clarence said at Churchill Downs during the pre-race festivities before race day they were pretty much ignored. They weren't in the political circles that attracted the press and the other racehorse people didn't pay much attention to them either. On race day they were off and the horse Clarence was handling came in second in that year's Kentucky Derby. Clarence said there were so many blankety-blank press and people who had been ignoring them for the past week in his stall; he couldn't get his work done. Then they were interviewed and invited to all the activities that were going on.

One more thing Clarence mentioned that night was a trip he made to England. Clarence joined a group of cowboys that loaded their horses on a ship, crossed the Atlantic Ocean and performed for the Queen of England. I hope he was on his good behavior and not cussing when he met the Queen.

I have noticed along my 115,000 mile horseback ride that the cowboys who live and work with the horses and cattle on the big ranches of the west are in two categories. Some talk incessantly about things they have never really done, but most almost never talk about the important things in their lives that they really have done. It took an unbelievable thunderstorm, an old Monarch cook stove with the oven door open, a flickering lantern, and a creaky chair to get Clarence in the mood to talk about some of the things he'd done during his life.

One rumor I heard about Clarence that probably isn't true because I heard it second or third hand, got started when Clarence was cow boss for the Maggie Creek Ranch located west of Elko, Nevada. The Southern Pacific and Union Pacific Railroad tracks run along the north side of Maggie Creek Ranch headquarters and driving cattle across the tracks was always difficult. So the rumor goes, on this morning, to make extra sure that no trains were coming, Clarence placed a crowbar across the tracks shorting out the railroad switch off signals, thus stopping trains all the way from Elko to Winnemucca, Nevada. I do not know how railroads operate and I do not know if anything like this is even possible but I am doubly sure this rumor is not true because the rumor reports that when the railroad detectives came by asking questions that afternoon, neither Clarence nor his crew knew anything about what could have caused the problem. I rode with Clarence for twenty years and in all that time, he never mentioned this incident to me. However, knowing Clarence, something like this could have happened.

LOUI CERRI

Loui Cerri was inducted into the Nevada Cattlemen's Association Cowboy 100,000 Mile Club in 2000.

Loui's presentation was written and presented by his son, Ron Cerri and is as follows:

By and large, the men who qualify for the honor of membership in the Cowboy 100,000 Mile Club are riders, who knew the open range, before there were many fences, no stock trucks or goose-neck trailers to haul men and horses to work. They rode out at daylight, often going fifteen to twenty miles, sometimes even more, to start the day's circle. It was the land of ranches—no subdivisions—the time of the open range.

They knew of the dust and the heat of the mid-summer sun, the freezing misery of late fall roundups and of riding in winter blizzards. But in the spring and summer they fell asleep under the light of the stars. They knew trial and hardship as they worked among the cattle. They knew hunger, thirst, and weariness, but theirs was the best of the hardy life, the glory of work in the open and joy and satisfaction of a job well done. I believe these men were the "Long Riders" – the "Last Cavaliers" of the range cattle industry.

My father, Loui Cerri, was selected to receive this extraordinary honor this year.

(A family member escorts Loui to the podium.)

Loui Cerri was born in Paradise Valley, January 23, 1928. He lived with his parents Giovanni and Evelina Cerri, one brother, Leo, and a sister, Jeanette. His father owned and operated the Mica saloon.

Giovanni later bought the Tumbleweed Ranch. As Loui got older money was short, so at the age of fourteen he started riding as a rep for Elmer Cathcart. The Mica Saloon was sold and the ranch expanded.

Loui married Elaine Cosci, November 29, 1952 in Elko, Nevada. He brought a young girl that was not familiar with the ranching lifestyle to Paradise Valley. On the family ranch, with a lot of dedication and hard work they raised three children, Susie Hansen, Ron Cerri, and Anita Cassinelli.

Loui was the first to bring Black Angus cattle to the valley where they were bred to Hereford bulls producing black bally calves. Part of the ranch was sold in 1978. Loui and Elaine continued to live in Paradise Valley until 1988 when the remainder of the ranch was sold and they moved to Winnemucca. Loui continued to help his son and his friends brand and work cattle until 1989 when a roping accident left him with one eye.

Elaine passed away in July 28, 1999 and Loui continues to live in Winnemucca. He likes to fish, enjoys visiting with his friends, and spends a lot of time with his eight grandchildren.

I'll give a short account of how my dad amassed 100,000 miles. But first I'd like to give special thanks to Les Stewart, not only for nominating my dad for this award, but also for his help in compiling and sharing some of his memories.

Loui rode from the ranch to the Paradise Valley School and in those days many kids rode to school. There was a barn behind the school where the horses waited until it was time to go home.

7,200 miles

Loui rode with the 96 Ranch. A story I've heard from those days is as follows—one spring was exceptionally wet and stormy. While camped at Goat corral, the cavy was turned out with a bell mare at might. Dad was riding for Elmer Cathcart and was called a "rep". The reps had to wrangle their own horses so they got up earlier than the other buckaroos.

One especially wet and cold morning there was a lot of commotion and someone hollered, "Somebody come out here and help me."

The buckaroos ran out of the tent to find my dad had saddled a horse with a bad habit of cinch binding. The horse had thrown himself over backwards and my Dad was pinned under the horse, covered from head to toe with mud and water. He was holding the horse's head by the bridle so the horse could not get up. Dad wanted to make sure he wasn't hung up before the horse got to his feet.

As a rep, my dad remembers Albert Skeedaddle showing him how to shoe horses and also teaching him a lot about horses. He remembers riding with Jimmy Dewar, the Holt brothers, the Skeedaddle brothers, Vic Arriola and Woody Bell.

4,000 miles

Loui rode on the range from Bradshaw Cabin to keep cattle scattered and check general range conditions. A memory about my Dad told by Les Stewart happened in the late fall when they went back onto the summer range with packhorses to make sure there were no cattle left in the area. In order to get home they had to go over 8,000 foot Buttermilk summit. A storm and blizzard hit that was so intense they could not see more than a few feet in any direction. Giving their horses their heads to take them home didn't work. When given free rein, all the horses did was turn their tails to the storm and try to go with the wind. Les said they had better find some rocks or some kind of shelter, unpack and "siwash it." My Dad wanted to keep going, which in the end they both agreed to do. Finally they blundered upon a water trough they recognized, got their bearings and made it home.

1,800 miles

Dave's comment: "As anyone who has been caught in this kind of situation knows, this was a close call that could have ended differently. I remember one time I nearly blundered over a thirty foot high rim rock ledge while caught out in a blizzard where visibility was less than ten feet."

Loui amassed these miles riding on the open range for his family and later riding in the Buttermilk allotment.

42,000 miles

Loui rode these miles running mustangs, gathering horses and broodmares in from the range.

200 miles

A little story from those times— While gathering mustangs in late February, my Dad's horse stumbled and fell. My dad was thrown. His horse got up running and got away. Dad, now afoot, watched helplessly while his favorite saddle, silver mounted bit and headstall went drifting down the draw on the loose horse that soon joined the wild bunch. Luckily another rider saw what happened. He took Dad along behind his saddle and with the help of other riders they corralled the bunch of wild horses. They were able to catch my dad's horse with the saddle and fancy bridle still unharmed.

Riding lanes

23,760 miles

Rounding up strays from the Circle A catch lot and from other neighbors.

2,400 miles

Everyday work on family ranch

16.000 miles

Helping his son and friends ride and brand

4,800 miles

This totals 102,160 miles, but I am sure he has ridden even more.

I am proud and honored to be able to present this award to you – "A Long Rider" – "A Last Cavalier" and now a member of the exclusive Nevada Cattlemen's Association Cowboy 100,000 Mile Club. You are joining an elite group that includes Virgil Piquet, Hillery Barnes, Leslie Stewart, Bill DeLong, Frank Baker, Loyd Sorenson, Jess Sustasha, Harvey Dahl, Jack and Irene Walther, George Wilkinson, Bob Thomas, Tom Marvel, Tom Pedroli and others. Congratulations.

LITTLE THINGS

It doesn't matter what income group you are in. Most people think if they just had 10 % more they would be all right.

THE RANCHER

A cowboy is often made fun of and called a loose cannon shooting from the hip. I have spent a lifetime among ranchers and cowboys. This is what I learned.

Most take a common sense approach to things. This comes naturally because of their close association with the fundamentals of life. They are self reliant by necessity and early on learn to appreciate the things they are lucky enough to be surrounded by. They know that if they destroy the environment around them, they will self destruct their livelihood and way of life. They survive by using their own self confidence and after due consideration, they succeed or fail by making their own decisions. A handshake is still an important document in a business deal and is often used, though in today's world, written contracts and agreements are necessary. On the big ranches and rural areas of the west there is still a common belief that a check or written agreement isn't any better than the person who signs it.

You might outsmart a rancher once, but he has a long memory, and it is very unlikely you will get a second chance. The ranchers I know are community minded and good neighbors. They are progressive and seek advice. Just do not try to dictate how they should use this advice or tell them how to operate their own ranches. A rancher knows when evaluating a horse or cow the first impression is usually the best but he also believes in thoroughly studying a project before making a decision. He doesn't believe in studying a project to death just to keep from making that decision. His management and way of life keep untold millions of acres from being covered by asphalt, houses, shopping centers and cement.

Some environmental groups don't know it yet, but when they get rid of the rancher and cowboy they will get rid of many of the things they say they are trying to protect.

I have been a lifelong rancher and cowboy and I'm proud to say that most of the land I've owned or been the steward of was in better shape when I left it than it was in when I found it. Ranchers and cowboys learned long ago that you can't starve a living out of a cow or the range where it grazes.

LITTLE THINGS

A story that circulated through the ranch country many years ago went something like this. In an effort to cut expenses an eastern lawmaker proposed firing all the cattle guards in the west. He estimated the huge amount of money this would save. It seems his definition of a cattle guard was an armed person guarding areas where fences crossed roads. He thought this was done twenty-four hours a day. This seems somewhat far fetched, but it does point out the misunderstanding that sometimes exists between the people that make the laws in the east and our cowboy way of life in the west.

LITTLE THINGS

Now this cowboy hadn't had a free afternoon for weeks and he hadn't been down to the river all spring. It was a warm, pleasant day. Flowers were blooming, birds were nesting, and this young man was thoroughly enjoying himself wandering down the river bank when he heard splashing.

Thinking a family of geese or ducks were in the water he slipped around the turn in the river to have a look. To his surprise the first thing he saw was a neatly folded pile of ladies clothes stacked on a rock above the water. Now this ol' cowboy wasn't born yesterday and he realized that sooner or later that young lady skinny dipping was going to have to come back to her clothes so he settled down and made himself comfortable.

When she looked over and saw him sitting there she ducked under the water. When she came up for air and he was still sitting by her clothes with a lazy grin on his face, she realized she had a problem. The afternoon wore on and the stand off continued.

The shadow of the trees along the river reached across the water. The young lady was getting cold, goose bumps were forming and she was beginning to shiver. As she moved around the pool of water her foot bumped something solid on the river bottom. She traced the object with her toes and realized it was an old wash tub with hinged handles on either side. She dove under, grabbed the handles on each side of the tub and holding the tub up in front of her, she came storming out of the water. She was cold. She was mad and she marched up to the young cowboy still sitting beside her clothes and demanded he go home. She finished by saying, "Young man I know what you are thinking." The young man's grin got a little bigger and he said, "Yes, Ma'm and I know what you're thinkin' too." She asked. "What am I thinking?" and he replied, "Your thinking there is a bottom in that tub."

STORIES

Max Casperson, a retired sheep rancher, farmer, and successful business man told me a story about his father that illustrates what I've learned about ranching families that have spent generations living on the big ranges of the west. The philosophy of other people I have crossed paths with during my 115,000 mile horseback ride, who live and work in rural America, is also reflected in this story. Their feelings for the country they live in and their way of life runs deep.

After four years in the Army during the Korean War, Max and Charlene, with their growing family, returned to the family farm and sheep operation near Oakley, Idaho. During the war things had changed and were still changing. Because of advancing age Max's father was having a harder time managing the ranch. So, through a natural transition, Max, with Charlene's help took over the management of the farm and sheep operation. After a couple of seasons, partly because of better record keeping, it was determined the sheep operation was financially becoming a burden to the rest of the farming activities. Times had changed. Some grazing leases had been lost and it was getting harder to trail the sheep to and from the summer ranges. The permits and leases were more expensive and harder to get, predators in the area were taking their toll and, partly because of imports from Australia and New Zealand, the lamb and wool markets were in the tank. With all these factors, Max set out to convince his father that this particular sheep operation was no longer profitable.

This was a big decision to make. Max knew his father would not be receptive to the idea, so he painstakingly compiled the financial statements, separating the sheep operation from the rest of the farming expenses and income. He gathered information from the past several years. He drew charts showing exactly why this sheep operation was no longer profitable and, in fact, was losing money.

At an opportune time, Max sat down at the kitchen table with his father and presented his case for selling the sheep. The table was covered with sheets of paper, charts, and graphs backing up Max's presentation. When he was finished Max looked up and said, "Dad we have to sell the sheep. They are costing us too much money." After a long silence his Dad looked up and replied, "What in tarnation has money got to do with it? This is what I do."

This story happened to be about a sheep operation but my experience tells me it could have taken place at any kitchen table in a home where the family derives its living from the land they live on. The reality of the situation may have won out but those words, "What in tarnation has money got to do with it?" would basically be the same with any family that has lived on the land for generations. Of course, everyone expects to make a living but the sentiment and feelings for the land and a way of life reflected in this story about says it all.

LITTLE THINGS

A sheep herder once told me sheep herders were dumb. They spend all summer on top of a mountain, with sheep all around, talking about girls. Then they spend all winter near town, with girls all around, talking about sheep.

Betty driving Rowdy and Darky - 1976

Betty on Tinker stuck in deep snow of 1945

Betty on Bunny - 1939

BETTY REED BEAR

Betty Bear was inducted into the Nevada Cattlemen's Association Cowboy 100,000 Mile Club in 2010.

Paula Wright, Betty's daughter, wrote the presentation using Betty's own words when Betty was inducted into the Club and it is as follows:

Robert Y. Reed and Alta Eva Reed lived at North Fork, Nevada. The ranch consisted of three creeks: Deep Creek, Clear Creek and Riff Creek. They all run off the Independence Mountains into the Owyhee River.

The Reeds had three daughters: Jean, Lois and me, Betty. I was born in 1925 in Elko, Nevada. I was the youngest daughter and remem-

ber my first rides sitting behind my Dad on a horse. When he galloped
he would put his in hand back of him on my leg to hold me on.

When I started school I rode Baldy. He was an elegant horse given
to me by our neighbors, Emery and Mrs. Johnson. During one blizzard,
Baldy got off trail and got into a very deep snow drift and floundered
around and couldn't get out. I was frightened and my Dad rescued me
by making a trail with his horse so Baldy could get us out and back on
the trail.

We rode to school for eight years. My Dad gave me a colt he called
Bunny because he was a little like a rabbit. He took Bunny to a friend's
son to break for me. Then when Bunny was about three and I was in
third grade, I got to ride him to school. Bunny would run away with me
almost every day so I rode many more miles going and coming from
school than I should have.

One weekend my Dad saw me racing across the field. He took
Bunny and rode him a few times and he never ran away with me again.

My Dad saved all the cow work for weekends so we could help him.
We loved it. In the summer, my nieces came and we rode all day, almost
every day. I had to wrango the work horses for haying and find the milk
cows every evening.

The cattle were turned on to the Taylor Grazing in the spring. We
had big rodeers to gather our cattle before driving them to the forest permit. There were a lot of ranches that ran cattle in common with ours:
Vegas, Aguirres, the PX, Rutherfords and Moffats. We thought it was
great to go on these big round-ups. Most of the horses ran on open range
during the year and we gathered them late in the winter and before haying
started in early July. When my Dad passed away, I was the only one
that knew the horses. I remembered all the two and three year olds—
there were about 100 horses.

After my Dad was gone, I did most of the riding when I wasn't in
school. When I was sixteen, I didn't go back to school. The war was on
and help was really hard to get so I stayed home to take care of the cattle.

I met Paul Bear about this time. He was the cow boss for the PX
outfit. On our first date he took me to a dance at North Fork. Then he
said, "Why don't you go around my trap line with me?" We trotted and
galloped for about thirty miles checking the traps. It was a long night
and day because we started riding as soon as the dance was over.

My friends at Mountain City, the Bieroths, were driving cattle to
Halleck to ship on the railroad. Hugh Bieroth was a great horseman.
His wife, Mabel, the cook, his daughter Margie, Carl Ratliff, Frank
Baker, Ted Baker, Loyd Baker and I were the crew. The drive took six
days. It was fun. The longest day was 28 miles from the Cotant to

Devil's Gate. We left at 2 a.m. and were in the field at 9 p.m... There was a windmill field after we reached Devil's Gate with two big corrals. We put the cattle in one field and the saddle horses in the other. There were four kids in the crew and we got bored so we decided to show each other what good horses we had. We got on our horses and rode them bareback with no bridles to the end of the lot. There, the horses took over and raced back to their buddies with the four kids on them. We sure got chewed out! What if we had stampeded the cattle and they lost a lot of pounds before they reached the scales and got weighted?

Paul went into the service for four years during World War II. I was tired of the Reed Ranch and went to work for Moffat at the Rancho Grande where my sister, Lois, and her husband, Charlie Chapin, were working. I rode with Charlie all that year, almost every day. It was a great experience on the big outfit.

Paul and I were married the year before in 1944 when he was home on furlough. He was discharged on December 1945 and we spent the winter of 1946 on the Reed ranch. We broke seventeen head of work horses and started a couple of saddle horses. Paul had been in the service for four years and was restless so we went to Lee and Verna Reborse's Ranch at Golconda. It was different for us, more of a desert, and not what Paul had expected. He got to irrigate and Verna and I did most of the riding. We had to ride around a big mountain and keep the cattle away from the Getchel Mine because there was arsenic in the water ponds below the mine.

Once Lee took Paul and me the other direction to look for his cattle. I rode my mare, Penny. Paul sent me one way and he went the other. I ran into a bunch of wild cattle; about ten head. They took off running across the hillside and I couldn't see the brands. I was running Penny flat out and she jumped an old open mine shaft located in the sagebrush. It sure looked big, wide and deep. However, I didn't go back and check it out. If we had gone in that gaping hole, I doubt they would ever have known where we went. After that close call, I decided the wild cows could just stay where they were.

When we lived in Charleston, Paul would cook breakfast and I would wrango the horses on Doc. The Shively horses were tough and hard to corral. It was a lot of fun to go there early in the mornings and really come in fast while corralling the horses.

When we moved to Devil's Gate there were not many fences. Paul and I worked many cattle along the few fence lines there were. In the spring we would push the cattle to the high country and brand in a rodeer out on the open range. In the fall I would go over to Halleck and bring our cattle back to the ranch two or three times a week.

Once on Christmas Day, Paul decided I needed some fresh air and a chance to get out of the house. There were a few head of cattle below the Nine Mile Lane so I went after them. There was drifted snow on the ground so it was a slow, cold trip. I got home before dark. My little boys were still in their pajamas and Paul had a nice dinner cooked. I think it was one of the best Christmases Bob and Bill ever had – no Mom to make them do anything. They just had to play with their new stuff.

One time Alma Smiraldo asked me to go to the Owyhee Desert with her. We drove to the IL Ranch and rode our horses over the desert to Starr Valley. She knew the country and the horses. We rode over that range to the 45 Ranch on the Owyhee River. It was a real trip and a new experience for me.

We always did all of our work on horseback. When we bought the Fernald Ranch, we put on ropings and gynkhanas. We did many 4-H rides and trail rides and camped in the Ruby Mountains at different lakes. I rode on the bi-centennial wagon train across Nevada in 1975. I rode from Carson City to Montello, Nevada, a distance of about 400 miles, as an out-rider and met lots of nice people across the state.

I have enjoyed my life...I have ridden with some wonderful "top hands" that taught me a lot. Some of them were my Dad, Robert Y. Reed, Hugh Beiroth, Charlie Chapin, Jerry Merrick and Paul Bear. When I was growing up there were no horsemanship clinics and all of these people gave me good advice. I got to ride some fine horses. I've been very lucky to live in the era that I have ...It has been fun.

Dave's note-Betty and her family have owned and operated the J.M. Capriola Saddle and Western Store in Elko, Nevada, for fifty-one years. They build and sell top quality saddles and equipment while continuing to carry on the famous Garcia legacy.

BETTY BEAR'S MILES RIDDEN HORSEBACK

Miles ridden to grade school   5,600 miles

Miles ridden weekends and summer plus cattle drives with Hugh Bieroth   5,400 miles

Age 14 -16 ran cattle for her mother, drove horses for Earl Prunty
14,600 miles

Miles ridden on the Reed, Golconda, Moffat and McKnight Ranches   15,000 miles

Miles ridden mostly at Devil's Gate where we started a family (easily 150 miles per month because some days were sixty miles rides)
21, 600 miles

1958 moved to Elko. Started the 4-H horsemanship Program, helped at Devil's Gate, also rode to, from and in all parades.
                                                                                3,000 miles
1965 bought Fernald Ranch, lots of riding and rode the Ruby Mountains three times, running mustangs   32,600 miles
1975 divorced, bought ranch, rode across Nevada from Carson City, to Montello, Nevada, with Bi-Centennial Wagon Train
                                                                                400 miles
Rode Grindstone Mountain with Manzoni   600 miles
Riding meadows, Cancer Trail rides, riding with Neighbors and "up the hill to get strays"   6,000 miles

TOTAL OF MILES RIDDEN HORSEBACK   104, 200 MILES

One story Betty recalls from her youth: Betty said, "Mother sent me to a neighbor's to get a dozen eggs with very firm instructions to be careful and not break any. It was cold and snow was on the ground. On the way home my horse stumbled into a snow covered ditch, then came up running and bucked a couple of jumps before I again gained control. I was carefully holding the sack of eggs out to the side when this happened and the rest of the way home I worried about the condition the eggs were in. When my mother opened the sack, to my relief, not an egg was broken."

LITTLE THINGS

An old saying: Another day, another dollar. Thirty days, thirty dollars.

DAVE SECRIST'S SALMON RIVER CATTLEMEN'S ASSOCIATION
WESTSIDE RERIDE

We started early- five cowboys to ride.
The draws and rims along the west side.
I have the low circle so I'm slow starting out
Now the cowboys above are starting to shout.
I gather a few then I pick up some more
There's a bunch up above and they're coming full bore.
I get them together; we've a long way to go
Some are real fast and some are real slow.
A Stiegemier turns left and a Fuller turns right
Lierman stops back behind, Boies' she's about out of sight.
I holler and cuss and throw a real fit
Some still want to run and some want to quit.
I keep them together. I don't quite know how
I don't need help later. I need help right now.
My horse knickers and looks up a draw
I rise in the stirrups to see what he saw.
Around a rim cows burst into view
And back in the dust there's a cowboy, no - two!
We all grin at each other, the cowboys they know
They've been up above; they've been watching the show.
The day wears on the miles worry by
The sun's gone over the top part of the sky.
We reach the highway along old ninety-three
There's dust in my throat and an ache in my knee.
Four more miles, we sure aren't there yet
The closer we are the slower they get.
We finally make it. Just the highway to cross.
Four tired cowboys and a crotchety boss.
We all cinch up you never can tell
Cow don't cross a paved road very well.
I wave my slicker and ask the traffic to stop
Somebody yells "He's not a real cop."
A lady gets out of her little sports car
And starts taking picture for her VCR.
In spite of all this the cows are crossing just fine
'Til a Shewmaker looks down and sees the white line.
She doubles back –She kicks like a mule.
Her speed indicated she's been drinking jet fuel.
She doubles again –someone makes a good throw
Takes his dallies and across the highway they go.
Now she's across, give her some slack!
She's starting to jerk and her eyes are rolled back.
We gather them up the last cows through the gate.
The sun's out of sight. It's sure getting late.
I hope this stirs memories for old cowboys that's rode
From Burnt Meadow to the highway and crossed the paved road.

SMOKY

Through the years, especially in the early half of my lifelong horse-back ride, nearly every ranch and pleasure horse owner in the west at one time or another had a horse named Smoky. Except through the eyes of the boys and girls that owned these Smokys, few if any, lived up to the image of Will James' legendary horse made famous in his book Smoky The Cow Horse. I know the horses named Smoky that I have ridden certainly did not; but one Smoky I came to own, when he was middle aged, has always stuck in my memory

Smoky was the most unlikely horse you could imagine to be named after Smoky The Cow Horse. In the first place he was a catch colt out of a bay mare named Annie and this Smoky was coal black. He was a short, thick bodied horse with big feet. Shaggy hair protruded from his fetlocks and I think it would be safe to say Annie had been scared by some draft horse eleven months before Smoky was born. Smoky was a hearty eater, boss at the feed rack and with the exception of his looks, he was just an average ranch horse. Smoky was honest but lazy, smart to a fault and easy to catch, so I often used him in an emergency. Smoky never did one thing he did not have to do, but he was smart enough to know when a cowboy was on his back. A good rap under the belly with a romal would start his ears working and he could head cows, drag calves, hold a rope and do a reasonable job of doing what a ranch horse was expected to do. On the other hand, you could pack salt, pack a buck, put a dude or inexperienced rider on him and he would poke along just doing what he had to and that usually wasn't much.

The incident I remember Smoky for started early in the morning on a hot summer's day. We were moving about two hundred head of cows and calves from the valley to the Haw Creek pasture which was in the foothills at a higher elevation. It was a five or six mile drive and the sagebrush was saddle horn high. It got hot and it turned out to be a hard drive. As is normal, I was short handed and a member of the haying crew had been pestering me to let him help work cows. He was a good hay hand and had apparently ridden horses somewhere along the line, so this day I took him along. I rigged up an extra saddle and bridle and of course, Smoky got the call.

I can see this hay hand in my mind's eye but I can't put a name to him so I will call him Joe. Joe had on street shoes, baggy pants and if he had socks on they were not visible. All of this was topped off with a floppy straw hat.

The drive started out with four cowboys and Joe and it was a hard drive from the start with the usual problems of calves breaking back in the tall sagebrush. We reached the Haw Creek pasture about one o'clock in the afternoon.

When we started out that morning, it didn't take Smoky long to figure out what kind of a day he was going to have. He plodded along behind the cows doing as little as possible with Joe working overtime to get that much out of him.

When we got through the gate at the Haw Creek pasture we mothered up the cows and calves before we let them go out onto the range. We were busy keeping calves from breaking back, so when one old cow broke out of the herd I yelled at Joe, saying something like, "Joe, wake that old horse up and head that cow!" The urgency in my voice startled Joe and he rapped Smoky over and under with his romal. That woke Smoky up and forgetting who was on him, Smoky took off like a shot. He headed that cow in nothing flat, but in true Smoky style of not going one step further than necessary, he came to a jolting, three hop, front-legged stop. Each time Smoky hit the ground Joe's baggy street pants crawled another foot up his boney legs. By the time Smoky turned the cow, Joe's pants were hiked up nearly to his waist. Joe lost his hat but to his credit he stayed on while Smoky brought the cow back to the herd.

We finished mothering up the cows; rode to a spring surrounded by a small meadow, watered our horses and unsaddled them. We put our wet, sweaty saddle blankets upside down on top of the saddles to let the blankets air out. Joe, being tired, just dropped his saddle on the ground and left his saddle blanket underneath it. We led the horses into the meadow, hobbled them except for Smoky and left them to graze. Knowing that one old horse could travel faster hobbled than a man on foot, we settled down to rest between the grazing horses and the ranch headquarters. We were visiting, maybe teasing Joe about his bare legged stop, when I noticed Smoky stop grazing and walk over toward the saddles. I didn't think much about it. Smoky walked around through the saddles lying at the meadow's edge, stopping to smell each saddle as he passed by. By the time I realized what he was doing it was too late. When Smoky found Joe's saddle that had been on his back, he walked spraddle legged over that saddle, struck the classic pose all stretched out with head and tail up, reeled out his tallywhacker and cut loose. You may have heard the old saying, "It's raining as hard as a cow peeing on a flat rock." Smoky had dead aim on the seat of that saddle. We jumped up, hollering and waving our hats. Smoky was not impressed. He paid absolutely no attention to our efforts to move him off that saddle. He took his time and when his mission was finished, he farted three times, walked spraddle legged off of the saddle, turned his head and looked at us while sticking his nose in the air. He then rolled his upper lip up showing us all of his teeth in a horse laugh like horses sometimes do when they are unhappy about something. Then he walked back to the rest of the horses and continued grazing.

I know Smoky was attracted to Joe's saddle because of the smell of sweat or some other animal reason but I've never seen another horse methodically pick out the saddle that had been on his back and pee on it. It seemed like Smoky looked straight at me and said, "That will teach you to put a dude on my back."

I have ridden and owned a number of horses named Smoky during my 115,000 mile ride but this incident plus this Smoky's personality will keep his memory in my mind forever.

LITTLE THINGS

See that old cowboy limping along. Put him on a good horse and he will look twenty years younger.

SMOKY NUMBER 2 AND THE RANCH MANAGER

I didn't own this Smoky but I rode him for several years. He was an ordinary, honest ranch horse. He was half Arab and half Quarter horse, a smoky grey color with a big heart. His disposition leaned toward the Quarter horse and I used him to gather the ranch saddle horses as well as the stud band of ranch brood mares. The brood mares ran free on the open range, being gathered once in the early spring, when they were vaccinated for sleeping sickness and the stallion was turned out with them. The brood mares were again gathered in the fall when the colts were weaned. During this time frame the stallion being used was a registered Quarter horse named Little Red Jack and he was kept at the ranch headquarters during the winter months.

Every horse's disposition isn't suitable for running other horses. Some horses get too excited, rear up, lunge, run sideways and break out in a sweat even before the horse gather gets started. To keep these horses under some kind of control, a cowboy has to pull too hard on the horse's mouth. Smoky was reasonably calm and easy to control so I used him when running horses. His memory probably would not have been etched in my mind all of these years if it hadn't been for an incident that happened when I was riding him. In the early spring it was my job to gather the saddle horses that wintered out on the range. They consisted of broke horses that were less honest for winter use, green broke horses and colts that were to be started. This round-up happened several times a year but the spring gather was the wildest.

The horses had been on green grass long enough to shed their winter hair and become fat, slick and shiny. The old horses were the wise leaders that knew the routine. I learned from experience that if I just poked along, those old horses would slip off with several young horses following when we left the open grassy ridges where the trail continued down through oak trees and brush. I found that if I "hooped it up" the first mile while going through the open grassy country, the horses would hit the trail at a full run, stay together, eventually slow to a long trot and go directly to the Two Mile Corrals. The corrals were appropriately named because they were two miles from ranch headquarters.

The ranch manager, Roland Williams, would be at the corral with the winter horses that were to be turned out on the range after he picked out fresh horses to take back to the ranch. The fresh horses would be ridden during spring and early summer round ups and calf brandings.

To a bunch of young cowboys, Roland seemed to be gruff and tough. He didn't talk much and we approached him with a little apprehension. He was fair, but when he gave you a job he expected you to do it in a manner he thought was right. Roland believed if cowboys and horses were working together there was going to be horse wrecks and he accepted that. He didn't accept unnecessary chowsing or harassing a bunch of livestock. He had no patience with a cowboy who couldn't think like a range cow or horse and anticipate what the animal was likely to do.

Even though this happened sixty years ago, Roland managed the Eden Valley Ranch in the time frame of the past, combining things learned years ago with modern improvements of that day. He still used a rawhide riata and the throws he could make were remarkable. He believed when gathering cattle, an hour at daybreak was worth two hours in the afternoon. He thought a man with good dogs was worth two men when gathering cattle in the brushy draws and mountain ranges of northern California.

He thought you should ride out from the home ranch or line camp early enough to be in the area of the range being gathered by daylight. This meant getting up at three to four o'clock in the morning, wrangling horses and eating breakfast in the dark. I remember watching the sun come up in the mountains six or seven miles from where we started. I can still remember following Roland single file up a dark winding trail watching an occasional spark fly up when his horse's shoe hit a certain kind of rock. After we reached our destination and Roland gave his brief explanation of where he wanted each cowboy or pairs of cowboys to go, he would ride off without a backward glance. Because I knew the country and Roland's ways, I could explain to younger cowboys where Roland wanted them to go as they circled back toward home.

Anyway, this was the background when I saddled Smoky and started out to gather the forty head of saddle horses that were running somewhere on Bald Mountain seven or eight miles from the home ranch. It was a nice spring day. It was warm with a light breeze blowing and the grass and tree leaves were new and green. The birds had returned after a long winter and a couple of eagles were circling in the blue sky. It was a great day to be alive. Smoky shied at rocks and shadows along the trail, making it a fun ride. About midmorning I reached the top of Bald Mountain and on the green slopes to the south I located the horses. They were all in the same vicinity except for two small buddy groups that were away from the main herd. This was bad news because each buddy group would be led by a wise old leader that would be hard to keep with the other horses. I slipped around below the horses unseen, got them together, lined them out and headed toward home. I had to keep them moving. If the leaders of those buddy groups had time to think, they would slip away unseen when they got into the trees and brush. Then when I reached the Two Mile corrals, I would be short horses. Invariably the horses missing were amongst the horses Roland wanted. I never knew for sure if he really wanted those horses or if he was teaching me a lesson. Either way I had lots of time to think about it while I went back to find the strays.

Knowing all of this, I let out a Comanche yell, emptied my pistol in the air and the race was on. We crossed that mile and a half of open ground in nothing flat. The horses were running flat out when they reached the trees and Smoky and I were in hot pursuit. Smoky was eager to keep up with the herd so when we reached the trail going down through the trees and brush, I could nearly reach out and touch the running horses. The trail went down an especially steep hill and then abruptly benched out flat for about twenty yards before going downhill again.

When Smoky hit the flat at the bottom of that steep hill, his front feet went out from under him and he fell flat on his left side. He skidded ten or fifteen feet over the gravely ground with my leg pinned underneath before he came to a stop. As Smoky struggled to his feet, I kicked free. Luckily I was still holding the lead rope and when Smoky came to the end of it, he turned to face me while I got up slowly to survey the damage. The hide and hair on the point of Smoky's shoulder was ground away and the bare muscle was showing.

The leather, rawhide and some of the wood was worn away from the swell on the left side of my saddle. I looked down and the Levis on the outside of my left leg were gone. Gravel was lodged in the muscle of my leg from my hip to my knee. I could still bend my leg but this picture perfect day had turned into a serious situation in just a split second. The running horses were out of sight and everything was quiet. Even the birds were silent while I stood there with my hand on Smoky's sweaty neck. I realized as bad as things were, they could have been worse. If my foot had hung up in the bottom stirrup when Smoky struggled to his feet, I knew in spite of his sore shoulder, he would have taken off running, bucking and kicking, trying to catch up with the horses and my story may have had a different ending.

I learned later that the horses reached the Two Mile Corrals traveling at a fast trot, all together and corralled themselves. Roland, who had been waiting to turn out the winter horses and pick out fresh ones, closed the gate. He waited for awhile and when I didn't show up, he started up the trail the horses had just come down. Smoky and I were limping down the trail about a half mile from the corrals when I saw Roland coming. He was traveling at a fast trot and I wasn't sure what was going to happen. When he rode up and realized Smoky and I had been in a wreck but didn't appear to have life threatening injuries, the stern look on his face turned to genuine relief.

After I explained what had happened and why I was bringing the horses at such a fast pace, I thought I almost saw a pleased look cross his face. I realized under that tough exterior he had been reliving some of the serious wrecks he had been in or seen during his younger years. His face reflected the relief he felt when he saw that Smoky and I were going to survive.

As we started back down the trail at a slow walk, Roland said, "You were riding too fast coming down that steep hill and when you hit the flat at the bottom, you rode Smoky into the ground. You better remember that the next time you get into that kind of a situation." We slowly rode the rest of the way to the Two Mile Corrals in silence.

I went thirty miles to the hospital and was treated for my leg injury. I doctored Smoky's shoulder for several weeks and we both healed up and haired over at about the same time with no visible ill effects.

Smoky and I had many more rides together. As I mentioned before, Smoky was not an outstanding horse but he was honest, a good traveler and I liked to ride him. This type of horse is the backbone of the saddle horses used on the big ranches of the west. If it hadn't been for the incident I just described, the memory of Smoky probably would not have been etched in my mind and the understanding of a tough old ranch boss would have been slower to come.

As the years passed and I look back at this incident with more experience under my belt, I realized what Roland told me that day, in a very few words, was exactly what happened and I never forgot the advice he gave me. I worked for Roland for a number of years after that. I learned about the old time methods of working cows, breaking horses, and in general how to understand and think like range cows and horses. In other words, having an idea of what was going to happen out on the open range before it actually happened.

Another incident that happened in the very early stages of my horseback ride, making me realize Roland had a heart under that tough exterior, happened on a dark cloudy December morning. Don Linsteadt, my lifelong friend and partner, and I were young cowboys working for Roland. Roland had just purchased a brand new powder blue Chevy pickup and it was the pride of the ranch. Don and I asked to borrow it to run a short trap line we set out along one of the ranch roads. This was all right with Roland as long as we were back in time for breakfast and a day's work. This meant the night was our own and we had to get up and run our trap line in the dark early each morning.

Coming back to the ranch one dark morning, after checking our traps, we fell asleep and ran that shiny new pickup into an oak tree. We made a big dent in the shiny chrome bumper. Well, we thought we were going to get fired, so we rolled up our bedrolls before we went to breakfast that morning. We had a hard time getting up enough nerve to tell Roland what happened. When we did, Roland sat there with that stern look on his face for what to us seemed like forever before he said, "Boys, sometimes it doesn't pay to burn the candle at both ends." Then he got up and went into his office. The incident was never mentioned again.

Through the years I learned to understand Roland more. At the ripe old age of twenty I was promoted to ranch foreman and my sixty dollars a month wage plus room and board was raised to seventy-five dollars per month. I started working for Roland during summer school vacations for thirty dollars per month plus room and board and seventy-five dollars per month was good ranch wages at that time. In a few months I bought a brand new pair of hand made Blucher cowboy boots and I was riding on top of the world. This was just another learning experience along the early stages of my 115,000 mile horseback ride.

LITTLE THINGS

It was time to turn the clocks ahead to daylight savings time and an old Indian said to me, "Only the white man could take an hour off the beginning of the day, put it back on the end of the day and think they made the day longer."

GENE AND JODY CHRISTISON

Gene and Jody Christison were inducted into the Nevada Cattlemen's Association Cowboy 100,000 Mile Club in 2004.

Julian Smith presented their story as follows:

Ladies and Gentlemen:

Tonight we are going to honor a married couple that has always made their living horseback. In their fifty-five years of married life they have ridden together on their ranch out of Golconda, Nevada. Their ranch consists of the two Pinson Ranches and the Pettit Ranch on the south side of the Osgood Mountains, which are about thirty miles long in Clover Valley, near Winnemucca, Nevada. One of the Pinion Ranches is a Centennial Ranch, operated at least one hundred years by the same family. They have judged many horse shows, both singly and together in Winnemucca, Elko, Ely, Yerington, Gardnerville, Fernley, Lakeview and Sacramento. Gene, who held a judge's card in the National Reining Cow Horse Association, also judged in Canada and Idaho. He was one of the first group of Brand Inspectors in the State of Nevada, a position he held for nineteen years.

Gene was born in Bruneau, Idaho in 1925 as one of two sons in a family of seven children and spent his early years thereabout. His mother was from a pioneer family and his father came to Bruneau with his widowed mother. His father was a contractor and one of his accomplishments was building a trail into the rugged Bruneau River Canyon.

Gene's first job was a "rango" at Riddle, Idaho. He worked for various other ranchers in the surrounding area during the summers. He worked for such people as Claude Sullivan and Jeanne Hazle of Delamar, Idaho. Jeanne Hazle came from England for her health and passed herself off as a man in the Wild West.

Other ranchers Gene worked for were Hubert and Joe Nettleton of Reynolds Creek and Sinker Creek near Murphy, Idaho. Here, he and noted jumping horse rider, trainer and clinician, Gene Lewis, became lifelong friends. Among his many other honors, Lewis was named Horseman of the Year by the American Horse Show Association in 2002.

Gene's first introduction to Nevada was a cattle drive from Riddle, Idaho to Deep Creek, Nevada. Before the couple married, Gene buckarooed for Carl Hanks at the Horseshoe Ranch and for Roland Hill at the T Lazy S Ranch, both near Battle Mountain. Gene also worked for Phil Tobin and Tommy Hayes at the CS and for Jack Kearns at the Circle Bar near Winnemucca before returning to the TS for Elmor Hill. During this time Gene accumulated 38,808 miles horseback.

Gene was drafted into World War II while at the TS. While serving his country in the Philippines he was honored with a Purple Heart. When he was discharged, he returned to work for Joe Nettleton. He distinguished himself as a horseman and buckaroo, riding alongside the Jones brothers; Marvin, Melvin, and especially Everett, who was his closest childhood friend and later became his brother-in-law. Gene also rode with Ray Hunt. They all learned a great deal from Roland Hill, who had fine Morgan horses at the TS. Hill and his son, Elmor, gave great credibility and a sterling reputation to Nevada horsemen throughout the west.

In 1949 Gene went to visit his parents who were, at that time, employed at a mine in Golconda. Nevada. It was here he met Jody Hibbs.

Jody was born there in 1928 to Camille Pinson and Glenn Hibbs. Grandfather Paul Pinson was in Humboldt County in 1873 and founded the Pinson Ranch shortly thereafter.

Being the only child, at an early age she began to ride each and every day to gather a small bunch of sheep and the milk cows from out on the open range. That averaged being a four mile ride. During this time she accumulated 27,375 miles horseback. Another chore was riding to a spring that was a major watering spot for local cattle, driving and separating cattle alone over a period of twenty years. This added 14,440 miles. Even more miles were added gathering various fields during the past seventy years which totaled another 8,400 miles. After their marriage they bought the Pettit Ranch, where she added yet another 49,845 for a total of over 100,000 miles ridden.

Gene accumulated another 82,930 miles training his own horses, riding and showing horses for the public. He has ridden a grand total of over 120,000 miles horseback.

They have three children, two of which are on the ranch with them. Naturally they became 4-H horsemanship leaders and Gene has done many clinics, helping other people. Jody served on the third Ag District for twenty-two years bringing open horse shows and cutting to Winnemucca for the first time. She is also a member of the Nevada State Horseman's Hall of Fame.

They, like many others, have suffered disastrous range fires in the past few years and like anyone who has had fires on their BLM allotment they know the riding problems this causes. Also, like many others, they have had to take their livestock to other feed.

And yes, they both still ride. I would like to introduce Gene and Jody Christison.

Dave's comment: "The unusual thing about Gene and Jody's fifty-five year partnership is they have combined traditional Nevada ranching with professional horsemanship, judging and showing horses at many of the top shows around the country. During their lifetimes they excelled at both of these endeavors."

LITTLE THINGS

Jane and I have been married a long time. I usually try to take things as they come and accept what happens. One time however, not long after we were married, at some function we were attending I introduced Jane using her maiden name. I didn't know what I had done or why I got such a big laugh.

HAYING AND HAYSTACKS

In the northern California coastal mountains where I was raised, the annual rainfall is forty to sixty inches per year. In these conditions hay is harvested differently than it is in the big sagebrush basins and high deserts located in the more arid areas of the west.

In the earliest days along my long winding trail, I mowed hay using horse drawn number five John Deere mowers, raked hay using horse drawn dump rakes and made windrows into hay shocks by hand, using a pitch fork. After these shocks of hay cured, they were pitched upon flat bed hay wagons and hauled to surrounding barns.

Hay crews worked hard. They laughed and kidded each other and took pride in what they were doing. Losing a load of hay before it reached the barn was a disgrace. The hay wagons were pulled from shock to shock, stopping long enough to let two men working together, load a hay shock on the wagon. The two men stood with their backs to the wagon, placed their pitchforks into the far side of the hay shock and with their pitchfork handles bowing, they lifted the shock up over their heads, turning as they lifted and put it upside down on the wagon.

The man loading the wagon placed the hay around the outside part of the wagon bed before filling the center. By keeping the outside part of the load a little higher than the center, the loose hay was woven together. This process was repeated until the wagon load was as high as the hay could be pitched. The load was then topped off and hauled to the barn. When I was loading loose hay, I had one of the hay hands go to the back of the wagon when it was about half full and hold a pitchfork up in the center so I could make sure the load was centered on the wagon bed. If it wasn't I could still make adjustments. One time when Don and I were pitching hay shocks as high as we could reach, topping off a wagon load of hay, a very agitated rattlesnake came slithering down between our pitchfork handles. As you can imagine this caused some unplanned excitement.

Horse barns were located at ranch headquarters with a large hay loft built in the top half of each barn. Horse stalls were underneath along the sides and there were hay chutes going down to individual mangers. In the winter we climbed the ladder going to the hay loft and pitched hay into the chutes where it fell to the mangers below. Other large barns were located in strategic spots around the valley and filled from the ground to the rafters with loose hay. In winter the hay was pitched into feed racks built along the sides of the barn or pitched onto wagons and hauled to portable feed racks. These feed racks were built on runners so they could be moved to clean areas of ground when necessary. During most years in the coastal mountains of northern California, where the main cow herds ran out on the range during the winter, this type of supplemental feeding was adequate. In extremely hard winters, cotton seed cake, also stored in these barns, was packed out and fed on the open range.

When the wagon load of loose hay reached the barn it was parked at the front end of the building. Each barn's hay loft was equipped with a Jackson Fork. This fork was a large three tined fork equipped with pulleys. A cable attached to the Jackson Fork ran through several pulleys like a block and tackle, before it went along a track in the top of each barn. The cable eventually went through more pulleys before it ended on the ground outside the far end of the structure. The cable had a loop in the end that was hooked to a singletree behind an honest work horse. This horse was the power that lifted the Jackson Fork load of hay to the top of the barn and pulled it along the track installed there.

The Jackson Fork had a trip mechanism attached to a long rope controlled by the hay hand unloading the wagon. That man shoved the three foot long Jackson Fork tines into the top of the wagon load of hay and hollered, "Take it away." The boy (in previous years the boy was sometimes me) drove the work horse away from the back end of the barn. The Jackson Fork load of hay was lifted to the top of the barn and pulled along the tracks. The Jackson Fork had a trip mechanism attached to a long rope controlled by the man unloading the wagon. When the fork load of hay reached the spot where the man inside the barn wanted it dropped he hollered, "Whoa." The man unloading the wagon pulled the trip rope and the fork load of hay was released. The boy outside stopped the horse, unhooked the cable and returned to his previous position. The man on the wagon pulled the Jackson Fork toward him and let it back down on the wagon load of hay and the process was repeated until the wagon was empty. Hell, now I am getting myself confused.

This sounds complicated but in reality it was simple. In days gone by, this system of handling loose hay was on the cutting edge of technology. In high moisture areas of the west, tons upon tons of loose hay were stored in barns using this method.

I once got in trouble for fooling around too much while driving the derrick horse.

A boy from a neighboring ranch stopped by. We hadn't seen each other since school let out and we were excited. We were hollering at each other and the man unloading the wagon, who happened to be my Dad, mistook our hollering as the signal from the man in the hay loft. So Dad tripped the Jackson fork full of hay in the wrong place. A quarter of a ton of hay fell dangerously close to the hay hand working inside the barn. Didn't take Dad long to straighten that little problem out.

Putting up hay in the big sagebrush and cold high deserts of the more arid west was different. The basics were the same but the methods used differed drastically. In the white sage and browse areas of central Nevada, cows can winter out on the range, but in the northern counties and along the mountain ranges, a ranch's entire herd of cows is fed hay during the winter. The wild grass hay that is grown on the big natural meadows is mowed, stacked and fed back out on the same meadows that produced it. An old rancher once told me you need a ton and a half of hay for every animal on the ranch to get through the winter. He added, that means every cow, calf, horse, elk, and if you want to be really safe, put the dogs and cats into the count. His rule of thumb calculations were probably correct but I've seen winters when two ton of hay per cow wasn't any too much. Maybe I didn't add enough dogs and cats to his formula.

A cow's feed requirements vary greatly with the weather. The hay consumption of one four hundred head cow herd I was winter feeding, increased by forty eighty pound bales of meadow hay per day when the temperature dropped from thirty degrees above zero to thirty degrees below.

During the same time period that I described haying operations in northern California coastal mountains, loose hay was being put up in the Great Basin and high deserts of Nevada using different methods. Because many more tons of hay were needed and the much dryer climate allowed hay to be stacked outside, volume methods of putting up hay were developed. Large stack yards were built and huge stacks of loose hay dotted the meadows. Horse drawn mowers and dump rakes cut and raked the hay into windrows. Buck rakes brought the loose hay to stack yards where it was stacked using beaver slides, overshot stackers and hay derricks, along with a lot of man power. Not everyone could make a good loose hay stack that would stand and shed some moisture. Men that could, took pride in their work and were sought after during the haying season.

When the hay baler was developed and became reliable, it gradually replaced the loose hay methods of putting up hay. Existing equipment was modified but the bales of hay were still picked up and stacked by hand and baled hay stacks just replaced loose hay stored in the old stack yards. Slips replaced buck rakes and baled hay elevators replaced the beaver slides, overshot loaders and hay derricks.

In spite of these modified changes and improvements, haying on the big cattle ranches of the west was still labor intensive and didn't change much until the invention of the swather and the harrow bed. Up to this point, putting up hay on these big meadows was a labor intensive operation that still used large numbers of transient labor.

Even then, this change didn't happen overnight. I remember the first swather I owned. I cut the first swathe and back swathe around the meadow with a mowing machine before the swather came into the field. Then when opening up a new meadow, I led the swather on the first round by riding a saddle horse ahead of it. This helped to avoid getting the machine high centered and stuck in boggy places or head ditches. What old time swather operator doesn't remember spending an hour under the swather unplugging the hay conditioner several times a day? As swathers improved and the operators became more knowledgeable, the swather became the machine of choice when mowing hay.

Harrow beds were soon to follow and went through similar growing pains that the swather had endured. Ranchers, including me, took pride in their hand built baled hay stacks. We swore we would never let one of those new fangled machines on our ranches. At first our reasoning was pretty well founded. Wild hay bales are harder to stack than domesticated hay crops like alfalfa. Several varieties of grass hay grow in the same meadow. Some bales are firm while other bales are spongy and soft. This mix of bales is hard to stack even by hand and those first harrow bed hay stacks were a disaster. When these hay stacks settled, bales fell out in all directions. As the harrow beds evolved and got better and the operators' skills improved, the harrow bed also became the ranchers' method of choice when stacking two twine bales of hay. The starting columns of baled hay in a harrow bed stack are always prone to falling and are often propped up by long poles. This is the source of one of my hay stack experiences.

I've spent half a lifetime telling kids to not play around baled hay stacks and I cautioned ranch hands to be careful when feeding from them. I increased my vigilance when the harrow bed was developed and came into use. The machines automatically pick the bales up in the field, haul them to the stack yard and stack them up in three to four ton columns. These columns of hay are nine to ten bales high and stand fifteen feet into the air. The amount of hay available determines the length of the hay stack.

When this incident happened I was retired from the big ranches and slowing down. Through the years I'd watched my old cowboy friends break that last colt or rope that last steer long after their bodies could handle what their brain still wanted them to do. In some cases they were badly crippled for the rest of their lives. When I was young I told myself if or when I reach that stage of my life, I hope I have the common sense to quit. I didn't mean quit, quit. I think if you do that you are a dead duck. I meant quit doing the high risk things that you no longer had to do. What I didn't realize at the time is how hard quitting was going to be, especially after spending a lifetime of hard work I enjoyed doing. Finding the balance between what I could do in the past and what I can now do is difficult.

An example of this is a snorty, not so honest, bald faced horse named Charley grazing out in the pasture. I've ridden Charley many miles and I know what he is capable of doing. I would dearly love to get on him one more time and I know he would like to have me ride him now and then; but after having two shoulder replacements, plus two rods, twelve plates and twenty three screws placed in my back, I just go out into the pasture where Charley is and we talk things over. For now we leave it at that but even I wonder how long this common sense approach will last.

Anyway, that is the background when I started out to help my neighbor, Laurie, feed their cows and horses. My horses run with theirs so we feed together. This morning we had to open up a new harrow bed hay stack. The way the stack was situated we had to open up the end of the stack that was propped up by poles. Laurie said, "Let's wait until Ed comes home and he can open up the new stack for us." I told her, "I've done this hundreds of times and it won't be a problem." Laurie went around the barn to break ice on the water troughs while I drove the tractor with the front end loader up alongside the hay stack. I intended to use the loader to knock down the end bales so they would no longer be a danger. I got off and very carefully removed two long poles propping up the end of the harrow bed stacked hay. I was now on the opposite side of the stack from the tractor. I stood there for maybe two minutes watching. When I was satisfied that the end wasn't going to fall out of the stack, I started walking across to the tractor. I was about half way when the first hundred pound bale of hay silently fell from fifteen feet up and hit me in the back of the neck. I went down and a half a ton of hay bales tumbled down around and on top of me. My chest was crushed so tightly every drop of wind was squeezed out of my lungs and I couldn't breathe. Every time I felt another bale fall I was squeezed tighter.

When Laurie came around the corner of the barn all she could see of me was my two boots sticking out from under the fallen bales of hay. Now Laurie probably weighs about a hundred twenty pounds wringing wet. (I'm treading on thin ice here.) Somehow she lifted the hay bales above me high enough to let me take in hoarse, rasping breaths of air, then she ran for help. When they dug me out from under that pile of fallen hay, they said my face was blue and I was a sorry looking sight; but I soon recovered and we finished feeding the cows. Later when I was talking to Laurie about this incident, I asked how in the world she was able to lift that much weight high enough to give me a little breathing room. Laurie just stood there shaking her head and said, "I don't know. I just knew I had to." I don't know how she did it either but I'm glad she did. I came out of the wreck with only a couple of cracked ribs.

I sure would have hated to end my 115,000 mile horseback ride with two feet sticking out from under a fallen stack of baled hay.

I've often wondered how a person can come through a number of life threatening incidents with barely a scratch and then, doing something very simple, nearly come to the end of the trail. I guess this particular incident comes under the heading of, "Do as I say not as I do" and remember, you're never too old to stop paying attention to your own advice.

LITTLE THINGS

If you are bored and time is dragging by too slowly, go down to the bank and borrow thirty thousand dollars payable in full with interest in six months. Now see how fast time flies by.

JOHN FALEN

John Falen was inducted into the Nevada Cattlemen's Association Cowboy 100,000 Mile Club in 2003.

John's wife, Sharon, wrote and gave the following presentation when he was inducted:

John Falen was born in Caldwell, Idaho in 1937. As soon as possible he was taken home to Jordan Valley, Oregon, where his Dad had a ranch leased on Cow Creek. In 1941 his dad, Les Falen, bought a ranch. He called it the L-F Ranch, at Cliff, Idaho, forty-three miles of gravel road from Jordan Valley. It was here on this beautiful, isolated ranch on the south side of South Mountain in the Owyhee Mountain range that John began to amass his 100,000 miles horseback. He rode horses to school every day for eight years and his brother, Loyd, says that should account for about 6,000 miles.

Brother Loyd's favorite story about this time took place when John was about ten. It was John's turn to wrangle the horses before breakfast. Their dad was on his way to the barn to milk the cows but stopped at the outhouse on his way. Loyd says he was only an observer, but became highly amused at what happened next. John got on a horse named "Rex" whom he hadn't ridden much at this time. Now Rex was a young horse and believed in "early morning calisthenics". He apparently wanted to see if the young cowboy on his back could stay up there. John didn't—- as he soon departed his lofty roost for the ground. As he descended from the heavens, he came down on a mowing machine tongue and dislocated his elbow. Dad, observing the beginnings of the short episode bolted from the outhouse with his pants still down below his knees, hollering, "Stay with him John—- Stay with him." Loyd is sure his dad wondered what he thought was so funny.

Other than Rex, Loyd does not recall John ever being bucked off. He said his dad gave them this advice, "There is not much to staying on a bucking horse. Just sit there in the middle and keep one leg on each side of the horse and you will be just fine." It always worked for us – as long as we followed his advice.

The Falens only went to town once a year in the fall. They would sell their calves at the livestock auction, visit all the relatives and buy groceries and supplies they would need for the next full year. Other than that trip, most everything they did was on or with horses.

They ran their cattle in the spring in common with several other ranchers. Neighbor, Frankie Dougal, figures John put in somewhere close to 20,000 miles turning out and gathering those cattle. There was no use of trailers at that time. You were up early and trotting to the allotment in the dark before dawn and coming home in the black of night.

In the summer the cattle ran in the mountains. It was rugged country with creeks running through deep narrow canyons. This doubled the miles and added another 20,000 miles to his riding. John worked on the ranch all of his growing up years. He missed some of the rides while in college, but after college he spent weekends and vacation time, along with his family, going up to help his dad.

In the years after college John did a variety of things in the beef industry. 1963 found him located in Rupert, Idaho, with his wife, Sharon, and two small children, Cindy and Frank. He built and ran a feedlot there for three years. The miles there would probably not add up to more than 5,000. After the family left Rupert, John started buying cattle for Idaho Meat Pack. The horseback miles went down during those three years. He began to put miles of another sort in several different Chryslers as he bought cattle all over Southern Idaho. It was at this time his old friend and sidekick, Dick Rogers, entered the picture.

In 1969 John bought into a feedlot in Wilder, Idaho, and moved his family, which now includes Judy, to that location. For the next three years he hit the road trading cattle. Dick says, "John put more miles on a car in a month than most people do in a year."

He got to know a lot of his future neighbors at this time as he bought a lot of cattle not only in Idaho, but also in Oregon, Utah and Northern Nevada as well. During this time John sold a bunch of cows off the MacKenzie Ranch, north of Jordan Valley, to an outfit in California. The California outfit sent two of their boys to help John. They would eat breakfast at Falen's place in Wilder at about 3:30 in the morning and head to the Jordon Valley ranch to ride all day. They would get back at 9:30 or 10:00 at night, eat supper, and then go to their motel room. On the fourth morning Sharon asked them how they were doing.

"I know one thing ——a pair of sheets lasts a long time in this country!" says one. Dick figured John probably put in another 10,000 miles horseback at the feedlot and a few more at some of the ranches they leased for pasture, and he was still putting in time at the L-F Ranch. John's last daughter, Johnna, was born in Wilder.

In 1973, he sold his interest in the feedlot and got back to his first love —- a cow/calf operation. For the next three years, he leased the Spivey Ranch at Oreana, Idaho, his dad's L-F Ranch in Owyhee County, Idaho, and the very remote C Ranch in Jordan Valley, Oregon. It seemed to Sharon that they were scattered out all over the place. She would pick up the kids after school in Grandview, Idaho, on Fridays and drive to the top of the mountains, eighty miles of dirt road, to the L-F Ranch, or the C Ranch. She and the kids would help buckaroo all weekend, and then head back to Grandview on Sunday night to get the kids back for school the next morning. John was buckaroo'n full time now and thrived on it. You could probably add another 15,000 to 20,000 miles at this time. By the way, John did get bucked off for maybe only the second time in the Cherry Creek allotment when he was leaning to the right to see down in the canyon and his horse stepped on a rock with a rattlesnake under it. The horse jumped left and John hit the ground real hard.

Dick tells a story about this time. He says John is the only guy he knows who will go buckaroo'n in a rowboat. A steer had been quitting the herd all day. When they got to the Dougal reservoir on the way to the L-F Ranch, the steer headed for the willows, so Dick set the dog on him and just followed the rest of the cattle on by. All of a sudden he heard a "kersplash" and turned to see the steer headed straight across the reservoir. His first thought was to just go ahead and let him drown. His second thought was," Oh Hell, he can't make it across and I ain't swimming after him." Then along comes John, the boss, in some kind of shock state watching that stupid steer swimming in circles out in the water. He drug Dick back to an old leaky wooden rowboat and with only one oar, they set sail in order to save that steer. Probably not the smartest thing to do, but it did work. They lined the steer out for the bank and got him on dry land. After his ordeal, the steer stayed with the herd.

The end of these three years had John looking toward Nevada. It would be nice to have everything in one place. He was short on money but long on desire to make things work and no one worked harder than John. The first two years on the Home Ranch, the family was the only buckaroo crew. Even six year old Johnna was enlisted in the effort. The miles started before daybreak and they would all be trotting back to the horse trailer in the dark.

One time Judy was following her Dad on a really dark night. Every so often you would hear her say, "I can't see you any more Daddy!" He would pull up and wait for everyone to catch up.

Son-in law, Loyd, joined the crew in 1979 and is probably the only one who has put in more miles than John on the Home Ranch. Loyd says, "It is about seventy miles from the south end of the winter range to the far side of the summer country." He isn't sure how many times John has made the trip, but he figures it is enough to put him over the 100,000 mile mark. The days are long. One time they came into Jordan Meadows camp all worn out after dark. They all unsaddled and put their horses out, but John just turned his loose with the saddle still on. After they rounded the horse up to unsaddle him, they gave John a bad time about wanting to be ready early the next morning.

In 1979 John also signed a lease for the UC Ranch. Loyd says that he can tell several good stories, but one of his favorites happened on a nasty day when the crew (including eight year old Johnna) left the Quinn River Cabin at about 4:00 a.m. They brought four hundred head of pairs over the Bayber Trail back to the UC Ranch. They were not packing any lunches and at about 4:00 in the afternoon, Johnna started saying, "Daddy, I'm tired and hungry." This was repeated every little bit until the sky turned black and lightning started to flash around them.

"Daddy, I'm tired and hungry," was replaced with, "Daddy, I'm scared!" They were all glad to reach the UC Ranch that night, at about 11:30 with what seemed like a million pairs. For the most part, the rides at the UC were shorter and son-in–law Hank would have to fill in the miles there, should they need to be counted. Dick Rogers says, "If there is any possible way John could be short miles after all of this, I'll give him some of mine."

In the last decade or so, John has become more and more active in the issues that affect the cattle industry. He feels a driving commitment to help preserve an industry, a culture and a way of life called "Ranching." He drives more miles (over 100,000 miles a year) as he travels all over the state to various meetings. He has flown to Washington, D.C.

twice just this year and I can't tell you how many other trips he has made back there. For years now he has not missed a National Cattlemen's Convention or a Nevada State Convention. In October, he not only made one of his trips to D.C., but he also flew to North Dakota for a regional meeting for the Public Land Council. Besides being chairman of the Nevada Public Land Council (PLC) John is Nevada's representative to the National PLC. He is a member of the Sierra Front Resource Advisory Council (RAC). He is on the Eastern Nevada Landscape Coalition, which is part of the Great Basin Restoration Project. He is a State of Nevada representative to Nevada director Bob Abby's committee to address issues concerning all the state district managers. John serves on a Grazing Regulation Committee and on a Range Monitoring Committee with Dr. Lynn James of Utah. He is co-chair of a Sustainable Working Landscape proposal and just last week gave a speech to the Idaho Cattlemen on the method and progress of the Wildfire Support Group John is working on in Nevada. Although this has nothing to do with the cattle industry, he is finishing up his seventeenth year as a Humboldt County school board member. I believe that is his entertainment. At any rate, Sharon says to not judge her too harshly if you call the ranch for John and she says he is not there and she isn't sure where he is or what meeting he is attending.

On his days off from meetings, John still heads to the barn to throw a saddle on his horse and, I guess, work on his second 100,000 miles, or he could have a need to prove that he can still keep ahead of the younger guys. The girls say he is getting softer as the years go by. When the grandchildren are the only crew he can come up with, he stops and buys ice cream at the Texaco. The earlier generation says, "He never did that for us."

Dave's comment: In later years the time John has spent representing the livestock industry all over the United States is greatly appreciated. It's a tribute to John, Sharon, Dick Rogers and the entire Falen family that this big range ranching operation can continue to operate smoothly giving John time to spend representing the cattle industry along many fronts. I've said somewhere along my ramblings that living the life of a big range rancher and cowboy does not necessarily mean living the life of a hermit. John is a good example of this.

LITTLE THINGS

A ranch wife was getting along in years and the family hired a woman to come in and clean once a week. The ranch wife was heard to complain, "I don't know about that woman. The more I clean before she comes the less she does after she gets here.

EAGLES

Years ago I was riding through the west side of Bald Mountain. It was mid-afternoon in the late winter and I was headed to the home ranch when I saw a small herd of deer above me. The west side of the mountain is open grassland, the deer had seen me and they were walking along a trail single file headed toward brush and timber that was about an eighth of a mile away. A yearling deer was walking along the trail maybe ten or fifteen feet behind the main deer herd. The interesting thing about this sight was the two bald eagles silently circling over the deer. These were big birds with five or six feet wing spans. The eagles were circling at a lower altitude than normal. Even so the sight wasn't really unusual until one of the eagles suddenly gulled its wings and dove down toward the yearling deer that was lagging. The eagle came down like a bullet and attacked the deer from behind. The deer didn't seem to know the eagle was there until the eagle's talons dug deep into its back just behind the deer's hip bones. The eagle pulled up flapping its wings vigorously and lifted the deer's hind feet off the ground. The force of the dive shoved the deer forward and when the deer's weight became too heavy, just before the eagle stalled out, it let go of the deer, circled out and re-gained altitude. By this time the second eagle's wings were gulled and he was in mid dive, his talons dug deep into the same spot on the deer's back and the force of the dive again forced the deer forward. This time it caused the deer's front legs to buckle. The eagle pulled up, flapping its wings wildly, until the deer's hind feet were about a foot off the ground. When the weight of the deer again became too heavy for the eagle to lift, and just before the eagle stalled out, it too, let go of the deer and circled out and again gained altitude. By now the first eagle was back in position and again diving at the deer. This sequence repeated it-self three more times and the deer was down before I rode out of sight. Later, on a return ride through this area of Bald Mountain, I found the deer carcass. The bones had been picked clean by the eagles and other predators that took advantage of the eagles' kill thus receiving a free meal.

I have seen coyotes work together to kill a calf. In these attacks, several coyotes kept the mother cow occupied while other coyotes slipped in from behind and pulled her calf down. Coyotes do work to-gether, but their attacks are more unorganized and less disciplined than the eagles were when I watched them take down that deer. The amazing thing to me was the precision the eagles displayed while working to-gether. Their timing was perfect. This wasn't a haphazard game of chance. These eagles worked together with military precision to do something neither could have accomplished as an individual. This may be a more common occurrence than I am aware of, but this is the only time I actually saw eagles using this technique while I traveled along my 115,000 mile horse back ride.

There is little doubt that eagles are masters of the sky. On a clear day when the sky is cloudless, it is fascinating to watch them making effortless circles or unbelievable acrobatic maneuvers high up in the blue. Sometimes smaller birds, especially crows, blackbirds and starlings will harass eagles, screeching and screaming while diving down until nearly touching the eagle's back before pulling up and gaining enough altitude to dive again. On this afternoon an eagle was flying at a low altitude. The air was still and hot. The eagle was laboring and couldn't find an up draft to lift him out of the area when a lone crow began to harass him. The crow knew he had the advantage and made the best use of the situation. He crowed, cawed and dive bombed the eagle at will, getting bolder with every pass. About the fifth dive the crow made, the eagle watched and when the crow dived, the eagle turned over in mid air with his legs extended up toward the crow with his claws wide open. I can image the look on that crow's face when he saw the claws he was diving into. Somehow the crow lived to crow another day, but he lost a lot of feathers. The crow was visibly shaken as he gained altitude, turned tail and flew silently back in the direction from which he came. Then the eagle turned right side up and continued his flight undisturbed.

Another incident involving eagles also happened at the Eden Valley Ranch. It was winter and the roads were closed to the outside world. Don, Harold and I were batching at the ranch headquarters. During this time about a thousand Canada Geese spent the winter in the valley and the surrounding hills. They were scared and watchful when an eagle appeared in the sky. We could tell when eagles were around by the excited honking and the swift flight as geese left the valley. On this morning Harold was working on the east side of Eden Creek when geese began to honk and rise up off the field. The geese were up and in full flight when Harold looked up and saw the eagle with gulled wings dive down and catch an airborne goose in full flight. The eagle continued down with the goose in its claws. Suddenly, it saw Harold, dropped the goose and gained altitude.

That afternoon when Don and I returned from a short horseback ride, Harold brought the goose over to the cook house and explained how he got it. Well, we looked the goose over, except for claw punctures in its back it looked all right. So, like any other predator that roamed the mountains, we decided to eat it. I was cooking on this particular night so after Don and Harold picked and cleaned the goose, I cut the drum sticks, thighs, breast and wings up into pieces, dunked them in milk, rolled them in flour and put them in a sizzling hot skillet like I had done with chicken or quail a hundred times. When the ranch cook was there she also cooked geese, but she went through some time consuming rig-a-ma-role and the geese always came out tasty and easy to eat. This evening I didn't have that much time and I didn't know what the cook did anyway, so I thought I would take a short cut. I put the pieces of goose in a hot skillet, covered it with a lid for a while then took the lid off and let the goose fry until it was golden brown. Meanwhile, I fried some potatoes, baked some biscuits, made gravy and when the whole thing was done I said, "Come and get it." And we sat down to eat.

Don was the first one to pick a drum stick up in his fingers. He took a bite and pulled back and pulled back and pulled back. The skin on that drum stick stretched and stretched and stretched until it finally slipped out of Don's teeth and snapped back into place. By now Harold and I were trying to eat the goose with the same results. We were hysterically laughing. We tried to bite it, we dropped it and it bounced, we tried to cut it and when I finally got a bite size piece of meat whittled off, I couldn't chew it. That was the toughest bird I ever tried to eat. We finally gave up. We simply couldn't eat that goose, but the fried potatoes, gravy and biscuits weren't too bad.

The lessons learned from all this: don't try to fry an old goose in a frying pan and next time an eagle catches a goose, let him have it. If he can eat it, he earned it.

LITTLE THINGS

Harold, my old cowboy friend, and I used to get so thirsty during long rides on hot summer days, we would blow wiggles out of the way and drink water standing in old cow tracks. Harold maintains they are now making things so sterile, they are making us sick.

A VISIT FROM DOWN UNDER

One time the College of Agriculture, University of Nevada Reno arranged a tour to learn how Elko County ranchers irrigated the high elevation wild hay meadows located along the northeastern Nevada mountain ranges. Many of these meadows raised high quality grass hay used to feed cow herds wintering in the high elevation valleys. The tour included several faculty professors from Reno and two visiting professors from Australia. The purpose of the tour was to show the Australians how the high meadows were irrigated.

When the tour arrived at Lee Livestock Company, I explained the company owned all the water rights to the water coming down from the three canyons above. I explained our irrigation water came from snow melt and at the higher elevations it was still cold at night, so the high water flows for the day reached the meadows below between three o'-clock in the afternoon and midnight, about half a day behind the thawing process in the higher mountains. Some of the meadows were a mile long and I proudly showed the professors my extensive irrigation system consisting of manure dams held in place by wooden stakes and broken boards and poles. It is said that an Elko County rancher, with a load of manure and some broken boards from last winter's feed wagon, could dam up the Humbolt River. This may be true, especially in a drought year.

Well, the tour ended and one of the Australians, in his Aussie accent said, "Mate, I am impressed with your irrigation system and find it amazing that you can irrigate this big meadow with such a simplistic irrigation system that doesn't use any man-made energy." He added, "Your irrigation system is all natural." Then to make his point he said, "In fact, your irrigation system is just one step above the engineering ability of a beaver."

Now I do not know if I received a put down, a little Aussie humor, or a compliment. Either way it was an interesting day and the Australian visitors were genuinely interested in what they were seeing.

BILL MAUPIN

Bill Maupin was inducted into the Nevada Cattlemen's Association Cowboy 100,000 Mile Club in 2001 and Julian Smith gave the following documentation:

Bill Maupin's dad was the resident stockman for the Indian Department on the Apache Reservation in Arizona where Bill was born in 1932. The story is that Bill's first ride was on a five or six year old burro when he was about four years old. His dad packed a burro when going to work and put Bill on top of the pack. The burro ran under a tree scraping Bill off, but he wasn't hurt and enjoyed the ride.

When World II broke out, Bill's dad was working on a barge in the Colorado River and the job was immediately closed down. They moved to Hurlong, California but did not stay long and his father went to Wyoming to help build POW camp buildings. He was injured on that job and while in the hospital was offered a job on the Moore Sheep and

Cattle Company Ranch in Wyoming, which he took. The ranch raised cattle, sheep and horses. They crossed some of the horses with Shetland ponies to produce a shorter animal that the sheepherders could more easily use. Bill rode a three quarter Shetland pony fourteen miles round trip to school each school day. During these years he rode about 6,000 miles. The family lived there from July 1942 until 1945.

About this time his uncle, who owned a ranch in South Dakota, asked Bill's dad to come and help him run the ranch. This was a great opportunity for Bill's family because they now owned some cattle themselves and they could run them on that ranch.

Bill's first paying job was raking hay with a sulky rake in the summer of 1945. He and his brother also helped his dad and rode about 1,000 miles during that summer. He earned seventy-five dollars for the entire summer's work.

In the spring, Bill got his first real cowboy job as wrangler for the Diamond A Cattle Company in Eagle Butte, South Dakota. It was the first time he ever saw a rope corral. The company built all rope corrals. Bill said, "The Company's operation was unusual because they didn't have a permanent ranch headquarters. They just operated from wagons and permanent camp sites. Before the 1900s the ranch was owed by Thatcher and Bloom of Trinidad, Colorado. The company leased a full county in South Dakota before 1900. The lease lasted until 1947. Bill's dad became the jigger boss on the Diamond A wagon and he took Bill with him to ride. During this period Bill estimated he rode 4,000 miles.

In 1947 the ranch was sold to an outfit from Chicago. Bill stayed on from 1947 to 1952. They ran 7,000 head of cows and Bill rode about twenty miles a day five or six days a week. In this time Bill rode a total of 10,800 miles.

One of Bill's winter jobs was to ride the ice line fifteen miles down the Missouri River from a cow camp near Big Piney, Wyoming. At that point the Missouri River was a mile wide. The ranchers learned that if they chopped holes in the ice near the edge of the river bank, the cattle would water there and not try to reach air holes further out where the ice was thin and the cattle could break through and drown. From camp, Bill and another cowboy each went opposite directions on the river and chopped holes through ice that was up to an axe handle thick. These holes filled with water so cows could safely drink. This was about a thirty mile round trip. During the winter Bill made the ride five or six days a week for six years. He also rode for the ranch during the summers until 1950 when he started taking summers off to try his hand at bronc riding, but he still rode the ice line in winter. He added 13,800 mile in this time frame. Bill says, "Not very many of those miles came on the back of the broncs he was riding."

Bill worked six years for a stock association in Melrose, Montana, where they rode ten to fifteen miles a day from April fifteenth to December first. They had six different brands in the association and he added 14,400 miles horseback during this time.

About then Bill also took time out and for four years he built saddles. This didn't pan out and wasn't profitable so Bill decided to go back to the cowboy life.

In October of 1956 Bill went to work for the MC Ranch in Oregon. This job entailed riding pens in a feedlot. While there he was offered a manger's job on the Island Ranch in Burns, Oregon, for Taylor Lawrence's Company and he took it. He rode ten miles a day five days a week for eighteen months totaling 3,700 miles. When the cow boss job opened on the MC Ranch, Bill was hired and again worked for the MC. The MC ran 8,600 head of cows on 800,000 acres in one pasture while he was there. The BLM cut the ranch grazing permit due to the number of wild horses that were grazing in the area. This changed the way cattle were managed and the ranch sold, so Bill decided to move on.

Next Bill went to California to work for the Newhall Cattle Company headquartered in Cascade Junction. Here he added 1,500 more miles to his lifetime ride. Bill had a couple more jobs in California one in Imperial Valley and another in Paso Robles adding 2,000 more miles to his horseback ride.

In January of 1976, Bill went to work for Bob Halliday at the Allied Ranch in Elko County, Nevada. In just a few months he was transferred to the Roaring Springs Ranch in French Glen, Oregon. Bill rode every day and during this time rode 12,500 miles.

Bill then got a job at the IL in Elko County, Nevada. He ran the wagon and wanted to be out with the cows. To Bill, the Owyhee Desert was a unique and special place and he really enjoyed the work. Bill stayed for fifteen years.

The ranch started to run a wagon that left the fifteenth of May and had established places to make camp. There were four horses on the mess wagon team and two horses pulling the bed wagon. On the mess wagon there was a cook and a horse wrangler who herded the horses and put them in the holding fields at night. The wagon was out until November first. The cowboys worked straight through the month then had four days off. The cowboys on the round-up wagon averaged riding about twenty miles a day. During the fifteen years Bill worked for the IL Ranch, he documented riding about 28,000 miles.

Peter Jackson asked Bill to help him some after he left the IL Ranch. Bill says, "I got by luckier than some." But he remembers once when working for the Jacksons at the shipping corrals a big Riddle Ranch heifer ran under his horse. Bill thought his horse was going to go down and he reached for the pole fence, but the horse turned the opposite direction Bill's macarte that was tucked under his belt got stuck. Bill was hung up. The horse was spinning around in a tight circle; Bill was swinging around with his head nearly touching the ground. Finally the headstall broke and Bill was thrown free. He says he was lucky to come out of the wreck with only a damaged knee. While here, he added another 5,800 miles to his horseback ride. This made a conservative grand total of 103,500 miles ridden horseback during Bill's lifetime.

Bill's favorite horse was named Ringo. He bought him from Dan Opie in Jordan Valley, Oregon. He was a big stout horse and Bill team roped on him and kept him until he was nineteen or twenty years old.

Dave's comment: For four years in the 1960's Bill built saddles in Montana. During the 1990s after he retired, Bill again started building saddles. You can still find him building bronc saddles for rodeo contestants in his Spring Creek, Nevada workshop.

LITTLE THINGS

Jane said to her friend with excitement in her voice, "Have you been to the new mall? There are dress shops, shoe stores and department stores with all the latest fashions." The friend turned to Jane's husband and asked, "Have you been there yet?" He said,

"Yes, one afternoon I spent a weekend there."

Don

Forty Degrees Below Zero

Dave

REPLACING HORSES AND COWS
WITH MOOSE AND BROWN BEAR –III

Having made our decision, the next step was to get from our trapper's cabin to the highway at Copper Center. We set about building a toboggan out of poles thinking we could pull our winter catch of furs and the few personal belongings we had down the snow covered ice on the Tonsina River. During the time we were in Alaska, the ice covered rivers and lakes were used as trails during the winter. This was long before the snowmobile became a trusted method of winter travel.

Our sled took shape and it looked usable. Empty, it skidded along over the snow covered ice with little effort. On the trial run with weight on the sled, we found out we could not pull it. After several adjustments and trials with no better results, we abandoned the project. There was no way we could pull that sled down the Tonsina River for twenty-eight miles. The best option we had left was for one of us to take our winter catch of furs and walk down the ice covered river to Copper Center, find a fur trader and sell our furs. Then we could hire a bush pilot to fly in and pick us up. I don't remember how we decided who would make the trip, but Don got the call. I was going to stay at the cabin and finish taking up traps and get things ready to leave.

We bundled up our furs; put a cooked moose roast, some sourdough biscuits and the few things Don would need to survive in his backpack. The next morning, with a wave of his hand, Don disappeared down the Tonsina River and I turned my attention to picking up traps. I was busy and the first two or three days slipped by quickly. As the days stretched toward a week, I began to get that nervous feeling that comes when a partner is late coming into camp. I refused to let myself speculate about what might have happened and late the next day I saw Don coming up the river. He gave me that hand wave and it is hard to explain the relief I felt when I saw him. I would rather have made that trip myself than been anxiously waiting to see how it ended.

I was eager to hear the news and Don was anxious to tell me. He reached Highway 4 farther west of Copper Center than we planned. He'd made the trip down the river in one day, but it took an extra day to get to Copper Center. He spent another day finding a fur buyer and selling our furs. Don found Fred's cabin and made sure our Jeep was there, hired a bush pilot to fly into Tonsina Lake and then made the return trip back up the Tonsina River on foot. I filled Don in on my activities while he was gone. I'd picked up traps along all of the trap lines and had the cabin ready to close down.

The bush pilot told Don to pick out a smooth stretch of lake ice that was free of cracks and ice heaves and mark out a landing strip by placing green spruce boughs around it. They picked out a day and time for the plane's arrival and on the designated day, Don and I had the landing strip marked with our belongings stacked along one side. When the plane came into sight it was a small Cessna or Piper Cub equipped with skis. The plane landed without incident and taxied up to our small pile of equipment. The pilot was concerned about taking off. He said the snow was granulated and sticky. I got in the plane laying flat on my back with my head in the small part of the fuselage close to the plane's tail. Don and the pilot placed our bedrolls and belongings around me and they climbed into the front seats. The pilot taxied up the lake for a reasonable distance and turned around. The engine roared, the plane vibrated and we were off.

Well not quite, the pilot couldn't get the plane airborne. After another unsuccessful try, and much to my delight, the pilot said, "We have to reduce the weight." It was decided that I would stay at the lake and Don and the pilot would fly our belongings to Copper Center where Don would stay while the pilot returned to fly me out. I watched as the plane roared down the snow covered ice and again failed to take off. We unloaded weight two more times before the plane finally got airborne with the pilot, Don and two bedrolls aboard.

The pilot made two more trips flying our equipment out before he returned to pick me up and from the air I saw our little log cabin silently sitting in the cold Alaskan wilderness for the last time. We loaded the Jeep with our belongings, spent the night with Fred and started home the next morning.

By now we were old hands and took the Al-Can Highway in stride. We reached Dawson Creek and headed for Edmonton. Somewhere in the south part of Alberta, Canada, on a cold desolate stretch of highway, a car crossed the center line and hit us head on. At the time Don was driving and I was asleep. When I came to I was lying in a snow bank trying to figure out where I was and what happened. Our Jeep had turned completely over and was now sitting back on it's wheels out in a field. Our belongings were scattered everywhere and Don was no where to be seen. When I found him, he was just getting up out of the snow. The car that hit us was on the other side of the highway with three men still sitting in it. The rest of that night is really hazy.

We picked up what we could find of our things and someone gave us a ride to the next town where we found a room. The next morning we began to understand the reality of our situation. We were bruised, battered and extremely sore but we didn't appear to have any broken bones.

Someone from local law enforcement took us back to the scene of the accident and we picked up the rest of our belongings and made arrangements to have the Jeep taken to the only garage in town. We found out the Jeep could be fixed but it would take about ten days to get the parts and repair it. So we settled down to nurse our wounds.

The next surprise we had was unbelievable. The Pastor of the church Don and his family belonged to in Willits, California, was from Canada and his folks lived in this little town where we were stranded. You can believe this or not but it was true.

The little room Don and I were renting was primitive but we were used to that. It wasn't costing us much so we were satisfied. It had heat, two bunk beds, a kitchen chair and a naked light bulb hanging from the ceiling. This is the back drop for what happened next.

We had been in the room for about two days when midmorning there was a knock on the door. Don and I looked at each other and being too stiff and sore to get up, one of us hollered, "Come in." The door opened and there stood a Royal Canadian Mounted Policeman. His red uniform was immaculate. It was topped off with a wide brimmed Stetson, black belt and black boots. He was a strapping young man with a solemn looking face and the contrast between the Mountie and our condition was immense. We were speechless. His stern expression turned to an easy grin and he asked if he could come in while he was already sitting down in the only chair we had. Conversation came easy and we began to relax. He asked a few questions about our background. He wanted to know where we came from. Did we drink? Why were we out on that cold highway in the middle of the night? We explained why we were there, assured him we didn't drink, and explained where we were born.

We asked him questions about the Royal Canadian Mounted Police and he told us a little of his experiences in the wilderness of northern Canada. He thanked us for our time and left. The next day Don and I were sweeping out the cabin when we noticed a paper sack in the corner of the room. When I picked it up I was surprised to find a fifth of whiskey and several cans of beer inside. Knowing we had just told the Royal Canadian Mounted Policeman we did not drink it made us nervous. Thinking someone before us forgot to take the whiskey with them when they left; we decided to throw it out in the morning. Faced with much more important problems, we forgot about the whole incident and left the paper sack and its contents in the corner of the room.

The days dragged by and when our Jeep was ready, Don and I were fully recovered and anxious to get going. The day before we were leaving there was another knock on the door and the same Royal Canadian Mounted Policeman was standing there. We invited him in and we visited. He said he was glad to see we had recovered from the wreck and wished us luck on the rest of our trip. We shook hands and the Mountie walked over to the corner of the room, picked up the paper sack containing the whiskey and beer and said, " I guess you boys were telling me the truth. You really don't drink." He grinned and walked out the door. Don and I just stood there and looked at each other. We couldn't believe we had been that naïve.

The rest of the trip was uneventful and when we got home, we picked up where we left off. We were five months older and five years wiser. Don continued along his long winding trail and I continued to travel along my 115,000 mile horseback ride.

Our Alaskan experience was something like the Pony Express. It was challenging, exciting and it didn't last very long, but it left a lifetime of memories. I know we had a lot of luck along our Alaskan experience but I would like to think our hard work, dedication and a common sense approach to things we didn't fully understand made some of that luck happen.

LITTLE THINGS

This old rancher was semi-retired. The younger generation had pretty much taken over the ranch operation but he and his wife still lived on the home place. He still kept a couple of saddle horses and a few cows around.

He'd seen the old two track rutted wagon road of his youth that went by the ranch house transformed into a graveled county road. Then in more recent years he'd seen the old county road turned into a paved state highway with cars constantly zipping by. This didn't set too well with the old timer but as the years slipped away he came to accept it.

It was calving season and he had a little bunch of cavy cows in a small pasture close to the house where he could watch them. On this morning he went out to feed his horses and check the cows. He saw right away that one cow was having a calving problem. Two hind feet were sticking out and the calf was coming backwards. Apparently the calf's hip bones were wedged against the cow's pelvis. The cow had been trying to calf for quite awhile. She was gentle so the rancher decided to rope the cow, snub her up to a fence post along the highway and pull the calf. This he did.

He was just starting this procedure when a little red convertible sports car with the top down skidded to a stop in the gravel beside the pavement. The Hippy inside the car jumped out, climbed the fence, positioned himself behind the rancher and intently watched what was going on. This was an interesting sight. The old rancher behind the cow pulling the calf, the Hippy standing behind the old rancher, watching every move he made, while in the background cars continued to zip by.

The old timer finished the job. He pushed the calf back in a ways, twisted it around until the calf's hip bones unlocked from the cow's pelvis and pulled the calf out backwards. The Hippy finally said, "I just have to ask one question before I go." Without turning around the old timer said, "What do you want to know?" While the cars continued to whiz by the Hippy asked, "How fast was that little cow going when it hit that big cow?"

Hugh Reed about age 18 on Hezzekiah

HUGH REED

Hugh Reed was inducted into the Nevada Cattlemen's Association Cowboy 100,000 Mile Club in 2001.

Loretta Reed wrote and presented the following when Hugh was inducted:

The year was 1918, when our one hundred thousand mile cowboy, Hugh Reed, first hit the saddle a little before the age of four, and he stayed there on a regular basis for about the next eighty years. His first horse, Chappo, a big dark brown gelding, was outfitted with a small saddle to accommodate Hugh's short legs. It was on Chappo's back that the little boy began a lifelong love affair with horses. Hugh was crazy about riding old Chappo. He'd ride around the barn and corrals for hours upon hours, enjoying the view from the tall rangy horse's back, watching the cowboys work on the barn they were building at the White Rock Ranch and looking out over the mountains and valleys that surrounded him. Finally, the cowboys would take pity on the old horse and pry a loudly protesting Hugh out of the saddle and set him on the ground to give poor old Chappo a chance to eat and drink. Hugh would run to tell his mother, Anna Reed, and complain long and loud, but no help there for the frustrated little boy. Anna would just shake her head in sympathy ....for the horse.

Hugh remembers that at four years old, he had reached a milestone when his horse could hit a hard gallop, and he could stay on without falling off even once. Hugh's horse wanted to keep up with those of his brothers, John and Lawrence, who were fast becoming seasoned cowboys at the ages of six and eight. Lawrence was impressed and complimented Hugh when he could finally ride at a gallop. He would sometimes watch out for Hugh and make sure he stayed up on tall old Chappo, but in later years, Lawrence, the family jokester, was more often responsible for Hugh's falling off than staying on. Brother John was more "true blue" rescuing Hugh more than once from dangerous situations.

At about five years old, when riding with the real cowboys like his father, Jake Reed, older brothers and ranch cowboys, Hugh's orders were to stay out of the way, don't get in trouble and keep up on the long horse round ups so he wouldn't get lost. That was not always easy for a young rider whose feet barely touched the stirrups, riding a horse that was running at full speed, dodging badger holes, leaping over sagebrush and jerking little arms out of their sockets, while pulling on the bridle reins trying to get the horse's head. Hugh and his brothers grew up fast cowboying on the harsh Owyhee Desert, and their glorious tales of adventure in pursuit of the Owyhee Desert mustangs have become family treasures that keep the memories of days that are gone forever.

Hugh remembers when the crews from all the ranches worked the big rodeers; the cowboys would always warn him about keeping his horse out of the way of the bull fights. Two, three or more bulls would begin bawling, pawing dirt and butting heads. The more those bulls bawled, the more other bulls would be incensed into joining the fight. Sometimes ten or twelve bulls would be fighting at one time. Then suddenly they'd break, stampeding in all directions. The cowboys were afraid the kids' horses would be knocked down when the bulls blindly broke out of those fights. Anna's brother-in-law Uncle Jimmy Dove, would finally get Hugh and Lawrence out of the way and make them sit on a hill out of harm's way. John was cowboy enough to stay and help work the herd, and that irked both Lawrence and Hugh. Hugh's comment about the situation was, "I used to just hate Jimmy for that. I had to sit on the hill with Lawrence and miss all the excitement."

Hugh figures by the time he was ten he accumulated about 4,000 miles riding with his dad and brothers. This includes the twenty miles between the family headquarters at White Rock and the Desert Ranch, gathering cattle on drives that averaged a minimum of fifteen miles, and best of all, helping chase the thousands of mustangs that roamed wild over the endless miles of open range on the Owyhee Desert.

Jake Reed was a hard task master and he had his boys working like men before they ever hit their teens. In fact, in the eighth grade, each boy left school and was expected to take on a man's responsibility. It was a standing joke among the ranch hands that when Jake would try to sell a horse to a hesitant buyer, Jake would say, "Shucks, this horse is plumb gentle. My kids ride him all over." Anyone who knew the Reeds knew "those kids" were seasoned hands and could ride some pretty rank horses.

At the age of twenty, Hugh estimates that his number of miles on horseback increased to approximately 50,000 as he and his brothers continued to work cattle and chase horses. They rode the Owyhee Desert's great expanses of rocks, sagebrush, rim rocks and canyons that stretched thousands of miles, extending into three states: Nevada, Idaho, and Oregon. This desert was home to lizards, ground squirrels, antelope, jack rabbits, rattlesnakes and at one time during the 1920's and 1930's, it was home to thousands of wild horses. Hugh and his brothers pursued them in frenzied day long chases to the far reaches of the desert, through places known as Coyote Holes, Devil's Corral, Corral Lakes, Oregon Buttes, Monument Hill, Squaw Valley and Lake Creek, riding with skill and wild abandon over the rough terrain. Hugh describes those rides as the greatest thrill he has ever known. Nothing could compare to those heart pounding chases on the desert. The Reed boys rode many times from dawn to well after dark, with average horse round ups being seventy-five to one hundred miles in one day.

In his reminiscences of the mustanging days, Hugh mentions a horse by the name of Pally as his favorite of all the horses he has ever ridden. Pally was a big black horse with a white strip on his face and two white feet. He could take after a bunch of mustangs and no matter how far or fast they went, he could stay with them. Hugh says, "It took a lot of grain to get Pally in shape, but it was worth it because he was a tough horse who was sure footed enough to take Hugh safely through treacherous and rugged stretches of ground, running at top speed through rocks and badger holes, plunging down steep rim rocks and gullies and racing over the craggy terrain of the desert.

Hugh accompanied his father and brothers as they chased the elusive mustangs that roamed the Owyhee Desert, captured them and used them to do their ranch work or sold them for profit. During the Depression years, Jake and the boys were able to keep their ranching operation afloat when others were going under by catching wild horses. When they were gentled and well broke they used them on the big ranches or sold them to local ranchers and horse buyers for a good price. Older mustangs were sold to California buyers for about five dollars a head.

During the 1920's, about three times a year, Hugh along with his father and brothers and some of the ranch hands would trail about 150 horses they had gathered from the Desert Ranch down to a train loading station near Golconda called Red House. This was about a three day trip of about seventy miles, with cowboys starting at the Desert Ranch, camping at two camps along the way, Squaw Valley and the Lower Clovers, and arriving at Red House on the third day. On one of these drives, Hugh tells of brother John's bronc ride at Red House on an ornery roan horse and of horses stampeding when they saw one of those new fangled things called an automobile. But they always made it, and the horses would be loaded on the railroad cars and shipped to California. Most times the cowboys would get about a day's rest and then make the return trip horseback.

Hugh continued to ride and work with his father and brothers on the White Rock Ranch and the Desert Ranch until Jake Reed's death in 1939. Jake was killed in a logging accident in Silver Creek Canyon above the White Rock Ranch when he was thrown from a wagon onto some rocks in the creek bed. After his death, the family decided to leave the area and sold the White Rock Ranch to the Petan Company and relocated in the Lee, South Fork area. Hugh was twenty-six at the time and figures that between the time the family left the desert and his thirtieth birthday, he had ridden his first 100,000 miles horseback.

Hugh's days on horseback did not end with the leaving of the desert, for he continued the cowboy life with his brother John on the Willow Creek Ranch near Jiggs, Nevada. It was in this area where he met and married Mary Arrascada whose family owned what is now known as the Circle L Ranch. Mary and Hugh took up a ranch on the South Fork below the present reservoir, and it was while they were here their first son, Johnny, was born. Their second son, Kin, was born several years later when the family relocated to Old Uncle Kin's Ranch in Columbia Basin. Hugh bought a couple of places in the area from uncle Chester Woodward and Lee Reborse and ranched there for a time. He relocated to Idaho for a few years and then returned to his Uncle Kin's Ranch about 1961. In 1963 he went to work for Charlie Van Norman as a buckaroo and says, "I always enjoyed cowboying with Charlie and Bill."

In 1965, Hugh and his family started building fence for area ranchers in the summer and moved to the Sadler Ranch south of Jiggs to cut posts and run mustangs in the winter. It was a real treat for family members to travel to the old adobe house at Sadler, eat some of Mary's great cooking and look at the mustangs Johnny and Hugh caught during the winter. Brother John and his kids, Bob and Shirley, occasionally joined in the mustang chases among the junipers of Sadler Basin, Cherry Springs, and Sherman Creek. In fact, Hugh and Johnny named one of the Cherry Springs mustangs "Cherry" and kept him as a saddle horse for many years. These good times were ended, however, by Wild Horse Annie's Wild Horse and Burro Act in 1971.

Hugh also worked on the Raymond Gardner Ranch in Ruby Valley until the early 1970's. In 1970 he went to work for the 2U Ranch in the Lee/Jiggs area and was able to again join brother John who still lived at Willow Creek. He spent many long hours in the saddle gathering cattle in areas around Red Rock, Robinson Mountain, The Adiegos, Crane Springs and Cedar Ridge. John and Hugh's two families were able to have some really good times as they rode and branded together. Hugh and his son, Johnny, worked on the 2U for twelve or thirteen years until they relocated to Starr Valley in 1983, where Hugh continued cowboying, gathering, working and branding cattle until he reached the age of 83. He was thrown from a horse and had to have a hip replaced, but that little accident didn't slow him down much because he kept on riding, roping and branding until he retired in 1997. In almost sixty years after he left the desert, riding in areas like Bull Run Basin, Tuscarora, Ruby Valley, South Fork, Jiggs and Starr Valley, Hugh rode approximately another 80,000 miles. His lifetime horseback ride totals about 180,000 miles.

Hugh Reed is the epitome of someone who truly lived the cowboy way of life. Horses were his friends and work mates, and he lived close to them and close to the land in a way few are privileged to live. His family relishes reliving the history of his days working horses in the hay fields, riding on cattle drives and chasing mustangs on the desert. Hugh continues in his deep abiding love for horses, and even though at 87, he still has a keen eye and a great appreciation for a good horse.

Dave's comment: The following are excerpts from Loretta Reed's major class project entitled "Their Days on the Desert" and "A Sad Farewell". This gives an insight into the Reed family and Hugh's relationship with his brothers, especially his older brother John, because they spent so many years together on the desert.

Loretta's excerpts:

The desert in winter or summer was a harsh place, and the brothers soon learned to look after each other. On one occasion, John and Hugh were out after horses during the winter when a blinding blizzard with temperatures well below zero developed. The brothers became separated in the white out. Hugh got off his horse to gather kindling and try to start a fire to get warm. His horse was kind of wild and got away from him. When John finally managed to find Hugh, he was dismounted from his horse and was just sitting hunched over down under a sagebrush with a match held in his nearly frozen fingers. John rode up to him and asked, "Hugh, are you going to light the fire"? Hugh answered vaguely, "No, I'm not cold anymore." John said, "Give me the match. If you aren't cold, I sure am." John built a fire and made Hugh jump up and down and run in circles to get his circulation going. After he got Hugh warmed up, he helped him find his horse. He also had to help him mount the horse which was kind of a bronc and wouldn't let Hugh get on. John had to twist the horse's ears so it would stand still long enough for the still cold and stiff Hugh to mount. Hugh reported many times afterward that if John hadn't come along when he did, he surely would have frozen to death out on the unforgiving desert.

****

John developed quite a reputation as a bronc rider and was able to ride some pretty rank broncs. Sometimes, just for fun, he and his brothers would run in a bunch of horses and ride them just to see how hard they would buck. One of John's main jobs was to wrangle in the horses each day. Every night, he would catch his wrangle horse and tie it in the barn. If his younger brothers had trouble with a horse that bucked, they would wait until John went to bed, turn out his trusty wrangle horse, and tie the ornery one in its place. In the dark before daybreak the next morning, John would have no choice but to ride the substitute horse out to wrangle, even if it did buck. Hugh related he would stay in bed until he heard John leave and then scoot down to the barn and hide where John couldn't see him to see how hard the horse would buck. Usually, John would be so mad at his prankster brothers, he would take the entire buck out of the horse by the time he returned. He would give his brothers a lecture and tell them not to do it again, and they would promise faithfully with sly grins to never again substitute a bronc for his wrangle horse… The solemn promise was only good, however, until one of them had another hard bucking horse he couldn't handle.

****

Lawrence always seemed to get the best of John, because in another trickster incident, John was riding a buckskin horse at Red House that Lawrence wanted to ride. The horse was only half gentle, didn't have too many rides on him and John had him saddled, bridled and ready to go. The two brothers had an argument, John jumped on the horse, preparing to ride off, thinking he had won the argument. Lawrence, not willing to give up that easily said, "See how you like riding him this way." And he reached up, jerked off the bridle and spooked the horse, sending him crow hopping and bucking up the canyon. Again, John managed to survive and returned from the fiasco vowing revenge. Lawrence pulled a similar trick on Hugh who had one leg slung over his saddle horn while he rested his horse. Lawrence whacked the horse with his romal and the horse bucked Hugh off. Lawrence had a good laugh and thought he had won, but a couple of days later, Hugh threw his hat under a work horse Lawrence was riding and turned the tables on him. Lawrence's horse bucked him off hard and Hugh finally had the last laugh.

One favorite family story was of the time John, having an errand in the house, thought he would just tie his horse for a minute to his mother, Anna's, brand new wringer washing machine that was sitting in the yard. Something spooked the horse which took off dragging the washing machine bumping and clanging behind it. The faster the poor horse ran trying to escape the monster attached to him, the louder it clanged and banged. The sight that sent the family into peals of laughter was the wild eyed horse fleeing down the hill with John in frantic pursuit, and Anna in hot pursuit of both, flailing at John with her broom.

****

On June 28, 1939, Jake Reed was thrown from a wagon load of logs and he died seven days later from a blood clot on the brain in the Rio Tinto hospital. Jake's death took the heart out of the family. His wife, Anna, could not bear to remain in the area and live with the memories, so the family sold the White Rock Ranch to Petan Company and the days on the desert were over.

****

Many years later we took a trip back to the desert with Hugh and John. The caravan halts and two Levi clad figures wearing battered, weather beaten cowboy hats alight from the first vehicle, a 1962 Dodge Power Wagon. The two old cowboys move stiffly forward and lean on the hood of the truck. They remove their hats, run gnarled fingers through surprisingly abundant hair for men their age, and look with faded, rheumy eyes out over the vast expanse of land before them. We who rode in the trucks to the rear of the caravan hear fragments of conversation as we approach: "Do you remember the time when....?" "Right on top of that ridge to your right..." "Yep, the old horse tipped end over end coming down that hill..." Stiff backs straighten, bent shoulders square and clouded eyes clear as hard hearing ears ring with pounding of hooves and the excited shouting of cowboys in hot pursuit of stampeding horses, and the two old timers on a pilgrimage of remembrance, reach into the back roads of their memories to relive the days of a bygone era.

Watching them standing there lost in their reminiscences, I feel a lump in my throat and a sting of tears in my eye for I know in my heart, for a brief time these two are home, reliving what for them was the best of times, their height of glory, their hey day, the days when the desert abounded with the wild horses, and they pursued the horses in frenzied daylong chases to the far reaches of the desert.

Anna and her two sons, John and Lawrence have gone to join Jake. Hugh, now 85, his two sisters, Janie Staley, 81, and Charlotte Kump, 80, still survive. In July 1997, we stood with tearful eyes and aching hearts to witness an emotional parting of the two brothers. Hugh stood quietly by John's casket and gently touched his brother's shoulder, saying the words they often said when parting for a time, "See ya' in a little while."

LITTLE THINGS

If you can remember the size, number of cows you ran, the horses you rode and the date you signed the lease on a ranch you rented 10 years ago but can not remember your anniversary in time, you are probably a rancher or cowboy, who has a very understanding wife.

HORSE TRADERS

One time when I was at the Dinner Station Ranch north of Elko, Nevada, I had ten or twelve horses in the corral. These horses came with the ranch sale. Late one afternoon an old stoved up cowboy seeing the horses in the corral stopped, got out of his pickup, came over and asked if I had any horses for sale. I explained I had just gathered these horses off the range the day before and I didn't know much about them but they were for sale.

Anyway we climbed up on the corral fence and I pointed out the young unbroken horses, a couple of gimpy horses and some sound horses with saddle marks that I didn't know anything about. We talked the same language and while he was looking the horses over, we swapped stories and before we knew it, it was getting dark. I invited him in for supper and he ended up staying in the bunk house overnight. Early the next morning after breakfast we went back to the corrals. We climbed the fence and while we were visiting he asked what I wanted for the horses. I had what I figured was a fair price and I told him. He scarcely stopped talking about the story he was telling when he said, "I'll take them. If you can get a brand inspection I will get a truck here this afternoon." Now I have bought, traded and sold many horses during my 115,000 mile horseback ride but seldom if ever before or after this incident do I remember a horse trader accepting a deal without haggling over the price. My first thought was that I had under priced the horses but I felt the price I set was about right. The deal was made and the check he gave me turned out to be good. It just goes to show there are exceptions to every rule. I have made many horse trader friends and I am not saying they are not honest. The transaction is sometimes more like a contest and if you are not on your toes you may come out on the short end of the stick. I'm just saying when you are buying or trading horses keep your wits about you and don't go to sleep.

LITTLE THINGS

Like the little boy said after listening to the conversation around the dinner table. "Gee, it sounds like there is something wrong with everyone but us, doesn't it Dad?"

HILLERY BARNES

Hillery was inducted into the Nevada Cattlemen's Association Cowboy 100,000 Mile Club in 1981.

Dave's comment: I met Hillery Barnes and his family about 1959. The Barnes family is one of the most dedicated second and third generation ranching families I know. Hillery passed away in 1997. Harvey, Hillery's youngest son and Suzy, his wife, with the help of their family now operate and maintain the Barnes Ranch located in the lower end of Mound Valley near Jiggs, Nevada. Harvey followed in his Dad's footsteps and became Nevada Cattlemen's Association President in 1995.

Harvey said his Dad didn't talk much about himself, but Harvey remembers him saying that during World War II, when they were out on the wagon working cows, there wasn't much contact with things going on outside of the area. Hillery said, "It was like being in our own small world."

Harvey remembers one other story his Dad told about a cowboy named Lynn that worked for him. This happened sometime during the twenty years Hillery was cow boss on the River Ranch. Every morning after breakfast Lynn would take two left over biscuits, fill them with jelly, roll them up in a gunny sack and tie them behind the cantle of his saddle. This was his "lunch." One spring when the Mary's River was near flood stage, Hillery and the cowboys had to swim their horses to get across the river. This particular morning Lynn's horse would not enter the water and follow the other horses across. Lynn rode back about twenty yards and rapped his horse over and under with his romal. When they reached the water's edge that horse was running flat out and he jumped as far into the river as he could. Horse and rider sank completely out of sight in the swift, ice cold water. The horse came up swimming with Lynn still on his back. When horse and rider climbed out of the water on the other side of the river the first thing Lynn said was, "Damn, I got my lunch wet."

Harvey presented this documentation when Hillery was inducted into the Cowboy 100,000 Mile Club:

Hillery Barnes was born in 1903 in Rising Star, Texas. He was the fourth child in a family of seven. The family moved to a ranch near Roswell, New Mexico, when Hillery was three years old, and he lived there until he was twenty. From New Mexico, he went to California for three years and then to Nevada, where he still resides. Hillery has three sons: Charles, Warner and Harvey, plus ten grandchildren.

The first horseback rides started at the age of seven when it became necessary to go three miles to school. This made a six mile trip each day during the school year and Hillery rode horseback to school for three years. A horse and buggy became transportation when the younger brothers and sisters reached school age. This was the means of transportation near Roswell in 1913. Summer months were spent riding horses for fun and helping move cattle to pastures, so a conservative estimate of horseback miles being ridden between ages three and ten were 4,040 miles.

The next five years were spent as ranch boys spend them today except the horse was ridden instead of a tractor or pickup. It would be easy to clock the distance ridden at 6,000 miles during this time.

The family operation included buying and selling small bunches of cattle and assisting neighbors with cattle drives during the next sixteen to twenty years of Hillery's life. Cattle were driven to the delivery destination. There was also a screwworm infestation in their area at that time. Daily cattle inspections were necessary with treatment consisting of range roping, tying down and then pouring creosylic ointment into the infected area. Bull calves seemed the most susceptible to screwworms. Boys in the area developed into pretty good ropers. Later Hillery not only found this skill useful in his daily work, but liked the diversion of competing in calf roping events at the Garcia rodeos in Elko.

Short supplies of stock water required daily windmill inspections, and this also became Hillery's duty to ride from well to well making sure the water troughs were full. All these duties added 20,000 miles of horseback time.

In 1923 Hillery joined his older brothers in California. His first job was with a former New Mexico operation, the Tannehill Brothers. They were near King City. Weekly market deliveries of about twenty-five miles plus cattle selection beforehand and fence riding and general ranch duties chalked up about 3,500 miles during the year and a half of employment there.

In 1925 Hillery started working for John E. Marble and William B. Wright at Rancho Tilarcitos in Carmel Valley. This association lasted for twenty years. In 1926, William B. Wright moved to Deeth, Nevada, to the 71 and Mary's River Ranches and Hillery moved with him. His activities as a horseman became a daily duty with an average of more than 7,200 miles a year ridden while cattle foreman for this company. 144,000 miles were spent in the saddle during this time.

In 1945, Hillery decided to purchase a ranch in Lamoille and ended his long association with the Marbles and Wrights. The fenced operation did not require the many horseback miles that Hillery was used to traveling, but he still used his horse to irrigate as well as move cattle from one pasture to another. Again 3,000 miles could conservatively be added to the distance Hillery rode horseback. The flat-heel rubber irrigating boots really were not appealing to Hillery during his Lamoille tenure from 1945 to 1947. When an open range operation became available, the Lamoille ranch was sold and the presently owned Jiggs ranch was purchased in 1948.

With U.S. Bureau of Land Management and Forest Service unfenced ranges connected to the Jiggs ranch, cattle movement required many more miles of horseback riding a year for twelve years, totaling at least 24,000 horseback miles.

Salting the range before Jeep days was an eight or nine day operation with four blocks of salt on a pack horse. Many hours and miles were added to Hillery's lifelong ride.

Gasoline transportation cut the circle in half and salting shortened to a three or four day job. Fence work became half Jeep riding and half horse transportation. This still totaled 12,000 miles until 1979 when Hillery decided it was time to watch his grandchildren ride. He says his son, Harvey, placed some steps out by the barn for him and his grandchildren to mount their horses. In the late 1970's Hillery's legs started cramping while he was riding so he stopped after seventy-five years and approximately 216,540 miles in the saddle.

Hillery joined the Nevada Cattlemen's Association when it was formed in 1934. He served as president of the association from 1960-1962. He received the Cattleman of the Year award in 1963. Until the last few years, he had not missed a state convention.

Later Harvey remarked, "This information was a little hard to gather because as Hillery said, "I'm not too much on letting people know what I've done, anyway."

LITTLE THINGS

The old teamster said when referring to his wife, "We could go down life's road together if we just had one tongue between us."

A SHORT INTERLUDE

One time during the middle part of my 115,000 mile horseback ride, Jane and I boarded a plane and took a trip to visit relatives in Alabama. We had a week long visit and enjoyed being with family and grandkids.

The first things I noticed, besides the humidity, were the overwhelming abundance of trees, brick houses, green lawns and people. It reminded me of a quote, I think from Will Rogers that went something like this: "When I was in Oklahoma I thought there were not enough people in the world to eat all this beef. Then I went to New York City and I thought there is not enough beef in the world to feed all these people." Being from Nevada and being used to seeing thirty to seventy miles in one look, things did seem to be closing in. I soon realized the only way I could see any distance was by looking straight up. There were lots of interesting things going on and everyone made an effort to show them to me. Because I am an exploring type I appreciated their efforts.

Sometime during the week I was taken to a University of Alabama football game. After we entered the stadium and got seated, one of the first things the announcer said was,   "Today we have a capacity crowd of eighty thousand people." After looking around I concluded the announcer had underestimated the number. We did the wave, stomped our feet, ate hot dogs, yelled and I was proud of myself for doing some of these things at the right time. The Alabama Crimson Tide won and the day turned out to be an interesting experience. By staying close (well, actually by hanging onto the people I knew) we miraculously found the car we came in, loaded into it and got safely home.

On this trip, I learned that going to the mall was not only a necessity but a form of recreation and a good place to get exercise, miles and miles of exercise. On another day we loaded into the car, left the relatively quiet residential district, made a turn and were in the middle of a swarm of cars on a six lane freeway. The amazing thing to me was the cars on our side of the median were all going the same direction. In due time we arrived at a parking lot that must have covered at least forty acres. We parked and made our way into the mall. I had been in big box stores and malls before but this thing was huge. After about an hour of following along through grocery stores, dress shops, kid's stores, and jewelry outlets, I saw a couple of oak benches positioned at a cross roads inside the mall. I said, "I think I will sit here and wait for awhile." In a voice that sounded like a mother taking to a six year old I heard, "O.K. but be sure and stay put so we can find you when we come back." This sounded good to me.

The place was jammed with people and as I watched them go by, I noticed most were dressed in shorts or some sort of similar clothing and my thoughts turned to what I was wearing. I left my hat and neckerchief at home and I was wearing a borrowed loose fitting grey sweat shirt. I still had my belt and Levi's on but I'd traded my boots for a squeaky pair of white tennis shoes. All in all I thought I was doing a good job of fitting right in. After about an hour, knowing from other shopping experiences that I still had lots of time, I decided to look around. I started out glancing back frequently trying to locate land marks that would help me get back to the designated oak benches where I was supposed to be. I found sporting good stores, a L.L. Bean store with down coats, and even a Western shop that had a saddle department. Most of the things in the western store were made for English style riding with a few Western type saddles thrown in. The Western saddles were made out of pink or blue plastic and I wasn't impressed.

As I continued along I noticed several oak benches situated at similar looking crossroads within the mall. While I was approaching one of these bench areas I noticed two old timers watching me. They had on clean bib overalls; they were relaxed and obviously waiting for someone that was on a shopping spree. When I got closer they started to smile and as I passed by one said, "Hey fellow, you're not really from around here, are you?" Well, my cover was blown and I was having trouble locating the right oak benches when I heard a familiar voice saying, "There you are. Where have you been?" I was in a little trouble but we all got together, had something to eat and that ended my big mall experience.

The week slipped by quickly and almost before we knew it we were saying good byes. We were taken to the airport and within twelve hours I was back in familiar surroundings. This was just "a short interlude" that sticks in my memory while traveling along my long winding trail.

LITTLE THINGS

Who hasn't spent more time and energy trying to start a chain saw than it would have taken to get the job done the old fashioned way, by chopping the limb off with a double bitted axe.

TOM PEDROLI

Tom Pedroli was inducted into the Nevada Cattlemen's Association Cowboy 100,000 Mile Club in 1992

The following sketch of the miles Tom's ridden was written and given by his wife Honorine.

Tom Pedroli of McDermitt, Nevada is one of the most avid supporters of the school's basketball team. In fact, he can probably count on one hand all the home games he has missed. Tom is also a renowned horseman. Tom Pedroli, born in 1913 at the hospital in Winnemucca, started his first 100,000 miles on horseback somewhere a round the age of four.

One of his earliest memories is of the Winnemucca Fourth of July parade and a white mare he rode. He was six or seven years old at the time.

Now down to serious business of making a living. Tom's first job was in 1921 at the age of eight, haying at the Pine Forest Land and Livestock Company with Will Delong and his son, Bill. Bill was also eight years old at this time. The senior DeLong contracted many hay fields in the area. This entailed riding several hundred miles to and from each ranch. They included the Taylor's at Deer Creek, across the valley from the Pine Forest to Capelli's Mary Sloan Ranch that was another twenty miles across the desert. From there they went around the mountain to the Alexander Ranch, another forty miles to ride back and forth during the course of the haying summer. These haying jobs lasted from 1921 to 1924 or 25. The only mode of transportation these young hayers had was horseback. Most of their time was spent getting the haymaking horses to and from the various ranches. This young feller even trailed a milk cow with the work horses when traveling form haying jobs on different ranches. He probably even milked the cow after they got to their destination!

The DeLong crew he was contracting with called the Clark Field the home place and most of the contracting was done from the homestead. They also hayed the Piaute Field and the Battle Creek Ranch on the side of the Mountain. They used green broke mules for putting up hay. These animals were broke to drive using a stone boat. The Miller and Lux outfit furnished their own horses for the contractors to use.

Upon entering high school in Winnemucca, Tom went to work cutting meat for his older brother, Pete, at the Winnemucca Market Spot. He had to do one half of a beef before school and the other half after school was over. He was very picky about his meat cutting.

The two summers of 1926 and 1927 were spent running horses on the Owyhee Desert and Jordan Meadows. This all sounds very exciting and wild western. To be sure, there were wild western incidents, but for the most part, dusty and tired young men made up the crew. This bunch of horsemen made three trips to the Winnemucca shipping corrals per summer. Each trip was eighty miles each way. After gathering the horses, these miles could easily be tripled while trailing the animals to market.

Sometime in the latter part of the era, Tom became part of the crew that rode for Miller and Lux's Big Creek wagon under the cow boss, Harry Wilson. Of that crew only Tom and Harold Woodward are left.

Tom left the Pine Forest area in 1928 and rode to McDermitt. He hayed around there for the Utah Construction Company in 1928 and 1929. In 1930 he went back to Alan. For three days his career as a sheepherder survived. The original herder was sick, so Tom filled in. The owner was so impressed with Tom's sheepherding; he would not go get another herder in spite of Tom's protests. In Tom's whole life this is the only job he ever quit, but he did give warning.

After graduation in 1931, Tom swore no more meat cutting. He hit the racetrack trail for a short period of time. He had two fast horses, a blue and a sorrel. He made money running them and more than likely betting on them. He had a woman friend who jockeyed in the then-popular women's races.

About this time and shortly thereafter, Tom hayed at the Quinn River Ranch and Otto Danglemayer's Sod House Ranch. At the Quinn River Ranch he worked for sixty dollars a month riding horses. The man wouldn't pay him rough string wages for riding half broke horses, so he moved on to the Happy Creek Ranch and then back to McDermitt. He stopped at Nouque's Ranch in McDermitt on July 13, 1932 and has been there ever since. He is now partners with John Nouque.

Nouque's is an outside riding outfit, even now. Tom has ridden the Owyhee Desert from one end to the other on various wagons: north to Highway 95 for Wilkinsons and Echave at the old Jaca Place, west to Wilkinsons, Jaca, McCullough and Andersons, from the IL and YP Ranches on the east and Les Stewart's 96 Ranch to the south. The Rocking A owned by Ables (later by McClearys) was also to the south. He has ridden on the Indian Reservation at Fort McDermitt also to the east. That's a lot of miles on horseback, covering lots of ground.

Tom's only lay up could have ended in a grave instead of a hospital room with lots of pretty nurses around. His horse fell on top of the mountain in the 1950's. Someone found Tom and brought a pickup to transport him off the mountain. He spent six weeks, laid up, after that wild ride. Not that he minded. Everyone visiting the hospital and not finding nurses had only to go to Tom's room. He had them all spellbound with his wild stories.

Tom ended his bachelorhood with his marriage to Honorine Bengoa in 1988. Basically, his life hasn't changed much. He still does most of his cattle work from the back of a horse. He has discovered his four-wheeler doesn't buck on early mornings and is the same temperament day in and day out, so he has started using it more for short trips. He still uses the horses for the long rides.

For most of his life, Tom worked for a living working cattle, branding calves, anything to do with cows.

Now he plays. Neighbors ask him to help brand and he never has to get off his horse, just rope calves. Now isn't that play for this man who still works full time in the cattle business?

Dave's comment: "Tom is another cowboy that doesn't go much for documenting distances but everyone that knows him says Tom's long winding trail is over 175,000 miles long. The Nevada Cattlemen's screening committee was satisfied Tom had ridden over 100,000 miles horseback in his lifetime."

THE RUNAWAYS

During my lifetime I have ridden three real runaways. I am not talking about the colt or young horse that bulls its neck and runs that can eventually be doubled, turned or stopped. I am talking about the blindly stampeding runaway horse that runs until he gives out completely or kills himself and you by going over a cut bank or cliff. Riding this kind of runaway horse is one of the most uncontrollable, scary, bone-chilling experiences I've ever had. The fear of getting hung up is frightening. Though neither is appealing, I would rather ride a bucking horse than ride a real runaway. When a horse bucks, you either make a ride or get bucked off. It is usually over in a short period of time and you do not have much time to think. A blindly stampeding runaway can end quickly in a tremendous wreck or last for a long time giving the cowboy time to think about the hazardous terrain that is coming up.

The longest distance I've ridden such a stampeding horse is four miles. The shortest distance was about one hundred yards. I have ridden with cowboys that said their first impulse when riding this type of runaway horse was to kick free and fall off. I could never do that. Win, lose or draw I am going to stay in the saddle as long as possible.

The first blindly stampeding runaway horse I rode was during the early stages of my 115,000 mile horseback ride. I was young and riding a small half Quarter–half Arab four-year-old gelding with the unlikely name of Wildfire. He did have a lot of fire and a stubborn streak but I had ridden him for about a year and felt comfortably in control. This particular morning I was about a mile from the ranch gathering a breeding herd of registered horned Hereford cows. The pasture was relatively small, close to the ranch and especially steep (some old timers would have said that hill was as steep as a cow's face.) The fence corner was over the top of the hill in a small swale just out of sight from down below. I hated to climb that hill. I'd climbed it before and found no cows shaded up out of sight. Other times I hadn't climbed the hill and I would come up five or six cows short then I had to re-ride and climb the hill anyway. To be on the safe side I started the switchback climb. In an hour or so I reached the top and looked over. No cows shaded up over the top this time, though the cow sign indicated they had been there sometime during the previous day. I sat relaxed with my hands crossed over my saddle horn looking down on the roofs of the ranch building some half mile to my left. I hadn't flown before but I thought this view must be something like looking out the window of an airplane. I leaned forward and nudged Wildfire intending to start the trip back down the hill. In my wildest dreams I could not have predicted what happened next. That little gray horse lunged forward, hit the ground on a dead run, and I was off on one of the wildest rides of my life. I pulled on the reins, hollering, "Whoa!" It is amazing how many times you call holler, "Whoa" in a few seconds when your life depends on it. I may as well have had that horse by the tail. We were covering ten to fifteen feet per leap and about half way to the bottom of the steep hill, Wildfire stumbled, went down to his knees, and my heart was in my throat. Miraculously he recovered and seemingly ran faster than before. Oak limbs tore my shirt and scraped my ribs. A limb slapped across my face. My eyes burned and my vision blurred. My saddle slipped further up on Wildfire's withers, dangerously close to his neck, and just before I thought I was going over his head saddle and all, the ground began to flatten. A hundred yards out on the valley floor, Wildfire's blindly stampeding run slowed to an uncontrollable lope and not long after that he stopped.

He stood spraddle legged, his sides were heaving in and out, his head hung down nearly touching the ground. White foam and streams of sweat ran down his flanks and front legs. When I stepped off, my knees buckled and I nearly fell. I put my hand on Wildfire's shoulder and every muscle in his body was quivering.

It wasn't far so I led Wildfire back to the ranch, got him cooled out, and he had no ill effects from this experience. He never again offered to run away and became a good, honest, ranch horse.

In my experience this runaway was unusual because the blindly stampeding runaway horse is typically an old, spoiled, cold jawed horse that, given the right opportunity, will never change his ways.

Why this runaway happened is another of the unsolved mysteries I encountered in the early part of my 115,000 mile horseback ride.

The next time I rode a blindly stampeding, runaway horse was about thirty years later. I needed five or six ranch horses and the Elko Livestock Auction advertised the complete dispersal of saddle horses from an eastern Oregon ranch that had recently sold. I am not a big fan of buying horses through a sale yard but this sounded interesting and it was close to home. The afternoon before the sale, I stopped by the auction yard to get as much information about the horses as I could before sale day. I was looking for some sound, middle aged, broke ranch horses.

While I was talking to ranchers and horse traders, I noticed two old, beat up, ton and a half ranch trucks with Oregon license plates backing up to the chutes. The trucks had stock racks with four horses loaded in each truck. Each horse was saddled and haltered. While I was watching, two sagebrush type cowboys wearing beat up hats and chaps climbed out of each truck. (This was before the days of goose neck trailers.) As

I got closer I heard the man that apparently was the boss says, "Boys, don't take the saddle off those dirty S.O.B.'s."

Now I'm not too bright but I scratched those horses off my "to bid" list. As it turned out those horses were not part of the dispersal sale and I did buy five or six horses that day, and all but one turned out to be usable ranch horses.

This one horse was a big, stout, solid colored bay horse. He seemingly had a good disposition, his feet were easy to pick up, he had white saddle marks on this withers, and he reined fairly well. In spite of all of this, the horse gave me my second, blindly stampeding, runaway horseback ride.

The first time I rode this old horse we were driving cows across a sagebrush flat below hay meadows at the base of the Ruby Mountains in Elko County, Nevada. Because this flat was located below irrigated wild hay meadows, several small springs or seeps surfaced in the sagebrush and through the years they sodded over, causing water boils or jelly bogs twenty to thirty feet in diameter. You could carefully walk out on one of these bogs, jump up and down and the whole area would quake and the sod would roll in waves. We were a ways out on the flat when a cow broke back. I ran out to head her but before I reached the cow, that bay horse turned into a cold jawed monster. I passed the cow as if she was standing still and I was headed out across the sagebrush flat in a cloud of dust. Every time I put pressure on the reins, that horse found another burst of speed. The whole situation was completely out of control. About this time I looked ahead and realized we were headed directly for one of those jelly bog holes.

One second we were on solid ground, kicking up dust and the next second we were belly deep in a bog hole with blue muck, water, and sod flying in all directions. Every time that old horse lunged, his back feet sunk lower into the bog and his front end rose higher. Each effort brought him closer to solid ground but he still had quite a ways to go. I knew if I jumped off and sunk to my knees there was a good chance the horse would lunge around and catch me with one of those flaying front feet and stamp me down underneath that slimy blue muck. As he got closer to solid ground, his hind quarters sunk lower so that when he did lunge, it felt like he was going to go over backwards.

When I finally thought the ground was solid enough to hold me up I jumped, rolled and scrambled out of his reach. Once on dry ground I pulled on my lead rope while he lunged and with one final effort he came free.

I was standing there trying to gather my senses when I heard a horse running toward me. As I looked up, Walt slid to a stop and he asked me if I was hurt. When I said, "No" he started laughing so hard I thought he might fall out of his saddle. I guess I was a sorry looking sight. Walt said the only thing not covered in blue muck were my eyeballs and hat.

Walt and I cleaned the mud off me and the bay horse the best we could. Walt rode his horse in front of the bay while I mounted, but the bay had all of the running he wanted for that day and the rest of the ride back to the herd we were driving was uneventful. In fact, the rest of the day was uneventful except for the ribbing I took for wallowing in the mud to cool off.

The cowboys also named that old bay horse, "The Mud Dobber." It didn't really matter because I called the horse trader that consigned the horse to the sale, explained the horse was a cold jawed runaway that was going to kill somebody, and in true horse trader fashion he was surprised. He said to bring the horse back. He had a little sorrel horse I could have that was really cowy and foolproof. To finish off the sales pitch he said, "Hell, even my wife can ride him." Experience tells me at this stage of a horse buying deal you are usually trading downhill.

Now, during my 115,000 mile horseback ride I have learned that when a horse trader finishes a sales pitch about a horse he wants to sell by saying, "Hell, even my wife can ride him," you had better take a look at the wife. In this case the wife was about five feet six inches tall, weighed about a hundred thirty pounds, had a black hat pulled down over her eyes and a snuff box ring on the right hip pocket of her Levi's. She was wearing a silver belt buckle bigger than she was; inscribed with, "Champion Cowgirl Something" from some ranch hand rodeo.

While the horse trader took my halter off the bay horse and replaced it with his, he said, "There is a rodeo stock contractor I know that is trying out bucking horses. I think I'll take this bay over there and see if he can buck." To his credit, I did come out of the deal with a usable ranch horse, but I could have been tromped to death in that jelly bog hole.

I've bought, traded and tried out horses with friends and strangers all along my 115,000 mile horseback ride but two things I have learned: "BUYER BEWARE!" and keep your eyes open when a horse trader says, "Hell, even my wife can ride him."

The third and last life threatening blindly stampeding runaway happened during the last part of my 115, 000 mile horseback ride. We were gathering a stud band of twelve brood mares. They were running in the Pie Creek allotment about four miles north of the Dinner Station Ranch located along the Mountain City Highway.

It was a cold December morning and it was freezing with eight or nine inches of snow on the ground when three of us started out to gather these horses. The stallion had been pulled and these were wise old range mares that knew the country. They knew every canyon and trail in the mountain they lived on. We were well mounted and we were lucky because we saw the horses before they saw us. They were in a little grassy basin off in the distance.

I was riding a big bay eight-year-old, long circle, snaffle bit horse, the kind found on many of the large ranches throughout Nevada. This bay didn't particularly like people. You needed to catch him, saddle him, do your day's work, turn him loose and above all don't do something stupid while you were on or around him. He was just a fairly ordinary cowboy type horse. I rode him during the fall round up and got along fine but I had not run horses on him. Some horses do not have the right disposition to run other horses. I was somewhat concerned about controlling the bay but because of his stamina and sure footedness, I decided to ride him.

After we spotted the horses, we dismounted, reset our saddles, tightened our cinches and worked out a plan of attack. Clarence and Les would station themselves at the mouth of two long canyons that would lead the horses south back toward Lone Mountain instead of north the way we wanted them to go. I slipped around and came up on the far side of the horses so when they started to run they would go north.

When I topped the ridge the horses instantly spotted me. For a moment they stood like statues, and then they whirled and started running north. The big bay whinnied and every muscle in his body tensed. When I tried to hold him back, he reared up and started dancing sideways. In spite of the fact that it was below freezing, sweat broke out on his neck just ahead of his shoulders and he took the bit in his mouth, lunged forward and the race was on. I was probably a hundred yards behind the horses that were now running flat out. With the snow cover on the ground it was impossible to see the badger holes or dry washes that were drifted over with snow.

By the time I reached the first canyon and Clarence turned the horses north, the big bay had closed the gap and was now within fifty yards of the running horses. We went by Les who took up the chase and when we reached the gate and went out of the Pie Creek allotment onto the Mountain City Highway right-of-way, frozen chunks of snow, kicked up by the running horses, were hitting my face. At this point the highway right-of-way was fifty yards wide. The horses had to make a sharp turn to the right and when they hit the black ice on the highway, five horses fell flat on their sides. Instantly I was in the middle of floundering horses all trying to get up at the same time. The big bay's legs flew in all directions and he missed some of the downed horses by inches. Somehow he managed to keep his feet and by the time all the horses were up and back in the sagebrush along the highway right-of-way, he was in the middle of the running horses. Their nostrils were flared and I was being bumped on both sides. Everything was out of control. The only thing I could do was keep the big bay between my legs and hope he stayed on his feet.

In a while the horses began to slow and that big bay worked his way through the herd until he was in the lead. We remained in the lead until we turned into the open gate at the Dinner Station Ranch corrals and slammed into the corral poles on the far side. The horse herd followed with Clarence and Les close behind. With the corral gate closed and the big bay under control, there were grins of relief all around.

Sometimes it is easier to be involved in a wreck than watch it unfold and not be able to help. Through the years, all cowboy have, at one time or another, been involved in watching similar life threatening situations without being in a position to help. They experience the same emotions as if they were involved, so everyone was relieved when the runaway ended on a positive note.

This was the last blindly stampeding runaway ride I encountered on my 115,000 mile horseback ride and it reaffirms the feelings I expressed earlier. Though neither prospect is appealing, I would rather ride a bucking horse than ride a blindly stampeding runaway.

LITTLE THINGS

An old saying, "He's wild and wooly and full of fleas. He's never been curried below the knees."

FRANK "SHORTY" PRUNTY

Frank "Shorty" Prunty was inducted into the Nevada Cattlemen's Association Cowboy 100,000 Mile Club in 1986.

The presentation was given by Linda Morse when "Shorty" was inducted. The following was written by his granddaughter, Becky Lisle.

Charleston, Nevada, is a rural community located in northern Elko County. It is 85 miles north of Elko. This community has been the home of a cowboy who was born, raised and has lived all his life on the Prunty Ranch. He is a rancher, a hunting guide, a buckaroo, a rawhide craftsman, a former rodeo stock producer and a family man. But above all, he is one of Nevada's pioneering cowboys of today—- he is Frank "Shorty" Prunty, a man who has spent over 100,000 miles horseback. From this point on he will be called by his nickname "Shorty".

Shorty was born on May 24, 1923, on the family ranch in Charleston, Nevada, which is about ninety miles north of Elko. His parents were Earl and May Prunty.

When Shorty reached school age, he rode to and from school every day. The school house was a mile from home, and he attended school there for his first eight years. Shorty then went to high school in Twin Falls, Idaho, graduating in 1941.

Shorty made his home and a living for his family on the Prunty Ranch which he acquired from his parents. He married Marjorie Bieroth in 1948, and they have two sons: Dick, who is currently living on the

Prunty Ranch with his wife Jan and daughters Becky and Kyla. Son Gary, a self-employed carpenter, lives in Elko.

Earl Prunty was known for liking horses better than cows, so Shorty grew up with his young life revolving around horses. At any time during Shorty's youth the family had anywhere from 200 to 400 horses which, during a year's time, ranged from the Diamond A Desert in southern Idaho, which is a forty mile ride from the home ranch, sixty miles to the northern most point of the desert where the horses ran, to Deeth, Nevada, which is another fifty mile ride south from the home ranch.

In 1929 Shorty began riding at the age of six. Young Shorty learned quickly that his major form of transportation and the most valuable animal on the Prunty Ranch was a horse. As a self-taught rider, Shorty spent much of his childhood with his father, Earl, working horseback on their ranch. There were cattle to be gathered in the fall, cattle to be ridden through in the spring and fall, cattle drives to be made, and horses to be broke for ranch use. Shorty spent many hours as a buckaroo for his uncle Mack on his ranch as well as for his Father.

Shorty started making very long rides at about the age of nine, putting in full days and doing a man's work. Most days would involve at least a twenty to thirty mile ride, just doing what needed to be done with the horses that ranged throughout northern Elko County and into southern Idaho. It was standard procedure to make four to six trips a year to the Diamond A to gather, sort and brand horses. In addition to the distance from the home ranch to the desert, there were, of course, the many miles put in gathering the big country. They often left for these week long trips with not so much as a pack horse. They traveled with a blanket and a bag of jerky tied to their saddles. At the age of ten, Shorty made a long distance horseback ride with his Father. They left Charleston with 19 head of mules on a four-day drive to the railroad station in Wells. The mules had been sold to a buyer to resell to plantations in the south. It was a 120 mile round trip to Wells and was made one to three times a year delivering cows or horses. Shorty made these trips with his Father until he entered high school in 1936.

During World War II, about the time Shorty graduated from high school and returned to the ranch to live full-time, the Pruntys participated in the Cavalry Remount program and provided horses for the military. Many trips were made to Deeth to load horses on the trains. In addition, from 1941 to 1945 Shorty had a mail contract with the United States Postal Service to deliver mail from Charleston to Deeth, Nevada. It was his responsibility to deliver mail twice a week during the winter months with a team of horses and a sleigh or wagon. In the spring when the snow was too deep for wheels or there was too much mud for the sleigh,

Shorty would ride horseback leading a pack horse. These travel conditions usually existed for at least one month of the winter season. These trips were tough on the rider as well as the horses. The distance from Charleston to Deeth round trip was 110 miles. Shorty made the trip twice a week for four weeks during the winter months for five years. As a mail carrier, Shorty accumulated an additional 4,400 miles horseback.

Since 1916, the 150 mile trips to and on the Diamond A Desert have always been a part of the Prunty Ranch operation. These trips were made in the spring and fall. Shorty Prunty has never missed one of these trips in the last 54 years. During this time Shorty rode 25,000 miles on the Diamond A Desert.

As a young cowboy and buckaroo, Shorty broke horses not only for himself but for others. Shorty said, "Breaking a horse takes patience. A young cowboy with a strong body and a solid attitude will succeed if he remains patient while working with his horse." Shorty broke horses for Albert Black in Bruneau, Idaho, in 1946. He rode 30 miles a day for 100 days giving him an extra rough earned 3,000 miles horseback.

Shorty also worked as a cowboy for neighbors, and of course did much of the riding needed for Prunty's cattle, however over-shadowed they were by horses.

In 1946 Shorty trailed a string of bucking horses to the Mountain City Rodeo in Mountain City, Nevada. The round trip horse drive was 80 miles and he made this trip for at least six different years. The excitement and adventure of the rodeo led Shorty to invest more time in selecting rodeo stock. He expanded his service as a rodeo stock producer by trailing horses to rodeos in Wells, Nevada seven times, to Elko four times and once to Battle Mountain. The round trips to Wells were 120 miles; to Elko 140 miles and the trip to Battle Mountain was 150 miles, 300 miles round trip, and he only made this trip once. Shorty was also the arena pick-up man for these rodeos and would ride another ten miles on horseback during three performances per rodeo at least ten times a year. These early years as a rodeo stock producer added another 1,850 miles horseback to Shorty's lifelong ride.

In 1959 Shorty and his brother, Corky, started the Diamond A Rodeo Company. When the demand for the rodeo stock increased, he moved the Diamond A Rodeo Company headquarters to Jerome, Idaho. From 1960 to 1964 his children went to school and his wife taught Elementary Education in Jerome. The highlight of Shorty's rodeo career as a rodeo stock producer was from 1962 to 1964. By this time he had acquired an outstanding string of bucking horses of which five made it to the National Finals Rodeo.

In 1961 Shorty joined the Rodeo Cowboys Association (now known as the PRCA) and of course, started hauling horses by trucks to more and more rodeos throughout the west. He leased horses to many other contractors and took horses to the National Finals Rodeo (NFR). In 1964, the bareback horse called Broken Blossom was the third best bareback bronc of the year at the National Finals Rodeo. The final rodeo Shorty and Marge put on was the High School Finals Rodeo in 1967 and 1968. After that the bucking stock was sold to Christensen Brothers.

Although the Prunty horses have always been in the spotlight and are first in the hearts of the Prunty family, the cattle business has been the main source of income for the Prunty Ranch. In the early years before fences and allotments were introduced, Shorty's father had a winter range located on the Bruneau River. The rides to the Bruneau River were cold and tough. Shorty made a number of trips with his Father to check cattle on the winter range. They kept this range until about 1964, when the cattle started wintering at the home ranch and were fed hay. During the calving season, Shorty is constantly on horseback riding through his herds. The summer range for the cattle has always been located in the Stone Flat, 76 Creek and Copper Mountain areas. Shorty has ridden about ten miles a day caring for his cattle for at least 150 days a year for the past fifty years. This gives him over 75,000 miles as a buckaroo.

As I said before, as a young man, Shorty made cattle and horse drives to Deeth with his Father to ship livestock to market. These round trips were 110 mile drives averaging three trips a year. However, today the cattle and horses are shipped by truck. When an early winter set in at Charleston, in the early 1980's, Shorty had to go back to the cattle drives of the past. This was a sixty mile round trip to the highway for Shorty and his riders. They made the trip twice with cattle and once with horses in 1983.

From the fall of 1941 to the present time, Shorty and his family have operated a hunting guide service in the Jarbidge Wilderness area. They provide each hunter with a horse and guide the hunters into the wilderness in groups. These daily hunts averaged about 20 miles a day and the deer season lasted a minimum of 25 days for a total of 500 miles per season. Shorty has accumulated another 22,500 miles riding horseback while guiding hunters for 45 years.

There were funny stories that involved hunters. Some of the bucking horses used in the rodeo string were also used as pack horses during the hunting season, and more than once, hunters would ask why the horses had number brands on their rumps. The "dude" hunters often provided entertainment as the wise old saddle horses got the best of them.

One hunter got scraped off under a tree when his horse decided to just circle the tree until the tree limbs raked the rider out of the saddle. All the while this was happening, the hunter was saying, "Whoa baby, whoa baby, whoa baby." When the hunter hit the ground "whoa baby" turned to "kiss my ass, you son of a bitch." Shorty would tell this story and laugh so hard tears would come to his eyes.

Shorty loved to tell stories. One of his favorites happened one winter. Neighbor Kent Howard at Miller Creek Ranch (about ten miles north of the Prunty Ranch on the Bruneau River) was running out of feed for his cattle. The snow was so deep he couldn't move the cattle out. Shorty was able to save the cattle for Howard by driving a herd of horses through the deep snow, breaking a trail to make moving the cattle possible.

Summary of miles ridden during Frank "Shorty" Prunty's lifelong horseback ride:

Miles ridden gathering and branding horses on the Diamond A Desert	25,000 miles
Miles ridden breaking horses in Bruneau	3,000 miles
Miles carrying the mail from Charleston to Deeth, Nev.	4,400 miles
Early rodeo miles	1,190 miles
Guiding hunters for 45 years	22,500 miles
Miles ridden taking care of his own cattle for 50 years	75,000 miles
A Grand Total of miles ridden horseback along Frank "Shorty" Prunty's long winding trail	131,090 miles.

Today, Shorty still makes his three trips to the Diamond A Desert each year and he continues to ride, caring for his own cattle year round. For a man who has gone through eight saddles during his cowboy career of well over 100,000 miles horseback, Frank "Shorty" Prunty is truly deserving of the Cowboy 100,000 Mile Club award.

Becky says, "With the many different horse centered ventures of Shorty's life, from rodeoing to mail carrying, it would be much easier to count the days he didn't spend in the saddle than those he did. When he won the Cowboy 100,000 Mile Club award in 1986, he was still very active and undoubtedly added several more thousand miles before his death in 1997. His wife, Marge, says that the 131,090 miles ridden is a very conservative estimate of Shorty's true lifetime horseback ride."

LITTLE THINGS

A cowboy that had too much to drink was driving home in his pickup when he crashed through his neighbor's fence. The deputy sheriff investigating the accident asked the old cowboy what happened. The old timer said, "I turned out to let a bridge go by and I don't know where that fence came from."

HORSE WRECKS

Anyone who has spent a lifetime working with horses has been in horse wrecks. Some are minor, some are serious, and some are comical. I've mentioned a few I remember that happened along my lifelong horseback ride but there are two incidents that really stand out in my memory. One happened in the early part of my 115,000 mile horseback ride and the other took place much closer to the end of my long winding trail.

The first wreck happened while we were cutting strays out of a ranch herd of cows and calves. During this time frame in my part of the world, ranch raised cattle were mostly British breeds that were predominantly Hereford. The neighboring ranch to the east had been sold and turned into a yearling steer operation so the Mexican steers they were running were somewhat of a novelty. These steers weren't any wilder than the native cattle that were raised on the mountain ranges of northern California but they were a little different.

On this day we had a herd of cows and calves bunched up along a drift fence and we were cutting Mexican steers out that were to be driven back to the range where they belonged. The Mexican steers had been running with the cows long enough to be attached to them and it was hard to keep the steers from returning to the cow herd. One big long legged steer started to break back and I ran out to head him off. That steer and my horse were both running flat out. As I edged by the steer and got to the point where he should have turned back to the left, the steer instead ducked to the right and tried to go under my horse's neck. The point of my horse's shoulder plowed into the running steer just behind his right shoulder and the steer went down, turning completely over. While this was taking place my horse's front legs were knocked out from under him and he turned upside down while going over the upside down steer. I was squashed between the steer's belly and my horse's back during the few seconds it took my horse to roll over the downed steer. We all got untangled and up at about the same time. My horse wasn't hurt. The steer, somewhat dazed, went back in the direction I wanted him to go and I unsteadily got to my feet.

About this time the boss's wife drove by along the road leading to the ranch headquarters and she called out, "What happened? Did he fall off of his horse?" I found out later that I had a broken nose, some broken ribs, and a banged up leg. But to a young cowboy the worst thing that could possibly happen was having someone think he had fallen off his horse. Getting bucked off or having a horse shy out from under him was bad enough but falling off his horse! Even to this day when I remember this incident from long ago, the first thing that comes to mind is those eight words. "What happened? Did he fall off his horse?" To this young cowboy I think hearing that comment was worse than the actual wreck itself.

The next horse wreck I started out to remember at the beginning of this story happened many years later. The forgiving muscles and bones of youth were long gone and I was in the shatter on impact stage of my horseback ride.

It was spring and the first herds of cows had arrived at the Canyon Ranch which was part of the Salmon River Cattlemen's Association range, located in northeastern Elko County Nevada. There is a long steep sided mountain that runs south from Gollaher Mountain to Devil's Gap, Angels Pass and Texas Canyon. Several times during the grazing season we would drive cows and calves up the steep trail on the west side of Angels Pass, go through the pass, and trail down a steep draw to lower range on the east side. It was only a five mile drive but it was very difficult because of the steep, rugged terrain. It was the shortest route to the area of range we wanted the cows to summer in and because of the steep, rugged mountain, few cows back tracked over Angels Pass to the Canyon Ranch area until fall.

With this background, three or four cowboys and I gathered about two hundred cows with calves at their sides and headed for Angels Pass. We left the Canyon Ranch meadows not long after daylight and worked our way up through the stringer meadows along East Trout Creek. About two miles into the cattle drive we left East Trout Creek and started up the steep trail toward Angels Pass. As we got closer to the top of the mountain and the trail got even steeper, we stopped to let the cows and our horses rest for several minutes every fifteen or twenty yards as we traveled up the mountain. During one of these stops, when the cows were fairly well under control, I got off and reset my saddle, let some air under my saddle blanket to cool my horse's sweaty back and remounted. I knew that once we got through Angels Pass and started down the steep draw to the east there wouldn't be time to do this. It was important to keep the cows strung out and in the bottom of the canyon for the first quarter of a mile downhill where they would then get on a trail leading to a stock water pond along the Side Hill water line. I knew some of the cows would want to go north following the narrow rim rock ledges instead of going down the draw and we would have our hands full keeping the herd together.

We had the lead cows strung out down the bottom of the canyon and were working hard to keep other cows from rimming around to the north. I was busy turning cows down the canyon when I looked above and saw cows heading for a rocky ledge. I turned Brown Jug, the horse

I was riding, uphill. The hill was so steep Brown Jug started lunging up through the rocks. On the third lunge my saddle slipped and the back cinch ended up around Brown Jug's flanks.

Now Brown Jug was another old horse that just tolerated people. Get on him, do a day's work and leave him alone. This fit his personality just fine. He had papers and his registered name was Desert Wine. He was an average sized brown horse so in true cowboy fashion that name was soon changed to Little Brown Jug, then shortened to Brown Jug. He was a good, sure-footed big circle horse. Just don't do anything stupid and everything was fine.

I do not know if I did anything stupid or not but when that back cinch touched Brown Jug's flanks that was all the spark he needed. Up there, in the rim rocks on that steep mountain side he exploded. I was bucked off almost before I realized what was happening. As strange as this may sound, that might have saved my life. I lit a long way down hill on the back of my head and shoulders. I dimly remember seeing Brown Jug bucking over me making huge leaps on his way downhill. I was told later that he was found about a mile below with his head down, his sides heaving with my saddle turned under his belly with one hind foot through a stirrup.

By the time Dale, who had seen the accident, came running to see if he could help I was sitting up with blood running down my face. We found out I could stand up and slowly walk. It was obvious Dale could not do much more for me. We were in an inaccessible area so we decided the best plan was for Dale to continue with the trail herd, help mother up the cows and calves at the stock water pond, and he or someone else could look for Brown Jug. I knew I could not get back on a horse so I started slowly walking back over Angels Pass to get to a spot where help could reach me. From Angels Pass I could look down to the west and see the ranch horse trailers a mile and a half below. That distance looked like forever but I soon found out that by stooping forward and slowly walking, I hurt less than when I sat down to rest. So I kept limping along.

I finally reached the ranch pickups and horse trailers. Luckily, from this spot I had a signal on my cell phone that was in one of the ranch pickups. So I called Jane and asked her to find Claude, who would know where to come, and tell him to come and pick me up as soon as possible, that I needed a little help. An hour later Jane and Claude showed up about the same time the cowboy crew came riding down the hill. They had Brown Jug, who wasn't hurt, and the only thing broken on my saddle was the rope strap.

At the emergency room we found out that besides cuts and bruises I had jammed vertebrae in my neck and lower back, some broken ribs and a damaged rotator cup in my right shoulder.

These two horse wrecks were like book ends. One happened in the early stages of my long winding trail and the other took place near the trail's end, with a number of less memorable horse wrecks sandwiched in between. After this experience I used a breast collar when riding Brown Jug and I rode him many more miles without another incident.

LITTLE THINGS

A sign on the front door of a veterinarian's office read: Lost one dog. He is a Border Collie. He is black and white. One ear is lopped off. He only has three legs. He's been castrated. He answers to the name of "Lucky."

Bob and Linnea Thomas

ROBERT "BOB" THOMAS

Bob Thomas was inducted into the Nevada Cattlemen's Association Cowboy 100,000 Mile Club in 1995.

In 1994 Mary Branscomb visited Bob Thomas and wrote a brief story about some of the incidents that happened along his long winding trail and Dave Secrist documented the miles Bob Thomas has ridden horseback in his lifetime. They are as follows:

"Bob's three loves in life were airplanes, horses and me – in that order," said his wife Linnea Thomas trying to describe her husband of nearly fifty years.

"Bob Thomas can still outwork any young man in Paradise Valley, and he will drop his own work in a second to help a neighbor," said Pete Marvel whose ranch and range are next to Thomas, "and he knows how to ranch in this valley. When I need to know something I ask Bob."

A man who doesn't want to "sound like he is braggin'," Bob is not likely to offer advice, but when he does explain something, for instance how he might grow a crop, he's careful to qualify his remarks with, "but my fields may be different from yours."

Bob and Linnea met in high school in Merced, California, and married on February 13, 1945. He flew a fighter plane from 1942 to 1946.

His North American P-51 "Mustang" took him on 85 combat missions into Germany from bases in England, France, and from Normandy Beach after D-Day. As he returned from one of these missions half way through his tour of duty, his low-flying plane was hit by anti-aircraft fire over a forest near the French/German border. He bailed out, landed on the right side of the line and was not mistaken for the enemy by American infantrymen. He lived to fly another thirty missions or more.

Bob earned the nation's Distinguished Flying Cross, the French Croix De Guerre with a Palm Leaf and the Air Medal with fifteen Oak Leaf Clusters (which means he was awarded the Medal fifteen succeeding times.)

After the war, Bob and Linnea began to look for a ranch to buy. In the end they returned to the first one they considered in Paradise Valley.

Linnea, a graduate nurse, explained, "I worked for a couple of years, but after we married, had children and began ranching, I was busy enough practicing my skills during calving season."

Their children are Keith, who now lives with his family on the 7HL Ranch in the north end of Paradise Valley, and Marilyn Loveseth, a registered nurse living in Reno. There are three grandchildren.

Bob remembered, "Since I was a boy I always knew I wanted to be a rancher.....but I had to run a dairy in California until I saved enough for a down payment on this, the old Elmer Cathcart place, in March of 1957. I bought it from J. C. Stearns who acquired it from Jack Utter."

"When I got out of the service about all I did was trade my Mustang plane for a mustang horse. I could have enjoyed either one."

"Fighter planes require a lot of thought," he said, "kind of like horses…. There's always some problem that comes up or some way to get a little more out of them. A way to gain more understanding, maybe."

Maybe it was Bob Thomas' lifetime efforts to understand what he observes that made him an efficient squadron commander at 24 years of age and a thoughtful caretaker of the land thereafter.

For his ability to husband his allotment, he was recognized last January by the Santa Rosa Ranger District of the Humboldt National Forest with its "Nevada Excellence in Rangeland Award."

District Ranger Scott Bell wrote, "Bob has been the sole permittee in the North Fork Allotment since 1965. He takes great pride in the allotment and is responsible in his management practices. Most of the allotment is in satisfactory condition due, much in part, to Bob's efforts. Bob is conscientious in not overusing the range. He comes on to the allotment well after range readiness is met, keeps the improvements maintained and rides often to keep the cattle distributed. Bob carries a tape measure with him when he rides to measure the utilization levels. When the proper levels have been reached, he takes the initiative to move his cattle to the next pasture or takes them home."

He continued, "Currently we are completing a new allotment management plan (AMP) for the North Fork Allotment. This has been a cooperative effort between the Forest Service, Bob, NDOW, USF & WLS and other publics…He is using his cattle as a management tool.

One of his tools is rest and rotation. He has divided his allotment into three fields and moves cattle as conditions warrant.

Bob said, "Years ago Holloway Meadows dried up every summer but now the moisture rises and it has water on it year round. Long before riparian was a catch word, Bob recognized the value and beauty of grass and trees along stream banks and encouraged them with proper use and non use."

Although Bob works well with the rangers who come and go in the Santa Rosa office, his ideas are different about beaver and how they affect the trout and riparian areas. Bob's record keeping photos show cattle and aspen live well together, but beaver and aspen – that's another story.

He explained sadly, "Beavers fell hundreds of 40 foot tall aspen trees in a season that took 25 years to grow."

He explained how big beaver dams will blowout one day during a spring flood or else high water will flood around the ends. Either way, when this happens, shrubs will be washed away and gravel will be deposited along the stream banks. Nothing grows in gravel, he observed. Stream banks will be undercut and erode and a riparian area will not be reestablished for decades.

Bob described how beaver in his canyon are chewing their way to the top, leaving a wasted riparian behind. He is trying to convince the forest service people the riparian is more important than the beaver dams.

(Dave's comments: "I've had a lot of experience with beaver and riparian areas in my fifty years of ranching in the great sagebrush basins of the west. I have observed and documented with pictures the same results Bob describes in his comments above. I do not believe that Bob meant to imply that beaver, living in forest areas or other places where trees and willows grow profusely and reproduce themselves much faster than the beavers need for food and dam material present a problem. They at times may be a nuisance but their presence in this type of environment probably outweighs the trouble they cause.

In the arid areas of the west, where aspen and willows usually grow in small isolated groups along small streams or springs, it is a different story. The beaver is a very prolific hard working animal that reproduce themselves and form large colonies in a short period of time. In this environment the beaver do not have any other areas to pioneer into. I've seen a lone beaver out in the sagebrush several miles from its colony trying to find a new food source. I've seen first hand the devastation left behind years after they have moved into the bottom of a drainage that didn't contain enough forage to sustain them. The beaver stripped the area bare as they worked their way up the canyon eating themselves out of house and home. When they reach the top they starve out and die or move on to another small food source that might be miles away. Years later, during a heavy thunderstorm the deserted beaver dams wash out like dominoes causing a flash flood effect. This leaves a deep wash in the bottom of the canyon with not enough surface water left to maintain re-growth.

Sadly the rancher is often solely blamed for the destruction left behind. I have observed that it is not wise to introduce or use beaver colonies as a management tool in this kind of environment.")

Bob continued, "They argue that pools left behind dams are spawning places for Lahontan Cutthroat trout (designated as an endangered species)", but Bob says, "I don't see how fish will benefit if streams wash out and riparian areas are dried up"

Bob has always been involved in his industry by serving as a member of the Nevada Cattlemen's Association Board of Directors and as 1966-68 president of the Nevada Farm Bureau. He also is involved in the politics of grass as a member of the N-2 Grazing Board and its Central Committee. He is on the Farm Bureau Land Management Advisory Board and the Agriculture Advisory Council for the University of Nevada –Reno.

"We grow alfalfa on 350 acres of my land. Linnea has always run the swather, but we usually have one hired hand during haying, and we sometimes have part time help....But this valley is not farming country. It's cattle country. I've got a permit for 1,000 AUMs on the forest and 600 on the BLM. If I lose the permits I'm out of business."

Bob continued, "I don't think I will see it in my lifetime, but I predict the government will beg ranchers to graze land one day. Right now the environmentalists have the upper hand. They have a lot of power, money and friends in government, but when it becomes apparent that what they are doing is destructive, the country will need ranchers more than you think.... Between now and then, a lot of people will be hurt."

Bob likes beef on the hoof and on the table. He says, "I'm a meat eater and beef is the Cadillac of meat."...still strong at 76 and able to work 16 hours a day, he adds, "I don't have any plans to retire. I'll probably die here."

Documentation of miles ridden during Bob Thomas's life long horseback ride;

Bob Thomas grew up working on his parents' ranch near Yosemite Park's west entrance. From 1926 until 1956, a time span of thirty years, four of those years Bob was in the service, so for 26 years Bob averaged riding five miles a day for 275 days a year. Many of these rides were 25 to 35 mile circles made while taking care of the family's cattle that ranged in the foothills along the west side of the Sierra Nevada Mountains. By the time he was thirty-six years old he had ridden at least 35,750 miles horseback. During 1956 Bob purchased the Cathcart Ranch and moved his family to Paradise Valley, Nevada. For the next thirty-nine years Bob became a typical Nevada rancher and cowboy. He ran mustangs, repped on round-up wagons and took care of his own ranching operations. During this part of Bob's life it is estimated that he rode another 75,000 miles by the time he was inducted into the Cowboy 100,000 Mile Club. The grand total miles Bob has ridden horseback along his long winding trail is 110,750 miles.

Dave's footnote: "Bob passed away August 4, 2010 at the age of 89. He was a quiet leader in the community and a good neighbor. He didn't agree with everybody but was respected by all."

RANCHING TWENTY-FOUR HOURS A DAY

This is a story Dave told when he accepted his Cowboy 100,000 Mile club award:

I want to tell you about an incident in my life that some of you ranchers might relate to. I have lived ranching 24 hours a day all my life and most of you folks that are here tonight have done or are doing the same thing. You do this partly because you like this kind of life and partly because you have to in order to survive.

We started out to drive 350 cows and calves on a one-day ten mile trip. From the very start the cows didn't want to go south the way we wanted them to go. Several weeks earlier the cows were trailed into Nevada from Idaho and they wanted to go back north in the direction they came from. That one-day drive turned into a three-day ordeal. All during the drive we fought with one old black bally cow. She had a big calf and she was really proud of him. She was in one side of the herd and out the other. Every time she got a chance, she tried to go north and it took one cowboy to keep track of her. Half way through the drive about a hundred calves broke back. After a three mile running battle the cows cleaned us and we ended up back where we started out earlier in the day. The next day we were back at daybreak with our bed rolls. We stayed with the cows that night and the next day we reached the pasture we were headed for. By the time we got the cows on water and the calves mothered up, it was getting late. We didn't get back to the ranch until about ten o'clock that night. We took care of our horses, Jane fed us, and we got to bed about midnight.

Now I don't dream very often, but about two a.m. I had a very vivid dream about that old black bally cow. She had me up against the corral fence hooking the devil out of me. I don't know why in my dream I didn't climb the fence, but I didn't. I just reached back, wrapped my arms around the corral poles and when that old cow charged me again, I kicked her along side of the head with both feet just as hard as I could.

That was mistake number one! I kicked Jane completely out of bed. I didn't just roll her over the edge of the bed. She landed about six feet out in the middle of the bedroom floor. The first thing I heard was a fairly agitated voice saying "What did you kick me for?"

Here is where I made mistake number two! I said "I didn't kick you I just kicked an old cow." She said, "Now you called me a cow." And I said, "No, I didn't call you an old cow."

Well for a while things went from bad to worse but after we both got completely awake and found out that Jane was not seriously hurt, it turned out Jane wasn't terrible upset because I kicked her out of bed but she darned sure was on the fight because she thought I called her an old cow.

Maybe there is a moral in this story for you fellows that are living ranching twenty-four hours a day.

LITTLE THINGS

I have been married a long time and I am boss of the family......
..just as long as my wife wants me to be.

FRANK BAKER

Frank Baker was inducted into the Nevada Cattlemen's Association Cowboy 100,00 Mile Club in 1984.

Jim Connelley wrote and gave this presentation when Frank was inducted in the Club. Jim's documentation of Frank's horseback ride follows:

I'd like to take a few minutes and tell you a story about a man I've known for about eighteen years and have come to respect as a cowboy's cowboy.

Frank was born in 1911 in Elko, Nevada, and raised at Gold Creek; about seventy miles north of Elko. His family worked in ranching and his father drove freight from Elko to the mines around Gold Creek and Mountain City. Frank rode his first miles horseback at a tender age while accompanying his father's six and twelve up teams on the freight runs. These trips took four days to go to Elko empty and seven to ten days coming out loaded. His Dad was the last commercial freight team that operated in the area.

Frank attended school in the Gold Creek, Wild Horse and the North Fork areas riding horseback.

In 1920 he took his first paying job as a buckaroo, riding for Emory Johnson in what is now Wild Horse Lake and Recreation area. For a whole summer's riding, he received one heifer. This calf became the foundation for what is probably the highest quality bunch of Hereford and Hereford-Saler cattle in Nevada.

During the mid 1920's he worked summers riding and breaking colts for various outfits such as Tom Tinnel, Em Johnson and the PX Company.

Due to the severity of the winters in this area, school was sometimes held in the summer when kids could more easily attend. However, boys will be boys, and he still managed to rack up approximately 3,000 miles during this early period of his life.

In 1926 after graduation from the eighth grade, he moved with his folks and went to work for William H. Moffat under cow boss, George Callaghan. The Moffat headquarters were in Osino, on the Clubine Ranch, at Rancho Grande and North Fork. For the next ten years he worked as a buckaroo for Moffat traveling between Osino and North Fork. During the summer season he rode the range and in the winter he fed cows.

Between 1930 and 1935 Frank was a designated representative for the Moffat outfit and would start a fall ride from Rancho Grande, go through Independence Valley, the Spanish Ranch, the Saval, Willow Creek and along the Humboldt river, finally winding up at Osino after the first of the year. As he got to know the brands, he would bring not only the Moffat cattle, but other strays as well, dropping them off at their respective ranches as he went along. He also repped for Moffat on the UC and the TS (Hillery Barnes outfit). For ten years on the Moffat ranches he spent ten to fifteen hours per day in the saddle for at least ten months of the year amassing 50,000 miles horseback.

In 1936 he rode one season for the Hinkley cattle operation driving cattle from the railroad to summer range in the North Fork-Gold Creek area then back again in the fall, adding another 5,000 miles on the back of a horse.

In 1936 he went to work for Homer Andrea whose home place and summer range was near Mountain City, Homer also had an early spring permit out in the middle of the Owyhee desert. In the early spring when the snow was melting, that desert ground would get saturated and every step a horse made he would sink up past his hocks in the mud making it almost impossible to drive cattle long distances. The cowboys would wait for a hard freeze after a Chinook, usually in February, then get the cattle up and leave Mountain City about midnight to drive them over Bull Run Mountain on the frozen trail to Deep Creek. The second day would get them to VN, the third day west on the IL and the fourth day they could rest——shoeing horses!

From February through April, living out of a cabin at Devil's Corral, Frank would ride the desert from Tuscarora north to the 45 Ranch at the base of the Juniper Mountains in Idaho. Old Homer always gave Frank a strong string of colts to break down on the desert. Frank, working alone, would have to fore-foot'em and tie'em down to get the saddle on. He would then release them and get in the saddle as the horse got up.

(Remarks by Dave Secrist: Jim Connelley told me he's been to the cabin at Devil's Corral and Frank Baker's initials are carved into the cabin wall. These "colts" Frank rode were three to five year old range raised horses, which had never been halter broke. Frank told Jim how he handled the horses. Frank would fore-foot the horses, tie the horse down, put a blind on him, fish the cinch under the horse's belly, place the saddle on him and tighten the latigo. Frank would then get on while the horse was getting up. Sometime in this process Frank would pull the blind and the ride was on.

During this time frame, the process just described or some variation of it was common practice all over the big ranges of the west. Remember Frank was forty miles from no-where, he was living alone in a line camp and he had ten of these horses to rough break before the cattle left the desert. By this time these horses were becoming trusted cow horses. The amazing thing to me is that many of these "old time cowboys" lived well into their sixties, seventies and eighties.)

Jim stated, "In the late 1930's it was still Depression times in Northern Nevada and there were quite a few unsavory characters: mustangers, moonshiners and men on the dodge from the law, holed up among the rims and gullies of the Owyhee Canyon. To this day it is one of the "wildest" places in the United States. During one fall when gathering strays in this area, Frank threw in with the IL wagon on John G. Taylor's outfit. John G. was in financial trouble and the bank's representatives rode with the wagon. One of them happened to be a good cook and was greatly appreciated. While working for Andrea, Frank logged another 16,000 miles horseback."

Then in the winter of 1938, he joined his folks and older brother, Earl, on a little ranch on California Creek, now part of the 101 Ranch near Mountain City. Here they eked out a living running dairy and beef cows while working for the Forest Service. This was hard work, but it was their own ranch, and they were determined to make a go of it. He added another 8,000 miles horseback.

In 1946 he, his brother, Earl, and younger brother, Ted, bought out Homer Andrea and built the place now known as the Baker Brothers 7 Diamond Ranch on Van Duzer Creek near Mountain City. From 1946 until the present day, Frank rides with his cows every day for a possible eight to twelve hours logging another 85,000 miles horseback. This brings the total to 167,000 miles in a saddle on the back of a horse. Although he carries all the marks of seventy three years in the saddle and looks at you through glasses thick as coke bottle bottoms, he can still see a cow on a ridge a half a mile away and tell you her life history and that of every daughter she's raised. Frank started a colt year before last and broke a feed team the year before that. You'll still find him in the middle of the saddle everyday from before the first calf hits the ground in late February until the last cow's gathered in the fall, and if I don't shut up and let him out of here he won't make tomorrow's ride.

I'd like to present the Nevada Cattlemen's Association Cowboy 100,000 Mile Club award to my friend, neighbor and mentor, Frank Baker of Mountain City.

LITTLE THINGS

Two old timers that had been friends and neighbors for a long time got into an argument one morning. They nearly came to blows. When they came in for lunch one said, "You are probably right." The other old timer said, "No, you are probably right." After some more back and forth they switched sides. Each took the other's position and continued arguing all afternoon.

MOTHERS

Along my 115,000 mile horseback ride one thing has been uncompromisingly constant: A mother's inherited trait of protecting her young. If push comes to shove it makes no difference if it is a two legged mom, a four legged mom or a winged mom. Their courage and complete disregard for their own safety is incredible. Each protects its young to the utmost of her ability. A country mom will face insurmountable odds to save a child. A killdeer will stand defiantly in front of her nest gallantly challenging an intruder a thousand times bigger than she is before flopping away as if crippled, hoping the intruder will follow her away from the nest. A nesting sage hen will sit motionless with a coyote only a few feet away hoping she will not be discovered. The wild sow or mother bear will charge straight forward with the intent to kill and sometimes at the fault of neither, it is your life or hers. At other times, a patch of grass left standing in a freshly mowed meadow gives testimony to the respect given a nesting blackbird, duck or pheasant.

One time, on my 115,000 mile horseback ride, I came around a sharp turn in the trail and saw a doe standing about thirty feet ahead, in the middle of the trail. Her head was down, her ears were flopped forward, she was stomping her front feet and the hair on her back and sides was turned the wrong way. I kept my dogs back and rode a few steps closer, but the doe didn't give an inch. I couldn't see any reason for her to be challenging me. On a second look, I saw a well camouflaged newborn fawn lying by her side. The fawn's neck was stretched out and its head and ears were pressed tightly against the ground. Then I saw the reason for it all. About half way between the doe and where my horse and dogs were standing, blending into the surroundings was a lynx. The cat was crouched flat against the ground, stone still except for the slight twitching of his stubby tail. For a moment we all stood frozen in time. Then I slowly lowered my hand toward the pistol holstered at my side. The cat lost its nerve first and bounded into the brush before I could get a shot off. The doe held her ground so I turned and rode back up the trail, circled around and rejoined the trail below. I marveled at the doe and the display of courage I had just seen.   A doe's normal defense against danger is flight. In this case she held her ground against a lynx, a man, two dogs and a horse while protecting her fawn. She put her life on the line. I was on her side, but she didn't know that. Even though I knew her battle might not be over, I hoped that cat, faced with the prospect of sharp hooves, plus a man, a horse and two dogs was gone from the area. I realize the lynx was only trying to get a meal, but in this kind of situation I usually tried to even the odds.

Another incident I remember involving a mother protecting her young, happened in the spring and this time the odds were fairly even.

It was a late spring day and Harold, Bob, and I were three young cowboys working for the Eden Valley Ranch in northern California. This day we were working fence along the south side of Bald Mountain, ten miles from the home ranch. Now, to three cowboys, that thought "anything that couldn't be done horseback wasn't worth doing," this job was not our favorite pastime. Fixing fence, in rough steep country too remote to get into with a vehicle, was a necessary spring job. We used honest horses that could pack staples, splice wire and fencing tools. When we reached the fences we dismounted and led our horses along the fence. We used them to pack fence supplies while we leap-frogged each other replacing staples and splicing broken fence wires.

It was a hard, hot day and about four o'clock in the afternoon we piled the few fence materials we had left at the foot of a post and started the long ride home. We were climbing up an abandoned road along a steep hill at the edge of a live oak canyon. We were feeling sorry for ourselves and conversation had long since ceased. Even our dogs seemed to catch our mood and trailed along behind. The only sound was the horses clomping along and saddle leather squeaking.

Suddenly like a shot out of a cannon, the dogs passed us on a dead run, yelping and barking. Out of sight over a low rise in the old road, we heard barking, snarling, and growling. A dog yelped in pain and a sound like a baby screaming at the top of its lungs reached our ears. When we topped the rise we saw a mother bear sitting upright in the middle of the road, snarling, biting and swatting at dogs with both front paws. Spike, my old dog, was just letting go of a partly grown bear cub and there was complete chaos. The cub quit squalling and started to climb a large live oak tree. The mother bear, instead of treeing as would have been normal, lunged over the edge of the old road and we could hear her rolling and tumbling down through the brush and rocks.

Now, Spike was as close to a junkyard cow dog as you could find. He was bull headed, tough and hard of hearing by design. He never saw a mountain lion, bear, cow or wild hog that he didn't think he was big enough to tackle. He had a missing toe, broken teeth and other scars to prove it. Through all of this, Spike was loyal and faithful.

I thought the excitement of the moment was over and things were calming down. But just before I reached Spike he made a flying leap at that live oak tree, grabbed the bear cub by the hind leg and they both came crashing down around my feet. The cub was again squalling at the top of his lungs. I was cussing Spike while Harold and Bob were hollering, trying to control dogs and frantic horses. I grabbed Spike by the collar and when I looked up, the Mother bear was back on the road charging toward me.

Absolutely no guess work was needed to tell what her intentions were. Her ears were pinned back, her teeth were clacking and when she got closer, her mouth was wide open. I jerked back on Spike's collar so hard, there was no room for misunderstanding, and he turned the cub loose. The cub immediately stopped squalling and lunged toward its mother. The mother bear skidded to a stop just a few feet from me. She hesitated for a moment, then whirled around and plunged back over the edge of the road with her cub following close behind. We heard them crashing through the brush. Then everything was silent.

After a few moments we were all talking at once while we untangled lead ropes, got reins unhooked from saddle horns and checked dogs for injuries.

This whole incident lasted less than a minute and with no time to think, the actions were completely instinctive. This could have been an example of kill or be killed by a mother bear protecting her young and at the time the odds were not in my favor. In those few seconds our depressed mood changed to excitement and the adrenalin rush stayed with us the rest of the way home.

With the passage of time this event became a memorable incident that happened in the course of everyday work while I traveled along my 115,000 horseback ride.

I also found, along my lifelong horseback ride, that some of the most formidable and aggressive domestic animal mothers are a range cow with a newborn calf or a range sow with a litter of pigs. An old sow will eat you alive if you give her a chance and a range cow with a newborn calf will charge, hook, kick and trample if you get too close. A lone coyote, being somewhat of a cowardly opportunist, is usually not much of a threat when facing one of these mothers head on. Instead, the lone coyote uses cunning and slyly hunts for the young calf the cow has hidden, while she goes to water or to graze maybe a half mile away. Even then the coyote is in great danger if the cow is close enough to hear her calf bawl, because the coyote that has already begun the harassing killing process, is reluctant to leave when that charging cow comes thundering in to protect her calf. After a few close calls with a furiously bawling, kicking, butting cow, the coyote usually retreats, especially if more cows are nearby and hear that loud low pitched bawl and come charging in to help. When coyotes run in packs of two, four, six or more it is a different story. Domestic and wild animal mothers are at much greater risk and far less likely to be able to protect their young.

I was once riding across the range in the early spring where cows were calving. A short distance ahead I heard a commotion and that loud low pitched bawl of a cow in trouble. I loped to the crest of a small ridge and below, in a little wild rye grass basin, I saw four coyotes. They were attacking a lone cow with a young calf huddled up against her flank. Two coyotes would attack from the front and the cow would charge forward. The other two coyotes were behind the cow and when the cow charged forward they would try to slip in and grab her calf. This scenario kept repeating itself and for the moment, the cow was holding her own. She was holding her own because her calf was staying beneath her and her hind feet were lethal weapons, but it was only a question of time until the cow trampled her own calf to death trying to protect it, or the calf got far enough behind its mother so the coyotes attacking from the rear could pull it down.

I started down the hill with my horse at a full run. I let out a war hoop and fired a shot in the air. The surprised coyotes took off. I passed the cow and calf still running flat out and fell in behind the coyotes now shooting in their direction with little or no chance of hitting one, but I was scaring the daylights out of them. Every time a bullet came close to a coyote it would wring its tail and find another burst of speed. By the time my pistol was empty, those coyotes were flying. I pulled my horse up and returned to where the cow and calf had been. The only thing left of the battle was a trampled piece of ground where the cow made her stand fiercely protecting her calf. That wise old cow was gone, getting her calf as far away from this area as she could.

Another activity I've witnessed many times, along my long winding trail is the range cow's ability to protect her calf by organizing and operating a baby sitting, or in this case, a calf sitting program. I once rode over a ridge in the spring time, when cows were calving and saw one cow with thirteen young calves lying around in a small grassy basin below. When the cow saw me approaching with my horse and dogs, she let out that low pitched, loud beller, cows use when being threatened and the calves got up and gathered around her. Within a minute cows came charging in from all directions bellering as they ran. Some of them were just over the hill grazing, while others were farther away going to or coming back from water. In any case, this was a formidable group of mother cows charging in to protect their young. Any predators, thinking they had found an easy meal, would have been in for a big surprise.

How the cows organize this program is still a mystery to me. The activity can happen any time of the year, but out on the big ranges, it happens mostly in the spring when calves are young and their liquid requirements are still sustained by their mothers' milk. This activity usually starts in the middle of the day when the cows are finished with their morning grazing. A group of up to a dozen cows and calves will be lying around on a grassy hillside.   One by one or in small groups, the cows will get up and start going toward water. That water might be a mile or more away, but every cow leaves her calf behind. Cows will often hide a newborn or young calf and leave it for a short period of time and the calf will never move until the cow returns, but calves old enough to travel usually follow their mother everywhere they go.

These calves were old enough to travel but not one calf got up or made an effort to follow its mother. The cows continued to leave until there was only one cow left. This cow was still lying down chewing her cud, surrounded by every departed cow's calf. Not one calf started to follow its mother. There was no visible communication or indecision among the cows. It was almost as if the calf sitter was selected in advance. Later in the afternoon after the mother cows returned, the calf sitter took her turn and started her lonely walk to water.

I know this is an inherited trait possessed by most mothers but the mystery to me is how the designated calf sitter is picked? She is just as thirsty as the rest of the cows. It doesn't seem logical to me that she is just the last cow left when the cows leave to go to water.   Is there some indistinguishable sign picking the calf sitter? If there is, I haven't been able to recognize it. Within the same group of cows, it doesn't seem to be the same calf sitter each day and at this time of the year calf sitting happens in numerous places throughout the big ranges.

Anyway, to me this is another of the mysteries encountered along my 115,000 mile horseback ride and probably the mothers involved are the only ones who understand what is going on and it is a fairly safe bet they do not spend much time thinking about it. Maybe I am over analyzing the situation and the laziest cow in the group or the last cow to get up, gets stuck with the job, but after a lifetime of watching range cows I do not think it is as simple as that.

EVAN ZIMMERMAN

Evan Zimmerman was inducted into the Nevada Cattlemen's Association Cowboy 100,000 Club in 2008.

Dave's comment: "Evan Zimmerman's story is something of a miracle considering the first twenty-seven years of his life were spent on a dairy farm in the Petaluma area of northern California. Evan wasn't born on the big range areas of the west but he was born to be a rancher and cowboy. His choice of a lifetime partner, his wife Tillie, his extrodinary work ethic that he was able to pass down to his five sons, and his burning desire to become a big range cowboy and rancher allowed him to put together a cattle operation that at one time encompassed 3.5 million acres in central Nevada. In the late 1970's Jane and I had a reason to visit the Zimmerman family at one of their ranch headquarters. They were a very gracious, conservative ranch family."

The following is an excerpt from the December 2008 issue of the Nevada Rancher:

The next award brought a tear to nearly every eye in the place and many were related to the recipient. Evan Zimmerman was awarded the 100,000 mile award for having ridden on horseback over 100,000 miles while attending to his ranching duties throughout his lifetime. The award and heartwarming speech given by his granddaughter, Rachel Buzzetti, was a brief look into the long ranching career of Zimmerman. He is a man who was humbled by the thought of being awarded for anything. The room rose to their feet as the 87 year old rancher walked to the podium. The room was packed with much of his family who joined together at the end of the evening for the rare opportunity for a family photo.

How all of this was accomplished and the documentation of Evan's 115,000 mile horse back ride is explained by his granddaughter, Rachel Buzzetti, in remarks she made when Evan was inducted into the Cowboy 100,000 Mile Club. Here is her presentation:

Evan Albert Zimmerman was born December 31, 1923 in Petaluma, California. He spent his first seventeen years growing up on a family dairy ranch in the Chileno Valley that had been homesteaded by his grandfather in 1869. Unlike today where dairy cows are fed alfalfa in troughs near the barn, at this time dairy cattle grazed pasture hills between milkings. Beginning at the age of six, he and his brother rode horseback, much of the time bareback, every morning and evening to bring the Holsteins that were scattered in the pasture to be milked. As you know, dairies operate 365 days a year. Evan rode about 1.5 miles out and back twice each day, so six miles every day for twelve years. When school was in session he did this before and after school each day. He had ridden 26,280 miles by the time he was seventeen.

In 1940 when Evan was seventeen, the family moved to a larger ranch in Marshall, California. It was located on the coast; the secluded Bodega Bay was visible from the tops of the hills. It had a cooler climate with fog creeping over the pasture hills and valleys, regularly, like the milking of the cows, every night and morning. Again Evan rode a horse twice each day to bring the cows to the dairy barn to be milked. Upon graduating from high school, not only did he gather the dairy cows. He and his brothers milked forty of them by hand twice a day. On these larger pastures, Evan clocked about four miles a day for another four years, adding about 11,800 miles horseback.

In 1944 Evan married his high school sweetheart, Tillie Antoinette Christianson. They left the family dairy and bought their own small ranch where they milked cows and raised chickens. Here, he did gather

Holsteins on horseback for milking, twice each day, about 2.5 miles each day for another six years, adding about 5,475 miles on a horse. Although Evan did not put many miles on a horse at the Fallon ranch, he did have three boys: Ross born in 1945, Ted born in 1946 and Dennis born in 1948.

Wondering how he could raise three active boys on 120 acres, he started looking for something larger. An advertisement in the Western Livestock Journal for a cattle ranch in Nevada caught his eye. Over Memorial Day weekend in 1950, he took Tillie and his Uncle Roy, a realtor, and drove to the Disaster Peak Ranch in central Nevada to have a look. He looked in awe at the beautiful green meadows nestled at the base of the lone pyramid shaped, Disaster Peak. The ranch had 3,000 acres of deeded land, 52,000 acres of BLM range and could hold about 1200 cows. On June 25, 1950, Evan, Tillie and the three boys moved to the Disaster Peak Ranch.

Now horseback riding began in earnest. Evan was not a greenhorn when it came to riding horses. Breaking them was another matter. He learned from the other ranchers, mainly Orville Doane and Charlie Maher. The horses won some rounds and he improved with practice. As a true Wild West cowboy he began smoking cigarettes and chewing tobacco, trading the pearly white teeth he had on the dairy for false ones. He and Tillie had two more boys: Arnie born in 1951 and Buzz born in 1952.

As they had no tractors, stock trucks or horse trailers, all work was done on the back of a horse or when haying horses provided the power. Loose hay was stacked, loaded and fed. For the eight years at the Disaster Peak Ranch, horses were ridden nearly daily the year round.

This is how Evan's years went for those first eight years:
Springs:
Evan had a lot of country to get acquainted with. He rode horseback with all of the surrounding ranchers to learn their ways and their brands. No fences existed between the ranches so cattle were frequently mixed together. In the spring, Evan and a couple of hired men or Evan and his sons gathered and branded cattle with the other ranchers and cowboys from the White Horse Ranch, McCormick Ranch, Washburn Creek Ranch, Bruno Ranch, King's River Ranch, Trout Creek Ranch and the Home Ranch. They saddled up and rode to cow camps each day for about six weeks for eight years. Evan rode about 8,400 miles during this time.
Summers:
Summer work from 1950 to 1958 included haying the Disaster Peak meadows. Not only were horses used to mow, rake and stack the hay,

they were used also to transport Evan and his crew from the barn to the fields where the equipment was located. For about eight weeks he rode another five miles a day for another 2,240 miles.

Falls:

In the fall, all of the cattle that were out on the BLM range were gathered and driven to the meadows at the main ranch. The gather took about eight weeks and each day involved riding ten to thirty miles. Evan separated all the weaner calves, sold them and turned the cows back onto the meadows for the winter. Evan rode 8,900 miles during these fall gatherings.

Winters:

The winter brought some additional daily horseback riding. Each day Evan and his crew rode horseback to three stack yards. There they harnessed the team of work horses that stayed in the stack yards, used a Jackson Fork to load the hay onto a wagon and fed cows. This amounted to about twelve miles a day for four months, so during the eight years 6,720 miles were added to Evan's long winding trail.

(69,765 miles of Evan's lifetime ride were documented up to this time.)

The next ten years, 1959 to 1969 brought a few changes to Evan's yearly riding patterns. In 1958 the BLM began fencing ranges so the big round up with neighbors became a family round up confined mostly to the Disaster Peak Ranch. Evan continued to ride a horse daily for the spring brandings and the fall gatherings. In 1959 Tillie and the five boys moved to Winnemucca, Nevada, so the boys could attend school. Evan was often alone or short handed. The boys helped on weekends, but returned to school during the week. Evan spent many long weeks without seeing another person. He spoke frequently to Queenie, his Australian Shepherd, and she was a good listener. So for these ten years he rode an additional 11,200 miles in the fall and 8,400 miles for the ten springs. By 1959, haying and feeding cows on the ranch became more mechanized. Travel to stack-yards was done with a piece of machinery and travel to field work was handled the same way.

Throughout the nineteen years that I have just covered, many of the miles Evan rode are not included in this total because the times he saddled up to perform chores that were not daily or even weekly events were more random. They do not lend themselves to easy calculations. For example, Evan did not own a horse trailer until 1969. So, from 1950 to 1969, if a neighbor called to say they had a couple of cows and calves or bulls, he had to ride a horse to the neighboring ranch and drive them home. Cattle on the range had to be tended, checked or moved, springs had to be checked, salt hauled, fences fixed usually in remote areas, inaccessible by pickup. So we added a conservative 500 miles a year spent on this type of activity, so an additional 9,500 miles was added to Evan's lifelong ride.

In 1969 Evan bought his first stock truck, allowing him to take horses on a truck to gather cattle, to pick up strays, to check cattle and springs, to fix fence and to haul salt. It cut back on the miles he rode, but an event in 1972 added many more horseback miles. Ross, his oldest son, had recently graduated from Veterinary Medicine School. Ted had a Master's Degree in Physical Education. Dennis had spent four years in the Air Force and Arnie and Buzz were attending Oregon State University. All were open to Evan's idea of getting together and purchasing and operating a ranch. Evan and his five sons purchased the RO Ranch in Big Smoky Valley. The RO is a Great Basin, high desert ranch which encompassed 1.5 million acres of BLM, Forest Service and Section 15 land. He did have his sons working with him and they did much of the riding, but for the first five or six years, he participated in the fall and spring gatherings. Each year cattle were gathered from the desert, BLM ranges, the calves branded, the weaner calves separated and then driven to the mountain ranges (pastures) for summer feeding. Then in the fall, these cattle were again gathered from the mountain ranges, the new calves branded, the calves to be weaned separated and driven back to the valley for the winter. Evan and his boys trucked the weaned calves to the Disaster Peak Ranch where they gained tremendous weight on the grassy meadows and were sold in the fall.

The use of stock trucks and horse trailers for transporting horses to gathering areas each day helped greatly, but there were still vast miles to cover to gather and drive the cattle. Each day cowboys covered 20, 30, 40, often 50 miles a day. Evan rode many of these days for five years. The same was true of the fall gathering which usually lasted from August 25th to about Thanksgiving. Gathering cattle in the rugged mountains of the Toiyabe National Forest is treacherous with steep ravines, rocky hillsides covered with junipers and vast stands of quaking aspen. This is a topography that is challenging to the best cowboys. This fall riding again entailed 20, 30, 40, 50 miles a day. So for the first five years at the RO he clocked another 11,250 miles. In 1978 Evan was 55 years old. He continued to irrigate and put up hay on the meadows of the RO. He fed bulls and a few cows that spent the winter there. At this time he and his family added more ranches, more cattle and more land. In 1978, the Zimmermans bought the Triple T Ranch in Smokey Valley and the Monitor Valley Ranch in Monitor Valley. They ran cattle in Big Smokey Valley, Monitor Valley, the Toiyabe Mountains, the Toquima Mountains and the Monitor Mountains. This encompassed 3.5 million acres of land. Evan continued to saddle up, helping in the fall and spring round ups. The Zimmerman family owned these ranches until 1988 at which time they sold three ranches and went in different directions. He rode at least another 4,000 miles in this time.

Evan and Tillie moved back to the Disaster Peak Ranch. Instead of running cows and calves, as he had earlier, Evan started buying and selling steers. There was not a lot of riding, but he and his son, Arnie, moved cows from pasture to pasture for seven months of the year. In 1996 Evan had finished helping Arnie work some cattle and headed home alone. Trotting along, at a sharp curve where a culvert crossed the road, his horse spooked and he was thrown. He broke his thigh bone. His horse stopped and stood around for awhile, then headed for home. When Tillie saw Evan's riderless horse she became alarmed, called Arnie and went to look for Evan. Evan lay where he had fallen for about three hours before Tillie found him. She immediately called life flight and he was taken to a hospital in Boise, Idaho. He was 72 years old and it took about a year for him to completely recover. This did not keep him from saddling his horse when necessary. Evan continued to do some riding well into his seventies. He added about 1,000 miles to his lifelong horseback ride.

In adding up the miles ridden by my grandfather, it did not surprise me that the grand total was more than 115,000 miles. Although I have never known my grandfather to ride a horse for pleasure, you know just get on a horse and ride up a trail for fun, or to see the sights. He has always ridden for a purpose, a job or a task. But I do know that he has gotten tremendous pleasure from riding horses, and from living the life of a cattle rancher.

Gramps will be 85 next month on December 31st. If you see him today, walking directly away from you or coming directly towards you, it is easy to see that he still has a straight, long back and short bowed legs. I don't know if he got them from spending 115,115 miles horseback, but I like to think that he was born with those bowed legs to fit comfortably in a saddle, and that he spent most of his life doing exactly what he was meant to be doing.

INDIAN C0WBOYS

For fifteen years our family and I owned and I managed the Lee Livestock Company in Pleasant Valley, twenty miles south of Elko, Nevada. During this time, we lived next to the South Fork Indian Reservation.

For the next twelve years we owned and I managed the Dinner Station Ranch twenty six miles north of Elko, Nevada. During both of these periods of time, I hired and rode with many Indian cowboys. At the Dinner Station I continued to hire Indians from the Duck Valley Indian Reservation that is located sixty miles north of the Dinner Station Ranch. In this time period, I documented riding 34,781 miles of my 115,000 mile horseback ride.

At Lee Livestock Company I hired Indians from the South Fork reservation. I rode with them on the reservation and sometimes went to their council meetings. I made friends and learned some things about their heritage and way of life. In their own environment they are happy people with a good sense of humor. I learned about the thickness of a deer hide having something to do with forecasting a hard winter, and that there is sweet nectar in the Indian Paint Brush flower. Once when an old Indian told me it was going to be a hard winter and I asked how he knew, he answered with an emotionless face and said, "Because white man has a large wood pile." Sometimes you have to look for the humor, but it is there.

A young Indian cowboy, right out of the army, told me that people would come up to him and say, "How," an old Indian form of greeting. He said he would reply, "If you don't know how by now, there is no use for me to try to explain it."

On a cold winter morning when it was about zero outside and the wind was blowing the snow sideways, we were getting ready to go out and feed cows when an Indian cowboy looked up from the breakfast table and said to me, "This is all you fault! If the white man had not messed things up, she (he pointed to Jane) would be going outside to feed cows and we would be sitting in the house by the fire."

In many ways the Indian's and white man's cultures have come together, but the Indians still have strong ties to their histories and cultures, including the ancestral spirits. Some Indians take advantage of these traits. One fellow that worked for me spent his summers in Elko County on the reservation and his winters in Arizona. He posed as an Indian Chief telling about Indian folklore while, for a price, he would sit for pictures with inquisitive tourists. In the white man's world, we would call this working the system.

I was helping the reservation gather a pasture southeast of Haw Creek. We were holding about two hundred cows on a sagebrush flat while the Indians cut out yearlings that were going to be driven to the mouth of Echo Canyon, doctored for pink eye, then turned out for the summer. Erwin and I were the only non-Indian cowboys there. Erwin was also a rancher that bordered the reservation and we were there to cut out our strays and take them home. The reservation cowboys were laughing, joking and having a good time. It was a pretty wild scene. Any cow that needed to be roped or may need to be roped any time in the near future was fair game. Any cow being cut out, that ducked back into the herd got roped. Any cow that quit the herd without any intention of stopping got roped. All of the cowboys, even the cowboys that worked for me, spoke in their native Shoshone or Paiute languages, so I couldn't understand anything that was being said. Everyone was good natured and got kidded.

Erwin was an old time cowboy that had worked with the reservation for years. Erwin was sitting on his horse, at the end of the rodeer grounds, with his rope in his hand. When a cow that looked like it wanted to quit the herd came his way he would give her a little air, let her break out of the herd, and when the cow went by, Erwin would make a half hearted throw with his rope. He never intended to catch the cow. He would holler, "Catch that S.O.B." Then he would sit on his horse and watch the show, while three or four Indian cowboys took off in hot pursuit. The Indian cowboys knew what Erwin was doing but they didn't seem to mind.

On this day I was holding herd when a three year old steer, that had been missed on previous round ups, came around to my side of the rodeer grounds. I could tell from the look in his eye and the way he carried his head he was seriously looking for a way out. The steer was big, long, lean and his horns came straight out of his head making him look even wilder than he was. As luck would have it that steer worked its way around the rodeer grounds to Erwin's position before he decided to break out. Erwin made his usual half hearted throw with his rope while hollering, "Catch that S.O.B." The steer was going by Erwin like a freight train, when to his surprise, the big loop in the end of his rope settled down over the steer's head. The rope slipped back of the steer's shoulder and by the time Erwin jerked his slack and took his dallies; he had that steer roped around the belly. The steer drug Erwin's horse out into the sagebrush, before the steer finally started bucking, bawling and kicking while it circled around at the end of Erwin's rope. The Indian cowboys hooped, hollered, and shouted advice. But no one made an effort to help Erwin until the steer finally wore down, and then the Indian cowboys roped the steer, took Erwin's rope off and put the steer back into the herd while the hollering and joking continued. Erwin joined in, giving as much as he was taking until at last things calmed down and everybody went back to working cows.

Johnny Temoke and Wesley Dick were two Indian cowboys that worked for me off and on for twenty-five years. Marvin McDade was a young Indian cowboy, who among others, worked for me during the early years at the Lee Livestock Company Ranch. These were good cowboys and friends and we rode many miles together.

It was early winter and I was feeding four hundred head of cows on the Griswold Ranch meadows, located in the foothills of the Ruby Mountains, ten miles from the Lee Livestock Company Ranch headquarters. Because it was at a high elevation, the Griswold Ranch was in a heavy snow zone and was at times inaccessible in winter. We were feeding the hay put up on these meadows the summer before. We fed this hay early in the season so we could drive the cows home to Lee Livestock headquarters before the calving season started. In the spring and summer Johnny Temoke irrigated the Griswold meadows riding a horse from dam to dam as was the custom at the time.

Another incident I remember involved my Indian friend, Wesley Dick. It was winter and there was a foot or two of snow on the ground. Wesley was staying in the old Griswold ranch house feeding cows, using a team of horses and a feed sleigh. The ranch had been deserted for a number of years and for some reason, the Indian cowboys were nervous when around the ranch house at night. I don't think, until this incident, I was ever told why. Wesley was using a flashlight and a kerosene lantern for light in the house after dark.

I knew there was an old Kohler light plant in a shed about fifteen yards from the house. I also knew that the house was wired for lights because a wire with a switch and a naked light bulb hung from the center of the ceiling in each room. A string was still attached to each light switch that could be reached and pulled to turn the lights on and off. I thought I might be able to get the old light plant started and Wesley could have lights and feel better about staying in the house at night. At one time these old light plants were on the cutting edge of technology. They ran forever and many isolated ranch headquarters had one. Each had a battery and a switchboard with breaker points wired to start the motor when the first light in the house was turned on. The points also shut the motor off when the last light in the house was turned off. Couple this with a refrigerator powered by bottled propane and, in days gone by, we were really living uptown.

While Wesley was feeding, I followed up on my inspiration and went out to the shed housing the light plant. Snow was piled high on the roof of the shed and the door was sagging. When I looked inside, what I saw was a little discouraging. A pack rat's nest was completely covering the motor. In about an hour I had the shed cleaned out and the motor looked fairly good. The oil level was all right, the motor block was drained and the pack rats hadn't chewed through the wiring. I came back the next day with a new battery, antifreeze, and several cans of gas. After cleaning the points, priming the carburetor, and tinkering around with the light plant, I turned on a light and the motor turned over. It coughed, back fired, sputtered, finally started and the light came on.

I thought, for a cowboy, I was some kind of mechanical genius. I tested the motor several times and it started the light plant when I turned a light on and when I turned the light off the motor shut down. The next time I came to the Griswold ranch with supplies for Wesley, we were having a January thaw and the snow was melting.

When I arrived, Wesley was standing out in the yard and I thought that was unusual. When I went by Wesley with an arm full of groceries he said, "I won't go back in that house." I asked, "Why not?" Wesley again said, "I won't go back in that house."

I finished packing the supplies in and finally talked Wesley into following me into the kitchen. We sat down at the kitchen table and I waited, Wesley finally said, "This house is haunted."

I said, "What makes you think so?"

Then Wesley began to talk and said, "Last night about midnight the light plant come on all by itself and woke me up. The wind was blowing, the house was shaking, there was a mournful sound, the screen door was banging and the light came on. When I pulled the switch to turn the motor off, the motor kept running. Later in the night the motor stopped running all by itself. The light over my head went out and everything was quiet." Wesley said, "There are ancestral spirits in this house." I told Wesley I realized this was a spooky situation but there must be a logical explanation.

At that very second the light plant started running all by itself and the light over the kitchen table came on. Even though it was broad daylight a little shiver ran up my back and the hair on the back of my neck stood up. For a moment I thought Wesley's theory might be right. He was ten miles back in the mountains. No one was around. It was a pitch black night. A sudden wind storm came up. The old house was creaking and groaning, the screen door was slamming and in the middle of all this, the light plant mysteriously started running and the light over his bed came on all by itself.

I've stayed many a night in an old house alone when about midnight the "old house" started to creak and groan as it cooled down from the heat of the day. I'd swear one night when I was staying alone in an empty house I heard someone walking across the floor upstairs above me.

Well, Wesley and I were sitting there looking at each other and I could see no amount of talking was going to change his mind, so I went out to the light plant shed and looked around. Snow was melting and water was running off the eaves. Inside the shed everything looked normal. When I turned to leave I heard water splash and when I looked back I realized I had found the ghost. There was a little leak in the shed roof. Water was seeping along on top of the rafter to a point just over the motor. When enough water puddle up on top of the rafter, it ran over the side, dropped down into the control box and shorted across the points, thus starting the light plant as if a light had been turned on. In between, when the points dried off, the motor would shut itself off, causing the light plant to start and stop on its own without turning a light on and off. I found a piece of corrugated tin and diverted the water.

When I left Wesley that day, after the mystery of the ghost had been solved, he said to me, "I think there is a ghost up in those rafters above the light plant and he caused the leak in the roof." A little lingering apprehension or a little Indian humor. I will probably never know.

The light plant ran normally until the hay was used up and we drove the cows back to the main ranch and closed the old house up for the rest of the winter. Once again the Griswold Ranch was left undisturbed and only the ghosts and spirits remained.

Dave on Babe about 1933

Dave on Sweet William 1980

DAVE SECRIST

Dave Secrist was inducted into the Nevada Cattlemen's Association Cowboy 100,000 Mile Club in 2002.

Jane Secrist, Dave's wife, made the following remarks and gave the documentation of miles ridden during Dave's lifelong horseback ride.

"This is Dave's story and he wrote it in the first person.

I am just here to read it. To remind you that it is Dave's speaking, I brought a prop. I selected a fairly presentable one and this should look

natural to those of you who ride and do ranch work."—- Jane   (I put on
Dave's hat with the hole burned in the crown.)

DAVE'S STORY

I have been nominated to be inducted into the Nevada Cattlemen's
Association 100,000 Mile Club. The following information has been
documented from people that were present at the time the events occurred and from information taken from my daybooks recording the
events of the time.

I was born in a private house in Willits, California on May 23, 1928.
I was taken home to a homestead in the mountains about twelve miles
east of Willits as soon as possible.

The first memories I have about my lifelong association with horses
probably aren't my memories but memories of family pictures and family stories many times retold. My first memories of horses that I know
are mine, because the horse and I were the only ones involved, began
when I started going to the first grade. I rode three miles round trip to a
one room school each day. The old mare that I rode was named "Babe".
Babe was old, a little sway backed and really tall. My folks would put
me on in the morning and the teacher would take me off at school. In
the afternoon the process was reversed. I guess nobody thought much
about the in-between. I did learn years later that my dad followed me all
the way to school that first day far enough behind so that I didn't know
he was there.

There were two instances during the two year period I rode old
"Babe" to school that probably bonded me to horses for the rest of my
life. The first occurred after a flood when the water in String Creek had
gone down enough so I could safely cross. A neighbor's horse had
drowned and the floodwaters floated it down stream. The carcass lodged
on a sandbar close to the creek crossing. This was a pretty scary thing
for a kid and an old bay mare and we depended on each other to get by
this spot. Several days went by and we were getting used to shying
around the area. Then one day as we were passing by, that horse carcass
began to grunt, squeal, groan, and shake. The squeals got louder and
that carcass kind of rose up and partly turned over. The hair on the back
of my neck was standing straight up! Old "Babe" was running much
faster than an old horse had a right to go. I looked back just before we
went out of sight and saw the neighbor's skinny old sow running for dear
life in the opposite direction. I was told the old sow had crawled up into
the rib cavity of that horse carcass and when she heard us going by she
panicked, got tangled up, and had trouble getting back out. Now to a
young kid and an old bay mare, there was absolutely no doubt. That
horse carcass had been possessed by some kind of super human horse
killing, kid eating demon and it was sure out to get us!

The other incident occurred soon after when my folks were involved in a meeting after school. There were only six students in school and when the neighbors got together they enjoyed visiting. It was almost dark when my dad put me on old "Babe" and started me toward home. In order to give me a head start, my folks stayed and visited a little longer. Well, they gave me too much of a head start and I got home before they did. By now it was dark and pitch black, old "Babe" stopped when she reached the barn door. I was trying to find the fence so I could get off when I heard the most blood-curdling scream I had ever heard in my young life. I'd heard owls hoot before but I'd never heard a screech owl so I had no idea what was making that ungodly sound. By now I was too scared to get off of old "Babe" so I just leaned forward, pressed my face against the old mare's neck and talked to her. She didn't answer me but somehow she sure was a lot of comfort while one owl was screeching out in front of me and the other owl was answering from somewhere back behind.

It wasn't very long before the lights of that old car came over the ridge but it seemed like forever to me and of course, after my folks arrived and I was trying to explain, those owls never made another sound.

I have had a lot of conversations with horses since that night but probably none more serious than that one was. During this period of time I documented riding 920 miles horseback.

From that time forward with the exception of two years during World War II when my dad was involved with the military, I have never lived for any length of time where I couldn't touch a horse or see a cow.

About now my folks left the homestead and we all moved to the Circle W Ranch. For the next four years my brother and I rode eight miles a day round trip to school. By now we had become fairly good horsemen. Everything we did was done horseback—we played, we worked, and we went to school horseback. Sometimes a couple of neighbor kids rode to school with us and one thing I remember very clearly was a big bald hornet's nest high up in an old oak tree about halfway to school. In the morning when it was cool the hornets didn't bother us much but sometimes coming home on a warm afternoon it was a problem. We usually ran through that stretch of road and sometimes it got very interesting for the kid that got a slow start or had a slow horse, especially if the kid in the lead made a good throw with one of the rocks he usually carried in his pocket. During this phase of my life I documented riding 8,960 miles horseback.

For a number of years counting summers while I was going to high school, I worked for the Eden Valley Ranch in Mendocino County, California. At this time about all ranch work in the back country with the exception of haying was done on a horse. During these years that I worked for the Eden Valley Ranch I cannot remember one time when a horse or a cow was hauled anywhere on the ranch in a truck or a trailer.

Every two weeks when the weather was bad in the winter I would saddle up and lead a packhorse on the thirty mile round trip to the mailbox. I would pick up ranch supplies and mail that had been delivered to the end of the county road.

I remember one winter in particular when I was going over the summit. The snow was up to the point of my horse's shoulder and nearly touching the lower edges of my saddle blankets. It was new snow and still soft enough to break through, so without getting off I would slip from my saddle horse to the back of the packhorse, break trail for awhile, then switch back to my saddle horse and break more trail. I continued to exchange horses until I got to a lower elevation where the snow was not so deep. During this phase of my life I documented riding 48,640 miles horseback.

The next forty-four years of my life I spent in Elko County, Nevada.

The first fifteen years of this time were spent at Lee Livestock Company. During this phase I documented riding 17,330 miles horseback.

The next twelve years I spent on the Dinner Station Ranch where I documented riding 17,451 miles on horseback.

The last seventeen years I spent on the San Jacinto Ranch for the Salmon River Cattlemen's Association and documented riding 21,900 miles horseback.

I guess I have just about come full circle. Seventy some years ago I started out on an old bay mare and when I retired from Salmon River Cattlemen's Association, they gave me a shiny new stick horse. His name is "End of the Trail." He is about three feet tall, made of wood, with a brown yarn mane. He has real leather ears but I have to be careful when riding him because his maker forgot to install eyes.

I have ridden many horses in between, some good, some bad, and a few outstanding and while doing so I have documented that I have ridden 115,201 miles. I still have a couple of horses out in the pasture and I intend to ride a few more miles before I hang up my chaps and put a pad lock on the saddle room door.

When Dave was asked what he would like to be remembered for he replied, "I would like to be remembered for being just an ordinary big range rancher and cowboy that enjoyed and respected the people, animals and environment that surrounded me while I traveled along my 115,000 mile horseback ride."

LITTLE THINGS

If you can't laugh at yourself, you are taking yourself too seriously.

A CHANCE ENCOUNTER

In the early part of my 115,000 mile horse back ride I had a chance encounter with an old lion hunter that became a legend in the back country in his own lifetime. It was a late fall day and the feel of winter was in the air. I saddled up well before daylight, rolled a sandwich up in my slicker and tied it behind the cantle of my saddle. Then I turned Spike and Will, two over anxious cow dogs, loose. I released an excited hound named Rex and started the forty mile ride that would take me by the summer camp, past Rackout Springs, and up the steep climb to the back bone of Mt. San Headron. I would pick my way through the loose shale of the partially hidden trail that worked its way through an unlikely shaped outcropping called Impassible Rock. At first look this rock appeared to block any chance of passing through the area. The swale in the middle of Impassible Rock was only a few feet wide. I would be able to look down the steep slopes on the east and west sides of Mt. San Headron while standing in the same spot. I would have to work my way through this area carefully while looking down at the tree tops on either side of the mountain. From here on the mountain top abruptly widened out and passed by springs and small meadows ringed with skunk cabbage. I would now be at an altitude where the Douglas fir and Ponderosa pine forests thinned out and I would be traveling through Oak brush and scrubby White fir thickets until I climbed to the highest point on Mt. San Headron. There a forest service fire lookout station would be precariously perched on the highest rock. It was held in place by numerous guy wires anchored to surrounding rocks. I would have to reach this lookout station to get to the trail head that went down the steep timbered mountain side to the north before I reached the Crocker place homestead. Once I reached the Crocker place I would turn toward home and hope to get off the mountain and close to the ranch house before dark. This was the plan when I untied my dogs, mounted my horse and started out on that early dark fall morning.

The purpose of this late fall re-ride was to make sure all the cows were gone off the summer range. In these coastal mountains that are about a hundred miles from the Pacific Ocean it was not uncommon for a storm to bring in two to four inches of rain in twenty-four hours. Under winter conditions an early storm could mean three or four feet of snow and twenty foot drifts in the high country almost overnight. When this happened any stray cows caught in the high country couldn't get down and worried ranchers in the lower country couldn't get to them.

On this day the hours and miles went by and when I reached the steeper part of the mountain, I stopped to let my horse rest and my mind began to wander. We had ridden the summer range well in the early fall and any cows left would just be stragglers that slipped away.

My thoughts turned to a story a rancher once told me. It was late spring almost early summer and he was packing salt and checking cows that were returning to the high summer range. He was going up a steep switch back trail when he stopped to rest his horses. While looking around he happened to look up. His first thought was, "What the hell?" He said he could not believe what he was seeing. There, fifteen feet above him, next to the trunk of a big fir tree, cradled on two large limbs, was a cow. At first glance it looked very much alive. After he had regained his senses he theorized the cow had gotten trapped by last winter's storms, thin and half starved she wandered out on the frozen crust of a huge snow drift that had formed on the north side of the ridge above. She was probably looking for shelter or reaching for anything green to nibble on when the softer part of the snow drift, protected by the trees trunk and limbs, gave way. The cow fell through and was trapped on the two big branches she was now laying on. He further theorized the cow had frozen solid until the spring thaw came along and the wind and sun turned the cow's skin to rawhide thus holding the cow together in the life like form she was in now. When the snow drift melted away, there she was, lodged fifteen feet in the air on the two big branches of the fir tree.

This is another of the stories I encountered on my 115,000 mile horseback ride where truth is stranger than fiction. I know the cow was fifteen feet up in that tree and I know she didn't climb that tree. I know she couldn't jump that high and I know from my own experience that the theories the rancher explained were feasible. Anyway the thoughts of this story made my ride a little more urgent.

I was now on top of the mountain, past Impassible Rock, through the springs and meadows and stopped in front of the Forest Service fire look out station. It was all shuttered up; the glass windows that circled the entire building were hidden. The building shook while the wind whistled through the guy wires that held it down, making a mournful sound. The little building looked pitiful and was a far cry from the scene I remembered when I was last here. It was summer then and I had a pack horse loaded with salt I was scattering along the top of the mountain. The short wave radio was crackling and the man at the look out station was surprised and pleased to see another human. On that summer day I loaded his four empty five gallon water cans on my pack horse, went an eighth of a mile down the steep hill to a spring, filled the cans with water and packed them back up to his look out station. He was so excited he got on his short wave radio and called several look out stations located on distant mountains and told them a cowboy from the ranch had taken his water cans down to the spring, filled them and packed them back to him on a horse. In the summer time the days were long and I had plenty of time to make the trip and the man stationed at the lookout followed me down the trail for a ways visiting.

Now, the days were short, the wind was blowing, the place was deserted and I had to keep moving. I ate my sandwich while I was riding down the steep trail to the Crocker Place. I hadn't expected to see any cows or tracks on the windy mountain top I'd just traveled over, but I had to look. This was wild country and though I was looking for cows, I brought Rex the hound along thinking I had a good chance of picking up a hot bear or lion track. Both Spike and Will were good varmint dogs and would be quick to pick up on Rex's lead. When I got to the Crocker Place area I spent forty-five minutes looking for any tracks or signs of cows. This was a cowy place and any cows in the area would come through here every week or two. Spike and Will ranged out looking for any fresh cow sign. Rex was plodding along behind me. He had no interest in cows so he was bored with the whole thing. Satisfied there weren't any cows in the area, I called the dogs in and was getting ready to start down the trail back towards the ranch. If I picked up any cows on the way, my plan was to start them on a long trot until they slowed down, then drive them as far off the country they had been running in as I could before I had to leave them. I would then trot out of this rough country before darkness set in. If I got to open country by dark I could give Sandy his head and he would take me home. The next morning I would return. If the cows hadn't continued traveling to lower elevations, I would drive them the rest of the way down from the high country.

While I was running all of this through my head I noticed Rex was coming to life. His tail was swishing from side to side, his nose was on the ground, and his big loose lips were flopping in and out. Rex didn't let out that first long drawn out bawl that was usual when he found a fairly cold track, so I thought whatever he was tracking was probably pretty old. Spike and Will couldn't pick up the scent Rex found so they just got excited and ran around peeing on everything.

I got off and while I was looking, I found several panther scratches in the pine needles that covered the ground. These scratches are the way the big cats mark their territory. Now I knew what Rex was trying to track. About thirty yards back in the pine timber I could tell Spike and Will had found something. When I walked over I saw the panther's kill. It was a forked horn buck all covered up with pine needles and sticks that had been raked from the immediate area. The only thing sticking out of this pile was one of the deer's forked horns. I uncovered the deer and there was little left of the carcass, just hide, some gnawed ribs, leg bones and the head. Nothing had been disturbed recently and I realized the big cat had made the kill five or six days earlier. He probably hung around for several days, gorged himself, then left looking for the next kill. At this time the general consensus compiled by experts that should know was that a panther in the wilderness of northern California averaged killing a deer a week or fifty-two deer a year.

Now I had a dilemma on my hands, everything in me wanted to run that big cat. He may still be bedded down close by. Besides the excitement of the chase, either the county or state, I don't remember which, was offering a thirty dollar bounty for killing a panther and turning in the hide.

Well common sense won out. I was twenty miles from home, the afternoon hours were slipping away, the fall days were getting shorter, and I still had a lot of country to ride through looking for cows. I mounted Sandy and kept an especially close eye on Rex, I couldn't afford to let him slip away and start working that cold panther track. He may tree the panther right away but more than likely it would take hours before he could catch up with the big cat and there was a good chance he never would. I had gone about a hundred yards down the trail toward home when I heard a sound that brought me straight up in my saddle. I pulled Sandy up. I listened intently for maybe a minute and this time there was no doubt I heard the long drawn out trailing bawl of a hound with a second hound chiming in. I knew it wasn't Rex but I looked down to make sure. I had been lost in my own thoughts and having a tug of war with myself about running the big cat. I had been secure in the knowledge that on this blustery day in the late fall in the wilderness on the east side of San Headron Mountain, no one was within forty miles of me. I rode back to the pine trees and an uneasy feeling settled in. I coupled Rex to Spike's collar knowing Spike would not let the hound get far away from me. I remounted Sandy. Somehow I felt better mounted than standing on the ground. At first the hounds long drawn out trailing bawls were fairly frequent, but as they came closer they were further apart. After a long silence, the loud booming voice of a hound trailing a cold track came out of the nearby trees and startled me. This caused the hair on my dogs' necks to stand up.

Instantly, a scene from the past appeared before my eyes, out of the pine trees stepped two old hounds followed by an old mountain man leading an old bay horse. They looked ancient. The hounds' muzzles were grey clear up to their ears. The old man was stooped, a mop of grey hair stuck out from under his battered old hat, he had a pistol holstered on his hip and the two old hound were pulling on the leashes he was holding firmly in his right hand. His left hand was pulled back from leading an old bay horse that didn't want to travel as fast as he was. That old horse was another picture, his muzzle was also grey. He was bare footed and sway backed with his withers and hips almost as high as the old saddle that sat on his back. The scabbard that held a rifle, probably a thirty caliber, was old but the gun's stock that stuck out of it looked well taken care of.

I had the advantage because I'd known for sometime that he or someone was coming. I was much too close (less than twenty feet) to call, "Hello" to him while he was still a safe distance away, which was the custom, and for once my dogs had remained silent. The old man was so intent on holding on to his hounds and looking at the ground for panther tracks that he had not seen me. He was coming closer so in the friendliest sounding voice I could muster, I said, "Hello." The old mountain man's body stiffened and he stood straight as a string. That was the only sign of surprise he showed. His eyes were steady and unwavering and his right hand, that was full of hound leashes, dropped toward his pistol but he didn't let loose of the hounds and it was plain to see this was just a reactive movement and no malice was intended. I felt embarrassed at putting the old man in this kind of situation. The whole meeting had only taken a few seconds and at this close range I didn't know what else to do. His answer to my "Hello" came in a calm voice. He said, "Hello, young feller. Where in the hell did you come from?" We laughed a little about the awkward meeting we just had and introduced ourselves.

It wasn't until then that I realized I had just shaken hands with one of my boyhood heroes. This was the lion hunting legend and mountain man I had as a boy sat spellbound listening to stories of his exploits the old-timers told. He asked where I came from and after I told him he said, "Young feller you are a long way from home." I knew he was from the Potter Valley area about twenty miles to the south. But until he introduced himself I didn't even know he was still alive. I hadn't heard anything about him for years.

I asked him if he had seen any cows or tracks and he had not. He asked me if I had seen any panther sign. I pointed to the panther kill I'd just discovered. He told me that his hounds had picked up what he thought was a fresh panther track about a quarter of a mile from where we were. By the time he realized his hounds were back tracking in the wrong direction and he caught up with them to turn them around, he heard my hello, looked up and there I was.

After looking at the panther kill he said he couldn't visit any longer, it was already afternoon and he had to get back to the spot where his hounds first picked up the cat's scent so he could get them going in the right direction. After a few more words he gathered up his hounds, his old horse and just melted into the pine trees going back the way he came. He was intent on treeing that big cat and though I had a short distraction, I was intent on making sure there were no cows left on the mountain.

When I topped the next ridge I stopped to listen. The hounds' long drawn out bawls were much shorter now with more excitement in their voices and they were moving along at a fast pace. I smiled to myself, tipped my hat in his direction, and wished the old lion hunter luck. I realized I had more time left to tree the next big cat I came across than he did.

I didn't find any cows the rest of the way home and reached more open country by dark. I gave Sandy his head and he took me home without incident. The lights in the window were a welcome sight and after I took care of my horse and dogs, a hot meal was waiting. I haven't missed many meals along my 115,000 mile horse back ride but I sure have postponed a lot of them.

This meeting took place fifty years ago and lasted less than five minutes, but I can still see it in my mind's eye as clearly as if it were yesterday. I can see the old lion hunter's floppy hat, his weathered face, his

two grey muzzled hounds, the worn out saddle, and his old bay horse. But for the life of me after fifty years have gone by, I can't remember his name. It must have been a strange sight, this old mountain man and his long time partners facing a young cowboy surrounded by his horse and dogs all in the prime of their lives. His roan horse standing with its ears pointed forward, his dogs standing at attention, with his saddle, rope and chaps showing signs of use but well maintained. Yes, the contrast must have been striking during that chance meeting out there in the mountains forty miles from nowhere. Of course, at that time I didn't realize all of this and probably wouldn't have thought about it if I had. But as the years slipped by and my mind occasionally revisits this incident, I realize that at this meeting, one lifelong horseback ride was coming to a close and another lifelong horseback ride was in its early stages. Now that my 115,000 mile horseback ride is nearing its end, it is my firm belief that somewhere out there in the mountains and big ranges of the west there is a young cowboy, mounted on a roan horse whose ears are pointed forward, while his dogs stand at attention, that is just beginning his 100,000 mile horseback ride. I wish him good luck through all of the experiences he is going to have while traveling along his long winding trail.

INDEX